Arbitration Law of Pakistan

Arbitration Law of Pakistan

Ikram Ullah

Wolters Kluwer

Published by:
Kluwer Law International B.V.
PO Box 316
2400 AH Alphen aan den Rijn
The Netherlands
E-mail: international-sales@wolterskluwer.com
Website: lrus.wolterskluwer.com

Sold and distributed by:
Wolters Kluwer Legal & Regulatory U.S.
7201 McKinney Circle
Frederick, MD 21704
United States of America
Email: customer.service@wolterskluwer.com

Printed on acid-free paper.

ISBN 978-94-035-1702-5

e-Book: ISBN 978-94-035-1710-0
web-PDF: ISBN 978-94-035-1714-8

Printed and bound by CPI Group (UK) Ltd, Croydon, CR0 4YY

This book is dedicated to
my mother, Sughra Bibi,
my wife, Aisha, and
my sister, Asifa

Table of Contents

Acknowledgements

I will always remain indebted to Professor Ilias Bantekas – my friend and mentor – who is truly a person of head and heart. I am always blessed with his guidance, support and encouragement on each and every step from my LLM till now and believe to have this in the future also. His hard work, effectiveness, vision and honesty always inspire me. From him, I learned that research is a passion and hard work is the code of life. He reviewed the earlier drafts and gave invaluable, detailed and very constructive comments. I am profoundly grateful to him.

I am also very thankful to Professor Sébastien Manciaux, my PhD supervisor. I developed several chapters of this book on my PhD thesis. He was generous in giving me time to discuss my chapters, patient with my work and helpful in all academic and non-academic matters coming in my way during my PhD in France. It was a great privilege to do a PhD under his supervision.

My sincere thanks go to Farqaleet Khokhar and Tauqir Bhatti, who were always there to help me in collecting data and reviewing the draft to give their critical views thereon.

My parents, you are brimmed with positivity, love, optimism, honesty, humility, respect, discipline, hard work, and so much more and taught us these values. You are always with me, like seeing me working, smiling on my good deeds and putting me on the right path when I am wrong. Words are not made for the sublime purpose of counting your blessings or expressing my love in words.

I would also express my deepest gratitude to my sisters, Uzma, Asifa, Arifa and Faika. Their prayers and best wishes made my journey easy and smooth.

I also owe a huge debt of gratitude to my parents-in-law for their care, love and best wishes for the accomplishment of this task.

My wife made this book possible and my life beautiful. Despite being a teacher herself at a university with pressing research and administrative engagements with gruelling deadlines, she excellently took care of everything at home to create a space for my research. She sustained me throughout this research to make me realize that this is the partner who makes every moment of life worthwhile.

My son Yusha and daughter Mahlail are an unending inspiration for love for me. They are the best things that have ever happened to me. From my professional life, they take me to their own world to make me perceive the precious moment I miss – each moment spent with them makes me feel fulfilled.

CHAPTER 1

Introduction

Arbitration is rooted in Pakistani culture, and people trust and utilize this mechanism for the resolution of very complex disputes. Unfortunately, the Pakistani legal regime on arbitration could not keep pace with the developments followed in other jurisdictions. This introductory chapter gives an account of the development of arbitration in Pakistan, the current legal regime governing arbitration, the judicial hierarchy interpreting and enforcing that regime, the system of precedent and its reporting being followed in Pakistan and the lack of institutionalization of arbitration in Pakistan.

The legal and cultural landscape of Pakistan reflects the recognition of arbitration as a well-established and reliable system of dispute resolution. Arbitration has been recognized in Pakistan by its Constitution[1] as a legal method for the settlement of disputes. Specifically, for the regulation of administrative relations between the Provinces of Pakistan and the Federation, it relies on this mechanism.[2] Arbitration has ancient roots in the culture of Pakistan and the subcontinent in the form of the Panchayat and Jerga. Both of these dispute resolution mechanisms not only maintain their social acceptability but also continue to flourish to the present day. This is evident from the words of the Bombay High Court, whereby it was held that submission of disputes and controversies to the Panchayat is one of the natural mechanisms to resolve said disputes and controversies in India.[3]

1.1. DEVELOPMENT OF ARBITRATION LAW IN PAKISTAN

Arbitration, i.e., the resolution of disputes by a forum settled upon by the mutual agreement of the parties to a dispute or otherwise agreeable to them, has an ancient

1. Constitution of Islamic Republic of Pakistan 1973 ('Constitution of Pakistan').
2. Constitution of Pakistan, Articles 146(3), 152 and 159(4).
3. *Chanbasappa Gurushantappa Hiremath v. Baslingayya Gokurnay Hiremath*, AIR 1927 Bombay 565, 568-569.

lineage and a rich heritage in the subcontinent. Formalization of arbitration on the Indian Subcontinent's legal scene started to concretize by the promulgation of the Indian Arbitration Act 1899. The very limited scope of this instrument was apparent from its applicability, which was restricted to the territories of Calcutta, Madras and Bombay. Thereafter, the Code of Civil Procedure was promulgated in the Indian Subcontinent in 1908, being applicable to the whole of India. In the Second Schedule of this Code, provisions for arbitration were also enacted, but these provisions governed only matters in pending suits; that is, these were relevant only in respect of past disputes and did not govern future disputes. The need for a comprehensive law on arbitration for British India was felt and reflected in the recommendations proposed by the Civil Justice Committee in 1925, which were materialized into the present Arbitration Act 1940. It is to note that the 1940 Act, which is applicable only to domestic arbitration, is still current law in Pakistan but was otherwise repealed by the Arbitration and Conciliation Act in 1996 in respect of India. By enacting the 1940 Act, the purpose of which was to resolve disputes through arbitration, the effect was to curtail civil proceedings in the Civil Courts. Therefore, the technicalities of procedural law as enshrined in the Civil Procedural Code 1908 ('the CPC' hereinafter) do not extend to arbitration proceedings; yet, the provisions of the CPC govern civil proceedings before civil courts, including court proceedings emanating from arbitration.[4]

Despite being part of the British Empire before the partition in 1947, British India (Pakistan and India) was recognized under international law as a separate entity for particular purposes associated with international law. In that distinct capacity, British India signed the Geneva Protocol 1923 and the Geneva Convention 1927. These instruments were enacted domestically by the Indian legislature in 1937 by promulgating the Arbitration (Protocol and Convention) Act 1937. The 1937 Act governed matters pertinent to international arbitration in Pakistan until the enactment of the Recognition and Enforcement (Arbitration Agreements and Foreign Arbitral Awards) Act 2011,[5] which repealed the 1937 Act and incorporated the New York Convention into the domestic law of Pakistan.[6]

Pakistan was among the first countries that signed the New York Convention and ICSID Convention,[7] having ratified the New York Convention on 30 December 1958 and the Convention on the Settlement of Investment Disputes Between States and Nationals of Other States, 1965 ('the ICSID Convention' hereinafter) on 6 July 1965. In September 1966, the instrument of ratification was duly deposited. It is also noteworthy that the world's first bilateral investment treaty (BIT) was concluded between Pakistan and Germany on 25 November 1956. Based on these developments, Pakistan

4. *M.S. Port Services (Pvt.) Limited v. Port Qasim Authority*, 2006 CLC 1678; *See also Haji Hasham Haji Ahmed & Bros. v. Trading Corporation of Pakistan Ltd. Karachi*, PLD 1977 Kar. 480 and *Abdul Sattar Mandokhal v. Port Qasim Authority*, 2000 YLR 758.
5. *See also Cummins Sales and Service (Pakistan) Limited through authorized Signatory v. Cummins Middle East FZE through Chief Executive and others*, 2013 CLD 291.
6. *See for detail, International Arbitration in the Context of Globalization: A Pakistani Perspective* by Mr Justice Mian Saqib Nisar, judge Supreme Court of Pakistan. http://pakistanlawsite.com/LawOnline/law/contents.asp?CaseId=2008J4 (Last accessed on February 2015).
7. The Convention on the Settlement of Investment Disputes Between States and Nationals of Other States, 1965.

could justifiably be included in the leaders' group of arbitration. But the situation metamorphosed drastically in the last half of the twentieth century. While the rest of the world undertook, evolved and promulgated the new and modern norms and approaches towards international arbitration, Pakistan did not move with that pace. Pakistan might never be considered safe to host arbitral proceedings (due to the interventionism prevailing in its judicial system), nor can it be perceived as a secure destination for enforcement of awards (due to, along with interventionism, the obscurity and uncertainty in the scope and grounds of review of awards, their interpretation and application).[8] The absence of modern arbitration-friendly laws, as well as judicial attitude, are the chief reasons for the effective ostracization of Pakistan from the global arbitration map.

The adverse disposition of the Pakistani judiciary towards arbitration will become manifest throughout this work, but this is largely because of the legislature's heedlessness rather than any particular opposition to arbitration. This is evident from a very brief history of the Recognition and Enforcement (Arbitration Agreements and Foreign Arbitral Awards) Act 2011 ('the 2011 Act' hereinafter), which incorporated the New York Convention into the Pakistani domestic legal regime. Before narrating that history, it merits mentioning that law in Pakistan can be enacted either as an Act of Parliament or as an Ordinance. While an Act is passed by Parliament, Article 89 of the Constitution of Pakistan provides that when neither house of Parliament (National Assembly and Senate) is in session, the President can enact a law by issuing an Ordinance that will be in force for four months. If within these four months the Parliament does not transform the Ordinance into an Act, it will expire, and upon such expiry, the President can reissue it as an Ordinance. The Recognition and Enforcement (Arbitration Agreements and Foreign Arbitral Awards) Act 2011 was first enacted as the Recognition and Enforcement (Arbitration Agreements and Foreign Arbitral Awards) Ordinance, 2005, on 7 July 2005 (Ordinance VIII of 2005). This Ordinance was to be passed by the Parliament as an Act within four months of issuance, but this did not transpire, and hence this Ordinance expired accordingly. It was reissued as Ordinance of XX on 3 December 2005. After its expiry for the same reason, it was enacted again as Ordinance III of 2006 on 18 March 2006 and thereafter as Ordinance XVI of 2006, on 13 July 2006. This lapsed, and then it was re-enacted as Ordinance XLII of 2006 on 28 December 2006. After its expiry, it was again issued as Ordinance XXV of 2007 on 2 June 2007. Finally, the Recognition and Enforcement (Arbitration Agreements and Foreign Arbitral Awards) Act 2011 was passed by Parliament.

At present, the Recognition and Enforcement (Arbitration Agreements and Foreign Arbitral Awards) Act 2011 ('the 2011 Act' hereinafter) governs the enforcement of foreign arbitral awards as well as arbitration agreements. The 2011 Act incorporated the New York Convention into Pakistani domestic law. This statute

8. Tariq Hassan, *International Arbitration in Pakistan A Developing Country Perspective*, 19(6) J. Int'l Arb. 591 (2002); Shahid Irfan Jamil, *International Commercial Arbitration in Pakistan, Navigating Between the New York Convention and the Draft Arbitration Act 2005*, Paper Prepared for the ICC Arbitration Conference held at Karachi, Pakistan 23 November 2005. http://jamilandjamil.com/wp-content/uploads/2010/11/papericc.pdf (Last accessed on February 2015).

abolished the Arbitration (Protocol and Convention) Act 1937 ('the 1937 Act' hereinafter). The 1937 Act was enacted to integrate the Geneva Protocol 1923 and the Geneva Convention 1927 in Pakistani domestic law and applied to foreign arbitral awards. For domestic arbitration and awards, the Arbitration Act 1940 ('the 1940 Act' hereinafter) continues to be the current law.[9] The 1940 Act pertains exclusively to arbitral proceedings seated in Pakistan and was not repealed by the 2011 Act. More specifically, sections 32 and 33 of the 1940 Act in domestic arbitration and section 4 of the 2011 Act in foreign arbitrations are relevant to the powers of the court and arbitrators to determine jurisdictional claims, including the validity and existence of arbitration agreements.

The most noticeable characteristic of the 2011 Act is its applicability to both the arbitration agreement and the arbitral award. However, Pakistan needs wholesale legislation to deal with matters relating to domestic as well as foreign arbitration because the 2011 Act only pertains to the enforcement of the arbitral award and arbitration agreement by setting out only ten provisions. The dearth of provisions in the 2011 Act in respect to a variety of other matters has tempted Pakistani courts to apply the provisions of domestic law, and the jurisprudence evolved under the old law, which might obstruct the attainment of desirable results envisaged in the 2011 Act.

1.2. JUDICIAL SYSTEM OF PAKISTAN

After narrating the historical background of arbitration law in Pakistan, it is important to provide an account of the courts and their hierarchy in Pakistan, which, of course, interpret and apply this law. Article 175 of the Constitution of Pakistan establishes the Pakistani judicial system, thereafter establishing the Supreme Court of Pakistan and a High Court for each Province, including a High Court for Islamabad's Capital Territory. This Article also allows the establishment of other courts by law.[10] In accordance with this Article, subordinate Criminal Courts and subordinate Civil Courts were established. Article 227 of the Constitution has also set up a Federal Shariat Court. In this way, the judicial hierarchy of Pakistan may be briefly set out as follows:

- Superior Judiciary of Pakistan comprising the Supreme Court, Federal Shariat Court and High Courts in Provinces.
- District Courts (Criminal and Civil) constituted by law functioning under the aegis and control of the High Court in whose territorial jurisdiction or Province they operate.

---

9. *See for detail*, Justice Mian Saqib Nisar, *International Arbitration in the Context of Globalization: A Pakistani Perspective*), CLD (2008).
10. For detailed discussion on Judicial system of Pakistan, *see* Dr. Faqir Hussain, registrar, Supreme Court of Pakistan, *The Judicial System of Pakistan*' at https://www.supremecourt.gov.pk/downloads_judgements/all_downloads/Judicial_System_of_Pakistan/thejudicialsystemofPakistan.pdf (Accessed on 8 May 2021); Justice (R) Tanvir Ahmad Khan, *Judicial System of Pakistan* at http://www.pja.gov.pk/system/files/Judicial_System_of_Pakistan.pdf (Accessed on 20 January 2016).

- Administrative courts, special courts and tribunals founded under various laws.

1.2.1. Supreme Court

The Supreme Court is the highest forum in the land, entrusted with original, appellate and advisory jurisdiction.[11] It is the ultimate forum of appeal.[12] According to Article 177 of the Constitution, it consists of a Chief Justice and sixteen judges. The Constitution of Pakistan also provides the procedure for the appointment of judges in the Supreme Court.[13]

1.2.2. High Courts

The High Court is established in each Province along with the one constituted in the Capital Territory of Islamabad. The High Court comprises a Chief Justice and a specific number of judges fixed for each Province. By way of illustration, the Punjab High Court has 60, the Sindh High Court 40, the Khyber Pakhtunkhwa High Court 20, the Balochistan High Court 11 and the Islamabad High Court 7. Like the Supreme Court, the High Court is also entrusted with Original and Appellate jurisdiction. Each High Court controls and supervises all courts subordinate to it.[14] It has been observed that the Sindh High Court is much more involved in cases relating to international trade and international arbitration due to the obvious reason that Karachi, which is the principal seat for the Sindh High Court, is the biggest city of Pakistan (around 280-300 million population) and is the Provincial Capital of Sindh. The other reason is that Karachi is on the coast of the Arabian Sea with Port Qasim, from where almost all trade either passes through or is otherwise undertaken.

1.2.3. Federal Shariat Court

It comprises eight Muslim judges.[15] The court, either *suo moto* or on the petition from a Pakistani citizen or Government (Federal or Provincial), may examine the conformity or repugnancy of a particular law with the injunctions of Islam as laid down in the

---

11. *See* Articles 184, 185 and 186 of Constitution of Pakistan. Supreme Court exercises its original jurisdiction with regard to disputes between two Provincial governments or between Federal Government and Provincial Government (Article 184(1)). It also exercises original jurisdiction, under Article 184(3) if 'it thinks that a question of public importance with reference to the enforcement of any of the Fundamental Rights conferred by Chapter 1 of Part II' of Constitution of Pakistan is involved and the concurrent power is also conferred on high Court under Article 199 of the Constitution. Under Article 186 of the Constitution, Supreme Court enjoys advisory jurisdiction to furnish opinion the Government on a question of law referred to it by President of Pakistan.
12. *Ibid.*, Article 189.
13. *Ibid.*, Articles 175-A and 177.
14. *Ibid.*, Article 203.
15. *Ibid.*, Article 203-C.

Quran and Sunnah.[16] The Shariat Appellate Bench of the Supreme Court of Pakistan (comprising three Muslim judges) hears appeals against the verdict of the Federal Shariat Court.[17] The decision of subordinate criminal courts on Hudood matters (Islamic capital offences) are heard by the Federal Shariat Court under its appellate jurisdiction, and such decisions of the Federal Shariat Court are binding on the High Courts as well as the subordinate judiciary.[18]

1.2.4. Subordinate Courts

The Subordinate Courts may be divided into two categories. Criminal Courts were established under the Criminal Procedural Code 1898, and Civil Courts were constituted under the Civil Court Ordinance 1962. The Civil Courts include District Judges, Additional District Judges, Senior Civil Judges and Civil Judges Class I, II & III. In the same way, Criminal Courts consist of Session Judges, Additional Session Judges, Judicial Magistrates Class I, II & III. Their territorial and pecuniary jurisdiction is fixed by law. Verdicts from civil judges may be appealed to the District Judge and then the High Court. It should be noted that under the 1940 Act, depending on the pecuniary value of the subject matter of the dispute, the Civil Court has jurisdiction to deal with arbitration. Under the 2011 Act, jurisdiction relating to matters falling within the purview of the 2011 Act is entrusted to the jurisdiction of the High Court.

In addition to these two streams, special courts, administrative courts, tribunals, etc., also exist, all of which are created under specific laws and statutes and which prescribe their functions and powers. Decisions from these special courts, tribunals, etc., are challenged in the High Courts in whose territory they are functioning and then Supreme Courts. Special courts and tribunal, as authorized by Constitution, are established by the Federal Legislature,[19] which mostly work under the control of the Federal Ministry of Law and Justice or some other governmental legal departments. They are large in number, but to refer to a few, they include Consumer Protection Courts, Anti-Corruption Courts, Accountability Courts, Anti-Terrorism Courts, Revenue Courts, Service Tribunals, etc.

1.3. PRECEDENT SYSTEM OF PAKISTAN

Precedents play a pivotal role in Pakistan because it is a common law regime. Article 189 of the Constitution of Pakistan says that:

> Any decision of the Supreme Court of Pakistan shall, to the extent that it decides a question of law or is based upon or enunciates a principle of law, be binding on all other courts in Pakistan.

16. *Ibid.*, Article 203-D.
17. *Ibid.*, Article 203-F.
18. *Ibid.*, Article 203-D & G.
19. *Ibid.*, Item 14 of Part I, the Federal Legislative, Fourth Schedule.

The same rule is enshrined in Article 201 of the Constitution with regard to the binding nature of judgments of High Courts on the subordinate Courts.[20] Similarly, the decision of the Federal Shariat Court decreed in the exercise of its jurisdiction shall be binding on the High Courts and all subordinate courts.[21]

Judgments from the courts of foreign jurisdictions, like India, France, England, and the United States (US), would not be binding on Pakistani courts and will only have a persuasive effect.[22] In Pakistani courts, Indian judgments are frequently relied on by lawyers in their submissions and by judges in their verdicts. Although the precedential value of Indian judgments is equal to the judgments from any other foreign jurisdiction, the reason for extra reliance on Indian judgments may be that India, like Pakistan, has inherited the bulk of its laws and legal tradition from England. So, often, on a given issue, the statutes or principles relied upon in India are similar to those in Pakistan. For that reason, Indian judgments are perceived as more familiar or relevant to the Pakistani legal system by the Pakistani Bar and Bench. Hence, with specific regard to judgments from Indian courts, even from the Indian Supreme Court, it has been held that they are not binding on Pakistani courts but rather produce a persuasive effect.[23] Disinclination to recourse to foreign decisions is more apparent in cases where Pakistani law is codified.[24] Hence, in the event where a verdict from Pakistan's superior judiciary conflicts with a foreign judgment, the principle laid down in the Pakistani judgment will prevail.[25]

It is not only the *ratio decidendi* of the Supreme Court that has a binding effect.[26] Obiter dicta rulings imparted by it will also be binding on other courts in Pakistan.[27] However, it should be noted that interim orders are not binding,[28] and the same is true in respect of opinions rendered by the Supreme Court in the exercise of its advisory jurisdiction.[29] The decision of a larger bench of the Supreme Court, particularly a five-member bench, will prevail over the decision of a three-member bench.[30]

As far as the High Courts are concerned, conflicting judgments exist, but the prevailing view is that the five-member bench can deviate from the judgment of a three-member bench. Similarly, a three-member bench can dissent from the decision of the divisional (two members) bench. The Division bench can dissent from the

---

20. *Ibid.*, Article 201 which says that 'subject to Article 189, any decision of the High Court shall, to the extent that it decides a question of law or is based upon or enunciates a principle of law, be binding on all courts subordinate to it'.
21. *Ibid.*, Article 203-GG.
22. *S. M. Ilyas & sons Ltd. v. Monopoly Control Authority, Islamabad*, PLD 1976 Lahore 834; *Abdul Mutaleb v. Rezia Begum*, PLD 1970 SC 185.
23. *A. K. R. Ahmed v. Government of East Bengal*, PLD 1951 Dacca 13; *Syed Ikram Gardezi v. State*, 1980 PcrLJ 941.
24. *Ahmad Din v. Abdullah Bhai and others*, PLD 1962 Karachi 663; *Abdul Mutaleb v. Rezia Begum*, PLD 1970 SC 185.
25. *Begum Samad Khan v. Muhammad Farooq Ayub*, 1989 MLD 3914 Karachi.
26. *Province of Punjab v. S. Muhammad Zafar Bukhari*, PLD 1997 SC 351.
27. *Ghous Mohammd v. The State*, PLD 1970 Lahore 1235.
28. *Mian Ghulam Jilani v. Federal Government through the Secretary, Government of Pakistan, Interior Division, Islamabad*, PLD 175 Lahore 65.
29. *Al-Jihad Trust through Raees-ul-Mujahidin Habib Al-Wahabul Khairi, Advocate Supreme Court v. Federation of Pakistan and others*, PLD 1997 SC 84.
30. *All Pakistan Newspaper society v. Federation of Pakistan*, PLD 2004 SC 600.

judgment of a single-member bench. But the deviation in the opposite direction is not allowed; that is, the larger bench can deviate from the verdict of the smaller bench and not vice versa.[31] Similarly, the equal member bench cannot deviate from the earlier verdict of its same-number counterpart, and hence the division bench cannot deviate from the verdict of other division benches, and the full bench will be bound by the decision of other full benches. These principles also apply to the Supreme Court.[32]

Although a High Court rarely deviates from other High Court decrees, the decision of one High Court is not binding on other High Courts.[33] If a subordinate court encounters conflicting judgments on the point of law from more than one High Court, it would be bound by the judgment of the High Court to which it is subordinate.[34] It also merits mentioning that the opinions of jurists and scholars are not binding on the courts.[35]

1.4. LAW REPORTING

In Pakistan, law reporting is governed by the Law Reports Act 1875, as amended in 1990 by the Law Reports (Amendment) Act 1989. In Pakistan, private publishers report the judgments of the High Courts and Supreme Court on a monthly basis. All Pakistan Legal Decisions (PLD) Publishers is the most renowned among its competitors. It publishes the judgments in almost all areas of law, including civil, criminal, tax, corporate, labour, services etc. Their monthly law reports include: the Supreme Court Monthly Review (SCMR), containing Supreme Court judgments; the Civil Law Cases (CLC), containing only civil decisions mainly from High Courts; the Pakistan Criminal Law Journal (PCrLJ), containing only decisions on criminal law; the Pakistan Tax Decisions (PTD); Yearly Law Reports (YLR); Pakistan Labour Cases (PLC); Monthly Law Digest (MLD) and PLD. The National Law Reporter is a private publisher, whereas the Punjab Bar Council publishes the Pakistan Law Journal (PLJ). It is noteworthy that PLD's Annual Law Digest (ALD) publishes the headnotes of all judgments with cross-referencing, as these are published in all law journals in the preceding year. The judgments published in these journals are also available on some websites. Each journal has a subject index in alphabetical order used as a table of contents at the start of the manual mentioning all the statutes and subjects on which judgments are given, including Arbitration Act 1940 and Recognition and Enforcement (Arbitration Agreements and Foreign Arbitral Awards) Act 2011.

Publishers prepare headnotes for each judgment and publish both together. These headnotes contain the legal principles laid down in the judgment. However, quite often, these headnotes miss some very important principles given in the

31. *Engineer Jameel Ahmad Malik v. Shaukat Aziz and others*, 2007 CLC 1192; *Faqir Muhammad Khan v. Mir Akbar Shah*, PLD 1973 SC 110; *Ch. Ajaib hussain v. Mst. Zareen Akhtar*, 2003 YLR 410 Supreme Court (A J & K).
32. *Province of East Pakistan v. Dr. Azizul Islam*, PLD 1963 SC 296; *Ardshir Cowasjee and others v. Karachi Building Control Authority*, 1999 SCMR 2883.
33. *Murad Ali v. Collector of Central Excise and Land Customs*, PLD 1963 Kar 280.
34. *Safa Textile Limited v. Babib Bank Ltd.*, 2004 CLD 279.
35. *Justice Sajjad Ali shah v. Malik Asad Ali*, 1999 SCMR 640.

judgment. Moreover, these headnotes do not contain an impressive narration of the facts of the case. For reasons similar to these, Pakistani courts have time and again warned the legal fraternity against using these headnotes and have declared that these are not to be considered official parts of the judgments.[36]

1.5. INSTITUTIONALIZATION OF ARBITRATION IN PAKISTAN

In Pakistan, there is no national arbitration centre. In the past, by adopting the United Nations Commission on International Trade Law (UNCITRAL) Model Law, an Arbitration Bill was tabled in the National Assembly; yet, no progress was made on that Bill in Parliament, and ultimately, it was abandoned by the legislature. In that Bill, the Pakistan Centre for Mediation and Arbitration was proposed with the aim of institutionalizing mediation and arbitration. It may be hoped that whenever a wholesale amendment of Pakistani arbitration law is envisaged, the idea of establishing such a centre would be situated there. This is also clear from the National Judicial Conference organized by the Supreme Court and Law and Justice Commission of Pakistan on the theme of foreign investment in Pakistan with special emphasis on the China-Pakistan Economic Corridor, for which the Islamabad Declaration was published. This declaration heavily focused on the establishment of a dispute resolution centre by institutionalizing arbitration and mediation.

1.6. LAYOUT OF THE BOOK

The second chapter discusses some fundamental principles, such as the attitude of the Pakistani regime to separability, the laws relevant to arbitration and the grounds on which Pakistani courts assume jurisdiction. The third chapter explains the concept of arbitrability as practised in Pakistan with its different variations. It also explains which disputes are arbitrable and which are not, along with the reasons defining the purview of arbitrability in Pakistan. The fourth chapter explores the principles of interpretation of the formal as well as substantive validity of an arbitration agreement. Chapter five discusses who, whether arbitrator or judge, has the power to interpret arbitration agreements. If a party in disregard of the arbitration agreement initiates legal proceedings on the merits of the dispute, the other party can seek a stay of such proceedings in favour of arbitration. Chapter six discusses all the legal issues pertaining to the stay of court proceedings in relation to both domestic and foreign arbitration. Chapter seven discusses anti-suit applications. Chapter eight gives a comprehensive account of Pakistani law on the constitution of arbitral tribunals. This involves an interplay between the power of the parties to arbitration and the court concerning the appointment, removal and reappointment of arbitrators. Chapter nine elucidates the

36. *Salah ud Din v. Zaheer ud Din*, PLD 1988 SC 22; *Farhat Nasreen v. Muhammad Hussain*, PLD 1997 Karachi 204. For a comprehensive note on law reporting and precedent, *see* Muhammad Munir, *Precedent in Pakistani Law* (OUP, 2014).

substantive and procedural law principles of the Pakistani regime on interim measures in relation to arbitration proceedings.

After the arbitration proceedings end and the arbitrator issues an award, the process of enforcement of the award commences. The enforcement of an arbitral award entails its judicial review. Chapter ten explains the intensity with which the Pakistani courts review an award (domestic and foreign) while enforcing it, whereas Chapter eleven, twelve and thirteen discuss the grounds on which awards may be evaluated by Pakistani courts. In this regard, Chapter eleven discusses the enforcement of domestic awards. Chapter twelve and thirteen explain the Pakistani approach to due process and public policy, respectively. Since the New York Convention does not prohibit an enforcing court to use its national concept of due process to decide the enforcement of foreign award, the principles discussed in this chapter are relevant for both foreign awards under the head of due process and for domestic awards under the head of arbitrator misconduct. This is also the case with public policy. The contents of the public policy chapter are relevant for the enforcement of domestic and foreign awards.

The other grounds of Article V of the New York Convention have not been discussed in separate chapters. The grounds not discussed include rejection of enforcement on the basis of an arbitration agreement (V(I)(a)), inappropriate constitution of the arbitral tribunal (V(1)(d)), annulment of an award at the seat (V(1)(e) and arbitrability (V92)(a)).

Because the 2011 Act is relatively new, no judgments have elaborated these grounds in detail. But it may be assumed that while the Pakistani courts decide the enforcement of a foreign arbitral award on the basis of these grounds, the principles developed in respect of domestic arbitration will be applied to foreign arbitral awards, where such principles are relevant. To that end, where the existence of an arbitration agreement is invoked as a ground for the enforcement of a foreign award, the principles discussed in Chapters 2, 3 and 4 will be relevant. For instance, Pakistani courts have held that an arbitral award will be set aside if the arbitration agreement is invalid or non-existent.[37] The sanctity of the arbitration agreement will not be recognized if it is against public policy or in violation of any law.[38] Similarly, an award beyond the scope of its underlying arbitration agreement will not be enforced,[39] and an agreement to recognize an award beyond the scope of the underlying dispute in the parties' reference shall be void.[40]

If the enforcement of a foreign arbitral award is resisted on the basis of Article V(1)(d), the Pakistani courts may declare that an award given by an arbitrator who is not appointed in accordance with the manner provided in the arbitration agreement will be void.[41] The mandate of the arbitrator emanates from the arbitration agreement.

37. *Pakistan v. Rajasthan Alloy and Steel (Pvt.) Limited*, 2002 CLD 61; *Resham Janv. Allah Ditta and others*, 1980 CLC 739; *Pakistan Agricultural Storage and Services Corporation v. Sheikh Muhammad Latif and another*, 1999 MLD 2773.
38. *Obaidullah Khan v. Inayatullah Khan and others*, 1998 MLD 1718.
39. *Muhammad Sharif v. Roze Deen and others; Masood Ahmad Bhatti v. Raja Imran Yaqoob and others*, PLD 2019 Islamabad 577.
40. *Abdullah and others v. Abdur Rehman and others*, 2004 YLR 295.
41. *Karachi Dock Labour Board v. Quality Builders Ltd.*, PLD 2016 SC 121.

He or she has to issue the award by remaining in the four corners of his mandate. If the parties have given their consent to the arbitrator for an award on a matter not specifically mentioned in the arbitration agreement, the arbitrator must receive that consent of parties in writing with their signatures on the agreement. He can also secure the consent of the parties with their signatures on the award.[42]

Similarly, by applying the domestic notion of arbitrability as discussed in Chapter 3, Pakistani courts may refuse the enforcement of a foreign award if they decide that a particular dispute is non-arbitrable. For instance, in *Ali Muhammad and others v. Bashir Ahmad*, the petitioner and Bashir Ahmad were partners, and the petitioner filed a criminal complaint against Bashir Ahmad on charges of misappropriation of the partnership funds. Bashir Ahmad filed a civil suit seeking the dissolution of the partnership and rendition of accounts. During the pendency of the civil suit, the parties agreed to refer their disputes, including the subject matter of the criminal dispute, to arbitration. The arbitrator gave an award on all the issues. As a settlement of the dispute in its entirety, the award directed the petitioner to withdraw its criminal case from the court where it was pending. The petitioner applied to the court to provide the award with the status of a court judgment. The court highlighted the fact that the arbitration agreement specifically mentioned the subject matter of the criminal case to be referred to arbitration. The court held that the award was in conflict with public policy because it dealt with the criminal matter by directing a party to withdraw a criminal case. The award sought the settlement of the underlying dispute by stifling the ongoing criminal proceedings. The court held that the criminal matters could not be referred to arbitration, nor can an arbitrator direct to withdraw any pending criminal proceedings. As a result, the court refused to enforce the award.[43]

No foreign arbitral award that is annulled at the seat has yet been presented before the Pakistani courts. Therefore, it is difficult to pass judgment with any degree of certainty on the disposition of Pakistani courts against such awards.

The last chapter discusses the orders of the court on matters pertinent to arbitration on which the remedy of appeal and revision is available. In this regard, the chapter expounds on the concept of appeal and revision and offers a comparison between the two.

42. *Farida Malik and others v. Khalid Malik*, 1998 SCMR 816.
43. *Ali Muhammad and others v. Bashir Ahmad*, 1991 SCMR 1928.

CHAPTER 2

Separability, Governing Laws and Jurisdiction of Pakistani Courts on Arbitration Matters

Pakistani regime has considerably accepted the principle of separability. Due to separate treatment to the arbitration agreement by Pakistani courts, there is the possibility of application of a law that is different from the law governing the main contract in which the arbitration agreement is incorporated. For the determination of the law applicable to an arbitration agreement, if parties have omitted to make that choice, the Pakistani courts apply the 'closest connection' test. It is encouraging that now Pakistani courts do not assume exclusive jurisdiction over foreign-seated arbitration if the governing law of arbitration agreement is that of Pakistan.

2.1. INTRODUCTION

Although an arbitration agreement is concluded as part of the main contract and is situated therein, it nonetheless remains a separate and independent contract. The principles of separability entail that the challenges against the main contract will have no impact on the arbitration agreement. The Pakistani legal regime has not accepted this principle in its entirety. Instead, it has accepted several variations where an arbitration agreement shares the fate of the parent contract.

Due to its separability from the main contract, the agreement to arbitrate may be governed by a law that is different from that governing the main contract. Along with matters falling in the scope of this law, the identification of such law becomes an important task where the parties have failed to designate such law in their arbitration agreement.

It is to note that Pakistani courts have been following the tradition of assuming exclusive jurisdiction to decide matters falling in the purview of the proper law of the arbitration agreement, especially where such a law turns out to be the law of Pakistan.

This chapter discusses separability in connection to the arbitration agreement because of the proximity of the two issues. This is also the case in respect of the need for a separate law governing arbitration agreements. The proper law of the arbitration agreement is equally the reason why exclusive jurisdiction is the subject matter of this chapter. The chapter first discusses the Pakistani notion of separability. After highlighting the need for a separate law governing the arbitration agreement due to separability, this chapter provides an account of laws relevant to arbitration, as explained by Pakistani courts; the proper law of the arbitration agreement is one of them. The method used by Pakistani courts to identify the relevant laws, if these are not agreed upon by the parties, is further discussed. Since the proper law of the arbitration agreement has been used by the courts as justification to assume exclusive jurisdiction over certain disputes, this chapter discusses all the possible grounds that may be used by the courts for that purpose.

2.2. SEPARABILITY

Arbitration agreements are of two kinds: arbitration clauses and post-dispute submission agreements. Arbitration clauses deal with future disputes, whereas submission agreements focus on present disputes. Submission agreements are normally more detailed and concluded after a dispute has emerged. They are typically recorded in a separate instrument and, as a result, are generally irrelevant as regards submission agreements. Rather the doctrine of separability is relevant to arbitration clauses embodied in the main contract, which is called a parent contract, carrier contract or matrix contract.

Separability means that the arbitration agreement is separable from its parent contract and survives the defects of the contract in which it is embodied. In other words, if the main contract is contested to be invalid on any ground, this challenge will have no effect on the validity of the arbitration agreement. The 1940 Act seems to have implicitly accepted in its sections 32[44] and 33[45] the principle of separability of arbitration agreements. Section 32 bars a suit from challenging the existence or validity

44. Section 32. Bar to suit contesting arbitration agreement or award:

> Notwithstanding any law for the time being in force, no suit shall lie on any ground for a decision upon the existence, effect or validity of an arbitration agreement or award, nor shall any arbitration agreement or award be set aside, amended, modified or in any way affected otherwise than as provided in this Act.

45. Section 33. Arbitration agreement or award to be contested by application:

> Any party to an arbitration agreement or any person claiming under him desiring to challenge the existence or validity of an arbitration agreement or an award or to have the effect of either determined shall apply to the Court and the Court shall decide the question on affidavits:

of an arbitration agreement, while the existence of the main contract may be challenged only by a regular suit under section 9 of the CPC. Similarly, the application under section 33 of the 1940 Act should be confined to challenging the arbitration clause to the exclusion of other clauses of the contract.[46] This demonstrates that the 1940 Act treats arbitration clauses as being separate and distinct from other provisions in the parent contract. From this, Pakistani courts could have evolved and modernized this tacit acceptance of separability into a well-established principle through the precedential value of their judgments.

The judicial disposition towards separability appears mixed. In *Federation of Pakistan v. Abdul Majid*,[47] Abdul Majid contracted with the Federation of Pakistan (FOP) to supply goods. He could not fulfil FOP's demand to furnish a bank guarantee as stipulated in the contract. However, Abdul Majid served on FOP a notice for the termination of the contract and then initiated arbitration under that contract. FOP did not appoint its arbitrator but rather prayed the court to revoke the authority of the arbitrator appointed by Abdul Majid. By denying the principle of separability, the court held that the party repudiating the contract and challenging the validity of the contract itself could not rely on the arbitration clause placed in it. On the other hand, in *Raja Muhammad Sarwar v. The Federation of Pakistan*, the Sindh High Court treated the arbitration agreement to be separate from the contract in which it was incorporated. It held that the arbitration agreement could not be declared void due to a party's supposed repudiation of the contract.[48]

However, in *Muhammad Aazam v. NA Industries Case*,[49] the Sindh High Court stated that a challenge of invalidity and non-existence of the parent contract went to the roots of the arbitration clause. On that account, as was held in this verdict, the scenarios arising from a challenge against the arbitration clause along with its carrier contract might be split into two parts. Disputing the validity and existence of the parent contract will equally ravage the arbitration clause, resulting in the simultaneous death or survival of both agreements. In this situation, jurisdiction to determine this issue will be placed in the courts. However, if the challenge to the arbitration clause concerns the interpretation of some other provision in the main contract, the arbitration agreement will survive to grant jurisdiction to the arbitrator to determine the validity of the arbitration agreement. In the same year, the Punjab High Court's view, as expressed in *WAPDA v. Abdur Razzaq*,[50] was compatible with the Sindh High Court's view in *Muhammad Azam v. NA Industries*. In the former case, the validity and existence of a contract encompassing an arbitration clause were contested for conclusion under

---

Provided that where the Court deems it just and expedient, it may set down the application for hearing on other evidence also, and it may pass such orders for the discovery and particulars as it may do in a suit.

46. *Badri Narayan Agarwala v. Pak Jute Balers Ltd.*, PLD 1970 Supreme Court 43; *Water and Development Authority v. Abdur Razzaq Muhammad Iqbal*, PLD 1977 Lahore 5; *Asian Mutual Insurance Co. Ltd. v. Pakistan Insurance Corporation*, PLD 1982 Karachi 778.
47. *Federation of Pakistan v. Abdul Majid Opel*, PLD 1956 Karachi 96.
48. *Raja Muhammad Sarwar Khan v. The Federation of Pakistan*, PLD 1958 (W. P.) Karachi 224.
49. *Muhammad Azam Muhammad Fazil & CO v. N. A. Industries*, PLD 1977 Karachi 21.
50. *Water and Development Authority v. Abdur Razzaq Muhammad Iqbal*, PLD 1977 Lahore 5. *See also Karachi Development Authority v. Mst. Haseena Begum* 1980 CLC 522.

duress. However widely drafted the arbitration clause was, the Punjab High Court held that a dispute regarding the existence and validity of a contract could not be subsumed into the scope of an arbitration agreement incorporated in the parent contract because the arbitration clause was part of the main contract and the denunciation of the parent contract would entail the denunciation of the arbitration clause. Such eventuality would ultimately result in the arbitrator denied jurisdiction. Hence, the court held that the existence and validity of the arbitration clause would be determined by the civil courts.

The jurisprudential landscape started to become encouraging with the emergence of judgments establishing the separability of the arbitration clause from the main contract. For instance, in *Port Qasim Authority, Karachi v. Al-Ghurair Group of Companies*,[51] the Sindh High Court held that the contract did not come to an end when it was frustrated because of the impossibility for one or both parties to perform it; rather, the frustration of contract only absolved the parties from the performance of contractual obligations. The same result is true in the event of repudiation arising where a contractual obligation ceased to exist, even though the contract remained alive for ascertainment of contractual liabilities and claims created thereunder. It was further held that an arbitration clause, in this case, would survive because the arbitration clause had to determine the mode of such ascertainment in both cases of frustration and breach. Even though frustration and repudiation violated the purpose of the contract, arbitration was not the purpose of said contract. In the same year, in *Sezai Turkes Feyzi Akkaya Construction Co. v. Crescent Services*, the Supreme Court of Pakistan held that the arbitration agreement would survive due to its separability, even in the event of repudiation or frustration of the parent contract and also even if both parties had novated or modified the main contract or its clauses.[52] This was because the disputed arbitration clause was not suppressed in a subsequent contract as its binding nature between the parties continued to remain intact.[53] Similarly, in *Province of Punjab v. Industrial Machine Pool*, the Punjab High Court held, by making a specific reference to the principle of separability, that arbitration agreements did not die with the death of their parent contract and that the repudiation of the main contract or its terms had no effect on the arbitration agreement embedded in it.[54] However, where the court went on to find the main contract non-existent for the reason that it was never concluded between the parties, the arbitration agreement embodied in that contract would also be non-existent.[55]

51. *Port Qasim Authority, Karachi v. Al-Ghurair Group of Companies*, PLD 1997 Karachi 636; *Lahore Stock Exchange Limited v. Fredrick J. Whyte Group (Pakistan) Ltd.*, PLD 1990 SC 48.
52. *Sezai Turkes Feyzi Akkaya Construction Company v. Crescent Services*, 1997 SCMR 1928.
53. *Nawab Brothers Limited v. Project Director, Office of the Project Director, Special Projects, Planning and Development Department, Karachi*, 1981 CLC 638.
54. *Province of Punjab v. Industrial Machine Pool*, PLD 1978 Lahore 829.
55. *Cosmopolitan Development Company Ltd. v. Alfred C. Toepfer International*, 1991 CLC 1087. *See also Associated Agencies Ltd. v. Industrija Masina/Tractors*, PLD 1993 Karachi 459. In this case, an original agreement between the parties concluded aiming to manufacture and supply the tractors, contained an arbitration clause to resolve 'all differences arising out of … or in relation to' that agreement through arbitration under ICC. The original Contract was not substituted by

Some judgments discarding separability may also be viewed like *Munawar Ali v. Health Vision*,[56] where the main contract was terminated. There, the Sindh High Court held that the arbitration agreement incorporated in it would also lose its sanctity and thus could not be invoked. However, more recently, the Sindh High Court acknowledged the principle of separability more forcibly in *LPGCL v. Karkey*.[57] The Supreme Court of Pakistan declared by pronouncing a judgment (*Power Rental Decision*) that the main contract was void due to the involvement of illegality and corrupt practices and ordered that it be rescinded along with the reimbursement of funds from Karkey (defendant) to Lakhra Power Generation Company Limited (LPGCL) (plaintiff). The Supreme Court also held that the public officials involved in these contracts had committed corruption and corrupt practices and that civil and criminal actions be launched against them.[58] The main contract provided for London-seated arbitration under the London Court of International Arbitration ('LCIA' hereinafter) Rules. The Sindh High Court, while hearing the case of the plaintiff for the recovery of the aforementioned amount from the defendant, assessed the effect of the *Power Rental Decision* on the arbitration clause in the main contract. The Sindh High Court referred to the Supreme Court's decision in *Hitachi v. Rupali*,[59] wherein the principle of separability was recognized explicitly. Thereafter, the Sindh High Court also alluded to *Shipyard and Engineering Works Ltd. v. General Iron and Steel Works Ltd.*[60] and *Muhammad Sarwar Khan v. Federation of Pakistan*[61] wherein it was held that frustration and repudiation, respectively, of the main contract, did not have any impact on the separability of the arbitration agreement.

By narrating the aforementioned, the Sindh High Court then held that in the Supreme Court's *Power Rental Decision*, it was only the main contract that was declared *void ab initio* and which was ordered to be rescinded. It also noticed that the Supreme Court did not hold anything about the dispute resolution mechanism as laid down in the arbitration clause contained in the main contract. This conclusion, the Sindh High Court said, was supported by the Supreme Court's direction to recoup the amount through 'civil actions' and not exclusively through criminal actions and that 'arbitration proceedings' fell under the scope of 'civil actions'. It also held that the arbitration agreement being separable from the parent contract would survive the voidness, invalidity and rescission of the main contract as targeted by order of the Supreme Court.

FAL Oil Company Ltd. v. PSO[62] is yet another instance wherein the Sindh High Court reinforced the principle of separability by discussing it from another angle. By issuing tenders, Pakistan State Oil (PSO) invited offers for the procurement of LSFO

---

any new contract but the original contract was modified with regard to unpaid dues. Court held that the arbitration agreement along with all other provisions will be enforceable.

56. *Surgeon Munawar Ali v. Health Vision*, 2008 CLC 1476.
57. *Lakhra Power Generation Company Limited (LPGCL) v. Karadeniz Powership Kaya Bey*, 2014 CLD 337.
58. 2012 SCMR 773.
59. *Hitachi Limited v. Rupali Polyester*, 1998 SCMR 1618.
60. PLD 1971 Karachi 501.
61. PLD 1958 Karachi 224.
62. *FAL Oil Company Ltd. v. Pakistan State Oil Company Ltd.*, PLD 2014 Karachi 427.

(Low Sulphur Oil) and HSFO (High Sulphur Oil). A bid from FAL, a company incorporated in the UAE, was accepted, and two contracts, similar in all aspects except quantities, were concluded. Both contracts will be referred to hereinafter as 'Contract'. English law governed the Contract. FAL was required to furnish a performance bond regarding the Contract from a Bank in Pakistan, which was duly furnished to the satisfaction of PSO to the tune of USD 7,771,600 and USD 1,305,600 for the HSFO and LSFO, respectively. The bonds were governed by Pakistani law. Each contract incorporated a similar arbitration clause with its seat in London under LCIA Rules.

On the emergence of disputes relating to the supply of both types of oils, PSO conveyed notice to terminate the Contact and sought to encash the bonds. On this, FAL filed a suit in Pakistani courts pleading for injunctions to restrain PSO from the encashment of bonds that were granted accordingly. In court, FAL denied the breach on its part and contended that a repudiatory breach was committed by PSO, which had issued the notice of termination. FAL also commenced LCIA arbitration, whereupon PSO submitted its counter claim. The arbitrator rendered an award finding that FAL had infracted the Contract by disentitling itself for damages and also held the counterclaim of PSO unsustainable. Relying on another ground, PSO sought from the arbitrator that ASL's proceedings in court for containing PSO from the encashment of bonds should be maintained to have been instituted in breach of the arbitration agreement and damages be awarded for the expenses incurred by PSO as a result. The sole arbitrator dismissed the argument from FAL that such proceedings were filed to secure conservatory measures and reasoned, *inter alia*, that FAL had submitted the same arguments to the courts, which had been proffered to the arbitrator and that in court proceedings FAL had attempted to persuade the court that it had no liability towards PSO. Therefore, by holding FAL to have breached the arbitration agreement, the arbitrator awarded damages of GBP 19,610.50 in favour of PSO. As was observed by the arbitrator that PSO could not quantify the loss it suffered on account of court proceedings, so for the quantification of such loss and for any other matter which might have come into being later, the arbitration remained open, and the award was held by the arbitrator not to be final.

On the enforcement stage, FAL asserted in the court that the award should be enforced under section 6 of the 2011 Act[63] for the amount awarded by the arbitrator and that PSO could not encash the performance bonds, whether for any claim on the parent contract nor for the sake of contravention of arbitral agreements. FAL was prepared to deposit the money for damages in the court. PSO did not put forward any objections on the enforcement of the award under section 6 of the 2011 Act but rather averred that it was entitled to the encashment of bonds for the damages awarded in the award and any

63. Section 6. Enforcement of foreign arbitral award:

(1) Unless the Court pursuant to section 7, refuses the application seeking recognition and enforcement of a foreign arbitral award, the Court shall recognize and enforce the award in the same manner as a judgment or order of a court in Pakistan.

(2) A foreign arbitral award which is enforceable under this Act, shall be treated as binding for all purposes on the persons as between whom it was made, and may accordingly be relied on by any of those persons by way of defense, set off or otherwise in any legal proceedings in Pakistan.

later amount quantified and awarded by the arbitrator. Therefore, the question arose whether the bonds, on their true interpretation, had secured the obligations under the main contract only or also encompassed the obligation to abide by the arbitration agreement.

PSO contested that the principle of separability of the arbitration agreement from the main contract was not relevant to the matter of performance bonds, but rather its application was limited to cases where it was contended that the parent contract was unenforceable, void or was suffering from some illegality or other infirmity. In the present case, as PSO asserted, allusion in performance bonds to the contractual obligations and the breach thereof was, in fact, a reference to both contracts, i.e., parent contract and arbitration agreement. Hence, PSO contended that it could encash the bonds for the violation of the arbitration agreement.

The Sindh High Court, by rejecting the submissions from PSO, held that a guarantee with regard to 'breach of any of its obligations aforesaid' appearing in bonds was limited to the obligations under the parent contract. The Sindh High Court, by employing the criterion of 'matrix of fact' as suggested by Lord Hoffmann in his speech in *Investors Compensation Scheme v. West Bromwich Building Society*[64] to construe the contract, found that the first element of the matrix of facts was the principle of separability of the arbitration agreement from the main contract, which it had pronounced to be a 'part of the very alphabet of arbitration law'.[65] According to this principle, the Sindh High Court stated that an arbitration agreement incorporated as a clause in the parent contract was an 'independent, separate and (if necessary) severable contract on its own. It has its own existence and takes effect accordingly'. The Court did not limit the applicability of the principle of separability to cases of failure of the parent contract but rather held that the context of the case in question in which this issue arose did not shrink the breadth of this principle due to the fundamental place it occupied in arbitration. Hence, bonds governed the main contract to the exclusion of the arbitration clause because the latter was not only independent and autonomous from the parent contract but was also independent of the applicability of bonds. Finally, the Sindh High Court decreed that PSO could not encash the performance bonds, and the award was enforced accordingly under section 6 of the 2011 Act.

Arbitration clauses and bonds are similar in their purpose in that both ensure the performance of the contract, and this statement demonstrates that the arbitration clause, bond and parent contract constitute three distinct entities. In other words, as based on its purpose to ensure the performance of a contract, a bond cannot be regarded as being part of a contract which it meant to secure. Similarly, an arbitration clause cannot be considered part of a contract whose performance it has to ensure. One may raise the question as to how an arbitration clause becomes part and parcel of a parent contract just like other terms just because its purpose is to ensure the performance of other clauses.

64. [1998] 1 All ER 98.
65. Court referred to *Lesotho Highlands Development Authority v. Impregilo SpA* [2005] 3 All, ER 79 (HL), para. 21.

Although the endeavours of the Sindh High to uphold the principle of separability are appreciable, it is not certain whether the principle of separability will be respected with the same vigour when matters such as fraud, corruption, bribery and illegality are involved. These concerns seem legitimate after the issuance of the Supreme Court's judgment in *Reko Diq*,[66] as discussed *infra*, wherein it held that 'the illegality of the agreement seeps to its root. As such, no operative part of the agreement survives to be independently enforceable and the principle of severability cannot be applied to save any part thereof. The agreement is, therefore, void and unenforceable in its entirety under the law'.[67] But the termination, frustration, cancellation and expiration of the main contract does not end the arbitration agreement in it.[68]

2.3. APPLICABLE LAWS AND RULES

The Supreme Court has dealt in detail with the subject of laws applicable to international arbitration *Hitachi Limited v. Rupali Polyester*.[69] In its judgment, the Supreme Court highlighted the laws relevant to international arbitration, the contents falling in the preview of these laws and their effect on the jurisdiction of the various courts.

The Supreme Court has grouped the laws relevant to arbitration mainly into three categories. First, the proper law of the arbitration agreement. This law governs the construction, validity, effect and discharge of the arbitration agreement; the scope of arbitration agreement; the constitution of the arbitral tribunal; whether the award comes within the jurisdiction of the arbitral tribunal; the formal validity of the arbitral award; and whether the parties have discharged their obligation to resolve their disputes through arbitration.

Second, the curial law regulates the manner for the conduct of a reference; the duties and procedural powers of arbitrators; the question of evidence; and ascertainment of the proper law of contract.

Third, the proper law of reference, which governs the dispute, such as whether the parties are discharged from their obligation to continue with the reference in respect of a particular dispute.

2.3.1. Determination of the Procedural Law of Arbitration

Parties are free to choose the law governing the arbitration agreement, as well as the procedure of arbitration. If they have not chosen these laws in their agreement, Pakistani courts apply a close connection test, i.e., the law which has the closest connection will be considered to have been chosen by the parties.

---

66. *Maulana Abdul Haque Baloch v. Government of Balochistan*, PLD 2013 SC 641 (*Reko Diq* Case).
67. *Ibid.*, para. 24.
68. *BNP (Pvt.) Limited v. Collier International Pakistan (Pvt.) Limited*, 2016 CLC 1772.
69. *Hitachi Limited v. Rupali Polyester*, 1998 SCMR 1618.

2.3.1.1. *Determination of Law Governing the Arbitration Agreement*

The Supreme Court in the *Hitachi* Case argued that the curial law regulates the determination of the proper law of the contract. If the parties have chosen no law to govern the arbitration agreement, the law governing the main contract will be applicable because this law has the closest connection with the arbitration agreement. In *Abid Associated Agencies International (Pvt.) Ltd. and others v. Areva and others,*[70] the Islamabad High Court recognized the separability of the arbitration agreement and the possibility and need for a separate law governing it. It claimed that the determination of such law becomes essential for the interpretation of arbitration agreements according to the law governing it. It then set out a three-staged process for the determination of such law. First, the court will see if the parties have expressly chosen some law to govern the arbitration agreement. Second, the court will determine if the parties have made some implied choice to that effect. Third, in the absence of any express or implied choice by the parties concerning the law governing the arbitration agreement, the court will identify the system of law with which the arbitration agreement in question has the closest and most real connection. The Islamabad High Court has stated that:

> in deciding an application under section 4 of the Act of 2011, the Court has to decide if there is an arbitration agreement, and in case the answer is in the affirmative, to consider whether the dispute(s) are covered by the arbitration agreement, then to determine the proper law governing the said arbitration agreement, so as to finally decide whether, under the applicable governing law, the arbitration agreement has become null and void, inoperative or incapable of being performed.

It is to note that the order does not seem practical because the law governing an arbitration agreement is essentially needed in its interpretation, but the court is saying that first, it will determine the existence and scope of the arbitration agreement, through which it is expected that the law governing it will be derived. It is not clear as to which law the court will apply to determine the existence and scope of the arbitration agreement. Unfortunately, the Islamabad High Court did not define the closest connection test.

2.3.1.2. *Determination of the Procedural Law of Arbitration*

In the *Hitachi* case, the Supreme Court also held that although the parties can choose a law other than that of the seat to govern the procedure of arbitration, this may create complications. Where the parties have failed to designate the law governing the procedure of arbitration, the arbitration procedures will be governed by the law of the seat of arbitration because this law has the closest connection with the arbitration proceedings. The validity and effect of an arbitral award can be challenged before the

70. *Abid Associated Agencies International (Pvt.) Ltd. and others v. Areva and others*, 2015 MLD 1646.

court of the seat of arbitration. There may be an alternative possibility, especially where the court other than that of the seat can decide a challenge on the validity and effect of the arbitral award. The Supreme Court held that the procedural law of arbitration governs:

- in so far as the arbitration agreement is silent, the appointment of the arbitrator and also if a party fails to make such appointment, as well as whether the court will appoint itself or the sole arbitrator will proceed, and also whether the authority of an arbitrator can be revoked;
- challenges against the arbitrator's authority on the basis of independence and impartiality and revocation of the authority of arbitrators;
- which law the arbitrator should apply;
- challenges as to whether the arbitrator has committed some kind of misconduct;
- remedies available for the discovery and security of costs;
- challenges against the award after it is pronounced by the arbitrator and where the winning party seeks to enforce the award abroad;
- circumstances in which these judicial remedies are excluded.

Matters pertinent to the interpretation and determination of the validity, voidness, effect and discharge of arbitration agreements befall the sphere of substantive law. Therefore, they are to be governed by the substantive law governing the arbitration agreement and cannot be governed by the procedural law of arbitration or the *lex fori* of the court called upon to enforce them.

2.4. GROUNDS OF ASSUMPTION OF JURISDICTION BY PAKISTANI COURTS

To decide arbitration matters, a party has to first persuade the Pakistani courts that it has jurisdiction over that matter. Given the difference in the nature of such matters, a variety of grounds may be contested in this regard. The law governing the arbitration agreement, the nationality of the parties and the territorial jurisdiction of the Pakistani courts over the subject matter of proceedings may be among several grounds justifying the assumption of jurisdiction by the Pakistani courts. However, it should be noted that with the repeal of the 1937 Act by the 2011 Act, the judicial approach over these grounds in relation to foreign arbitration is evolving.

2.4.1. Governing Law

The Supreme Court in *Hitachi* stated that although the arbitration agreement is separable from the main contract in which it is contained, and the parties can choose a law to govern the arbitration agreement that is different from the law that governs the main contract, in the absence of any such agreement, the law of arbitration agreement will follow the law of the main contract. By applying this approach, if Pakistani law is the governing law of the arbitration agreement, Pakistani courts will have exclusive jurisdiction to decide matters falling in the domain of this law. With the promulgation of the 2011 Act, Pakistani courts have considerably moved away from this approach.

2.4.1.1. **Hitachi *Case***

In *Hitachi v. Rupali*, a contract was concluded between Rupali (appellant and buyer), a Pakistani Company, Hitachi (respondent and seller), a Japanese Company and Mitsui (respondent and seller), a German Company for the supply and installation of some specific equipment and plants. The contract was concluded and was to be performed in Pakistan. The contract was governed by Pakistani law and contained an arbitration clause providing for arbitration under the International Chamber of Commerce (Hereinafter 'ICC') Rules with its seat in London if the seller was the defendant and Karachi if the buyer was the defendant.

A dispute arose as objections were raised by the petitioner with respect to the low quality of the material. The petitioner then initiated arbitration proceedings in London, and arbitrators were appointed who delivered two partial awards holding that the petitioner was not entitled to damages for the alleged breach of contract from the respondents. The petitioner filed an application to the district court of Sheikhupora (the District/city where the contract was entered) under sections 13 and 17 of the 1940 Act, impleading the sellers and three arbitrators with a payer that the arbitrators should be directed to file the awards in court so that the petitioner might challenge them and also filed another application under sections 5 and 11 of the same Act seeking from the court to remove the arbitrators for their misconduct. The sellers resisted these applications by raising objections on the court's jurisdiction to entertain the application relating to an arbitration seated in London. The Punjab High Court[71] held that both courts, i.e., the court of the seat of arbitration and the court whose law governs the arbitration agreement, would have *concurrent jurisdiction*, albeit Pakistani courts could rule on the substantive matters relating to the arbitration agreement. On appeal, the Supreme Court[72] held that the arbitration clause was an agreement separate from the main contract and thus, it might be governed by a law different from that governing the main contract. If the parties had not specified the law applicable to the arbitration agreement, the law governing the parent contract would be applicable to the arbitration agreement if this was indeed spelt out in the parent contract. The Supreme Court emphasized that if the law governing the arbitration agreement was Pakistani law, Pakistani courts would have *exclusive jurisdiction* to rule on matters coming in the purview of such law.[73] Even so, the Supreme Court referred to various authors[74] and judgments from other jurisdictions. It is noteworthy that while those authors have been elucidating the

71. *Rupali Polyester Ltd v. Dr. Nael G Bunni*, PLD 1994 Lahore 525.
72. *Hitachi Limited v. Rupali Polyester*, 1998 SCMR 1618.
73. This judgment was later followed by Pakistani Supreme Court in *The Hub Power Company Limited (HUBCO) v. WAPDA*, PLD 2000 SC 841.
74. Sir Michael J. Mustill and Stewart C. Boyd, *The Law and Practice of Commercial Arbitration in England* (2nd ed., 1989); Alan Redfem and Martin Hunter, *Law and Practice of International Commercial Arbitration* (2nd ed., 2009); David St. John Shutton, John Kendall and Judith Gill, *Russell On Arbitration* (21st ed., 1997); *Dicey and Morris on The Conflict of Laws* (12th ed.,

scope of the proper law of the arbitration agreement, no single author mentioned that the court whose law was applicable to regulate said agreement would have jurisdiction, whether concurrent to the courts of the seat or exclusive. The Supreme Court also admitted that no such indication existed in the scholarship, but it accoutred itself with exclusive jurisdiction to adjudicate matters falling within the ambit of the proper law of the arbitration agreement by relying on a judgment from Indian courts. Referring to the Indian Supreme Court in the case of *National Thermal Power Corporation v. Singer Company*,[75] the Supreme Court of Pakistan held that the jurisdiction of the courts of the seat (English court) was not concurrent to that of Pakistani courts for the purpose of determining the validity of matters coming within the purview of the law of the arbitration agreement; the jurisdiction of English courts was restricted solely to procedural matters encompassed under the curial law. However, in respect of issues encompassed under the proper law of the arbitration agreement, the courts administering such law would have exclusive jurisdiction.[76] It may safely be assumed from this judgment that exclusive jurisdiction may be invoked in respect of the existence, validity, effect, etc., of the arbitration agreement by filing an application under section 33 of the 1940 Act, provided the arbitration agreement is governed by Pakistani law. This is because the ICC rules cannot exclude the applicability of provisions of the 1940 Act.[77]

More recently, the Supreme Court in *Reko Diq*,[78] which was decided after the enactment of the 2011 Act, assumed jurisdiction to determine the validity of the main contract, which included an ICSID arbitration clause. This was justified on the ground that the governing law was that of Pakistan.[79] This approach, like the above-mentioned approaches, is without merit. Since the purpose of the law governing the main contract is to determine rights, obligation and their discharge under the matrix of that contract,[80] it should be utilized by the tribunal to ascertain the matters covered under it.[81] So, the effect of the reasoning of the Supreme Court in *Hitachi* could not be cured

1993), vol. 1 and also the 10th Edition (1981) of this book; Cheshire and North's, *Private International Law* (12th ed., 1992).

75. *National Thermal Power Corporation v. Singer Company and others* (1992) 2 Com LJ 256.
76. Such approach has also been adopted in *K. S. B. Pumps Co. Ltd. v. Islamic Republic of Pakistan*, PLD 1979 Karachi 269.
77. Supreme Court referred to *Eckhardt & Co. v. Muhammad Hanif*, PLD 1993 SC 42 and *Win Export and Import Enterprises v. M. Iftikhar & Company Ltd.*, 1993 SCMR 866, wherein this principle has been established after a detailed discussion. In that regard, Supreme Court in Hitachi pointed to some cases which held that the parties' agreement over ICC arbitration abroad will oust the jurisdiction court to apply the provisions of 1940 Act, was wrong. *Avari Hotels Ltd. v. Hilton International Company* PLD 1985 Karachi 445 (where arbitration clause provided for foreign-seated ICC arbitration, the section 34 to decide the stay application was not applicable). Similar principle was laid down in Meincke *Food Processing Equipment v. Danish Butter Cookies (Pvt.)*, 1992 CLC 1132. But Supreme Court said that this position cannot be followed.
78. *Maulana Abdul Haque Baloch v. Government of Balochistan*, PLD 2013 SC 641.
79. *Ibid.*, para. 106.
80. David St. John Sutton and others, *Russel on Arbitration* (23rd ed., 2007) 2.088, 78.
81. Alan Redfem and Martin Hunter, *Law and Practice of International Commercial Arbitration* (4th ed., 2007), 110.

even by the promulgation of the 2011 Act, as is evident from subsequent cases,[82] particularly *Taisei Corporation v. A.M. Construction Co.*,[83] which specifically relied on *Hitachi* to assume jurisdiction over a foreign arbitration and to apply the provisions of the 1940 Act.

2.4.1.2. **Taisei *Case***

In *Taisei Corporation v. A.M. Construction Co.*,[84] the petitioner (Japanese Company) and respondent (Pakistani company) concluded a contract for the improvement of a road which was governed by Pakistani law, without specifying a governing law for the arbitration agreement, which provided for ICC arbitration in Singapore. Both parties participated in the arbitral proceedings, and an award was rendered against the respondent. The Punjab High Court assumed jurisdiction, relying specifically on *Hitachi*, on the basis that Pakistani law, which governed the main contract, would also govern the arbitration agreement. Therefore, by holding that the award was domestic, it upheld its jurisdiction over set aside proceedings despite the fact that the foreign arbitral award has been defined by section 2(e) in the 2011 Act to mean 'an arbitral award made in a Contracting State[85] and such other State as may be notified by the Federal Government, in the official Gazette'.

Then court dealt with the dichotomy of courts created in the aftermath of the 2011 Act with regard to arbitration under this Act and under the provisions of the 1940 Act. Section 3 of the 2011 Act deals with the jurisdiction of courts, as follows:

> (1) Notwithstanding anything contained in any other law for the time being in force, the Court shall exercise exclusive jurisdiction to adjudicate and settle matters related to or arising from this Act.
> (2) An application to stay legal proceedings pursuant to the provisions of Article II of the Convention may be filed in the Court, in which the legal proceedings are pending.

'Court' has been defined by section 2(d) of 2011 Act as:

> A High Court and such other superior court in Pakistan as may be notified by the Federal Government in the official Gazette.

The Punjab High Court held that as regards matters arising under the 2011 Act, section 3 conferred exclusive jurisdiction on those courts constituted under section 2(d). It added that the jurisdiction of courts established under section 2(d) of the 2011 Act was confined only to matters concerning the enforcement of foreign arbitral awards, whereas in respect of other issues, remedies, and proceedings, which were covered by and enshrined in the 1940 Act but had not been contemplated or visualized

82. *Lakhra Power Generation Company Limited (LPGCL) v. Karadeniz Powership Kaya Bey*, 2014 CLD 337.
83. *Taisei Corporation v. A.M. Construction Company (Pvt.) Ltd.*, PLD 2012 Lahore 455.
84. *Ibid.*
85. Section 2(b) defines contracting state to mean a State which is a Party to the New York Convention.

by the 2011 Act, the civil courts (Court of First Instance which is the lowest court in the hierarchy of courts for civil matters) as empowered under the 1940 Act would have jurisdiction and legal competence, and the provisions of the 1940 Act would prevail. After mentioning that section 10(1) of the 2011 Act repealed the 1937 Act but not the 1940 Act in any way, the court highlighted that the 2011 Act did not contain parallel provisions concerning rights conferred on the parties under the 1940 Act; this is the case, for example, with section 14, read with sections 30 and 33 of the 1940 Act. As the 1940 Act had not been repealed, the remedies available under the 1940 Act could not be said to have disappeared by the promulgation of the 2011 Act. Hence, the court maintained that the parties could avail themselves, and the civil courts under the 1940 Act would have the power to dispense them for the reason that no jurisdiction to deal with these matters had been afforded to the court named in the 2011 Act. It is noteworthy that section 33 of the 1940 Act affords parties a right to have the effect, validity and existence of arbitration agreements and awards determined by the civil court and no such right is provided in the 2011 Act before the High Court. This grants exclusive jurisdiction to the courts under the 1940 Act to determine the validity, existence and effect of arbitration agreements, which may not be agreeable.

It is also noteworthy that if this judgment is followed, then the principles laid down in past judgments will be equally applicable as of today after the repeal of the 1937 Act and the enactment of the 2011 Act. In fact, these are the interpretations given under the Arbitration (Protocol and Convention) Act, 1937, which did not consider arbitral proceedings or awards to be foreign if their underlying arbitration agreement was governed by Pakistani law or was concluded between two Pakistani parties. These interpretations should have disappeared with the repeal of this Act by the 2011 Act, which ironically could not happen.

2.4.1.3. **Taisei, Hitachi** ***and the Current Trend***

After the judgment of the Punjab High Court, an application for the enforcement of the same award was also moved to the Sindh High Court in *Taisei Corporation v. A.M. Corporation Company (Pvt.) Ltd.*,[86] under section 6 of the 2011 Act. The Division Bench agreed with the finding of the single-member bench of the Sindh High Court that:

> subsection (1) of section 3 opens with a strong non obstante clause, displacing any other law for the time being in force. That obviously includes the 1940 Act. The High Court has been conferred exclusively jurisdiction to adjudicate and settle matters relating to or arising from the 2011 Act. These words are, on the face of it, clear and broad enough to encompass the question whether an award is a foreign arbitral award or not. Since the jurisdiction of the High Court is exclusive, it alone is the Court that can determine such question. It necessarily follows that the jurisdiction of the civil courts stands ousted and excluded. In my view, if it is shown that an award was made in a State that is party to the New York Convention, then the question whether the award falls within the scope of the 2011 Act can only be determined by the High Court. That is precisely the situation

86. *Taisei Corporation v. A.M. Corporation Company (Pvt.) Ltd.*, 2018 MLD 2058.

> here, and therefore, the civil court had no jurisdiction. In my view, and with respect to the civil court and the Lahore High Court decisions, the learned Civil Judge assumed a jurisdiction that vested in the High Court alone. The civil court ought to have stayed its hand; and either returned the defendant's application for presentation before the Lahore High Court, or stayed the proceedings pending a decision from that High Court (or possibly this Court) on the status of the award.

In this way, the Sindh High Court declined to follow the judgment of the Punjab High Court. As is clear from what follows, the judgment of the Punjab High Court in *Taisei* was equally not followed in subsequent judgments.

The prevalent trend concerning foreign-seated arbitrations is that the High Court has exclusive jurisdiction, and the 2011 Act is the only law to be applied.

In *Orient Power Company (Private) Limited v. Sui Northern Gas Pipelines Limited,*[87] the Division Bench of the Punjab High Court held that, as concerns the enforcement of foreign arbitral awards, there is no concurrent jurisdiction between the high court under the 2011 Act and civil courts under the 1940 Act. This is so because allowing a party to seek enforcement of foreign awards from a high court under the 2011 Act and at the same time seek other remedies for the award available under the 1940 Act from civil courts is impractical. Allowing this option will not only cause conflicting judgments but will also result in uncertainty as to the foreign awards. Similarly, the conferral of power on the high court to enforce arbitral awards under the 2011 Act and on the civil courts to set awards aside under the 1940 Act will result in absurdity and run contrary to the object and purpose of the 2011 Act and the pro-enforcement bias of the New York Convention. On this, it did not follow *Taisei* and *Hitachi*, arguing instead that:

> We also note that the Taisei Case relied upon 1998 SCMR 1618 (supra) which case interpreted the provisions of the 1937 Act which was repealed under Section 10 of the Act in 2011 where after for the purposes of the enforcement of a foreign award the Act is relevant, even if the arbitration takes place in a foreign country and the governing law of the agreement is of Pakistan, in such cases the 1937 Act will not apply. With the repeal of the 1937 Act, a foreign arbitral award under the Act is one made in a contracting state regardless of the governing law of the contract. The Act being the relevant law in terms thereof the High Court has exclusive jurisdiction.

The court also highlighted that exclusive jurisdiction is not new to the Pakistani legal landscape but existence since the 1937 Act.[88]

2.4.2. Territorial Jurisdiction

The 1940 Act, through its section 1, has been made applicable to arbitral proceedings taking place anywhere in Pakistan. Problems may arise with the interpretation of section 20 of the CPC, as rendered by the Punjab High Court in *Rupali Polyester Ltd v.*

87. *Orient Power Company (Private) Limited v. Sui Northern Gas Pipelines Limited*, 2019 CLD 1082.
88. For this court referred to *G.M. Pfaff A.G. v. Sartaj Engineering Co. Ltd., Lahore and others*, PLD 1970 Lahore 184: *Nan Fung Textiles Ltd. v. Sadiq Traders Ltd.*, PLD 1982 Karachi 619; *Marines Limited v. Aegus Shipping Co. Ltd and others*, 1987 CLC 1299.

Dr. Nael.[89] It was there declared that a suit might be registered before the civil court in whose territorial jurisdiction the cause of action, partly or fully, arose and that in contractual matters, the place where the agreement was entered, performed or breached would be taken as the place where the cause of action arose, thereby empowering the civil courts of that territory to entertain the dispute. It further stated that if jurisdiction was vested in the courts, it could not be taken away, even by the consent of the parties, as such agreement would be void and illegal under section 23 of the Contract Act 1872. Rather, such jurisdiction could be divested only by another statute. It may be fairly inferred that the creation of a cause of action in Pakistani territory pertaining to a contract containing a foreign arbitration clause will bestow irrevocable jurisdiction on Pakistani courts over that arbitration.

2.4.3. Jurisdiction on the Basis of the Nationality of Parties

In Hub Power Company Limited (*HUBCO*),[90] the Sindh High Court held that if both parties to arbitration seated abroad and under a foreign law were Pakistani, they would remain subject to the laws of Pakistan. To subject the agreement to a foreign law by mutual consent of Pakistani parties would be a temporary arrangement, and the moment the contract was performed, the umbrella of Pakistani law would automatically reappear. The court maintained that, as in this case, the parties had designated England as the seat of arbitration, this agreement was binding on the parties, but the moment arbitration was concluded and the award rendered, the temporary disappearance of the umbrella of Pakistani law would also, thereafter transforming the award into a Pakistani one and subject to Pakistani law. In that regard, the Sindh High Court extracted the following passage from the Supreme Court's judgment in *Rupali*:

> It cannot be urged that simpliciter the fact that the agreement is subject to arbitration under the I.C.C. Rules will divest the jurisdiction of the Pakistani Courts if otherwise it is vested in them.[91]

The Sindh High Court further held that the Pakistani parties' choice of foreign seat would be relevant only as regards the applicable curial law. However, the arbitration agreement would always be governed by Pakistani law, even though the Pakistani parties might temporarily come to an agreement to displace Pakistani law for the purpose of their convenience. For this purpose, in the words of the court, an award emanating from an agreement between Pakistani parties would be a Pakistani award, notwithstanding the fact that it was governed by foreign law.

Although the 2011 Act has enacted the criterion of seat to establish the nationality of an award, older judgments decided under the old law are being followed by negating the purpose of this new law (as discussed below), emphasizing, or best exaggerating the relevance of nationality of the parties and effectively disregarding the origin of the cause of action.

89. *Rupali Polyester Ltd. v. Dr. Nael G Bunni*, PLD 1994 Lahore 525.
90. *The Hub Power Co. v. WAPDA*, 1999 CLC 1320.
91. *Hitachi Limited v. Rupali Polyester*, 1998 SCMR 1618.

2.5. CONCLUSION

It is encouraging that the domain of 'separability' is widening, although with a very slow pace, with allegations of fraud and misrepresentation (e.g., concerning the main contract) are the key hurdles in accelerating this pace. Pakistani courts have, in principle, accepted the separability of the arbitration agreement and have assigned a separate law for its interpretation. The courts are gradually doing away with the principles (apart from separability) laid down in the *Hitachi* case, which violate the spirit of the 2011 Act and the New York Convention, like subjection of foreign arbitration to the 1940 Act and the exclusive jurisdiction of Pakistani courts on the basis of the governing law of the arbitration agreement.

CHAPTER 3

The Concept of Arbitrability: A need for Adjustment in Pakistani Legal Regime

Quite often, public policy is used as a ground to determine the nature of disputes as arbitrable or inarbitrable, which may be the reason, among others, that the Pakistani legal regime has restrictively interpreted arbitrability and seems to have considered it a principle concerning the validity of the arbitration agreement. An arbitrator cannot decide the arbitrability of a dispute, which may be due to the involvement of public policy in the subject of arbitrability. This anomaly can be resolved by, in general, trusting the mechanism of arbitration and, in particular, by offering correct interpretations to the relevant provisions of law.

3.1. INTRODUCTION

Consent to arbitrate involves party autonomy to submit disputes to arbitrators to the exclusion of the jurisdiction of courts, as well as the autonomy of arbitrators to resolve those disputes. These autonomies are not absolute, and that is why national laws place limitations by declaring certain disputes as being excluded from the arbitrator's jurisdiction. The ambit of arbitrability depicts a state's concern upon certain matters and also the magnitude of trust reposed on arbitration. These concerns and the attendant trust may be checked against the index of a regime's disposition towards arbitrability.

Arbitrability places limitations on the power of arbitrators and parties and emanates from the desire of states to protect their economic or social interests. In Pakistani law, there is no provision dealing specifically with arbitrability and how this is to be interpreted in order to ascertain if particular disputes are arbitrable. In Pakistani jurisprudence, there can be no presumption in favour of arbitrability of commercial disputes, nor is there any trend in Pakistani judgments to expand the ambit of arbitrability. Such attitudes might be the result of inherent constraints pertinent to the arbitral mechanism, which because of party autonomy, do not produce any impact on non-parties. This implies that inarbitrability is the inability of arbitral mechanisms to resolve some disputes effectively.[92] Similarly, substantial emphasis is occupied in the literature that arbitrations may be unable to enforce public policy rules fully, along with an apprehension that they, as commercial men, may not be able to deal with very complex issues. Also, the finality of arbitral awards increases these concerns even more.[93]

The narrow scope of arbitrability in Pakistan, which might be a reflection of these concerns, will be examined in this chapter, although this discussion is confined to objective arbitrability because Pakistani courts have not raised any objection to the government's capacity to enter into arbitration agreements. For the purposes of this chapter, arbitrability has been divided into three groups. The first category encompasses matters like fraud, misrepresentation, bribery, corruption, illegality, etc., which Pakistani courts normally consider non-arbitrable, treating them as public policy considerations involving complex legal points. The prevalent view is that they must be determined only by the courts. Although there are some judgments approving of the tribunal's power to rule on such matters, they are lonely voices in the wilderness. The second group pertains to matters such as termination, rescission, repudiation, frustration, performance, etc., which are normally declared arbitrable, subject to the condition that the arbitration agreement should be broadly worded to cover them. The third category includes matters that are not arbitrable under any circumstances, as is the case with criminal offences, family disputes, insolvency and intra-corporate laws.

3.2. ARBITRABILITY: WHEN MATTERS OF PUBLIC POLICY ARE INVOLVED

In *Sir E. Haroon Jaffar v. Haji Dossa,* the Sindh High Court held that if a prima facie case of fraud and misrepresentation, employed to obtain a contract, was made by a party alleging them, then the general principle is that the courts enjoy jurisdiction.[94] Even if the allegations of fraud in the performance of the contract were established by prima facie evidence, the jurisdiction would also rest with the courts to try the matter.[95] The

92. Stavros L. Brekoulakis, *On Arbitrability: Persisting Misconceptions and New Areas of Concern,* in *Arbitrability: International & Comparative Perspective,* eds Loukas A. Mistelis and Stavros L. Brekoulakis (1st ed., Kluwer Law International, 2009), 2-42, 48; Karim Youssef, *The Death of Inarbitrability,* in *Arbitrability: International & Comparative Perspective,* ed. Loukas A. Mistelis and Stavros L. Brekoulakis (1st ed., Kluwer Law International, 2009), 3-10.
93. Karim Youssef, *The Death of Inarbitrability,* in *Arbitrability: International & Comparative Perspective,* eds Loukas A. Mistelis and Stavros L. Brekoulakis (1st ed., Kluwer Law International, 2009), 3-9.
94. *Sir E. Haroon Jaffar & Sons Ltd. v. Haji E. Dossa & Sons,* PLD 1956 Sindh 4. Court gave the example of prima facie case by saying 'where accounts are fabricated and where there is evidence that the party charged with it (fraud) does not desire an independent or just inquiry into it, as where a close relative is appointed an arbitrator and circumstances are that he will not act impartially'.
95. *Haji Soomar Haji Hajjan v. Muhammad AMin Muhammad Bashir Ltd.,* 1981 SCMR 129.

reason for the assumption of jurisdiction by the courts was imparted in *Avari Hotel v. Hilton International,*[96] where the Sindh High Court noted that adjudication of issues relating to misrepresentation and fraud required the consideration of complex legal points, and the court would never leave such issues to the determination of the arbitrator.

3.2.1. *HUBCO* Case

The relationship of fraud, misrepresentation, bribery and corruption with the public policy was elaborated in detail by the Sindh High Court in *HUBCO.*[97] Although the judgment was overturned by the Supreme Court upon appeal, the logical arguments of the Sindh High Court are worth mentioning for their cogency and pragmatism. In this case, a contract governed by English Law was concluded between a foreign company HUBCO and the Water and Power Development Authority of Pakistan (WAPDA), containing a London-seated arbitration clause. In proceedings before the Sindh High Court, against the request from HUBCO to refer the matter to arbitration, WAPDA argued that the amendments to the Power Purchase Agreement (PPA) were induced by corruption, bribery, and fraud with the involvement of preceding government officials. It was equally argued that the matter related to public policy and hence was inarbitrable. The Sindh High Court, observing the prevalent trend, noticed that to attribute to one's predecessors false motives was endemic and the same was true concerning corruption and fraud, i.e., attribution without any content. The Sindh High Court stated that only the perception of corruption was pervading in the case because no proof about the fraud had been adduced, which could not be easily presumed in a country where 'the word "fraud" was banded around ceaselessly and even mercilessly often to discredit others or to explain one's failure'. The Sindh High Court held that arbitration would be the right forum to deal with the case of corruption if: (i) no indisputable evidence for corruption and bribe was available; (ii) if the parties had in their contemplation at the time of the entry of contract, the likelihood of corruption, and in addition incorporated a provision in respect thereof; and (iii) the accused party strongly denied such allegations. The Sindh High Court held that the parties had in their contemplation the issue of corruption and had included the provision to that effect.

With regard to public policy, the Sindh High Court expressed difficulty in defining the term 'public policy' and stated that the matter which was of a public policy nature for one government might not raise the same concern for another. It referred to section 23 of the Contract Act 1872, which reads as under:

> The consideration or object of an agreement is lawful unless it is forbidden by law; or is of such a nature that, if permitted, it would defeat the provisions of any law; or is fraudulent; or involves or implies injury to the person or property of another; or the Court regards it as immoral or opposed to public policy.

96. *Avari Hotels v. Hilton International Company,* PLD 1985 Karachi 445. For single bench decision from where appeal arose, *see Avari Hotels Ltd. v. Hilton International Company,* PLD 1984 Karachi 488.
97. *The Hub Power Co. v. WAPDA,* 1999 CLC 1320.

> In each of these cases, the consideration or object of an agreement is said to be unlawful. Every agreement of which the object or consideration is unlawful is void.

The Sindh High Court stated that this provision was phrased in a positive form, which presumed every contract positively to be of lawful consideration and object unless the court declared it to be immoral or against public policy. In the latter case, the contract would be void. It is manifest from the verdict of the court that the actual fact of being against public policy has to be proven and that mere perception is not enough to strike down a contract. The court further held that to declare an agreement, the state should not be a party thereto because the state is presumed as not entering into a contract violating public policy and hence could not ask for avoidance on such ground.[98] The Sindh High Court further maintained that section 23 was different from section 19, which says:

> When consent to an agreement is caused by coercion fraud or misrepresentation; the agreement is a contract voidable at the option of the party whose consent was so caused.
>
> A party to a contract, whose consent was caused by fraud or misrepresentation may, if he thinks fit insist that the contract shall be performed and that he shall be put in the position in which, he would have been if the representations made had been true.
>
> Explanation. If such consent was caused by misrepresentation or by silence, fraudulent within the meaning of section 17, the contract, nevertheless, is not voidable, if the party whose consent was so caused had the means of discovering the truth with ordinary diligence.
>
> Explanation. A fraud or misrepresentation which did not cause the consent to a contract of the party on whom such fraud was practised or to whom such misrepresentation was made, does not render a contract voidable.

By explaining that section 19 read that the contract in which the consent of one party was induced by coercion, undue influence, fraud and misrepresentation would be voidable at the option of the party so induced, the Sindh High Court made it clear that the case of fraud and undue influence was encompassed under section 19 rather than section 23. By holding so, it also rejected the argument that the amendments in the PPA were procured by undue influence and coercion, or bribes and hence that these actions were harmful to the public at large and contrary to public policy. The Sindh High Court, by declaring corruption to be a common phenomenon influencing certain officials in government, held that it was unable to see how it was against public policy. The court considered both public policies to be important, i.e., public policy to eradicate corruption by taking measures against its enforcement and the public policy of enforcement of international commercial contracts and arbitration agreements. The Sindh High Court seems to have preferred the second kind of public policy by allowing the arbitrability of corruption and bribes because the arbitral award would be reviewed subsequently by the courts at the enforcement stage.

98. For a detailed discussion, *see Dr. S Jalil Asghar v. Atlas Industries & Trading Corporation*, 1984 SCMR 1.

Upon appeal to the Supreme Court,[99] the decision of the Sindh High Court was vacated. The five-member bench was divided on the matter. The minority judgment held in favour of the Sindh High Court's finding by arguing that while the law governing the parent contract usually governed the arbitration agreement,[100] the arbitration agreement was separable from the main contract and was a self-contained agreement because, in a contrary situation, an attack on the main contract would also kill the arbitration agreement. Hence, it held that the arbitration agreement would survive and would endow jurisdiction to the arbitrator to adjudicate its validity and existence even if an allegation of a serious nature was made, such as the main contract being *void ab initio*.[101] The minority judgment held that 'considerations of public policy can never be exhaustively defined, but they should be approached with extreme caution' and 'the law reports contain ample warnings to judges to be cautious before striking down contracts in the name of public policy'.

The majority judgment, however, held that the prima facie level of evidence for corruption, fraud, and misrepresentation would be sufficient for the refusal to stay the court proceedings. It went on to say that disputes and allegations about corruption, etc., were not arbitrable due to public policy considerations. These disputes concerned the 'very existence of a valid contract and not a dispute under such a contract'.[102] It is worthy of notice that a prima facie level of evidence to establish fraud and misrepresentation, as was held in *HUBCO* by the Supreme Court, preclude arbitration, as was duly acknowledged in *the Government of Sindh v. Tausif Ali Khan*[103] and applied in *Nelofar Saqib v. Saiban Builders and Developers.*[104]

99. *The Hub Power Company Limited (HUBCO) v. WAPDA*, PLD 2000 SC 841.
100. *Ibid.*, para. 43.
101. *Ibid.*, paras 31 & 32.
102. *See also Malik Muhammad Anwar Khan v. Mian Wali Muhammad*, PLD 1956 Lahore 202. In *Island Textile Mills Ltd. v. V/O Technoexport*, 1986 SCMR 463 wherein the Supreme Court said that allegation of fraud and misrepresentation are not arbitrable. *See also Muhammad Yousuf Burney v. Muahmmad Ali*, 1983 CLC 1498. In this case, it was alleged that the contract containing an arbitration clause was procured by coercion and undue influence was alleged to have been exercised by a Lieutenant Commodore in the Martial Law Headquarters who exerted pressure on the Plaintiff for the execution of this agreement. The court held that whether the contract was entered into under the coercion and undue influence of the Lieutenant Commodore, it was not arbitrable.
103. In *Government of Sindh v. Tausif Ali Khan*, 2003 CLC 180, the Sindh High Court held that, although the court stayed the proceedings despite the allegations of fraud, it admitted that the *HUBCO* judgment rationale, whereby if the cause of fraud is substantiated with the prima facie level of evidence then the application for stay of court proceedings will be rejected. *See also Lever Brothers Pakistan Limited v. Qazi Muhammad Atique*, 1992 CLC 1062; *Syed Muddasar Shah v. Managing Director, N.-W.F.P. Forest Development Corporation, Peshawar and others*, 1999 MLD 736 in which it was held that mere allegations of fraud, misrepresentations and coercion will not dismiss a section 34 application.
104. *Nelofar Saqib v. Saiban Builders and Developers*, 2011 CLD 341. In this case, it is not clear whether the fraud was committed for the procurement of a contract, or later in the performance thereof. But the facts of the case imply that the fraud was committed after the conclusion of a contract, most probably in the performance of that contract. In relation to the allegation of such fraud and without elaborating the nature, intensity and evidence of fraud, the Sindh High Court held that in court proceedings if the plaintiff's allegation of fraud appears to be bona fide, weighty and substantial, the court will decide the matter and will not refer to arbitration. No reasons for assumption of jurisdiction were given.

3.2.1.1. *Criticism Against the* HUBCO *Case*

In *HUBCO*, the contract was governed by English law, with London as the seat of the arbitration under ICC Rules. The majority judgment did not give heed to this fact while assuming jurisdiction to determine the validity of the contract and to preclude arbitration. This point was relevant to this case as the courts in Pakistan had been assuming exclusive jurisdiction on matters related to the existence, validity and interpretation of arbitration agreements, as well arbitrability of disputes, on the basis that the law governing the main contract or arbitration agreement was that of Pakistan.

The Supreme Court did not differentiate between the application of two different provisions of the Contract Act 1872, i.e., sections 23 and 19. Section 23 of the Contract Act 1872 says that the contract whose object or consideration is unlawful or fraudulent is against public policy and hence void. Section 19 of the Contract Act 1872 reads that a contract wherein the consent is induced by fraud, misrepresentation or coercion will be voidable on the option of the party so induced. This point was also dilated upon by the Supreme Court in *Lahore Stock Exchange Limited v. Fredrick J. Whyte Group*, whereby a contract made on the basis of fraud and misrepresentation was not *void ab initio* because it came under the purview of section 19 of the Contract Act 1872, which only declared such contracts voidable at the option of the party against whom fraud and misrepresentation had been committed.[105] This meant that said party might insist on the performance of the contract by asserting to be put in the place where it would have been had the misrepresentation not been committed. The same was taken by the Sindh High Court in *HUBCO*.

Inarbitrability of fraud and misrepresentation is the result of the inaccurate application of public policy, as laid down in section 23 of the Contract Act 1872. Pakistani courts in general and the Supreme Court in *HUBCO*, in particular, have considering matters under section 23 that should otherwise be encompassed under section 19. The Supreme Court in *HUBCO* had not differentiated between inducement of consent by fraud and misrepresentation, on the one hand, and fraudulent consideration or fraudulent object, on the other. In this way, the Supreme Court equated a contract obtained by fraud, misrepresentation, etc. (voidable) with a contract having fraudulent consideration (void). To obtain the consent of another party through fraud, misrepresentation etc., is easy to comprehend. To appreciate the utilization of fraudulent consideration in the making of a contract, the following two cases are instructive. These cases elaborate as to how fraud should be involved in a contract in order to render it void as a matter of public policy.

In *Muhammad Yousuf v. Badruddin Ahmed*,[106] two contracts over the same property were executed – one with the actual price while the second indicated the lower price. The intention of the parties to execute the second contract was to pay the lower amount of taxes and registration fees. The court enforced the first contract by declaring the second one void by reference to public policy because the object of the second contract was fraudulent, i.e., to defraud the collection of public revenues. The

105. *Lahore Stock Exchange Limited v. Fredrick J. Whyte Group (Pakistan) Ltd.*, PLD 1990 SC 48.
106. *Muhammad Yousuf v. Badruddin Ahmed*, 2007 CLC 427.

second contract was declared void despite the fact that the court could not conceive any intent among the parties to defraud each other.

Similarly, in *Sultan v. Nawab Mouladad,*[107] a contract was declared void by applying section 23. Benami Transaction, in reality, comprises two agreements. One agreement is, expressly or impliedly, between the ostensible owner and Benamdar, wherein Benamdar agrees to purchase the property in his name for the benefit of the ostensible owner who advances the consideration. In the second agreement, Benamdar purchases a property from a seller in his name, and the ostensible owner is not privy to this agreement. In the Benami Transaction, the ostensible owner cannot enforce his right against the Benamdar if the object of an agreement between the two is fraudulent. In this case, Mr N was not legally entitled to purchase certain Government land. So, he established Mr S as his Benamdar to purchase that Government land that Mr S purchased in his name. Later, Mr N filed a declaratory suit in court to get himself declared as the actual owner of the land for Mr S was just a Benamdar who purchased land for the benefit and on the consideration of Mr N. The court appreciated the fact that, in the first agreement, Mr S had allowed Mr N to use the former's name to purchase the Government land and in the second agreement, Mr N had used Mr S's name to make the purchase from the Government. Mr N's suit was for the enforcement of the first transaction, i.e., an agreement that the land is purchased by Mr S in his name but for the benefit of and on the consideration of Mr S. The court referred to section 23, which says that agreement would be unlawful if the object or consideration of such agreement was fraudulent. The court interpreted 'object' by meaning 'design' or 'purpose' and held that the purpose and design of this agreement were to deceive the Government to make it believe that the real owner of the land was Mr S and not Mr N. This object of the agreement was held to be clearly fraudulent and the agreement between Mr N and Mr S that the latter would purchase and hold the land for the benefit of the former was void.

These cases regarding fraudulent consideration are completely different from those cases where consent is induced by fraud or misrepresentation with the fact that the latter come under section 19 because in these cases, the consent of neither party was induced by fraud or misrepresentation; rather, the consideration was fraudulent.[108]

3.2.2. *SGS* Case

In this vein, the mention of Societe Generate de Surveillance (*SGS*)[109] seems very much pertinent wherein the respondent, in its application to the court, alleged that the contract was induced by corruption, bribe, and kickbacks and also demanded to refer

107. *Sultan v. Nawab Mouladad,* PLD 1969 Karachi 221.
108. A contract will be void for its consideration being unlawful where it is concluded for consideration that the criminal proceedings initiated for non-compoundable offences will be withdrawn. *See Pro Booh Chandra Barman v. Abdul Rehman – Abdul Ghani,* PLD 1960 Decca 983; *Qasim Khan v. Jalal,* PLD 1987 Lahore 398.
109. *Societe Generale De Surveillance S.A. v. Pakistan,* 2002 SCMR 1694.

the suit to arbitration seated in Pakistan. The appellant raised the point that corruption and bribery were not arbitrable and prayed not to send the suit to arbitration because the contract as alleged by the respondent was entered into by corruption and bribe. The Supreme Court held that disputes arising from the contract concluded by corruption and fraud would be arbitrable if the corruption and bribery did not become part of the claim to be arbitrated. In view of the Supreme Court, corruption and bribery had been explained by the respondent as factual background to expound as to how the contract was concluded, and the respondent was, in fact, not demanding for arbitration over these matters. Rather, it was the terms and conditions of the contract which would be arbitrated. The Supreme Court further differentiated between the *SGS case* and the *HUBCO* case by saying that 'in *HUBCO*, there was no dispute about any claim determinable under the terms and conditions of either the original agreement or about the rates of tariff, etc., embodied in subsequent disputed amendments made in the original agreement but it was a case of a dispute regarding the commission of a criminal act, therefore, it was held that the same was not arbitrable'.

This judgment is inconsistent with *HUBCO*. Pakistani courts normally deny the jurisdiction of an arbitrator if there is prima facie evidence to establish that the contract is induced through bribe or corruption. When these allegations are established with this level of evidence, they outrightly declare the contract, including the arbitration clause, *void ab initio*. The question then arises in situations where an arbitration clause dies, where does the arbitrator get his jurisdiction to decide the validity of the terms and conditions of the contract. In *SGS*, both the respondent and appellant seemed to be in consensus that the contract was induced by a bribe, kickbacks, and corruption, which amounts to indisputable proof of corruption and bribery. This proof of corruption and bribery should have made the whole contract, including the arbitration clause, void had the Supreme Court followed the *HUBCO case.*

3.2.3. *Reko Diq* Case

The issue of arbitrability came again to the limelight after the Pakistani Supreme Court's judgment in *Reko Diq*,[110] wherein it held illegality, corruption, and fraud to be inarbitrable. On 29 July 1993, Broken Hill Proprietary ('BHP' hereinafter) Minerals Intermediate Exploration Inc. incorporated in Delaware (BHP), and Balochistan Development Authority ('BDA' hereinafter) concluded a Joint Venture Agreement (JVA) aiming to explore copper and gold in the Reko Diq area of Balochistan Province of Pakistan.

Article 15 of the JVA referred to ICSID arbitration for the resolution of future disputes. Were ICSID Centre to refuse jurisdiction for some reason, then the dispute was agreed to be finally resolved under the ICC Rules with London as the seat of arbitration. Regarding the applicable law, Article 16 of the JVA stipulated that 'the Law

110. *Maulana Abdul Haque Baloch v. Government of Balochistan*, PLD 2013 SC 641.

applicable to this agreement is the law of Pakistan which the Parties acknowledge and agree includes the principles of international law'.[111]

On 4 April 2006, the Governor of Balochistan, by representing the Government of Balochistan ('GOB' hereinafter), made an agreement (novation agreement) through BDA with BHP and the Australian company Tethyan Copper Company Limited, ('TCC' hereinafter) to novate JVA to assign all BHP's rights under the JVA to TCC. In the same year, however, the legality of the JVA was contested before the Balochistan High Court, which pronounced it to be valid. This judgment was then appealed to the Supreme Court of Pakistan. Some other petitioners also filed direct constitutional petitions to the Supreme Court under Article 184(3) of the Constitution of Pakistan, relating to the same subject, and all of these petitions and applications were heard together by the Supreme Court.

On 2 August 2011, while the appeal was still pending before the Supreme Court, TCC made an application to GOB for a mining lease, which was not granted by its Mining Committee.[112] To challenge this verdict, the TCC then opted for an administrative appeal to the Secretary of the Department of Mines and Minerals of the GOB, as provided under the Balochistan Mineral Rules, 2002, which too was unsuccessful. The TCC avoided challenging this dismissal before the Balochistan High Court[113] and submitted its claim for ICSID arbitration under the BIT between Pakistan and Australia.[114] Meanwhile, the Supreme Court overruled the judgment of the Balochistan High Court and declared the JVA *void ab initio* on the ground that it was contradictory to the provisions of the Mineral Development Act 1948 and the Mining Concession Rules 1970 framed thereunder, the Contract Act 1872 and the Transfer of Property Act 1882.[115]

The Supreme Court assumed jurisdiction and then invalidated the JVA, *inter alia*, due to the involvement of corruption. In its reasoning to support its assumption of jurisdiction to determine the validity of the JVA, the Supreme Court also referred to four cases[116] decided by ICSID tribunals, wherein they denied jurisdiction to rule on investments conducted in contravention to the host state's law.

The Chairman of the BDA, who was also Additional Chief Secretary in the GOB, signed the JVA. He was convicted in court under the National Accountability Ordinance 1999 on charges of 'having assets and living beyond his means'.[117] Because such conviction was put forward but was not confuted before the Supreme Court, it was held that 'having assets and living beyond his means' were tantamount to corruption under

111. *Ibid.*, paras 3, 25.
112. *Ibid.*, paras 92, 93, 96.
113. *Ibid.*, para. 97.
114. Agreement between Australia and the Islamic Republic of Pakistan on the Promotion and Protection of Investments (Islamabad, 7 February 1998) Entry into force: 14 October 1998, 1998 No. 23.
115. *Maulana Abdul Haque Baloch v. Government of Balochistan*, PLD 2013 SC 641, para. 122.
116. *World Duty Free v. Kenya* (ICSID Case No. ARB/00/7), Award, 25 September 2006; *Tokios Tokeles v. Ukraine* (ICSID Case No. ARB/02/18), Decision on Jurisdiction and Dissent, 29 April 2004; *Inceysa v. El Salvador* (ICSID Case No. ARB/03/26), Award, 2 August 2006; *TSA Spectrum de Argentina SA v. Argentina* (ICSID Case No. ARB/05/5), Award, 19 December 2008.
117. *Maulana Abdul Haque Baloch v. Government of Balochistan*, PLD 2013 SC 641, para. 49.

the Balochistan Civil Servants (Efficiency and Discipline) Rules 1983.[118] It is noteworthy that the link between the purported conviction of the BDA Chairman and the procurement of the JVA was never established by the Supreme Court. The other fact in respect of corruption came to fore when the GOB, who was pleading for the validity of JVA in the Balochistan High Court, backed out from his stance while the case was still pending before the Supreme Court, where it contested the validity of the JVA. The departure from his position ensued from the GOB's perusal of the record furnished on the direction of the Supreme Court with respect to the case, which 'made shocking disclosures of extensive irregularities and corruption'. It may be noted that extensive irregularities and corruption provided justification to assume jurisdiction and then to strike down the JVA could not receive from the Supreme Court the account of more than these very few words in the judgment.[119] These were the facts about the existence of corruption in relation to the procurement of the JVA that convinced the Supreme Court to lean on Article 34 of the United Nations (UN) Convention against Corruption and conclude that this provision from the Convention affords another ground under international law to determine the validity of the JVA to the exclusion of arbitration.[120]

In the end, it merits mentioning that in *Lahore Stock Exchange Limited v. Fredrick J. Whyte Group,*[121] the Supreme Court held fraud and misrepresentation to be arbitrable. Afterwards, this judgment was relied upon by the Punjab High Court, in *Aswan Tentage and Canvas Mills Ltd, Lahore v. MA. Razzaq,*[122] which held that the questions of whether the contract is procured through fraud, misrepresentation or coercion should be decided by the arbitrator and not by the courts.

3.3. ARBITRABILITY OF NON-PUBLIC POLICY MATTERS

The matters of repudiation, frustration, novation, rescission, and performance of a parent contract, as well as its conclusion by unauthorized persons, have been declared arbitrable by the courts in most instances.[123] The reason for such deference towards arbitration seems that these matters are not of a public policy nature. But for that purpose, the wording of the arbitration clause should be wide enough to confer powers on arbitrators to determine such matters. In this regard, phrases like 'any dispute in respect of interpretation of the agreement or concerning anything contained therein'[124]

118. *Ibid.*, para. 50.
119. *Ibid.*, paras 63, 116.
120. *Ibid.*, paras 50, 63, 106, 116.
121. *Lahore Stock Exchange Limited v. Fredrick J. Whyte Group (Pakistan) Ltd,* PLD 1990 SC 48.
122. *Aswan Tentage and Canvas Mills Ltd, Lahore v. MA. Razzaq & Company,* 1993 MLD 243. *See also S. Ghous Mohiuddin National Refinery Ltd.*, PLD 1968 Karachi 652, wherein Sindh High Court held that arbitrator may settle the question of fraud or dishonesty.
123. *Muhammad Azam Muhammad Fazil & CO Karachi v. N. A. Industries, Karachi,* PLD 1977 Karachi 21; *Water and Development Authority v. Abdur Razzaq Muhammad Iqbal,* PLD 1977 Lahore 5; *Lahore Stock Exchange Limited v. Fredrick J. Whyte Group (Pakistan) Ltd.*, PLD 1990 SC 48; *Port Qasim Authority, Karachi v. Al-Ghurair Group of Companies,* PLD 1997 Karachi 636; *Sezai Turkes Feyzi Akkaya Construction Company, Lahore v. Crescent Services, Lahore,* 1997 SCMR 1928.
124. *Lahore Stock Exchange Limited v. Fredrick J. Whyte Group (Pakistan) Ltd.*, PLD 1990 SC 48.

and 'dispute in respect of, or concerning anything herein contained',[125] or more specifically expressions like 'in respect of', 'arising out of', 'in connection with', 'in consequence of' or 'in relation to' used in arbitration agreements have been said to be of the widest amplitude.[126]

To sum up, from an overview of case law, it is clear that there is no consistency and hence predictability in Pakistani case law on the issue of arbitrability and the separability of the arbitration agreement. Due to flawed interpretations of section 23 of the Contract Act 1872, fraud and misrepresentation have been declared to be issues of public policy, without any differentiation from fraudulent and unlawful objects and considerations. These cases show that a crystallized and clear categorization of the separability and arbitrability issues is not possible. Even after the incorporation of the New York and ICSID conventions into Pakistani domestic law,[127] the courts are still sensitive to preserving their own jurisdiction by thinking of arbitration as an alien element. These cases also exhibit the concerns and importance attached to matters involving fraud, misrepresentation, corruption and illegality. This may be the reason that Pakistani courts have lowered the requisite level of evidence to preclude arbitration. In *HUBCO*, the Sindh High Court demanded indisputable and incontrovertible evidence to establish fraud and corruption, but in the same case on appeal, the Supreme Court felt prima facie evidence sufficient to have a hold on its jurisdiction.[128] This level even decreased in *Reko Diq*, where the allegations of corruption seem heretical on the basis of which the Supreme Court upheld its jurisdiction. When scholarly writings were not content with the Supreme Court's allocation of no more than a couple of pages to the elucidation of the fact of corruption in *HUBCO*, then how would a couple of words in *Reko Diq* about the reality of corruption, i.e., 'shocking disclosures of extensive irregularities and corruption' craft a fair and just look to the verdict of the Supreme Court's grad of jurisdiction.

3.3.1. *Fiona Trust* Case

In response to the Pakistani disposition to arbitrability, a reading of *Fiona Trust v. Privalov*[129] becomes very enlightening and instructive. This judgment gave a 'fresh start' whereby the Court of Appeal discarded the nice distinctions in phrases and words

125. *Port Qasim Authority, Karachi v. Al-Ghurair Group of Companies*, PLD 1997 Karachi 636.
126. *See also Punjab Province v. Zafar Iqbal Cheema*, 1983 CLC 513 wherein court said that 'only disputes arising out of or connected with a contract can be referred to arbitration'. *See also Mrs. Rashida Sayeed v. Metropolitan Development Corporation Ltd.*, 1982 CLC 1039. In this case, court held that 'all disputes' or 'all claims' is broader in its scope than the phrase 'all disputes arising out of the contract'. Court held the phrase 'all disputes arising between the parties', to mean 'disputes arising under this agreement' rather than 'disputes arising in relation to the subject-matter of the agreement'.
127. The Arbitration (International Investment Disputes) Act 211.
128. For further discussion on the discretion available to court to decide the stay of its proceedings on the availability of prima facie evidence, *see, Avari Hotels Ltd. v. Hilton International Company*, PLD 1984 Karachi 488. Appeal in *Avari Hotels v. Hilton International Company*, PLD 1985 Karachi 445.
129. *Fiona Trust & Holding Corporation & Ors v. Privalov & Ors.*, [2007] EWCA Civ 20; [2007] 1 C.L.C 144.

to decide what set of words attract what kind of disputes, ultimately arguing that when a businessman chose some specific forum for the resolution of his disputes, he did not expect that the nature of cause of action to be allocated to the arbitral forum for resolution would be decided on the basis of the words used in that dispute resolution clause. The court assumed that the party to arbitration wanted to get one-stop arbitration because he was not expected to repose the matter of rectification, avoidance or rescission of contract to the court, which if it had found the contract to be valid, would then refer the dispute to arbitration. Based on this assumption, the court held that 'arising under contract' and 'arising out of contract' should be construed liberally and that they should not be differentiated. The Court of Appeal then held that the allegations of illegality, bribery, duress, fraud, misrepresentation, repudiation and rescission exercised in the procurement of the main contract were arbitrable. This decision was not only upheld by the House of Lords but was rather applauded.[130] Lord Hoffmann endorsed the words of the Court of Appeals by saying that a rational businessman could not be expected to have intended that the question of repudiation of contract or disputes like the validity and enforceability of an agreement should be adjudicated by a tribunal and the inducement of contract by misrepresentation or the question about the performance of the contract should be determined by the courts. So, the businessmen were believed to make the submission of all of their disputes to arbitration and to prove an otherwise intention of the parties, the language of the agreement should expound expressly. He said:

> In my opinion the construction of an arbitration clause should start from the assumption that the parties, as rational businessmen, are likely to have intended any dispute arising out of the relationship into which they have entered or purported to enter to be decided by the same tribunal. The clause should be construed in accordance with this presumption unless the language makes it clear that certain questions were intended to be excluded from the arbitrator's jurisdiction.

Although contracts tainted with bribery are not enforceable in England because they are repugnant to the public policy,[131] *Fiona Trust* declared that disputes involving bribery arbitrable due to the principle of separability subject to the condition that the allegation of bribery was not directed to the arbitration agreement specifically.[132]

130. *Fiona Trust & Holding Corporation and others v. Privalov and others,* [2007] UKHL 40.
131. *Westcare Investment Inc v. Jugoimport-SDPR Holding Co Ltd* [1999] 3 All ER 865.
132. *Fiona Trust & Holding Corp v. Yuri Privalov* [2007] UKHL 40. For a comment on the English general approach toward the issue of bribery and its arbitrability, *see* John Zadkovich, *International Commercial Arbitration and the Bribery Act 2010 (United Kingdom): A Matter of Common Sense,* 14(4) Int'l Arb. L. Rev. 103-110 (2011). For an opposite view *see* Rose, Cecily, *Questioning the Role of International Arbitration in the Fight Against Corruption,* 31(2) J. Int'l. Arb. 183-264 (2014) wherein by surveying more than fifty awards, the author attempts to prove that a private forum like arbitration is not suitable to determine allegations of corruption due to the evidentiary challenges and lack of transparency.

3.3.2. Other Arbitrable Matters

Claims founded on the terms and conditions of the contract and the breach thereof would be arbitrable.[133] The courts have also found matters pertinent to the dissolution of partnerships and rendition of corporate accounts to be amenable to arbitration.[134] Matters pertinent to trade marks have also been declared arbitrable in *Zeeshan Nadeem v. Omer Aziz*. Under a franchise agreement, the plaintiff was running schools, namely 'The Lahore Lyceum', which was a chain of schools owned by the defendant. The plaintiff then unilaterally terminated the franchise agreement and established its schools under the name 'The Lyceum'. A dispute arose as to whether the plaintiff could use this name. The court held that the defendant cannot interfere with the business of the plaintiff before getting the dispute arbitrated according to the arbitration clause in the franchise agreement.[135]

3.4. THIRD CATEGORY: FAMILY, CRIMINAL, INSOLVENCY, INTRA-CORPORATE, RENT AND CONSTITUTIONAL MATTERS

Matters pertaining to the legal regimes of the family, criminal justice, insolvency, intra-corporate, rent, and the constitution are excluded from the domain of arbitration. The reason for such exclusion sometimes seems to be the nature of the subject matter and the significance associated with it, and sometimes the designation of an exclusive forum to determine those disputes. However, there are certain aspects, although very limited in number and scope, relating to some of these subject matters that have been determined as possessing an arbitrable foundation.

3.4.1. Criminal Disputes

Whenever a non-compoundable offence is committed, it becomes a matter of public interest and is to be punished according to law.[136] As a result, such disputes are not arbitrable, save for corruption-related disputes as discussed above.

3.4.2. Family Disputes

Under Pakistani law, matters regarding the restitution of conjugal rights, dissolution of marriage and custody of minors are not arbitrable,[137] but disputes regarding inheritance and distribution of property among the legal heirs of a deceased may be subjected

133. *Dar Okaz Printing and Publishing Limited Liability Company v. Printing Corporation of Pakistan Private Limited*, PLD 2003 SC 808.
134. *Sqn. Ldr. (R) Khurram Zaman v. Mrs. Afia Zafar and others*, PLD 2008 SC 368.
135. *Mst. Zeeshan Nadeem v. Omer Aziz*, 2002 CLD 706.
136. *Ali Mohammad and others v. Bashir Ahmad*, 1989 CLC 2194.
137. *Nadir Khan v. Zeenat Bibi and others*, 1990 CLC 293; *Haji Muhammad Suleman and another v. Kadir Bux and another*, PLD 1965 (W. P.) Karachi 326; *Razia Begum v. Khan Bahadur Allah Bakhsh Gabole*, PLD 1961 (W. P.) Karachi 225.

to arbitration,[138] and the arbitrator has authority to issue an award for the partition of ancestral property among legal heirs.[139]

3.4.3. Disputes Related to Bankruptcy and Winding up of Companies

Controversies concerning bankruptcy and winding up of corporations are not arbitrable in Pakistan. In *Pakistan Industrial Credit and Investment Corporation Ltd. v. Premier Rubber Belting & Manufacturing Co. Ltd.*,[140] the petitioner, by a loan agreement, agreed to advance a specific sum in foreign currency, payable in fourteen equal semi-annual instalments. The loan was secured by the mortgage of the company's fixed assets and was also pledged in the shape of a floating charge on the company's assets, along with a personal guarantee from the directors of the company. Despite many notices and demands from the petitioner for the reimbursement of the loans, the company failed to pay them back. Subsequently, a petition was filed by the petitioner in the court for the winding up of the company, which was resisted by the company under section 34 of the 1940 Act. The court was to consider if section 34 was applicable to the winding-up proceedings. Section 34[141] stipulates:

> Where any party to an arbitration agreement or any person claiming under him commences *any legal proceedings.*

In pursuit of the question as to whether 'any legal proceedings' as appeared in section 34 included the winding-up proceedings, the court stated that had the phrase 'legal proceedings' been used alone, it would without any doubt have included the proceedings initiated by the petitioner. The court held that this phrase is not alone and is surrounded by other words in section 34, encompassing the proceedings initiated by the party to an arbitration agreement in respect of any matter agreed by the parties to refer to arbitration. More specifically, the court held that the proceedings launched in the court were not meant for the enforcement of money claims in order to achieve a

138. *Shamim Akhtar v. Najma Baqai and others*, PLD 1977 SC 644; *Pir Omar Khayyam v. Ruby Hameedullah and others*, 2014 YLR 1654; *Bibi Najma and others v. Abdul Rehman*, 1998 SCMR 1304.
139. *Mst. Mehran Bibi and others v. Mst. Shakeel Fatima Alias Rani and others*, 2006 YLR 2275. *See also Jamal Khan v. Secretary Home Department and others*, 2015 MLD 972.
140. *Pakistan Industrial Credit and Investment Corporation Ltd. v. Premier Rubber Belting & Manufacturing Co. Ltd., Karachi*, PLD 1973 Karachi 326.
141. Section 34 of the 1940 Act:

> Power to stay legal proceedings where there is an arbitration agreement: Where any party to an arbitration agreement or any person claiming under him commences any legal proceedings against any other party to the agreement or any person claiming under him in respect of any matter agreed to be referred, any party to such legal proceedings may, at any time before filing a written statement or taking any other steps in the proceedings, apply to the judicial authority before which the proceeding: and if satisfied that there is no sufficient reason why the matter should not be referred in accordance with the arbitration agreement and that the applicant was, at the time when the proceedings were commenced, and still remains, ready and willing to do all things necessary, to the proper conduct of the arbitration such authority may make an order staying the proceedings.

decree for specific debt; rather, the prayer was intended so that the company should be wound up because it was unable to pay back its debt.

The question as to whether the parties expressly subject the dispute of winding up to arbitration, would it become arbitrable, was answered in the negative in *Orix Leasing Pakistan Ltd v. Colony Thal Textile Mills Ltd.*[142] In this case, the petitioner resorted to the courts to invoke its 'jurisdiction under section 305, 306, 309 and 319 of the Companies Ordinance 1984 for the compulsory winding up of the respondents', which were companies incorporated under the Companies Ordinance, on the ground that the respondents were unable to reimburse their debts. The respondents resisted by moving an application under section 34, seeking a stay of the winding-up proceedings in view of the arbitration clause, which expressly provided for the resolution of disputes between the petitioner and respondent through arbitration. The existence of the arbitration agreement was not disputed by the parties, although the petitioners raised objections that winding-up proceedings could not be stayed under section 34 of the 1940 Act.

The Punjab High Court held that it was true that section 34 contemplated the stay of proceedings and did not speak of the suit alone because there could well be proceedings not be in the form of judicial proceedings. This is because these proceedings had been initiated by derogating the arbitration agreement, so they might be stayed if applied by a party under section 34. After noting that the amplitude of 'legal proceedings' as appeared in section 34 was very wide, the court held that this wide scope was delimited by a condition enunciated in the same section 34 whereby a stay should be sought 'in respect of any matter agreed to be referred to arbitration'. The court held that in the instant case, the parties did not specifically agree to refer the matter of winding up to arbitration, but if the arbitration agreement showed the intention of the parties to refer such matter to arbitration, the court would not have stayed its proceedings due to the very nature of winding up dispute which must be decided by the court by exercising its special statutory jurisdiction. As a result, winding up could not be the subject matter of arbitration. It held that section 305 of the Companies Ordinance 1984 granted exclusive jurisdiction to the courts to wind up a company.

The court further reasoned that winding up could not be considered as the enforcement of any claim arising under the agreement. This was true even where winding up was sought as the direct result of default by a company in meeting its financial liabilities, since in that case, the courts would not issue the decree for the recovery in favour of the petitioner. Rather, the courts would have proceeded to settle the company's affairs by dealing in its assets, paying back its debts and the like. The court, while making this conclusion, referred to *Pakistan Industrial Credit and Investment Corporation Ltd. v. Premier Rubber Belting and Manufacturing Co. Ltd., Karachi,*[143] where it was held that even if the ground for seeking the winding up of a company was its inability to pay its debts, proceedings arising from winding applications could not be included into the 'legal proceedings' of section 34 of the 1940 Act

142. *Orix Leasing Pakistan Ltd. v. Colony Thal Textile Mills Ltd*, PLD 1997 Lahore 443.
143. PLD 1973 Karachi 326.

because winding up did not mean the recovery of a sum due from the company (or a suit for recovery).

3.4.4. Intra-corporation Disputes

The Supreme Court discussed the arbitrability of a dispute between a company and its shareholders based on an arbitration clause in the articles of association. It has been held that articles of association constitute a contract between the company and its shareholders, concerning only rights possessed as a shareholder and not rights possessed by a shareholder apart from membership. The contractual force of articles of association is confined to such clauses contained in it, which apply to the relationship of the company vis-à-vis shareholders. Articles of association do not give the company nor its shareholders any special contractual rights beyond those emanating as normal rights of shareholders. So, the rights which a shareholder can possess against the company in a capacity other than or different from that of a member would not be the subject matter of the contract enshrined in the articles and hence would not be arbitrable.[144]

3.4.5. Rent Matters

The rent controller has exclusive jurisdiction to deal with the eviction of tenants from rented premises. Such an issue cannot be considered by arbitrators, even if an arbitration agreement to that effect is incorporated in the tenancy agreement because such arbitration clause will be void. Proceedings before a rent controller are special proceedings, whereas those before an arbitrator are general ones, and special proceedings will prevail over general proceedings. The rent controller has exclusive jurisdiction over these matters to the exclusion of any other forum, including the civil courts. Even if an arbitrator gives an award on such a matter, such an award cannot be enforced under section 14 or 17 of the 1940 Act because the rent controller is not a 'court' as defined in section 2(c) of the 1940 Act.[145] The rent controller is a *persona designata* and does not fall within the definition of 'court' under section 2(c) of the 1940 Act.[146]

144. *G. M. Pfaff A. G. v. Sartaj Engineering Co. Ltd. and others*, PLD 1971 SC 564.
145. Section 2(c) reads as '"court" means a Civil Court having jurisdiction to decide the question forming the subject-matter of the reference if the same had been the subject-matter of a suit, but does not, except for the purpose of arbitration proceedings under section 21, include a Small Cause Court'. *Ch. Naseer Ahmed and another v. Rent Controller and others*, 2018 YLR 29. *See also Commissioner of Income Tax v. Sakina Karim*, 1979 CLC 644; *Abdul Wahid v. Ghulam Muhammad*, 1984 MLD 1198; *Muhammad Khalid v. Muhammad Naeem*, PLD 2012 Lahore 490; *Hakim v. Tassadaq Hussain Shah*, PLD 2007 Lahore 261. For different view, *see Nuricon Union (Pvt.) Ltd. v. Muhammad Nasar Sajjad and others*, 2005 CLC 882.
146. *Haji Muhammad v. Syed Manzoor Hussain Shah*, PLD 2003 Lahore 208.

3.4.6. Constitutional Matters

Constitutional matters are not arbitrable. In *K – Electric Limited and another v. Federation of Pakistan,*[147] the Karachi Electric Supply Company ('KESC') and the National Transmission and Despatch Co. Ltd. ('NTDC') concluded a PPA. The PPA authorized KESC to draw up to 650 MW from the national grid. Subsequently, owing to the decision of the Council of Common Interest ('CCI'), 350 MW were withdrawn from the ESC, and NTDC refused to supply power beyond 300 MW under the PPA. KESC filed a suit for injunction and declaration to the effect that it was entitled to draw up to 650 MW from the national grid. NTDC filed a section 34 application with the prayer to stay court proceedings in favour of arbitration pursuant to an arbitration clause in the PPA. This application was declined by the court. The court agreed that the dispute between the parties existed and stated that the KESC had, in fact, directly challenged the decision of the CCI by terming this decision in its plaint as without jurisdiction and *ultra vires* to the constitution. The court held that if such matter is referred to arbitration, they would be deciding on the constitutional validity of CCI's decision. The court stated if the matter is referred to arbitration, the NTDC could resist KESC's claim on the basis of CCI's decision, which in fact gave rise to a constitutional issue, and KESC could challenge this defence of NTDC. All this would require a ruling on the constitutional validity of CCI's decision, which becomes a constitutional issue that is not arbitrable. A legal issue can be referred to as an arbitrator, and the constitutional issue is to be decided only by the superior courts. If a constitutional issue arises incidentally or collaterally, that can be submitted to the jurisdiction of the arbitrator.

3.5. WHO SHOULD DECIDE THE ARBITRABILITY OF DISPUTES?

Public policy should not be the basis to define the arbitrability of a matter because inarbitrability of disputes pertains to the inherent limitations of arbitration due to its consensual nature. For that reason, inarbitrability of a subject matter covered by the agreement to arbitrate has no effect on the validity of such arbitration agreement for the reason that inarbitrability of a subject matter is related to the jurisdiction of the arbitrator and not the validity of an arbitration agreement. When looked at in this way, the jurisdiction to decide the arbitrability of disputes should be vested in the arbitrator instead of the courts.[148]

Arbitration agreements possess both a contractual as well as a jurisdictional dimension. They are distinguished from ordinary agreements on the basis of their jurisdictional aspect due to which, by ousting the jurisdiction of the court, they confer jurisdiction to the arbitrator. But on the contractual side, they are similar to other ordinary contracts. Just like other contracts, arbitration agreements require for their

---

147. *K – Electric Limited and another v. Federation of Pakistan,* PLD 2014 Sindh 504.
148. Stavros L. Brekoulakis, *On Arbitrability: Persisting Misconceptions and New Areas of Concern,* in *Arbitrability: International & Comparative Perspective,* eds Loukas A. Mistelis and Stavros L. Brekoulakis (Kluwer Law International, 2009), 2-3, 2-4.

valid formation free consent, and capacity of the parties and possible form requirements as stipulated by law. If some other condition is prescribed for the validity of arbitration agreements that is actually not mandated for ordinary contracts, it will put arbitration agreements in an unjustifiably more onerous situation compared to ordinary contracts. The very close connection between the validity of arbitration agreements and the jurisdiction of arbitrators cannot prove the similarity between the inarbitrability and invalidity of arbitration agreements as sometimes the arbitrator may lack jurisdiction over a matter despite the validity of the arbitration agreement, for reasons, *inter alia*, that they fall outside the ambit of the arbitration agreement or that they cannot be reagitated due to the res judicata effect of a decision from either the arbitrator or the courts. This group includes the factor of inarbitrability of a dispute over which the arbitrator cannot exercise its jurisdiction even if the arbitration agreement is valid. Hence, arbitrability, which is a condition precedent for the arbitrator's jurisdiction, is a jurisdictional requirement pertinent to arbitration, is not a contractual requirement for the validity of an arbitration agreement.

When a dispute is declared to be non-arbitrable, it will deprive the arbitrator of its jurisdiction to adjudicate over that dispute without having any effect over the arbitration agreement, which will remain valid by bestowing jurisdiction on the tribunal with regard to some other arbitrable matter. This is because under a single contract, various claims may emerge, and some of these may be arbitrable while others may not be amenable to arbitration. The subject matter of an agreement is normally arbitrable. It is actually the dispute that later arises and which may be inarbitrable. For instance, in insolvency disputes, the bankruptcy of debtors does not render the arbitration agreement to be *void ab initio*. For this reason, all issues that are not core to the insolvency may be submitted to arbitration despite the insolvency of the debtor. This means that the subject matter of the arbitration agreement cannot be termed as inarbitrable at the moment of entry of the contract; rather, if a dispute emerged subsequently, it is this that may or may not be arbitrable.[149]

When it is admitted that the arbitrability is a jurisdictional issue, then the courts, after conducting a prima facie review, should refer to the arbitrators the matter of arbitrability, which relates to the jurisdiction of the arbitrator, and the tribunal should have the power to determine all jurisdictional issues, including the scope of the arbitration agreement and the arbitrability of the dispute in question exclusively.

3.6. CONCLUSION

Laws should be modernized. Along with that, there is a need for an arbitration culture to be created by arbitration-friendly disposition from the bar and the judiciary, which should take into consideration the demands and dimensions of international business. This takes time. The change should come from inside the judiciary as well as outside, involving all stakeholders. The internal change requires instilling faith in the judiciary

149. *Ibid.*, 2-58 to 2-69. Haris Pamboukis, *On Arbitrability: The Arbitrator as a Problem Solver*, in *Arbitrability: International & Comparative Perspective*, eds Loukas A. Mistelis and Stavros L. Brekoulakis (Kluwer Law International, 2009), 7-17.

that arbitrators are no less competent and responsible than the courts and not merely a tool for reducing their case log.

There is no one except the state that can materialize the external change. Judges may be trained in arbitration, particularly by attending international training sessions and conferences, where they will have an opportunity to meet arbitrators, judges and counsels from other jurisdictions and exchange their experiences.

All this does not mean to put the sole responsibility on judges who at the end have to decide a matter in accordance with the law of the land, Rather, the promulgation of arbitration-friendly laws, such as the repeal of the 1940 Act, is also the need of the hour. In that respect, those on the helm of legislative affairs may realize that interference with arbitration may secure their short-term interests with regard to one individual case, but this will, in the long term, impair the inward investment flow by damaging the long economic interests of the country.

Pakistani society is very receptive to such changes favouring arbitration, which is manifest from the social acceptability of the Jerga and Panchayat. These are informal ways of dispute resolution where the adjudicators are appointed from within the society and even decide murder cases, despite the fact that no mechanism for the execution of these decisions exists because the Pakistani legal system has imparted no sanctity for their verdicts. It is only the social pressure that ultimately becomes the instrument for their enforcement. In the Khyber Pakhtunkhwa province of Pakistan and the Federally Administered Tribal Areas of Pakistan, 70.47% of people trust Olasi Jirga, which is the private dispute resolution system and 12.07% of people trust the FCR Jirga, which is a dispute resolution system established by the Government under Frontier Crimes Regulations, while Taliban Jirga receives only 0.67% support.[150] It is interesting to point out that despite the governmental recognition of the FCR Jirga's decisions, the percentage of trust for the Olasi Jirga, which lacks such recognition for its decisions, is much higher, which also symbolizes the social support for private dispute resolution mechanisms.

150. Understanding Jirga: Legality and Legitimacy in Pakistan's Federally Administered Tribal Areas was a report formulated after research conducted by Community Appraisal & Motivation Programme (CAMP) with the technical support from Max Planck Institute for Comparative Public Law and International Law, Heidelberg, Germany – 2011. Downloaded from http://archiv.ub.uni-heidelberg.de/savifadok/3124/1/Understanding-Jirga-07-2011.pdf (Last accessed on 24 March 2015).

CHAPTER 4

Interpretation of Arbitration Agreements by Pakistani Courts

Although a normal contract is enforceable even if it is orally concluded and an arbitration agreement needs to be in writing, Pakistani courts have applied the same principles to both the agreements for the purpose of interpretation. In this regards, this chapter discusses the cannons of interpretation employed by the Pakistani court to interpret the formal and substantive validity of an arbitration agreement. Generally, arbitration agreements are broadly and effectively interpreted by taking into consideration the 'in writing' requirement for an arbitration agreement.

4.1. INTRODUCTION

The question as to how an arbitration agreement is interpreted by Pakistani courts has far-reaching reverberations since sundry matters of arbitral legal regimes are controlled by judicial attitudes. The stay of legal proceedings started off in disregard of an arbitration agreement, and then referral of the matter to arbitrators, issuance of anti-arbitration injunctions and sometimes anti-suit injunctions pivot on the scope, existence, and effectiveness of arbitration agreements. Article II(3) of the New York Convention also waives the obligation of a state court to refer the matter to arbitration if 'it finds that the said agreement is null and void, inoperative or incapable of being performed', which condition has then been enacted into domestic legislation.[151]

Given the significance of the scope, existence, and effectiveness of arbitration agreements, it is vital to figure out the Pakistani way of interpreting these issues. Hence this chapter surveys comprehensively relevant Pakistani judgments to unearth the

151. Section 4(2) of the Recognition and Enforcement (Arbitration Agreements and Foreign Arbitral Awards) Act 2011 which has incorporated the New York Convention into Pakistani law.

canons of interpretation employed in that regard. This chapter also investigates the requirements of formal validity of an arbitration agreement and how those requirements are interpreted, along with another question as to what is the Pakistani attitude to the incorporation of an arbitration agreement by reference to another document. To embark upon the research, it is submitted that in Pakistan, the arbitration agreement is considered a normal contract and both are governed by the same principles of interpretation.[152]

Arbitration agreements like any other contract concluded between two parties having the capacity to contract with free consent, at *ad idem* regarding the essential terms of the contract and under section 29 of the Contract Act 1872, would be void if its meaning is not certain or capable of being made certain.[153] The main purpose of interpretation of an agreement is to find out the intention of the parties to the agreement.[154] The true meaning, scope and applicability of a contract is a question of law,[155] and it is the duty of the courts to interpret a contract in its proper legal perspective by applying correct law.[156] The arbitration agreement is to be interpreted separately and independently from the main contract.[157]

4.2. INTERPRETATION OF SCOPE OF ARBITRATION AGREEMENT

4.2.1. The Principle of Strict and Liberal Interpretation

Arbitration agreements should not be interpreted strictly. The argument in favour of a strict interpretation of arbitration agreements is premised on the fact that arbitration constitutes an exception to adjudication, and exceptions are construed restrictively. This argument has lost its strength because arbitration has become a normal mechanism of dispute resolution owing to its reliability and for many other reasons of a similar nature.[158] Since arbitration agreements deal with unforeseen matters, to

152. *Yasmeen v. Beach Developers through Managing Director and another*, 2003 YLR 1109; *Ibad & Company v. Pakistan Television Corporation Ltd. and others*, 1981 CLC 106.
153. *Mrs. Yasmeen v. Beach Developers*, 2003 YLR 1109; *Karachi Dock Labour Board v. Quality Builders Ltd.*, PLD 2016 SC 121.
154. *House Building Finance Corporation v. Shahenshah Humayun Cooperative Housing Society and others*, 1992 SCMR 19; *Haji Adam Ali Agaria v. Asif Hussain and others*, 1996 MLD 322.
155. *Captain Salim Bilal v. Pakistan International Airline Corporation (PIAC) and others*, 2013 PLC (C.S.) 1212.
156. *Concentrate Manufacturing Company of Ireland and others v. Seven-up Bottling Company (Private) Limited and others*, 2002 CLD 77.
157. *Abid Associated Agencies International (Pvt.) Ltd. and others v. Areva and others*, 2015 MLD 1646.
158. This viewpoint finds support by the French Supreme Court in its Judgment of 13 March 1978, 1979 Rev. Arb. 339 (French Cour de Cassation). The English Supreme Court's decision in *Fiona Trust & Holding Corporation and others v. Privalov and others*, [2007] UKHL 40 also adhered to the same approach, whereby Lord Hope stated that the liberal interpretation of arbitration agreements would create certainty. *See also* Joachim Delaney and Katharina Lewis, *The Presumptive Approach to the Construction of Arbitration Agreements and the Principle of Separability: English Law Post* Fiona Trust *and Australian Law Contrasted*, 31 U. New S. Wales L.J. 341 (2008). Emmanuel Gaillard and John Savage, *Fouchard, Gaillard, Goldman on International Commercial Arbitration* (Kluwer Law International, 1999), para. 478.

establish the scope of arbitration agreements, the sole reliance on the wording of the parties may not be sufficient. Rather, it may be necessary to explore the intention of the parties with a presumption in favour of the inclusion of disputes in the ambit of their underlying arbitration agreement. This presumption signifies that a valid arbitration agreement should normally be construed broadly so as to encompass all pertinent disputes when there is doubt about their inclusion.[159]

This approach appears to have been followed, to a very great extent, in Pakistan courts through the prohibition of restricting the scope of arbitration on the basis of a mere technicality.[160] For instance, the Punjab High Court held that agreements should be interpreted reasonably and liberally in accordance with the parties' intentions.[161] Similarly, in *Muhammad Azam Muhammad Fazil & Co., Karachi v. N. A. Industries Karachi,*[162] the question before the Sindh High Court was whether the seller had committed a breach by making the delivery with the ship VALL MOON by substituting the contractually agreed ship MARIE ANN and whether there was no new agreement needed for the purchase of a new ship. By maintaining that the scope of arbitration agreements was wide enough through the use of the words 'in case of dispute touching upon this agreement', the court concluded that these two matters in question pertained to the interpretation of the contract and thus fell within the scope of the arbitration clause. In another case,[163] the original construction contract was terminated by a Termination Contract whereby the Original Contract embodied an arbitration clause, while the Termination Contract did not. The Supreme Court ceded an expansive interpretation to the scope of the arbitration agreement built into the Original Contract by holding that the disputes springing under the Termination Contract would also be settled by the arbitration clause incorporated in the Original Contract.[164]

In *Island Textile Mills Ltd. v. V/O Technoexperts,*[165] for the resolution of future disputes, it was put in writing that 'the parties shall take all measures to settle amicably all disputes or differences which may arise out of this contract or in connection with it'. In case the parties' endeavour to arrive at an amicable settlement was inefficacious, all disputes and differences which might arise out of that contract were to be submitted to arbitration. As to the contention from the plaintiff that the discords did not fall in the scope of the arbitration clause, they argued that in the first subparagraph respecting the amicable settlement of disputes, a sentence 'all disputes or differences which may arise out of this Contract or *in connection with it*' was put down while in sub-para two, appertaining to the referral of the dispute to arbitration, only 'all disputes, and

159. Gary B. Born, *International Commercial Arbitration* (Kluwer Law International, 2009), 1066 & 1067.
160. *Waseem Construction Co. v. Government of Sindh and others*, PLD 1987 Karachi 575.
161. *Province of Punjab v. Malik Muhammad Ilyas and others*, 1994 MLD 476; *G.M.K. Enterprises v. Shaheen Builders*, 1999 CLC 1698.
162. *Muhammad Azam Muhammad Fazil & Co., Karachi v. N. A. Industries, Karachi*, PLD 1977 Karachi 21.
163. *Sezai Turkes Feyzi Akkaya Construction Company, Lahore v. Crescent Services, Lahore and another*, 1997 SCMR 1928.
164. *See also Karachi Shipyard and Engineering Works Ltd., Karachi v. General Iron and Steel Works Ltd.*, PLD 1971 Karachi 501.
165. *Island Textile Mills Ltd. Karachi v. V/O Technoexperts and others*, 1979 CLC 307.

differences which may arise out of this contract' was committed to paper, and the phrase '*in connection with it*' as employed in sub-para one had been omitted in sub-para two, implying that the parties, in point of fact, intended to restrict the scope of the arbitration clause. The court turned down this argument by unambiguously pronouncing that such distinction by the plaintiffs on the basis of language utilizing these two sub-paras of the arbitration agreement was not material, as prima facie, the claims of the plaintiffs arose out of the contract.

Sometimes, however, restrictive interpretation has been afforded to the scope of an arbitration agreement. For example, the Punjab High Court held that an arbitration agreement encompassed only business disputes, whereas the rendition of accounts, not considered as business disputes, did not fall in the scope of such arbitration agreement.[166] Under this approach, the court does not imply anything inconsistent with the express terms of the contract or stipulation in the contract that has not been expressed in it merely because it thinks this implication reasonable. The court can imply such stipulation only if, after having considered the terms of the contract in a reasonable manner, it is satisfied that the parties should necessarily have intended the implied term in the contract.[167]

In the same manner that restrictive interpretation should be avoided, so too an exceedingly extensive interpretation of arbitration agreements should not be resorted to. It is in accordance with the reality that arbitration has reliably become a normal mechanism of dispute resolution, but that does not entail that parties to disputes should be excluded from access to the courts. In other words, if a party has the intention of bringing its dispute to court, it should not be restrained from doing so on the mere allegation of the existence of an arbitration clause, on the basis of an immensely broad construction to the arbitration agreement. What is of essence is the construction of the arbitration agreement to ascertain the true intentions of the parties in order to determine if they were looking to truly submit their disputes to arbitration. If the answer is affirmative, then what sort of disputes did the disputants concur to submit to arbitration?[168]

4.2.2. Role of Words Used in Arbitration Clauses and Their Interpretation

Where an agreement is in written form, then nothing can be read more than what is written in it.[169] While interpreting the contract, the court looks to the words to ascertain the intention of the parties.[170] If words are clear and unambiguous, the courts should

166. *Syed Naushab Ali v. Lt. Col. Mehmood Khan Durrani*, PLD 1972 Lahore 766.
167. *House Building Finance Corporation v. Shahinshah Humayun Cooperative House Building Society and others*, 1992 SCMR 19.
168. Emmanuel Gaillard and John Savage, *Fouchard, Gaillard, Goldman on International Commercial Arbitration* (Kluwer Law International, 1999), para. 481.
169. *Muhammad Naveed v. Teejays Exclusive (Pvt.) Ltd. and another*, 2009 CLC 883.
170. *House Building Finance Corporation v. Shahinshah Humayun Cooperative House Building Society and others*, 1992 SCMR 19.

give them their ordinary and natural meaning[171] and should not make any addition, edition, modification, or variation of these on the basis of any evidence, unless the intention of both parties warrants such modification, addition, or other is obvious.[172] Where plain and natural meanings are inconsistent with other expressions used and defined in the contract or create absurdity, then the courts can modify the ordinary meaning to avoid absurdity and inconsistency, since the courts should keep the document alive and binding on the parties, according to the intention of the parties.[173] It is to note that along with the words, the courts also examine the conduct of the parties read into the contract and the eventualities not covered by it.[174] Intention is to be ascertained from the language of the contract, but this intention should not be defeated by too strict adherence to actual words.[175]

Hence, words employed by the parties in the arbitration agreement play a pivotal role in the judicial determination of the scope of the arbitration agreement. For instance, the matter of no claim certificate' was held by the Sindh High Court to fall within the arbitrator's jurisdiction, owing to the phrases 'arising out of' or 'relating to' as employed in the arbitration agreement.[176] Other phrases which have attracted broad judicial interpretation of arbitration agreements embrace 'dispute in respect of or concerning anything herein contained' or 'any dispute in respect of interpretation of the agreement or concerning anything contained therein'[177] or more specifically 'in respect of' or 'arising out of' or 'in connection with' or, 'in consequence of' or 'in relation to' are of the broadest amplitude.[178] Similarly, the expression in an arbitration agreement 'all disputes arising between the parties' was interpreted strictly to connote 'disputes arising under this agreement', rather than 'disputes arising in relation to the subject matter of the agreement'.[179]

These word-groups, although being all-inclusive in their outlook, do not encompass in the ambit of the arbitration agreement non-contractual disputes and disputes

171. *Khanzada Muhammad Abdul Haq Khan Khattak & Co. v. WAPDA*, 1991 SCMR 143; *Cantonment Board, Sialkot Cantonment v. Sheikh Nazir Ahmad*, PLD 1953 Lahore 400.
172. *Mian Absar Akhtar and others v. Zarai Taraqiati Bank Ltd. and others*, 2007 CLD 1620; *Muhammad Saleem and others v. Marryam Bibi and others*, 2007 CLC 1592.
173. *House Building Finance Corporation v. Shahinshah Humayun Cooperative House Building Society and others*, 1992 SCMR 19.
174. *Al-Abdullah Construction (Pvt.) Ltd v. WAPDA*, 2003 YLR 1535; *Habib Bank Limited v. Malik Atta Muhammad and others*, 2000 CLC 451.
175. *Ghazanfar Hussain v. Rehmat Bibi and others*, 1989 CLC 310 SC (A J & K).
176. *Karachi Electric Supply Corporation Ltd. v. Consortium 2000 P.E.C.H. Society, Karachi*, 1986 CLC 1350.
177. *Lahore Stock Exchange Limited v. Fredrick J. Whyte Group (Pakistan) Ltd.*, PLD 1990 SC 48.
178. *Port Qasim Authority, Karachi v. Al-Ghurair Group of Companies and others*, PLD 1997 Karachi 636; *Lahore Stock Exchange Limited v. Fredrick J. Whyte Group (Pakistan) Ltd.*, PLD 1990 SC 48; *Punjab Province v. Zafar Iqbal Cheema*, 1983 CLC 513.
179. *Port Qasim Authority, Karachi v. Al-Ghurair Group of Companies and others*, PLD 1997 Karachi 636; *Rashida Sayeed v. Metropolitan Development Corporation Ltd. and another*, 1982 CLC 1039. *See also Shabbir Ali Khan v. Rice Export Corporation of Pakistan Ltd.*, 1989 MLD 1144; *Punjab Province v. Zafar Iqbal Cheema*, 1983 CLC 513 wherein court said 'only disputes arising out of or connected with a contract can be referred to arbitration'.

arising from fraud, bribery, etc.[180] On the other hand, matters of termination, frustration and rescission of contract and whether a contract was indeed signed by authorized persons would be included in the scope of the arbitration agreement if the parties availed themselves of broad words, such as: 'any dispute in respect of interpretation of the agreement or concerning anything contained therein' or the words explained below.[181] The Sindh High Court elaborated these principles further in *Port Qasim Authority, Karachi v. Al-Ghurair Group of Companies.*[182] In this case, the conflict arose because the parent contract did not come into being since the 'effective date' specified to that end did not transpire.[183] The court, however, found that the phrase 'dispute in respect of or concerning anything herein contained' in an arbitration agreement embedded in the matrix contract was broad enough to bestow on arbitrator with power to determine the existence and validity of that contract. The Sindh High Court also maintained that the general principle was that an arbitrator did not have the power to rule on his own jurisdiction. Where an arbitration agreement was open to more than one interpretation, the parties would be presumed to have never intended to authorize the arbitrator to determine the validity and existence of the agreement. That is to say, parties can vest power in the arbitrator to resolve this jurisdictional issue with a perspicuous and all-embracing arbitration clause by bringing into use the expressions that are of widest import and encompass the jurisdictional issues. In this way, the Sindh High Court came to the conclusion that the question as to whether an arbitrator has the power to rule on the existence and validity of an arbitration agreement was a rule to be utilized in interpretation and construction, and it was the language of the arbitration clause which would determine the bestowal of such power on the arbitrator.

The unappealing extensive reliance on words to interpret the scope of an arbitration agreement might be seen as problematic if we look into the English experience on this point. English case law, which used to revolve around the issue of a narrow or broad interpretation of words inscribed in arbitration agreements to decide their scope came to an end with the decision of the House of Lords in *Fiona Trust.* These words included 'any dispute or difference', 'in connection with', 'in respect of', 'in relation to', 'arising out of' and 'arising under'.[184] In *Fiona Trust,* the Court of Appeals and then the House of Lords discarded these distinctions and held that businessmen would be presumed to have intended to bring all disputes within the scope of the arbitration clause. This presumption could be rebutted only if express

180. *Water and Development Authority v. Abdur Razzaq Muhammad Iqbal,* PLD 1977 Lahore 5.
181. *Travel Automation (Pvt.) Ltd. v. Abacus International (Pvt.) Ltd.*, 2006 CLD 497; *Lahore Stock Exchange Limited v. Fredrick J. Whyte Group (Pakistan) Ltd.*, PLD 1990 SC 48; *M. M. Ispahani Ltd. v. Pakistan Trading Company*, PLD 1966 Dacca 54.
182. *Port Qasim Authority, Karachi v. Al-Ghurair Group of Companies and others*, PLD 1997 Karachi 636.
183. It was provided in the contract that 'the "effective date" of the agreement shall mean the date by which the company has obtained all the necessary permissions and sanctions from the Government of Pakistan, towards establishing the terminal ... within 180 days'.
184. For review of cases interpreting these phrases, *see* Andrew Tweeddale and Keren Tweeddale, *Arbitration of Commercial Disputes; International and English Law and Practice* (OUP, 2005), paras 20-50–20-58.

words to the contrary were found in the arbitration agreement.[185] It may be suggested that Pakistani courts should also adopt the same presumption by freeing themselves from interpreting the niceties and distinctions of phrases used in arbitration agreements.

4.3. INTERPRETATION OF VALIDITY, EXISTENCE AND EFFECTIVENESS OF ARBITRATION AGREEMENT

From an interpretation viewpoint, the question of whether an arbitration agreement is effective and whether it can furnish a valid foundation for arbitration has often been resolved on the basis of elements external to it. For instance, when the association from where the parties were to opt for an arbitral tribunal ceased to exist, the courts found the pertinent arbitration agreement to be ineffective.[186] Similarly, when an office in which the incumbent was to be designated as a sole arbitrator was put to an end, the arbitration agreement stipulating the appointment of such office holder was pronounced to be infructuous.[187] In another case, an arbitration agreement provided that any controversy would be submitted to the: 'Secretary, Government Punjab, Civil Supplies Department', but later this office was abolished on account of the reorganization of that department. The court held that the arbitration agreement was incapable of being performed.[188] In *Taj Muhammad Khan v. NWFP Forest Development Corporation*, the arbitration agreement provided for the appointment of the Chairman of NWFP Forest Development Corporation for the resolution of future controversies. The NWFP Forest Development Corporation Act, 1977, which established this corporation, was subsequently repealed by the NWFP Forest Development Corporation Ordinance, 1980. The later instrument altered the structure of the Corporation and brought to an end the office, the bearer of which was to function as arbitrator. On account of this, the arbitration agreement was interpreted to be inoperative and infructuous.[189]

However, there are also instances where Pakistani courts, while interpreting the validity or the effectiveness of an arbitration agreement, did not pay any heed to elements extraneous to an arbitration agreement, whereupon the interpretation was effected by looking at both the externality and the words employed in the arbitration agreement. In this situation, various principles of interpretation appear to have been pressed into service due to their relevance, like the principle of good faith and the principle of effective interpretation.

185. *Fiona Trust & Holding Corporation and others v. Privalov and others*, [2007] UKHL 40.
186. *Hafiz Abdul Aziz Cotton Ginning Factory v. Haji Ali Muhammad Abdullah & Co.*, PLD 1966 (W. P.) 197; *Hafiz Abdul Aziz Yousufani & Co. v. Haji Ali Muhammad Abdullah & Co.*, PLD 1967 Karachi 698; *Oil & Gas Development Corporation v. Karachi Builders*, 1978 SCMR 278.
187. *Taj Muhammad Khan v. NWFP Forest Development Corporation and another*, PLD 1984 Peshawar 64.
188. *Province of Punjab v. Irfan & Co.*, PLD 1956 (W. P.) Lahore 442.
189. *Taj Muhammad Khan v. NWFP Forest Development Corporation and another*, PLD 1984 Peshawar 64.

4.3.1. The Principle of Good Faith

The principle that arbitration agreements should be construed in good faith is widely accepted and is applied while interpreting an arbitration agreement.[190] A challenge from a party to the validity or the existence of an arbitration agreement will not concern bad faith on every occasion, save only if that party contests an arbitration agreement, the existence or the validity of which has already been established, or presents arguments that are inconsistent with the basic fabric and objective of the contract. In such cases, it would certainly amount to be an instance of bad faith. This principle suggests that the arbitration agreement should be interpreted to reflect the true intentions of the parties, and for that purpose, sole reliance on the literal interpretation is not warranted.[191] To that end, Pakistani courts look to the substance of a document and not its form to determine the true nature of the said document.[192]

The call to ascertain the true and common intention of the parties from the arbitration agreement drives this very wide principle of interpretation in good faith to beget a variety of specific rules, *inter alia*, that the arbitration agreement should be construed by contemplating the ends which parties reasonably and legitimately considered to achieve[193] and that the agreement should not be interpreted piecemeal; rather, the agreement, along with all of its parts, must be construed in its entirety and collectivity.[194] Contracts are to be interpreted in a harmonious manner so that each part of the agreement expounds the other so as to make all the parts agree with each other, and a rationale meaning is assigned to all parts of the agreement.[195]

Pakistani courts have not clearly referred to the principle of good faith while interpreting arbitration agreements, but its employment may be inferred from the judgment of *Zohra Begum v. Abdul Razzak & Co.*[196] In this case, there was a partnership agreement carrying an arbitration clause as follows:

190. For instance, Article 1156 of the French Civil Code reads:

> One must in agreements seek what the common intention of the contracting parties was, rather than pay attention to the literal meaning of the terms.

191. *Amco Asia Corporation and others v. Republic of Indonesia*, ICSID Case No. ARB/81/1, Decision on Jurisdiction, (25 September 1983).
192. *Bayer Pakistan (Pvt.) Ltd. and others v. Board of Revenue and others*, 2002 CLD 823.
193. *Amco Asia Corporation and others v. Republic of Indonesia*, ICSID Case No. ARB/81/1, Decision on Jurisdiction, (25 September 1983).
194. *Mrs Shamim Javaid Zar and others v. Mst Wazir Begum and others*, 2002 YLR 1061; *United Bank Ltd. v. Mujahid Transport and others*, PLD 1986 Karachi 107; *Rasheedur Rehman Khan v. Mian Iqbal Hussain*, PLD 2006 SC 418; *Saeed Mahmood v. Halima Bai*, 1990 MLD 1789; *Saudi-Pak Industrial and Agricultural Investment Company (Pvt.) Ltd., Islamabad v. Allied Bank of Pakistan and another*, 2003 CLD 596; *Amco Asia Corporation and others v. Republic of Indonesia*, ICSID Case No. ARB/81/1, Decision on Jurisdiction, (25 September 1983); *American company v. Belgian company*, ICC Award No. 8694 (1996), 124, J.D.I. 1056 (1997), *see also* Emmanuel Gaillard and John Savage, *Fouchard, Gaillard, Goldman on International Commercial Arbitration* (Kluwer Law International, 1999), para. 477.
195. *Ibad & Company v. Pakistan Television Corporation Ltd. and others*, 1981 CLC 106; *Ghazanfar Hussain v. Rehmat Bibi and others*, 1989 CLC 310 SC (A J & K).
196. *Zohra Begum v. Abdul Razzak & Co. and others*, 1984 CLC 1643.

> That if any dispute shall arise in respect of the partnership or about the interpretation, operation or the enforcement of the terms of this partnership, among the parties or their legal representatives, the same shall be referred for adjudication to two arbitrators nominated by Mr. Abdul Ghaffar, the Deputy Managing Partner (defendant no. 3 in the suit), within one month of the receipt of the written notice from any of the partners. In case, no arbitrators are appointed by Mr. Abdul Ghaffar within one month then the managing partner Mr. Abdur Razzak (defendant no. 2) shall appoint two arbitrators within two months of the receipt of such notice from any of the partners. In case, Mr. Abdul Razzak also fails to appoint two arbitrators within two months then Mr. Abdul Karim (defendant no. 4) shall appoint two arbitrators within three months of the receipt such notice from any of the partners, and dispute shall be referred to such arbitrators who shall give their decision and the decision of such arbitrator shall be final and binding on all the parties and their legal representatives. Arbitrators must be from reputable business.

It was contended that the arbitration clause was not workable and would bring about a delay in the resolution of the dispute as a consequence of the lengthy procedure for the appointment of arbitrators. However, the court held that since the parties had entered into the agreement with open eyes, they could not raise those contentions. Apart from that, the court also held that the procedure for the appointment of arbitrators was not delaying, time-consuming, uncertain, or vague. In the court's view, the three-month period for the appointment of arbitrators was not so drawn out to justify the vitiation of the arbitration clause.[197]

Pakistani courts interpret the arbitration agreement by extending due regard to the objectives the parties intended to accomplish. For instance, as per the arbitration agreement for the resolution of prospective disputes, the 'Chief Account' of the State Bank of Pakistan was to be appointed as sole arbitrator. This office was later abolished by an amendment in the Regulations of the State Bank of Pakistan, and a new position of 'Director Accounts' was created. The Sindh High Court did not agree with the plea that the abolition of this office had turned the arbitration agreement infructuous. Rather, it held that the intention of the parties as inferred from their agreement would ascertain if the supervening incident had frustrated the arbitration agreement. The court maintained that the intention of the parties in choosing the 'Chief Accountant' as an arbitrator was to have their disputes resolved by a person who was very well versed with the subject of accountancy. It held further that the requirement of having this kind of knowledge would be fulfilled with the appointment of 'Director Accounts'. It was because, as was observed by the court, the modification in the State Bank's Regulations had not reshaped the functions and powers of 'Chief Account' and that only the nomenclature of 'Chief Accountant' was substituted by the designation of 'Director Accounts'.[198]

Pakistani courts, in order to construe an arbitration agreement, peruse their entirety some terms of the parent contract that are amended by a subsequent agreement without touching the arbitration clause incorporated in the first agreement. In such circumstances, the court will read both the agreements, first and second,

197. Stay of suit was refused for the dispute.
198. *Macdonald Layton Costain Ltd., Karachi v. State Bank of Pakistan*, PLD 1980 Karachi 87.

together. In such a case, the arbitration clause in the first contract will not be deemed to have been abolished by the second contract and will continue to be binding on the parties.[199] This judgment portrays the prevalent judicial approach to the effect that while interpreting an arbitration agreement, the ordinary sense of words should be applied by looking at the whole document with an objective to gather the parties' intention.[200] For instance, in *Island Textile Mills Ltd. v. V/O Technoexperts,*[201] the plaintiff contended that 'all disputes and differences which may arise out of this contract are to be submitted with *exception* of recourse of Legal Courts to arbitration' as appearing in the arbitration clause, enunciating expressly that the jurisdiction of the court would remain intact. The court, however, held that the arbitration clause should be looked through as a whole, and hence, it became clear that the intention of the parties was to exclude the jurisdiction of the courts. That is, if they failed an amicable settlement, the disputes were agreed to be submitted to arbitration, to the exclusion of the courts. The court concluded that if the view of the plaintiff were granted, it would make arbitration agreements nugatory, redundant and ineffective. Similarly, in *Shaikh Muhammad Umer v. Zakaria Adamjee Charitable Corporation,*[202] the arbitration clause referred the dispute to the 'referee', but the court, by taking into consideration the arbitration clause in its totality, concluded that the intention of the parties was not to refer the dispute for the mere recording of evidence; rather, the parties intended to have their dispute adjudicated by a third party whose finding would be binding upon them. In this way, the court declared the clause to be an arbitration clause despite the use of the word 'referee' in it.

However, in another case,[203] the court arrived at an opposite conclusion, wherein in accordance with a work order, respondents supplied specific building materials to the appellants. The work orders which were imparted under the signatures of Mr Shah, who was also the Deputy Chief Engineer of the appellant company, stipulated that: 'in case of dispute the order of the undersigned will be final'. Thereafter, some disputes regarding the costs of the materials came into the open between the parties. Assuming it to be an arbitration agreement, the respondent launched an application to the court. The plea of the appellant that this could not be termed an arbitration clause was rejected by the lower court, whose decision was then appealed to the Punjab High Court. It held that in order to decide if the above-mentioned provision was an arbitration clause, it was to be interpreted bearing in mind the parties' intention and the setting in which the words of that clause were placed. Furthermore, the court stated

199. *Nawab Brothers Ltd., Karachi v. Project Director, Office of the Project Director, Special Projects, Planning and Development Department, Karachi and another,* 1981 CLC 638.
200. *Province of Punjab v. Malik Muhammad Ilyas and others,* 1994 MLD 476; *G.M.K. Enterprises v. Shaheen Builders,* 1999 CLC 1698.
201. *Island Textile Mills Ltd. Karachi v. V/O Technoexperts and others,* 1979 CLC 307. In this case, stay of court proceedings was granted in favour of Moscow-seated arbitration but in appeal, the Supreme Court refused the stay, on forum non conveniens basis and due to involvement of questions of law and third parties. For Supreme Court judgment, *see Island Textile Mills Ltd. v. V/O Technoexport and another,* 1986 SCMR 463.
202. *Shaikh Muhammad Umer v. Zakaria Adamjee Charitable Corporation and another,* 1988 MLD 1131.
203. *Conforce Ltd v. K. U. Naeem Malik,* 1983 CLC 1005.

that it was not of the opinion that the Deputy Chief Engineer was intended to be clothed with the status of an arbitrator. The intention of the parties to get the dispute settled by him was evident, but this was not sufficient to render this clause an arbitration clause, as, in order to achieve that end, Mr Shah should have been assigned specific duties, like performing judicial functions and providing his decision on the basis of the evidence presented before him. Such a position could not be found in that case even if his decision was characterized as final. As a result, he was no more than a supervisor of the work, especially because he was also the employee of a company that was a party to the work.[204] Hence, the court refused to give this clause the status of an arbitration clause.

4.3.2. The Principle of Effective Interpretation

While interpreting an agreement, a court will attempt to save it rather than destroy or nullify the same,[205] and such meaning will be given to it so that every part is made effective and every word is made operable[206] unless it is inconsistent with some other part of the contract or the rest of the contract. To be inconsistent, a term must contradict or conflict with another term. A term may also be rejected if it contradicts the intention of the parties as gathered from the agreement.[207]

This principle was elaborated by the Punjab High Court in *Muhammad Akram v. Muhammad Salim*, where it was held that if two interpretations were possible, the interpretation making the agreement valid would be applied,[208] which is equally applicable to arbitration agreements.[209] In *the Board of Trustees of Port of Karachi v. National Construction Co. (Pakistan) Ltd.*, the condition precedent for the referral of the dispute to arbitration was the completion of 'works'. The court suggested that 'works' was divisible into two stages and that the first stage had been completed. So,

204. *See*, *Dar Okaz Printing and Publishing Limited Liability Company v. Printing Corporation of Pakistan Private Limited*, PLD 2003 SC 808. In this case, the Supreme Court held that because the sole arbitrator happened to be the Chief Executive of the respondent would not render the arbitration agreement illegal or against public policy.

205. *Mrs. Shamim Javaid Zar and others v. Mst. Wazir Begum and others*, 2002 YLR 1061; *Saudi-Pak Industrial and Agricultural Investment Company (Pvt.) Ltd., Islamabad v. Allied Bank of Pakistan and another*, 2003 CLD 596.

206. *Mian Zafar Iqbal and others v. Bashir Ahmad and others*, PLD 1989 Lahore 152. In *Bank Alfalah Limited v. Iftikhar A. Malik*, 2003 CLD 363, court held that where a transaction is contained in more than one documents, all should be read and interpreted together. For all purposes, they will have the same legal effect as if they were one document.

207. *House Building Finance Corporation v. Shahinshah Humayun Cooperative House Building Society and others*, 1992 SCMR 19. Supreme Court referred to *West Pakistan Industrial Development Corporation, Karachi, v. Aziz Qureshi*, PLD 1973 SC 222; *Paragadas Mathuredes v. Jeewan Lal (1928) Ltd.*, P I. D 1948 PC 162.

208. *Muhammad Akram and others v. Ch. Muhammad Salim*, PLD 1964 (W. P.) Lahore 490. This principle is also laid down in Article 1157 of the French New Civil Code, which reads that 'where a clause can be interpreted in two different ways, the interpretation enabling the clause to be effective should be adopted in preference to that which prevents the clause from being effective'.

209. For arbitration agreement specifically, *see Province of Punjab v. Malik Muhammad Ilyas and others*, 1994 MLD 476; *G.M.K. Enterprises v. Shaheen Builders*, 1999 CLC 1698 wherein it was held that the agreement should be interpreted with a purpose to save the agreement rather than demolish it.

regarding that stage, the referral to arbitration was valid.[210] If 'works' had been considered by the court to be indivisible, as was contended by one party, it would not have been able to give any effect to arbitration.

In *Ghulam Qadir & Co v. Government of Pakistan*, by an agreement, the Secretary of State for India-in-Council granted a lease of Army Manson in November 1932 to the appellants for the tenure of thirty years on terms including that the lease might be terminated by either party on one year's notice to the other without giving any cause. The other stipulation was that on such termination, the lessee would be entitled to the compensation for the building structures erected by him on the basis of costs of that structure or the value of building material, whichever was less. The lease agreement contained an arbitration clause as follows:

> In the event of any dispute arising as to the meaning or effect of these presents the decision whereof is not otherwise provided for the same shall be referred to the secretary *for the time being* to the Government of India in the Army Department whose decision shall be final and binding on both the parties.

The Indian subcontinent was divided into Pakistan and India in 1947. In December 1949, the appellant served a notice on the Government of Pakistan (respondent), conveying his intention to bring the agreement to an end. Thereafter, negotiations started to settle the compensation claims of the appellant for the building structure, but it was all in vain, and the appellant then lodged the suit. The respondent contended that the courts did not enjoy jurisdiction because the only remedy for this dispute was its referral to the Defence Secretary as provided in the arbitration clause of the Lease Contract. The trial court held that the respondent had not taken any steps in proceedings and that the matter should have been referred to arbitration, whereon the appeal was lodged with the Punjab High Court. Various issues were raised before the High Court, but in relation to arbitration, the High Court conceded that the respondent had not taken any steps in the proceedings. The other contention was that the arbitration clause was vague and ambiguous in the sense that the phrase '*for the time being*' as committed to arbitration clause was not clear in its meaning since it was not certain that the Secretary to the Government of India who was to function as arbitrator was the person serving on that post at the time of conclusion of the contract, whether at the time the dispute arose or at the time of referral. As to its meaning, the court stated that it might choose any of those meanings, and it could not be said that no meaning might be gathered from this phrase. It stated further that its meaning had to be marshalled from the context in which this phrase was resting and that such context and the facts to which this phrase was referring would make its meaning definite and ascertainable. By keeping this in view, the court held that the parties' intention was not to appoint the Secretary holding down that post at the time of execution of the contract nor when the dispute emerged. Instead, it was the person who would be at that post at

210. *Board of Trustees of the Port of Karachi v. National Construction Co. (Pakistan) Ltd and others*, PLD 1980 Karachi 123. *See also Juna Bunder Joint Venture, Karachi (Contractors) v. Board of Trustees of Port of Karachi (TPK)*, PLD 1982 Karachi 13.

the time of the referral of the dispute. So, it held that the clause could not be viewed to be ambiguous or unenforceable.[211]

It merits mentioning here that, like any other contract, the arbitration agreement would be regarded as void under section 29 of the Contract Act 1872[212] on the basis of uncertainty, i.e., in circumstances where the parties' agreement cannot be ascertained from the arbitration agreement. This is for the reason that in this situation, the parties cannot be demonstrated to have consented to the same thing in the same manner. For instance, in *Mrs Yasmeen v. Beach Developers*, the arbitration agreement stipulated that disputes between the parties regarding the contract for the sale of an apartment will be referred to the 'Authority' without defining 'Authority'. For that reason, the court held the arbitration agreement to be vague and uncertain. When the defendant contended that the 'Authority' referred to the Defence Housing Authority, the court held that a natural person and not a corporate entity can act as arbitrator. Hence, on these two accounts, the court found the arbitration agreement void.[213]

Similarly, in *Jamshed Alam Khan v. Haq Nawaz and another*, three partners concluded a partnership agreement. Thereafter, the plaintiff, a retiring partner, filed a suit for a share in the capital profit, goodwill of the partnership and interest. The other two partners resisted the suit on the basis of an arbitration clause in the partnership deed. The plaintiff contended that the arbitration agreement is vague and uncertain, which contention was accepted by the court. The arbitration clause encompassed:

> Disputes between the partners ... shall be referred to arbitration, the mode and manner of which shall be decided by the partners mutually.

The court noted that this arbitration agreement could be divided into two parts. Under the first part, parties have agreed to refer their disputes to arbitration, whereas the second part relates to the mode and manner of arbitration to be decided by partners mutually. It stated further that the arbitration agreement was silent on the identity and number of arbitrators, which was a matter, along with the mode and manner of arbitration, to be agreed upon by the parties. In the current state of affairs between the parties, the court stated, such agreement is hardly possible. In this way, the second part rendered the part uncertain and vague. The court said further that due to the involvement of three persons, three alternatives were possible: first, the appointment of a sole arbitrator by three persons involved; second, the appointment of two arbitrators – one by the plaintiff and one by the defendant, and; third, three arbitrators,

211. *Ghulam Qadir & Co, Sialkot Cantt. v. Government of Pakistan*, PLD 1962 (W. P.) Lahore 948. The court held arbitration to be unenforceable on other grounds. It held that the 'Secretary for the time being to the Government of India in the Army Department' ceased to exist after partition of Pakistan in 1947 and that the Defence Secretary could not be considered such officer to enforce the arbitration clause after analysing Indian Independence Act 1947, section 8 of Pakistan (Provisional Constitution) Order (22 of 1947), Indian Independence (Rights, Property and Liabilities) Order (18 of 1947).
212. Section 29 of Contract Act 1872 – Agreement void for uncertainty:

> Agreements, the meaning of which is not certain, or capable of being made certain are void.

213. *Mrs Yasmeen v. Beach Developers*, 2003 YLR 1109.

one by each of them and three arbitrators in total. The court said that the plaintiff had indicated his unwillingness for the third option because the majority of arbitrators would represent the defendant. As to the first and second option, the court could not make the appointment of a sole arbitrator or umpire because of the inapplicability of sections 8 and 9 of the 1940 Act. On these grounds, the court held arbitration to be unworkable unless the parties agreed to act upon the first or second alternative. The court justified the inapplicability of sections 8 and 9 by saying that this was not a case of 'mere omission of the names or the names or the number of the arbitrators but the agreement expressly states that the mode and manner of the arbitration would be settled later'. The constitution and the manner of such a constitution of the arbitral tribunal are matters to be determined primarily by an arbitration agreement.[214]

However, the agreement cannot be regarded as void if it is amenable to two meanings or interpretations. If there is a contradiction between the terms of the contract, the court will not be tempted to declare the agreement void; rather, it will attempt to purvey an interpretation to the various terms of contact so as to cede effect to all of them and give them a rational meaning.[215] Even so, in *Jugotekstil Impex v. Shams Textile Mills. Ltd.*,[216] the court did not opt for a reconciliatory interpretation but instead invalidated the arbitration agreement on account of its uncertainty. In this case, under an arbitration agreement embedded in a commercial contract, the petitioner approached an arbitral tribunal in Manchester and came by an award in his favour. When he filed that award in Pakistani courts for enforcement, it was resisted by the respondent on the contentions, *inter alia*, that the arbitration clause was vague, uncertain, and hence invalid. So, the award emanating from the arbitration clause should also be invalid because the arbitrators had no authority to determine the dispute. The arbitration clause was as follows:

> Any dispute or difference will be referred to the Federation of Pakistan Chamber of Commerce and Industry, Karachi (Pakistan) *or* Manchester Chamber of Commerce, Manchester.

The court stated that in ordinary usage, 'or' generally corresponded to the word 'either' and was a disjunctive word to be applied to furnish the alternative. The court held that the aforementioned arbitration clause, which provided for arbitration, might be interpreted in two ways. If the arbitral tribunal under the FOP Chamber of Commerce was named as Tribunal A and the other tribunal was termed as Tribunal B, then:

(a) The reference should first be made to Tribunal A of Pakistan, and a further submission should be made to Tribunal B of Manchester.

214. *Jamshed Alam Khan v. Haq Nawaz and another*, PLD 1973 Karachi 31.
215. *Hohnson and Phillips (Pakistan) Ltd. v. Sahibzada Muhammad Ayaz and another*, 1997 CLC 1177; *Muhammad Azam Muhammad Fazil & Co., Karachi v. N. A. Industries, Karachi*, PLD 1977 Karachi 21. *See also Noor Nabuwwat v. Moulvi Muhammad Noor Ali Khan*, 1999 CLC 1685.
216. *Jugotekstil Impex v. Shams Textile Mills. Ltd.*, 1986 CLC 879.

(b) If the word 'or' was given the meaning to mark the alternative, then the arbitration agreement would mean the reference to Tribunal A or to Tribunal B.

The petitioner emphasized the second interpretation by asserting that the clause mandated the submission of the matter to either of the tribunals. But the court, by turning down this interpretation, pronounced that the arbitration clause did not elaborate the circumstances where under the dispute would be referred to Tribunal A and the circumstances which would lead to a submission to Tribunal B. So the court held that under such circumstances, the arbitration clause was prima facie uncertain. The petitioner asserted that this uncertainty or vagueness might be cured by election, that is, through the respondent consenting to the jurisdiction of tribunal B, and hence the election by the petitioner in favour of Tribunal B should be valid. But the court held that there was nothing in the arbitration agreement to denote that the parties were vested with the option to determine the tribunal of their choice for the resolution of their disputes. The court further held that under an agreement to arbitrate, two arbitral tribunals could not have jurisdiction over the same subject matter at the same time and that 'an arbitration agreement is an agreement that the disputes or differences shall be settled by an arbitrator named or designated in the agreement or by an arbitrator appointed in accordance with the arbitration agreement'. Agreement to refer the dispute to Tribunal A or Tribunal B was not an agreement to hand the controversies on a named arbitrator because it was not certain as to who was the arbitrator in the Manchester Chamber of Commerce. The arbitration agreement also did not endow any authority to the parties to co-opt for either the FOP Chamber of Commerce and Industry or the Manchester Chamber of Commerce as an arbitrator by referring to it. Hence, the court held that the arbitrator did not have any authority to render the award on the basis that the arbitration agreement was vague, uncertain, and hence invalid.

4.4. INTERPRETATION OF FORMAL VALIDITY OF ARBITRATION AGREEMENT

4.4.1. 'In Writing' Requirement

The term 'arbitration agreement' as defined in section 2(a) of the 1940 Act[217] requires it only to be in writing so that the consensus of the parties, arrived at by their free consent to resolve their disputes through arbitration, could be deduced. Although the courts have rejected the existence of arbitration agreements contended to have been part of an oral contract,[218] in order for an arbitration agreement to be binding, it does

217. Section 2(a) of the 1940 Act says that:

> arbitration agreement means a written agreement to submit present or future differences to arbitration, whether an arbitrator is named therein or not.

218. *Cosmopolitan Development Company Ltd. v. Alfred C. Toepfer International and others*, 1991 CLC 1087.

not have to be incorporated in a formal document or be under seal, nor is there any need to have the signatures of the parties on it.[219] Since an arbitration agreement can be contained in more than one documents,[220] the 'in writing' desideratum would be fulfilled by letters or correspondence exchanged between the parties, their statements, or even from the statements of their counsels directly expressing their consent to submit disputes to arbitration. This outcome could be effected by a membership application for an organization imperatively signifying such an agreement or by any other kind of writing which may unmistakably be attributed to the parties' intention for arbitration.[221] For instance, in a dispute regarding the distribution of the property of the deceased among his legal heirs, the appellant and the respondent individually wrote letters to Martial Law Authorities wherein each party nominated its arbitrator with a request that he should act as arbitrator. Such a request was considered by the Supreme Court to be a valid arbitration agreement because both letters jointly made a legally binding arbitration agreement by which to refer the matter to arbitration.[222]

In *Metropolitan Steel Corporation Ltd v. Macsteel International U.K. Ltd,*[223] the court seemed to have applied the most favourable clause (Article VII) from the New York Convention. The defendant sought the stay of a suit filed for damages in favour of LCIA arbitration with its seat in London. The plaintiff opposed the stay application by asserting that the transaction of sale hinged 'upon a pro forma invoice, purchase order and correspondence by faxes and emails' and that the plaintiff never reached a sale agreement containing an arbitration clause. The plaintiff substantiated its assertions by arguing that no document existed to demonstrate the existence of an arbitration

219. *Nawab Brothers Ltd. Karachi v. Project Director, Office of the Project Director, Special Projects, Planning and Development Department, Karachi and another*, 1981 CLC 638; *Conforce Ltd v. K. U. Naeem Malik*, 1983 CLC 1005; *Development Construction Corporation Ltd. Karachi v. West Pakistan P.W.D. and others*, PLD 1971 Karachi 292; *Sheikh Hussain Bux & Co. v. Zaib Tun Textile Mills Ltd.*, PLD 1981 Karachi 28; *Hukumzada v. Samandaroon Khan and others*, PLD 1988 Peshawar 133; *Ahmed Constructions through Sole Proprietor v. Neptune Textile Mills and another*, PLD 1990 Karachi 216; *Shamim Akhtar v. Najma Baqai*, PLD 1977 SC 644; *Trading Corporation of Pakistan (Pvt.) Ltd. v. Nidera Handles Compagnie B. V and another*, 1998 CLC 1610; *Noor Sahib Khan and others v. Mir Jananson and others*, 1989 CLC 1666; *Meredith Jones & Co. Ltd. v. Quetta Textile Mills Ltd.*, 2002 CLD 1191; *Tribal Friends Co. v. Province of Balochistan*, 2002 SCMR 1903; *MA Khan & Co. v. Pakistan Railway Employees Cooperative Housing Society Ltd.*, 1996 CLC 45; *Muhammad Saleem v. Saadat Enterprises*, 2009 CLC 291; *Merdith Janes Co. Ltd. v. Crescent Board Ltd.*, 1999 CLC 437; *Haji Ilyas Haji Issa and others v. Haji Ahmad and others*, 1987 CLC 2509; *Water And Power Development Authority, Lahore v. Metropolitan Steel Corporation Ltd and others*, 1986 CLC 312; *Hashmi Can Company v. Hysong Corporation of Karachi*, PLD 1999 Karachi 25; *Metropolitan Steel Corporation Ltd v. Macsteel International U.K. Ltd.*, PLD 2006 Karachi 664; *Ralli Brothers & Coney Ltd. v. Muhammad Amin Muhammad Bashir Ltd.*, 1987 CLC 83; *Karachi Dock Labour Board v. Quality Builders Ltd.*, PLD 2016 SC 121; *Syed Munir Syed v. Sardar Muhammad Kamal Khan and others*, 2019 YLR 209. There is also an isolated judgment, *Din Muhammad v. Jan Mohammad and another*, PLD 1971 Quetta 30 which held that an award might be resisted by an application under section 30(c) of 1940 Act on the ground that the party did not sign the arbitration agreement.

220. *Hanover Contractors v. Pakistan Defence Officers Housing Authority*, 2002 CLC 1880.

221. *Hafiz Abdul Aziz Cotton Ginning Factory v. Haji Ali Muhammad Abdullah & Co.*, PLD 1966 (W. P.) 197; *Saleem Ali v. Akhtar Ali and others* PLD 2004 Lahore 404; *Province of Punjab and another v. Industrial Machine Pool, Lahore*, PLD 1978 Lahore 829.

222. *Shamim Akhtar v. Najma Baqai and others*, PLD 1977 SC 644.

223. *Metropolitan Steel Corporation Ltd. v. Macsteel International U.K. Ltd.*, PLD 2006 Karachi 664.

agreement between the parties. The court held that the arbitration agreement could be inferred from the conduct of the parties found in the exchange of correspondence between them and that the plaintiff could not disentangle himself from this correspondence. By that time, the Recognition and Enforcement (Arbitration Agreements and Foreign Arbitral Awards) Ordinance, 2005,[224] had been promulgated, incorporating the New York Convention into the domestic laws of Pakistan. The court acknowledged that the 1940 Act dealt with domestic arbitration and the 2005 Ordinance was primarily applicable to the stay application in favour of foreign arbitration. However, when the plaintiff averred that as required by Article II(2) of the New York Convention,[225] the arbitration clause did not exist because it was not signed by the parties, the court left the definition of 'in writing' as enacted in the New York Convention and plumped for the interpretation of the Pakistani Supreme Court, in consonance with section 2(a) of the 1940 Act, which did not necessitate the condition of signature to declare the arbitration agreement to be existent.[226] The Punjab High Court has extended this interpretation of 'in writing' equally to Article II of the New York Convention.[227]

The case of *Province of Sindh and another v. S. Zaheeruddin Hussain*[228] is also very interesting in this regard. In the face of a contention that the old arbitration clause was substituted by a new one, the court was to adjudge which is binding: old or new. The difference between both the clauses was that the new clause, on which the appellant relied, did not bear the signature of the respondent, whereas the old arbitration clause was signed by both of them. The court held that although the arbitration agreement needed only to be in writing and was not in want of the parties' signatures, the court would be inclined in favour of an arbitration agreement signed by both parties instead of the one signed by only one party.

4.4.2. Submission of Arbitration by Reference

Pakistani courts have held that if there is a written agreement between the parties containing a reference to the rules, by-laws, or regulations of some specific association, and such rules, by-laws, etc., determine that disputes be submitted to arbitration, then such arbitration agreement would be binding on the parties.[229]

The parties can import to their contract the arbitration agreement that is embraced in another contract only by mentioning such import in express words. A reference divulging nothing more than that the terms and conditions of a particular contract will apply to the agreement between the parties and cannot be declared to

224. Ordinance XX of 2005. The 2005 Ordinance was repealed and re-enacted by Recognition and Enforcement (Arbitration Agreements and Foreign Arbitral Awards) Act 2011.
225. Article II(2) of the New York Convention says that 'the term agreement "in writing" shall include an arbitral clause in a contract or an arbitration agreement, signed by the parties or contained in an exchange of letters or telegrams'.
226. Court referred to two judgments of Supreme Court in 2002 SCMR 1903 and 1977 SCMR 409.
227. *Louis Dreyfus Commodities Suisse S.A v. Acro Textile Mills Ltd.*, PLD 2018 Lahore 597.
228. *Province of Sindh and another v. S. Zaheeruddin Hussain*, 1982 CLC 175.
229. *Gul Ahmed Textile Mills Ltd, Karachi v. Starko Ltd. Karachi*, 1981 CLC 1667; *Hafiz Abdul Aziz Cotton Ginning Factory v. Haji Ali Muhammad Abdullah & Co.*, PLD 1966 (W. P.) 197; *Sheikh Hussain Bux & Co. v. Zaib Tun Textile Mills Ltd.*, PLD 1981 Karachi 28.

have effectively imported the arbitration agreement into the contract between the parties because the 'reference to arbitration must be specific either in incorporating the clause or in main instrument so that there may not be any ambiguity and the intention of parties be made clear'.[230] The Sindh High Court approvingly and in support of this conclusion, referred to *Nefield*[231] whereby a bill of lading articulated that all stipulations along with exceptions contained in a charterparty contract would be incorporated in that bill of lading, and those terms and conditions included the arbitration clause, but no specific mention was made to the arbitration clause itself. In that case, the English court did not halt its proceedings in favour of arbitration. In that respect, Lord Denning said:

> I would take the clauses in the charterparty and apply them to the bill of lading in so far they are reasonably applicable to it, and I would reject the others. I would say that a clause which is directly germane to the subject matter of the bill of lading (that is, to the shipment, carriage, and delivery of goods) can and should be incorporated into the bill of lading contract, even though it may involve a degree of manipulation of the words to fit exactly the bill of lading. But, if the clause is one which is not thus directly germane, it should not be incorporated into the bill of lading contract unless it is down explicitly in clear words either in the bill of lading or in the charterparty.

French and English approaches on this issue are also instructive. French law prescribes that the party against whom the arbitration agreement is being invoked must be proved to have been aware of the presence of an arbitration clause in the contract whose terms were so incorporated.[232] English law also allows the incorporation of arbitration agreements by reference.[233] Section 6(2) of the Arbitration Act 1996 says that:

> The reference in an agreement to a written form of arbitration clause or to a document containing an arbitration clause constitutes an arbitration agreement if the reference is such as to make that clause part of the agreement.

The English approach, however, differentiates between 'single contract case' and 'two contracts cases'. In the first scenario, a contract is concluded between two parties, and this contract incorporates the standard terms. The standard terms, thus incorporated, contain an arbitration agreement. In this case, general words in the contract for

230. *Macdonald Layton & Company Limited v. Associated Electrical Enterprises Limited and another*, PLD 1982 Karachi 786. *See also Syed Arshad Ali v. Sarwat Ali Abbasi*, 1988 CLC 1350; *Cosmopolitan Development Company v. SO DI.ME. S.P.A. and another*, 1987 MLD 2832.
231. 1971 Lloyd's. LR 1.
232. Cour d'Appel, Versailles, 23 January 1991, *Bomar Oil N.V. v. Enterprise Tunisienne d'Activites Petrolieres* – ETAP, Yearbook Commercial Arbitration Volume XVII, p. 488; Cour de Cassation, 9 November 1993, *Bomar Oil N.V. v. ETAP* – L'Enterprise Tunisienne d'Activites Petrolieres, Yearbook Commercial Arbitration, Volume XX, 1995, p. 660; *See also* Cass. 1e civ., 18 February 1992, *Firme Peter Biegi v. Brittania*, 1993 Rev. Arb. 103; Cour de Cassation, First Civil Chamber, 21 November 2006, *Groupama Transport v. MS Regine Hans und Klaus Heinrich KG*, No. 05-21818, Yearbook of Commercial Arbitration, Volume XXXII, 2007, p. 294.
233. *Welex AG v. Rosa Maritime Ltd*, [2003] 2 Lloyd's Rep. 509 (CA); *Axa Re v. Ace Global Markets Ltd.*, [2006] EWHC 216. *See* for detailed discussion, David St. John Sutton and others, *Russel on Arbitration* (Sweet & Maxwell, 2007), paras 2.44-2.56.

the incorporation of an arbitration agreement in those standard terms are sufficient. In the 'two contracts case', in addition to two parties, a third party is involved. Bills of lading are an example of the 'two contracts case'. The charterparty contract, which is evidenced in the bill of lading, is covenanted between two parties, i.e., ship-owner and charterer. Let's say the charterparty contract embodies an arbitration agreement, and the bill of lading concerning that charterparty contract, being a negotiable instrument, is transferred to a third party (bill holder) by a new contract between bill holder and charterer. The charterer incorporates the terms of charterparty (including arbitration agreement) into the new contract between him and the bill holder. In this case, to make the arbitration agreement binding on the bill holder, the specific reference to arbitration is mandatory. The strict rule in the 'two contracts case' aims to protect a third party who is assumed to lack the knowledge of such terms. This rule is also said to promote certainty in international trade.[234]

The Pakistani approach on submission of arbitration by reference is very strict as compared to the other two regimes because it asks for a specific reference in every case. It is milder than that the French approach, which does not require the specific reference but restricts its demand only to prove that the party against whom such invocation is claimed must be proved to have knowledge. The English approach seems more preferable than its French counterpart because, in the latter regime, the presumption seems to be in favour of the party resisting such incorporation. It seems more pertinent that when the conclusion of the parent contract is proved, in which case, a presumption should turn in favour of the party relying on the arbitration agreement incorporated by reference.

4.5. CONCLUSION

Pakistani courts should interpret the scope of the arbitration agreement broadly. In that regard, they should depart from the practice of relying on the words and phrases written in arbitration agreements to interpret their scope. Rather, the parties should be presumed to have intended to include all kinds of arbitrable disputes in the purview of arbitration agreements. The Pakistani approach of effectuating the arbitration agreement and giving arbitration-friendly interpretations to the 'in writing' requirement should be commended, although to free arbitration agreements from formal requirements might be a more appropriate disposition. It is also submitted that the English experience on the incorporation of arbitration by reference appears more refined and beneficial to arbitration, which might be taken into consideration by Pakistani courts while being burdened with the task of construction of such an arbitration agreement.

234. *Sea Trade Maritime Corp v. Hellenic Mutual War Risks Association (Bermuda) Ltd (The Athena)*, [2006] EWHC 2530 (Comm). For detailed analysis on these two scenarios, *see*, Masood Ahmed, *Arbitration Clauses: Fairness, Justice and Commercial Certainty*, 26(3) Arb. Int'l 409 (2010). *See also* Simon Allison and Kanaga Dharmananda, *Incorporating Arbitration Clauses: The Specific of Consistency at the Alter of Experience*, 30(2) Arb. Int'l 265 (2014).

CHAPTER 5

Power of Arbitrator to Interpret the Consent to Arbitrate in Pakistan

Jurisdiction of the arbitrator to rule on his own jurisdiction has slenderly been acceded by Pakistani courts. Judicial power to fix upon arbitrator's jurisdiction, although stemmed from a statute constricted exclusively to domestic arbitration, was extended to foreign-seated arbitration. Along with that, Pakistani judgments are inconsistent on waiver from a party of his right to call into question the arbitrator's jurisdiction and arbitrator's power to carry on arbitration proceedings after its jurisdiction is challenged in court. To put right the predicament ensuing from these authorities, the Pakistani regime should give its seal of approval to the principle of competence-competence in its entirety.

5.1. INTRODUCTION

Despite Pakistan's long history of arbitration, arbitration is treated as an exception to litigation in accordance with section 28 of the Contract Act 1872.[235] The country's legislature, after having treated arbitration as an exceptional system of dispute resolution, failed to modernize arbitration law in Pakistan. This disposition towards

235. Section 28. Agreements in restraint of legal proceedings are void:

> Every agreement, by which any party thereto is restricted absolutely from enforcing his rights under, or in respect of any contract, by the usual legal proceedings in the ordinary Tribunals, or which limits the time which he may thus enforce his rights, is void to that extent.
>
> Exception 1. –Saving of contract to refer to arbitration dispute that may arise. –This section shall not render illegal a contract by which two or more persons agree that any dispute which may arise between them in respect of any subject or class of subjects shall be referred to arbitration, and that only the amount awarded in such arbitration shall be recoverable in respect of the dispute so referred.

arbitration is also translated into judicial attitudes towards arbitration. For judges, the role of arbitration is to decrease the case logs of the courts. The other reason in favour of arbitration is that it is a whistle-stop mechanism to resolve controversies. Even so, it may well be contended, following our survey of Pakistani judgments, that arbitration has not been received as a reliable and self-sustained system of dispensing justice. This is clear from the low level of trust reposed on arbitrators by judges, who rarely allow arbitrators to rule on the validity and existence of arbitration agreements along with other jurisdictional issues.

This chapter deals comprehensively with the Pakistani approach regarding the interplay of powers in the construction of the consent to arbitrate between judges and arbitrators. The chapter has traced this interplay through a survey of Pakistani judgments discussing whether the power to hear jurisdictional matters is to be entrusted to judges or arbitrators; our finding is that almost universally, such power is assumed by the courts. The chapter also analyses under which circumstances a party contesting the tribunal's jurisdiction is considered to have waived its right to object and whether the challenge to an arbitrator's jurisdiction in court will result in the suspension of arbitral proceedings until the issuance of a judgment. This chapter concludes that the Pakistani arbitral regime should recognize the negative effect of *competence-competence* by highlighting the quandary arising from judgments pronounced in disregard of this principle.

5.2. COMPETENCE-COMPETENCE: ITS POSITIVE AND NEGATIVE EFFECTS

The principle of *competence-competence* means that the arbitrator has jurisdiction to determine his own jurisdiction, which includes the determination as to the validity of the arbitration agreement. *Competence-competence* does not imply that the arbitrator alone decides his own jurisdiction. Gaillard notes that:

> It would be neither logical nor acceptable. In fact, the real purpose of the rule is in no way to leave the question of the arbitrators' jurisdiction in the hands of the arbitrators alone. Their jurisdiction must instead be reviewed by the courts if an action is brought to set aside or to enforce the award. Nevertheless, the *competence-competence* rule ties in with the idea that there are no grounds for the prima facie suspicion that the arbitrators themselves will not be able to reach decisions which are fair and protect the interests of society as well as those of the parties to the dispute.[236]

Therefore, the principle of *competence-competence* has two effects: the positive and the negative. According to its positive effect, the arbitral tribunal has jurisdiction to rule on preliminary and jurisdictional matters pertinent to its existence. Its negative effect means that the ruling of a tribunal on its jurisdiction is not final. In other words, the arbitrator is only the first judge but not the sole judge. Hence, the function of the

236. Philippe Fouchard, et al., *Fouchard Gaillard Goldman on International Commercial Arbitration* (Emmanuel Gaillard and John Savage eds, Kluwer Law International, 1999), para. 400.

court is limited to the subsequent review of the jurisdictional award. In summary, *competence-competence* may be defined as 'the rule whereby arbitrators must have the first opportunity to hear challenges relating to their jurisdiction, subject to subsequent review by the courts'.[237]

5.3. HOW MUCH POWER HAS THE JUDGE KEPT FOR HIMSELF?

Under Pakistani precedent, where the validity and existence of the main contract incorporating the arbitration agreement are challenged, or the arbitration agreement itself is specifically contested, jurisdiction is vested in the court and not the arbitrator.[238] For instance, when the validity and existence of a parent contract, in which an arbitration agreement was embodied, was called into question for having been concluded under duress, the Punjab High Court held that the question as to the breadth of the scope of the arbitration clause required a judicial determination as to the existence and validity of the contract; such a question could not be conferred on the arbitrator.[239] Similarly, when the interpretation of the arbitration agreement is at stake, Pakistani courts have decided that this is a matter not befalling the tribunal's jurisdiction.[240] In one case, the arbitration agreement set out that all the disputes arising from the contract would be submitted 'with the *exception* of recourse of legal courts to arbitration'. The court seized the dispute held that the arbitration agreement was in need of interpretation as to whether the jurisdiction of the court was excluded and that such interpretation must be carried out by the court and not by the arbitrator.[241]

Pakistani courts have reasoned that the powerlessness of an arbitrator to rule upon the existence and validity of a contract incorporating an arbitration agreement was because the arbitration agreement is the basis for the referral of a dispute to arbitration and that a dispute subject to an arbitration clause might raise complex questions of law pertaining to the law of contract or an infraction of some other provisions of law. Such questions could not be left to the authority of an arbitrator since it would be a futile exercise for the court to first refer the matter to an arbitrator when,

237. *Ibid.*, para. 660.
238. *Province of West Pakistan v. Messrs Fakir Spinning Mills Ltd and others*, PLD 1962 (W. P.) Karachi 386. In this case, court by quoting an Indian Judgment, *Ratnji Virpal & Co v. Dhirajlal Manilal*, AIR 1942 Bom. 101, held that if the question with regard to the existence and validity of an arbitration agreement arises, that question will be decided by the court. For challenge to the arbitration agreement, *see also AGRICIDES (Pvt) Ltd. v. Ali Agro Supply Corporation Ltd.*, 1988 CLC 59. For challenges against the arbitration agreement on the ground that there exists no parent contract in which the arbitration agreement is included, wherein the jurisdiction of arbitrator was denied by the court, *see Cosmopolitan Development Company Ltd. v. Alfred C. Toepfer International and others*, 1991 CLC 1087.
239. *Water and Development Authority through Chairman and another v. Abdur Razzaq Muhammad Iqbal*, PLD 1977 Lahore 5.
240. *Ibid.*
241. *Island Textile Mills Ltd. v. V/O Technoexport and another*, 1986 SCMR 463. By this decision, the Supreme Court overturned the decision of the Sindh High Court. For the decision of the Sindh High Court, *see*, *Island Textile Mills Ltd. Karachi v. V/O Technoexperts and others*, 1979 CLC 307.

first, no evidence had been placed before that court and; second, if the arbitrator were subsequently to assume jurisdiction, to risk issuing an award that could be challenged in the court and declared invalid on the basis of the invalidity of the arbitration agreement.[242]

It has been held by the Pakistani courts that section 32[243] of the 1940 Act bar a suit seeking to secure a declaration about the effect, 'existence or validity of an arbitration agreement', in view of the phrase 'on any ground whatsoever' employed in that provision, rather, under section 33.[244] The courts have argued that 'any party to an arbitration agreement or any person claiming under him' to make such a challenge should submit an application to the court for that purpose, and the court should settle that question on the basis of affidavits.[245] Despite the fact that the 1940 Act is limited to arbitrations seated in Pakistan,[246] this power to adjudge the validity of arbitration agreements under section 33 was also made available to foreign-seated arbitrations.[247] More precisely, in section 33, 'shall' is construed in order to spell out when an application is lodged under section 33 to the court, in which case the court is obliged to adjudge the effect and validity of the arbitration agreement.[248] For instance, in *Hakimuddin Harmusji & Sons v. Ghafoor Textile Mills*,[249] the defendant brought an application under section 33 to challenge the validity of an arbitration agreement, but while the court proceedings were pending, an award was rendered and submitted to the court for a decree. The Sindh High Court stated that it was then well established that 'a right to remedy in a court of law is a substantive right and not a mere matter of

242. *Avari Hotels v. Hilton International Company*, PLD 1985 Karachi 445. For an example of a single bench decision from where an appeal arose, *see Avari Hotels Ltd. v. Hilton International Company*, PLD 1984 Karachi 488.
243. Section 32. Bar to suit contesting arbitration agreement or award:

> Notwithstanding any law for the time being in force, no suit shall lie on any ground for a decision upon the existence, effect or validity of an arbitration agreement or award, nor shall any arbitration agreement or award be set aside, amended, modified or in any way affected otherwise than as provided in this Act.

244. Section 33. Arbitration agreement or award to be contested by application:

> Any party to an arbitration agreement or any person claiming under him desiring to challenge the existence or validity of an arbitration agreement or an award or to have the effect of either determined shall apply to the Court and the Court shall decide the question on affidavits:
>
> Provided that where the Court deems it just and expedient, it may set down the application for hearing on other evidence also, and it may pass such orders for the discovery and particulars as it may do in a suit.

245. *Water and Development Authority through Chairman and another v. Abdur Razzaq Muhammad Iqbal*, PLD 1977 Lahore 5; *Abdul Karim v. Mirza Bashir Ahmad*, PLD 1974 SC 61. *See also Rab Nawaz and another v. Muhammad Abdullah*, 2001 YLR 24. In *AGRICIDES (Pvt) Ltd. v. Ali Agro Supply Corporation Ltd.*, 1988 CLC 59, the court held that question as to whether there was a supply contract between the parties was a question of fact, which would be decided after recording the evidence.
246. Section 1(2) of the 1940 Act.
247. *Pakistan Chrome Mines Ltd. v. Phibro Asia Ltd. and others*, 1976 SCMR 93.
248. *Kashmir Corporation Ltd. v. Pakistan International Airlines*, PLD 1995 Karachi 301.
249. *Hakimuddin Harmusji & Sons v. Ghafoor Textile Mills*, PLD 1978 Karachi 152.

procedure. Upon the jurisdiction of the competent court being lawfully invoked, the right to remedy matures into a vested right'.[250] The Court observed that the defendant came with a right to have the issue of existence and validity of arbitration agreement adjudicated, upon a proper application under section 33 of the 1940 Act, holding that 'the mere act of a party or an arbitral tribunal (passing of award) changing his position cannot be held to obliterate or set at naught such right to remedy'.[251] The Sindh High Court further held that the specific right afforded under section 33 had been invoked by the defendant prior to the pronouncement of an award, and the remedy to adjudge the validity of the arbitration agreement could not be taken away from the defendant simply on account of the reason that the award had been decreed. So, the court opted to rule on the application under section 33 because the fate of the award would be contingent on the fate of the arbitration agreement.

Challenges under section 33 are to be confined to the arbitration clause as this provision has nothing to do with other clauses in the contract. However, the arbitration agreement can also be contended to be non-existent, on the ground that the parent contract was never signed because the declaration sought by a party from the court to the effect that he had not signed the disputed matrix contract simply encompassed the declaration that the arbitration clause did not exist as well. In that regard, a person denying to have signed the contract can also have recourse to section 33, as encompassed under the phrase 'any party to an arbitration agreement' appearing in section 33.[252]

It is incontrovertible from a string of judgments[253] that sections 32 and 33 cannot be pressed into service to impugn the parent contract as a whole. This bar, as laid down in section 32, can only be resorted in cases where the relief is also available in section 33 of the 1940 Act. However, an independent relief, which does not involve the determination of the effect, existence, or validity of an arbitration agreement, is not prohibited by section 32. This is based on the ground that if it had been the intention of the legislature that all types of documents containing the arbitration clause should fall in the purview of sections 32 and 33, such intention should have been expressed in express and appropriate language. Hence, the main contract can be challenged in a suit under section 9 of the CPC because the power of the courts to try all kinds of civil suits and every party's right to bring suit to civil courts have not been curtailed by section 32. A party can be bereaved of its rights only by appropriate words or implications of the law. Unless expressly or impliedly proscribed by law, civil courts enjoy jurisdiction to consider all kinds of civil suits, and any law interdicting or limiting the jurisdiction of

250. *Ibid.*, p. 163.
251. *Ibid.*, p. 164.
252. *Badri Narayan Agarwala v. Pak Jute Balers Ltd.*, PLD 1970 SC 43. For judgment of High Court, *see Badri Narayan Agarwalla v. Pak. Jute Balers Ltd. Dacca*, PLD 1966 Dacca 262. *See also Ejaz Ali Siddique and another v. Rana Irshad Ahmed and another*, 1998 CLC 1684; *Trading Corporation of Pakistan (Pvt.) Ltd. v. Nidera Handles Compagnie B. V and another*, 1998 CLC 1610.
253. *Trading Corporation of Pakistan (Pvt.) Limited v. Nidera Handelscompagnie B.V. Meent 94, P.O. Box 676, 3000 AR Rotterdam the Netherlands and another*, 2007 CLC 462; *Trading Corporation of Pakistan (Pvt.) Ltd. v. Nidera Handles Compagnie B. V and another*, 1998 CLC 1610.

civil courts will be construed strictly. It is submitted that the confinement of sections 32 and 33 of the 1940 Act to the challenge of arbitration agreements might be an arbitration-friendly attempt; that is, had the challenge to the main contract been sanctioned under these provisions, the party delaying the arbitration would have an additional opportunity to indulge the court in a verbose contract ascertainment along with a single arbitration clause. Therefore, it may be submitted that the main contract from the purview of section 32 and section 33 was, *inter alia*, to save the time and money of parties abiding by their arbitration agreement.

5.4. COMPETENCE-COMPETENCE: HOW MUCH SPACE HAVE JUDGES LEFT FOR ARBITRATORS?

Arbitrators have been given power in very limited cases. The courts have acceded to the power of arbitrators to determine the validity and existence of a main contract only if it is challenged on the basis of termination, repudiation, frustration, or incompetence of a party to sign a said contract. In situations where the dispute arises under the contract, as in the case of disputes concerning the exact price of commodities, the courts have held that the arbitrator's jurisdiction should not be denied.[254]

In *Lahore Stock Exchange Limited v. Fredrick J. Whyte Group,*[255] the contract was contended to be *void ab initio* on the ground that an unauthorized person had signed it. The applicant prayed that the court, to the exclusion of the arbitrators, should rule on the validity of the contract. This argument was turned down by the Supreme Court of Pakistan, which held that on account of the 'widest amplitude and content' of the phrase 'any dispute in respect of interpretation of the agreement or concerning anything contained therein' contained in the arbitration clause, the arbitrators had jurisdiction to rule on the validity of the contract as well as the competence of the parties to sign it.

These principles were further elaborated by Sindh High Court in *Port Qasim Authority, Karachi v. Al-Ghurair Group of Companies.*[256] There, the dispute concerned the main contract, wherein it was argued that it had not come into existence because the effective date[257] stipulated for that purpose had not occurred. However, the Sindh High Court held that the expression 'dispute in respect of or concerning anything herein contained' in the arbitration clause, as this was integrated into the main contract, was wide enough to empower the arbitrators to rule on the validity and existence of such contract.[258] The Sindh High Court also held that the original principle was that the arbitrator did not have jurisdiction to rule on its own jurisdiction. Where

254. *M. M. Ispahani Ltd. v. Pakistan Trading Company*, PLD 1966 Dacca 54; *Travel Automation (Pvt.) Ltd. v. Abacus International (Pvt.) Ltd.*, 2006 CLD 497.
255. *Lahore Stock Exchange Limited v. Fredrick J. Whyte Group (Pakistan) Ltd.*, PLD 1990 SC 48.
256. *Port Qasim Authority, Karachi v. Al-Ghurair Group of Companies*, PLD 1997 Karachi 636.
257. It was provided in the contract that 'the "effective date" of the agreement shall mean the date by which the company has obtained all the necessary permissions and sanctions from the Government of Pakistan, towards establishing the terminal ... within 180 days'.
258. *Port Qasim Authority, Karachi v. Al-Ghurair Group of Companies*, PLD 1997 Karachi 636., para. 13.

more than one interpretations of an arbitration agreement were possible, the court would presume that the parties never intended to empower the arbitrator to rule on the validity and existence of the contract. In other words, the court held that the parties could confer authority on arbitrators to rule on its own jurisdiction with a broad and clearly worded arbitration clause by employing expressions like: 'in respect of', or 'arising out of', or 'in connection with', or 'in consequence of', or 'in relation to', which were of the broadest compass and encompassed the issues of existence, validity and scope of the arbitration agreement.[259] The court concluded that the question as to whether or not the arbitrator had jurisdiction to determine the validity of the arbitration agreement was not to be found in the law; instead, the arbitrator's jurisdiction was to be found in the construction and interpretation of the arbitration clause, with an emphasis on the language of the arbitration agreement, which determines such conferral of power on arbitrators. In addition to the broad wording of the arbitration clause, the other reason why the Sindh High Court conferred jurisdiction on the arbitrator was because the contract did not come to an end when it was frustrated, on account of the fact that the impossibility for one or both of the parties to perform only absolved them from the performance of their contractual obligations.[260] The same applied when the repudiation of the contract unexpectedly arose, whereupon the contractual obligation incurred by one party for the other ceased, albeit the contract remained alive for the purpose of ascertaining contractual liabilities and claims arising from such breach. The arbitration clause determined the mode of such ascertainment for both frustration and breach. Frustration and repudiation fail the purpose of a contract, but arbitration does not constitute the purpose of a contract.[261] Similarly, an arbitrator's jurisdiction could not be denied in the face of termination, novation or substitution of parent contract containing arbitration clause.[262]

The arbitrator's jurisdiction was also discussed by the Sindh High Court in *FAL Oil Company Ltd. v. Pakistan State Oil Company Ltd (PSO)*.[263] In this case, the court proceedings initiated by FAL by way of a suit in a Pakistani lower court was held by the arbitrator to be in breach of the arbitration agreement, who then awarded damages to PSO on account of those court proceedings.[264] This award was enforced under the Recognition and Enforcement (Arbitration Agreements and Foreign Arbitral Awards) Act 2011, but the Sindh High Court discoursed as to how the jurisdiction of the arbitrator to determine the breach of an arbitration agreement could be established. In

259. *Ibid.*, para. 21.
260. *Ibid.*, para. 25.
261. *See also Punjab Province v. Zafar Iqbal Cheema*, 1983 CLC 513 wherein the court said that 'only disputes arising out of or connected with a contract can be referred to arbitration'. *See also Rashida Sayeed v. Metropolitan Development Corporation Ltd. and another*, 1982 CLC 1039. In this case, the court held that the term 'all disputes' or 'all claims' is broader in its scope than the phrase 'all disputes arising out of the contract'. The court also held that the phrase 'all disputes arising between the parties' means 'disputes arising under this agreement', rather than 'disputes arising in relation to the subject-matter of the agreement'.
262. *Sezai Turkes Feyzi Akkaya Construction Company, Lahore through Project Director v. Crescent Services, Lahore and another*, 1997 SCMR 1928.
263. *FAL Oil Company Ltd. v. Pakistan State Oil Company Ltd.*, PLD 2014 Karachi 427.
264. For summary of facts and legal issues involved, *see* the topic of separability in Ch. 2 above.

that regard, the Sindh High Court noticed that the breach of the arbitration agreement was alleged on the basis of initiation of proceedings in court and that subsequently, the arbitration proceeded under such arbitration agreement. It observed that the arbitrator could not be considered to have the power to rule upon the question of breach of the arbitration agreement on the sole basis of that same arbitration agreement that was alleged to have been breached. The Sindh High Court then held that the arbitration agreement (this arbitration agreement was referred to by the court as 'Principal Arbitration Agreement') is 'an agreement in its own right … and it necessarily follows that a dispute as to whether this agreement has been breached can only be arbitrated if there is an agreement to arbitrate in this regard' (the court referred to this second type of arbitration agreement as 'Secondary Arbitration Agreement').[265] The court further held that the disputes falling in the ambit of the Principal Arbitration Agreement could not be considered to encompass the dispute regarding the breach of the Principal Arbitration Agreement itself. The court also admitted that such jurisdiction to determine the breach of the Principal Arbitration Agreement could be conferred on the arbitrator by the parties by using express words. In other words, when the parties agreeing on the resolution of a dispute in their Principal Arbitration Agreement, they must specifically agree to confer jurisdiction on the arbitrators to decide the breach of the Principal Arbitration Agreement, and such agreement would be the Secondary Arbitration Agreement. An arbitration agreement within another arbitration agreement (Secondary Arbitration Agreement within Principal Arbitration Agreement) would be a full-fledged arbitration agreement and must fulfil all pertinent requirements, such as the governing law of Secondary Arbitration Agreement. If there existed a Secondary Arbitration Agreement regarding the resolution of allegations that the Principle Arbitration Agreement was breached, as was stated by the court, the parties could agree whether the same arbitrators designated under the Principal Arbitration Agreement – and who had to adjudicate the breach of the matrix contract – could be appointed, or otherwise other arbitrators would be appointed. In this way, it would be a reference within a reference, but effectively two distinct references to arbitration. The Sindh High Court held that in the instant case, as FAL had accepted that the arbitrator had jurisdiction to determine whether it had breached the arbitration agreement and PSO did not object to the arbitral tribunal's jurisdiction in that respect, this amounted to the Secondary Arbitration Agreement. In this way, the court highlighted that two sets of proceedings were actually going on before the same arbitrator; one under the Principal Arbitration Agreement, aimed at determining disputes arising under the matrix contract, whereby the arbitrator rejected the claims of both PSO and FAL whereas; the second set of arbitration proceedings were taking place under the Secondary Arbitration Agreement, whereby the arbitrator had to consider if the Principal Arbitration Agreement was breached by FAL. By finding FAL in breach of the Principal Arbitration Agreement, the tribunal awarded damages in favour of PSO. The arbitrator left the award open, subject to the proper quantification of losses suffered by PSO because of the court proceedings. The court stated that the arbitration under the Principal

265. *FAL Oil Company Ltd. v. Pakistan State Oil Company Ltd.*, PLD 2014 Karachi 427, para. 12.

Arbitration Agreement was closed, albeit, under the Secondary Arbitration Agreement, the arbitrator had kept the arbitration open.[266]

It is submitted that this is a complex interpretation. Instead, the court could have recognized the principle that the arbitrator had the authority to determine the disputes regarding both agreements: namely, the parent contract and arbitration agreement encompassed within it. These disputes include the breach related to the main contract and the arbitration agreement. This view finds support from the fact that no additional agreement or 'secondary arbitration agreement' is normally concluded between the parties to empower the arbitrator to adjudge the validity of the arbitration agreement along with the validity of the parent contract because arbitrators possess inherent powers for that purpose. As is discussed in the chapter on anti-arbitration injunctions, the arbitrator seems to have been declared a judge, implying that the arbitrator should have inherent powers to perform judicial functions, such as ruling on his own jurisdiction as well as determining breaches of the arbitration agreement. It is suggested that the power of arbitrators to determine the beach of the arbitration agreement does not require express words in the arbitration agreement because if there is really some need for a secondary agreement to empower the arbitrator to determine the breach of the arbitration agreement, then there will also be a need for a tertiary arbitration agreement to empower the arbitrator to adjudge the breach of the secondary arbitration agreement if any. Consequently, the need for subsequent arbitration agreements to empower the arbitrator to rule on the breach of preceding arbitration agreements will become infinite.

5.5. WAIVER OF RIGHT TO CHALLENGE THE ARBITRATOR'S JURISDICTION

If a party wishes to challenge the arbitrator's jurisdiction as a set-aside challenge, he or she should first raise those objections before the arbitrator itself, and if unsuccessful, the said party may participate in arbitration proceedings in protest because in that case, there is no obligation to retire from the arbitral proceedings. In this regard, the plea that an oral protest was made will not be accepted until some record of such protest is presented before the court.

The rule of *estoppel* against the party will take effect by its physical representation, as well as by that party's intentions and actions, because 'when a man had been silent when in conscience ought to have spoken, he shall be debarred from speaking when conscience required him to be silent'.[267] Therefore, the courts would be inclined

266. *FAL Oil Company Ltd. v. Pakistan State Oil Company Ltd.*, PLD 2014 Karachi 427.

267. *Sh. Saleem Ali v. Sh. Akhtar Ali and others*, PLD 2004 Lahore 404. *See also WAPDA v. Khanzada Muhammad Abdul Haque Khan Khattak and Company*, PLD 1990 SC 359; *Muhammad Rafique v. Qamar Ali*, 2003 MLD 52; *Haji Soomar Haji Hajjan v. Muhammad Amin Muhammad Bashir Ltd.*, 1981 SCMR 129; *Karachi Electric Supply Corporation Ltd. v. Consortium 2000 P.E.C.H. Society, Karachi*, 1986 CLC 1350; *Meredith Jones & Co. Ltd. v. Quetta Textile Mills Ltd.*, 2002 CLD 1191. In *Pakistan Refinery Limited v. Pakistan National Shipping Corporation and others*, 1986 CLC 2555. The party appointed arbitrator had participated in arbitration proceeding by expressly saying in his letters that it was without any prejudice to his objection to the

to reject such a challenge if a party did not raise this issue before the arbitrator and failed to participate, from first to last, in the arbitration proceedings. Similarly, delays in raising the jurisdictional issue before an arbitrator, such as after the evidence has been completed and closed before the arbitrators, will also disentitle him from making such a challenge at the set-aside stage.

In *Development Construction Corporation v. West Pakistan P.W.D.*,[268] the power to appoint the arbitrator was transferred from a federal body to a provincial body with the prior consent of the petitioner. An arbitrator was accordingly appointed, who resolved the dispute in favour of the petitioner under a construction contract. There was a second dispute for which the same arbitrator was appointed by the same provincial body, before whom the petitioner again participated. When the award was about to be issued, the petitioner raised an objection against the arbitrator's jurisdiction, alleging that he had been appointed by a provincial body and not by a federal body, as mandated by the original contract. The court did not accept the challenge and ruled that the party had acquiesced to the appointment by the provincial body, as well as to the jurisdiction of the arbitrator appointed by it. The court declared the want of jurisdiction to be different from the irregular exercise or assumption of jurisdiction and held that it was only the latter that could be waived.

The position was later affirmed by the Supreme Court, which decreed that an inherent want of jurisdiction assumed by an arbitral tribunal would result in vitiation of the proceedings before it, and this defect could not be cured even by a waiver from the parties because it was only the irregular assumption of jurisdiction which could be redressed by such waiver.[269] A party's waiver of objection on the arbitrator's jurisdiction is conditional upon the knowledge. Thus, the party appearing before an arbitrator who, due to lack of knowledge, thought an arbitrator to be the member of the Karachi Cotton Association, as required by the arbitration agreement, was not considered to have waived its right to challenge the jurisdiction of such arbitrator before the court.[270]

However, in another case, the Sindh High Court went so far as disregarding a party's very elaborative challenge, lodged before the arbitral tribunal, rather the court held that the party waived its right to challenge the arbitral tribunal's jurisdiction before the court because:

> He was not able to show that he had acted with due diligence because instead of taking steps under Ss. 5 & 11 of the 1940 Act, to approach the court to cancel the appointment of the arbitrator or stay arbitration proceedings, the appellant only attended by sending letters from time to time to the arbitrator agitating the same plea.[271]

---

invocation of such arbitral proceedings and that these must not be deemed to be a submission to arbitration. The court held that in this circumstance, the party's right to challenge the arbitration clause and arbitration proceeding did not stand waived.

268. *Development Construction Corporation Ltd. Karachi v. West Pakistan P.W.D. and others*, PLD 1971 Karachi 292.
269. *Haji Soomar Haji Hajjan v. Muhammad Amin Muhammad Bashir Ltd.*, 1981 SCMR 129.
270. *Munawar & Co. v. S. A. Rauf & Co.*, PLD 1954 Karachi 30. On this ground the award was set aside. *See also Habib & Sons v. Virak & Co.*, PLD 1957 Karachi 245.
271. *Karachi Dock Labour Board v. Quality Builders Limited*, 2006 CLC 1060.

This judgment was very clearly rendered per curiam and cannot be followed because, in light of aforementioned authorities from the Supreme Court, a party only needs to raise an express challenge before the arbitral tribunal and is not obligated to apply to the court for the revocation of the authority of the arbitral tribunal.

5.6. SUSPENSION OF ARBITRATION PROCEEDINGS

Where the arbitral tribunal is admittedly entrusted with the initial jurisdiction to adjudge matters in relation to a contract concluded between the parties, the institution of some proceedings in the civil court will not deprive the arbitrator of his jurisdiction to continue the arbitration proceedings. It should be noted that if the existence of the parent contract is under attack, the arbitrator will be considered *functus officio*, and any award rendered in this case will be null.[272]

Section 35 is relevant to deciding whether the arbitration proceedings should be superseded or not. This stipulates that:

> (1) No reference nor award shall be rendered invalid by reason only on the commencement of legal proceedings upon the subject-matter of the reference, but when legal proceedings upon the whole of the subject-matter of the reference have been commenced between all the parties to the reference and a notice thereof has been given to the arbitrators or umpire, all further proceedings in a pending reference shall, unless a stay of proceedings is granted under section 34, be invalid.

In *Hakimuddin Harmusji & Sons v. Ghafoor Textile Mills*, the defendant, who filed a section 33 application to get the existence and validity of his arbitration agreement determined by the court, contended on the basis of such proceedings that even if the decision on the stay of court proceedings had not yet been made, the arbitrator did not have jurisdiction to proceed with arbitration. This was because section 35 of the 1940 Act did not prevent the arbitrator from proceeding with arbitration if the notice for the court proceedings on the whole of the subject matter had been communicated to him. On this contention, the Sindh High Court stated that while the invocation of section 35 constituted a statutory bar against arbitration, the applicant had to first prove that the subject matter of arbitration and court proceedings were identical. The court further elaborated by saying that the cause of action of the dispute between the parties, which was the subject matter of court proceedings, should encompass the dispute that is the subject matter of arbitral proceedings. In other words, the court proceeding should have been initiated as a whole on the subject matter of arbitral proceedings. The court also noticed that the prayers under a section 33 application normally include that that there was no contract for whatever reason, such as a mistake, etc., and hence no arbitration agreement. It then concluded that such prayer went to the very root of the contract, implying that there was no contract at all and consequently no arbitration agreement and hence these prayers could not be made the subject matter of arbitration. It held that when said prayers were lodged in the course of court proceedings, one

272. *M. M. Ispahani Ltd. v. Pakistan Trading Company*, PLD 1966 Dacca 54.

could assume they could not cover any part of the subject matter of a reference to arbitration.[273]

Kausar Oil & General Mills v. Muhammad Amin-Muhammad Bashir[274] expressed a more elaborate view. In this judgment, the Sindh High Court stated that by stipulating the condition of encompassing the whole of the subject matter, the legislature actually wanted to avoid conflicting decisions. It held that this possibility must not be superficial but arise only if both the judge and arbitrator are found competing as to the whole subject matter and not part of it. The expression 'whole of the subject matter' means that by giving its decision, the judge should decide the whole matter submitted to the arbitrator. For instance, in a suit to declare an arbitration agreement along with a note which was bought and sold, to be void and illegal, the whole of the subject matter before the arbitrator will not be considered as having been submitted for judicial consideration because if the plaintiff loses the suit, the court could not adjudge the rights and obligation of the parties to the arbitral submission. It held that it is right that if the plaintiff wins the suit by getting the arbitration agreement declared to be void, that the arbitral tribunal will not have any jurisdiction to proceed and render a valid award. The court stated that, to say that because the suit challenges the very basis of the arbitration clause, it covers the whole of the subject matter of the reference is to offer the most superficial view because the word 'whole' cannot mean whole if the decision in the suit is in one way and part or nothing at all if such decision is the other way. Such an approach would not be giving the plain ordinary meaning to the word 'whole', only a speculative meaning.[275]

The court noted that this interpretation would also prevent the parties from filing a suit under section 35 to subvert arbitration proceedings by holding up for a long time.[276]

The courts possess the power to revoke the authority of arbitrators,[277] but such authority does not exist with regard to arbitrations seated abroad.[278] This is because after the court revokes the authority of the arbitrator, it has to proceed under section 12 of the 1940 Act, where under it may supersede the arbitration proceedings or decide to appoint an arbitrator,[279] which is not possible in cases of foreign-seated arbitrations due to the absence of territorial jurisdiction. Despite the authority to revoke the authority of arbitrators under section 6(2), the Punjab High Court has counted the absence of any judicial power granted by the 1940 Act to revoke a valid submission altogether as a flaw in the 1940 Act. As a result, it demanded the amendment of this Act in order to give such discretion to the judge.[280]

273. *Hakimuddin Harmusji & Sons v. Ghafoor Textile Mills*, PLD 1978 Karachi 152. For this, the court relied on *Shiva jute Baling Ltd. v. Hindley & Co. Ltd.*, AIR 1969 SC 1357.
274. *Kausar Oil & General Mills v. Muhammad Amin-Muhammad Bashir*, PLD 1982 Karachi.
275. *Ibid.*, para. 6.
276. *Kausar Oil & General Mills v. Muhammad Amin-Muhammad Bashir*, PLD 1982 Karachi.
277. *Aj-Bag Corporation v. Pakistan through the Secretary, Ministry of Defence, Islamabad and others*, 1973 SCMR 98.
278. *Hitachi Limited and another v. Rupali Polyester and others*, 1998 SCMR 1618.
279. *WAPDA v. Naeem Trading Co.*, 1982 CLC 353; *Trading Corporation of Pakistan (Pvt.) Ltd. v. Nidera Handles Compagnie B. V and another*, 1998 CLC 1610.
280. *M. A. Ghani Soofi & Sons v. The Federation of Pakistan*, PLD 1957 (W. P.) Lahore 363.

In conclusion, Pakistani courts have interfered with arbitral proceedings seated in both Pakistan and abroad. They have forwarded half-hearted support towards arbitration. One is justified to arrive at this conclusion following a wholesale submission of arbitration to local rules and the jurisdiction of Pakistani courts. This has resulted in the infliction of stringent constraints on the *competence-competence* principle and a lack of trust in the institution of arbitration (whether domestic or foreign), which is why the *competence-competence* authority of tribunals is under immense pressure. The courts have exclusive jurisdiction to hear the jurisdictional disputes, including matters pertaining to the existence, scope and validity of arbitration agreements.

Let us assume the absence of the *competence-competence* principle. The resulting scenario would be that to arbitrate, a person must litigate. As to the time to submit the jurisdictional issue to court, two approaches exist, both with their own drawbacks. If the court decides the issue at the outset of arbitral proceedings, it will, in fact, enable the recalcitrant party to delay the arbitration. Whereas, if the court has to decide the jurisdictional issue after the arbitrator issues an award/order on jurisdiction, then the court's decision in favour of the absence of arbitral jurisdiction will be moot and a waste of arbitral time and money.

Despite the negative implications arising from the restrictions to the tribunals' *competence-competence* powers, if a court defers authority over jurisdictional matters to the tribunal, these negative ramifications may be cured. For example, if the award is very well reasoned, it may put the losing party on the way to strike a settlement with the award creditor. Even if the losing party is disinclined to make a settlement, the compelling and penetrating reasons of the award will most probably convince the court to enforce the award. Therefore, if the award is good, the likelihood of wasting time and money from setting aside jurisdictional awards decreases. If the award is unconvincing for the courts of the seat, it is not unlikely that it may still be enforced in other jurisdictions.

Deference to arbitration to decide jurisdictional matters also finds support in the wisdom of arbitration, which is, *inter alia*, the knowledge of arbitrators assumed to be more abreast of foreign governing laws as compared to courts, and this is the prime criterion for their selection. This assumption becomes stronger in cases where the seat of arbitration is aboard.

5.7. CONCLUSION: THE OPTIMUM APPROACH FOR PAKISTAN

The procedure to be followed to challenge the arbitrator's jurisdiction at the referral stage is not elaborated in the 1940 Act. The negative effect of constricting *competence-competence* powers does not mean that the court has to abjure its authority completely in favour of arbitration for ever; rather, this temporary abdication of authority means that the court will later have an opportunity to review the jurisdictional order/award of the arbitrator.[281] As discussed earlier, by rendering the arbitral tribunal the first judge of jurisdictional disputes, the delaying tactics may be remedied. This ensures that it is not prejudicial to the interests of the party challenging bona fide the arbitration agreement because once the tribunal gives its decision on jurisdiction in the form of a preliminary award (upholding his jurisdiction), the aggrieved party may challenge the award in court. It is suggested that unless promulgated by the legislature, the courts may enforce the positive as well as the negative effect of *competence-competence*. The disadvantage of disregarding the positive effect of *competence-competence* is an admitted fact but disinclination to accept the negative effect is also counterproductive, as is evident from the following Pakistani judgments.

The case of *Juna Bunder Joint Venture v. Board of Trustees of Port of Karachi Etc. (TPK)*[282] raises very interesting issues with regard to the principle of *competence-competence*. In this case, the respondents ('Contractor' hereinafter) were under a construction contract concluded with the applicant ('TPK' hereinafter) to construct four new shipping berths and two transit sheds within specific time limits under the supervision of consultants. Disputes arose, and the Contractor moved to arbitration. On the failure from TPK and the consultants to appoint their arbitrator, the Contractors' nominated arbitrator proceeded as sole arbitrator. TPK challenged before the Sindh High Court the arbitration proceedings, arguing, *inter alia*, that according to the agreement, the arbitrator was to assume jurisdiction only after the completion of the 'works', save with the parties' written consent to commence arbitration before such completion, and that the 'works' were in progress and the entire work was not yet completed.

The Sindh High Court held that from the agreement, the intention of the parties could not be inferred to the effect that they actually made the completion of the entire work a condition precedent for the invocation of arbitration. The Sindh High Court stated that the contract had divided the 'works' into two parts, i.e., construction of Four Berths and the construction of Two Sheds and that the time for the construction of each segment of the work had been defined separately. The Sindh High Court concluded that on the completion of the first segment, as asserted by the Contractor, the reference to arbitration was valid. The Sindh High Court also supported its conclusion on the divisibility of 'works' in the contract by arguing that even the arbitration clause did not make it explicit that the parties intended to refer disputes to arbitration only after the work was wholly completed.[283]

As to the question of whether the arbitrator could rule on the jurisdictional issues, the Sindh High Court only enunciated that in the matter before it, the jurisdiction of the arbitrator was not questioned as such and that the actual issue in dispute was the stage

281. Emmanuel Gaillard, *Prima Facie Review of Existence, Validity of Arbitration Agreement*, N.Y. L.J. (1 December 2005). Available at: http://www.shearman.com/~/media/Files/NewsInsights/Publications/2005/12/Prima-Facie-Review-of-Existence-Validity-of-Arb2__/Files/IA_NYLJ-Prima-Facie_040308_14/FileAttachment/IA_NYLJ-Prima-Facie_040308_14.pdf (Last accessed on 20 July 2020).
282. *Juna Bunder Joint Venture, Karachi (Contractors) v. Board of Trustees of Port of Karachi (TPK)*, PLD 1982 Karachi 13.
283. *Ibid.*, p. 29.

at which the arbitrator's referral begins, or in other words, whether the reference to arbitration was mature or premature.[284]

From the letters between the parties, the Sindh High Court can fairly be seen to have assumed the truth of the assertion made by Contractors that they already had completed the work on the four berths. This assumption becomes meaningful after the division of the work into two parts by judicial interpretation, which went on to declare the referral to arbitration valid after the completion of one part of the entire work. Some confusion is evident where the court mentions 'completion' as if it had granted approval to such contention. In more than three places in the judgment, it says that the 'question whether the work is complete or alleged to be complete can very well be left to the Arbitrators'. The question is how much space is left for the arbitrator to decide the issue after the court's affirmative description of the contractor's contention about the completion of one part of the work. The Sindh High Court seemed to have followed the principle that if the jurisdiction of the tribunal depended on the occurrence of some event, the arbitrator did not have jurisdiction to decide whether that event had really occurred; such authority is only vested to the courts. The precise time upon which the tribunal assumes jurisdiction is at the core of the negative effect of *competence-competence*, and the timing for the tribunal to assume jurisdiction is a jurisdictional issue.[285]

In a nutshell, the end result of sending the matter to arbitration was correct but was based on a wrong argument. The court referred the matter to arbitration by impliedly ruling in favour of the completion of half of the work, which means that the court accepted the jurisdiction of the arbitrator by first intervening in his jurisdiction. The preferable approach would have been to simply declare that the interpretation of the contract and its performance was the matter to be decided by the arbitrator and hence the referral of the dispute to the arbitrator.

In another case, the petitioner argued that the validity and justifiability of the reasons given by the Government of Pakistan to terminate the contract were supposed to be determined by the arbitrator. The court inferred from this argument that the petitioner was establishing that the arbitration clause would extend to encompass the matter regarding the government's powers to terminate the agreement or in other words, the powers of government to terminate the contract might be questioned before the arbitrator – up until that time the government had not exercised its powers to terminate the contract. The court held that whether the government had the discretion to terminate the contract in given circumstances was a matter to be determined by the court at a proper stage, i.e., when the merits of the case would be ripe for consideration by the court. The court also held that such power rested with the court to determine at a proper stage whether the arbitrator had the power to investigate the reasons the government intended to exercise its powers to terminate the contract under clause 11;

284. *Ibid.*, p. 30.
285. Emmanuel Gaillard and Yas Banifatemi, *Negative Effect of Competence-Competence: The Rule of Priority in Favour of the Arbitrators*, in *Enforcement of Arbitration Agreements and International Arbitral Awards: The New York Convention in Practice*, eds E. Gaillard and D. Di Pietro (Cameron May, 2008), 257; Giulia Carbone, *The Interference of the Court of the Seat with International Arbitration*, J. Disp. Resol. 217 (2012).

or whether the arbitrator possessed power only to investigate the propriety, validity and justifiability of the exercise of power by the government under clause 11 in order to ascertain if such power was used properly and justly. Furthermore, the court would decide if the government could exercise its powers to terminate the contract even before the decision of the arbitrator.[286]

When an action concerning an arbitration agreement is pending in the court, the arbitral tribunal can continue its proceedings, but the fact of pendency of proceedings in court with a thought that the court still has to rule on it may certainly disturb the efficiency and the progress of the arbitration in a way that both the parties and the arbitrator will not be as efficient in pursuing the arbitration proceedings as they are under normal circumstances. A very broad interpretation regarding the concept of 'whole of subject matter' in section 35 so that court proceedings do not justify the supersession of arbitration – and then the restriction of powers under this provision to domestic arbitrations – is commendable. On the other side, the absence of the negative effect of *competence-competence* has also been denied for foreign-seated arbitrations. It implies that the court will not stay its proceedings in favour of those foreign arbitrations until it has ruled on the existence and validity of the underlying arbitration agreement. This is due to the obligation incumbent on the courts to interpret 'shall' as this appears in section 33 of the 1940 Act.

Disavowal by Pakistani courts of the negative effects of *competence-competence* is a policy concern, given that in Pakistan, the purpose of arbitration is to provide a speedy system of dispute resolution.[287] This is different from the objectives pursued elsewhere through arbitration, as highlighted by Gaillard, who says that:

> For the French legislature, the risk of having the arbitrators wrongly retain jurisdiction in some cases, and have that decision reversed by the courts several months, if not years, later, seemed less serious than the risk that the parties acting in bad faith could disrupt arbitral proceedings by systematically challenging the jurisdiction of the arbitral tribunal not only before the arbitrators, but also before the courts.[288]

However, if the jurisdiction to rule on the arbitrator's jurisdiction is left to the arbitrator, this choice will also save not only the parties' time but also that of the judges, not to mention a significant decrease in expenses.

286. *Pak. Industrial and Commercial Corporation, Lahore v. The Republic of Pakistan*, PLD 1964 (W. P.) Lahore 431.
287. *Zakaullah Khan v. Government of Pakistan through Secretary*, PLD 1998 Lahore 132; *Abdul Salam v. Muhammad Yaqoob and another*, 1999 CLC 1005.
288. Emmanuel Gaillard and John Savage, *Fouchard, Gaillard, Goldman on International Commercial Arbitration* (Kluwer Law International, 1999), para. 680.

CHAPTER 6

Stay of Court Proceedings in Favour of Arbitration in Pakistan

The stay of court proceedings in favour of arbitration is one of the most important criteria which determine the efficacy of the arbitral system as a dispute resolution mechanism. It also reflects the measure of friendliness of a particular regime towards arbitration. In that perspective, this chapter looks at Pakistani judgments to explore the approach of Pakistani courts as to the enforcement of arbitration agreements by staying their proceedings; the principles they employ in order to deal with stay applications; and, more specifically, the interpretation applied to the grounds of being 'null and void, inoperative or incapable of being performed'.

6.1. INTRODUCTION

The arbitration agreement forestalls parties from seeking judicial resolution of their disputes. Safeguards are introduced in every legal system against the recalcitrant party who, deviating from its contractual obligations, initiates court proceedings and thus tries to negate and bypass the arbitration agreement. For instance, Article II(3) of the New York Convention provides that the court wherein such proceedings were commenced will refer the non-compliant party to arbitration unless the arbitration agreement is 'null and void, inoperative or incapable of being performed'. This provision is also incorporated in Pakistani law.[289]

In fact, the stay of court proceedings in favour of arbitration is one of the most important criteria for the efficacy of arbitration as a dispute resolution mechanism. Furthermore, it also reflects the amplitude of friendliness of a particular regime towards

289. Section 4 of Recognition and Enforcement (Arbitration Agreements and Foreign Arbitral Awards) Act 2011.

arbitration. This chapter looks into the practice of Pakistani judgments with a view to exploring the approach of Pakistani courts regarding the enforcement of arbitration agreements by staying court proceedings; in particular, the principles they employ in order to dispose of stay applications and, more specifically, their interpretation of the notion of 'null and void, inoperative or incapable of being performed' and the grounds thereof.

The Pakistani legal regime with regard to stay of court proceedings initiated in defiance of an existing arbitration agreement or in parallel to arbitration proceedings may be divided into two phases: (1) the pre-2011 Act regime and; (2) the post-2011 Act regime. The pre-2011 Act regime was predicated on section 34 of the 1940 Act, the applicability of which was supposed to be confined only to arbitrations seated in Pakistan, although in practice was frequently applied to arbitrations seated abroad. Under this regime, even though foreign-seated arbitrations were governed by the 1937 Act and more precisely by its section 3,[290] Pakistani courts did not refer to this provision in many cases while deciding stay applications in favour of foreign arbitrations; instead relied solely on the onerous provision of section 34 of the 1940 Act. Hence, the 1940 Act and the principles developed thereunder were extended to foreign-seated arbitrations with equal force. The post-2011 Act regime consists of the Recognition and Enforcement (Arbitration Agreements and Foreign Arbitral Awards) Act 2011('the 2011 Act' hereinafter) and specifically section 4 thereof.

An analysis of the pre-2011 Act regime is pertinent due to several reasons. First, applications concerning stay in favour of arbitrations seated in Pakistan (whether between a Pakistani and a non-Pakistani party or even between two non-Pakistani parties) should be governed by the provisions of the 1940 Act. The same result occurs even if the subject matter of the dispute is of an international character. Second, the principles laid down by the courts while interpreting the provisions of the 1940 Act are still relevant. For instance, in *Reko Diq*,[291] decided under the terms of the 2011 Act, the Supreme Court of Pakistan held that by participating in the proceedings before the court, TCC (defendant) had waived its right to challenge the jurisdiction of Pakistani court, and hence was estopped from invoking its arbitration agreement. This waiver is tantamount to the concept of *taking steps in the proceedings before the court*, which was developed under the old regime, as discussed below. The concepts and principles developed to ascertain the nullity, voidness, invalidity and ineffectiveness, of arbitration agreements under the 1940 Act similarly seem relevant for the interpretation of the notions of 'null and void, inoperative or incapable of being performed', as these appear in the 2011 Act.

This chapter comprises four main parts. The second part analyses the pre-2011 Act regime, while the third part examines its post-2011 counterpart. This is followed by a fourth part evincing further the relevance of the old regime for the interpretation of the 2011 Act.

290. The 1937 Act is still applicable to limited types of arbitral proceedings and arbitral awards.
291. *Maulana Abdul Haque Baloch v. Government of Balochistan*, PLD 2013 SC 641 ('*Reko Diq*' hereinafter).

6.2. THE PRE-2011 ACT REGIME

As mentioned above, the pre-2011 Act regime primarily consists of section 34 of the 1940 Act and section 3 of the 1937 Act. Section 34 of the 1940 Act reads as follows:

> Where any party to an arbitration agreement or any person claiming under him commences any legal proceedings against any other party to the agreement or any person claiming under him in respect of any matter agreed to be referred, any party to such legal proceedings may, at any time before filing a written statement or taking any other steps in the proceedings, apply to the judicial authority before which the proceeding: and if satisfied that there is no sufficient reason why the matter should not be referred in accordance with the arbitration agreement and that the applicant was, at the time when the proceedings were commenced, and still remains, ready and willing to do all things necessary, to the proper conduct of the arbitration such authority may make an order staying the proceedings.

Section 3 of the 1937 Act, which governs foreign-seated arbitration, read as follows:

> Notwithstanding anything contained in the (Arbitration Act, 1940) or in the Code of Civil Procedure, 1908 if any party to a *submission* made in pursuance of an agreement to which the protocol set forth in the First Schedule as modified by the reservation subject to which it was signed by India applies, or any person claiming through or under him, commence any legal proceedings in any Court against any other party to the submission or any person claiming through or under him in respect of any matter agreed to be referred, any party to such legal proceedings may, at any time after appearance and before filing a written statement or taking any other steps in the proceedings, apply to the Court to stay the proceedings; and the Court, unless satisfied that the agreement or arbitration has become inoperative or cannot proceed, or that there is not in fact any dispute between the parties with regard to the matter agreed to be referred, ***shall*** make and order staying the proceedings.

With regard to section 3 of the 1937 Act, two points need to be highlighted.[292] First, In order to invoke this section, there must be an actual submission of a dispute to arbitration by the parties in pursuance of an agreement to which the protocol set forth in the First Schedule to the 1937 Act applied. In that regard, the mere existence of an arbitration agreement is not sufficient. Second, the use of the word 'shall' in section 3 has been interpreted in a particular way by the courts. The Sindh High Court in *Transcomerz AG v. Kohinoor Trading (Pvt.) Ltd. and others*[293] held that 'it cannot be denied that the word "shall" is interchangeable with the word "may" and therefore if the context of the relevant provision of a statute demands, the word "shall" can be construed as "may" and vice versa'. It concluded that the word 'shall', as used above, gave the meaning of 'may' by investing discretion in the courts to grant a stay or decline it. This interventionist interpretation was further solidified by the court by emphasizing

292. *Akbar Cotton Mills Ltd. v. VES/OJUANOJO Objedinenije Tech/Amesh Export and another*, 1984 CLC 1605; *Transcomerz AG v. Kohinoor Trading (Pvt.) Ltd. and others*, 1988 CLC 1652; *Pakistan Insurance Corporation, Karachi v. P.T. Indones Oriental Lines and others*, PLD 1977 Karachi 562.
293. *Transcomerz AG v. Kohinoor Trading (Pvt.) Ltd. and others*, 1988 CLC 1652.

that it is bound to offer an interpretation to a statutory provision that results in the preservation of the court's jurisdiction

6.2.1. Ingredients of the Pre-2011 Act Regime

Under this regime, the party praying for stay is obliged to prove the following grounds to secure a stay of court proceedings initiated in disregard of the arbitration agreement.

6.2.1.1. Discretion of Court to Stay Its Proceedings

The general principle is that the mere existence of an arbitration agreement does not extinguish the jurisdiction of the courts.[294] The right of a party for a stay under section 34 is not absolute because by stating that the court 'may make an order staying the proceedings', section 34 effectively confers on the courts a discretion to stay their proceedings, despite the existence of an arbitration clause. No doubt, such discretion should be used judiciously and cautiously.[295] After delineating the same approach in *Uzin Export Import Foreign Trade Co. v. Macdonald Layton & Co. Ltd.*,[296] the Supreme Court of Pakistan justified this approach by stipulating that:

> It must be remembered that these arbitration clauses must be taken to have been inserted with due regard to the existing law of the land, and the law of the land, applicable to them is, as. I have said, that it does not prevent the parties coming to the Court, but only gives to the Court the power to refuse its assistance in proper cases. Therefore, to say that when we refuse to stay action we are not carrying out the bargain between the parties does not fairly describe the position, we are carrying out the bargain between the parties because that bargain to substitute for the Courts of the land a domestic tribunal was a bargain into which was written, by reason of the existing legislation, the condition that it should only be enforced if the Court thought it a proper case for its being so enforced.[297]

Hence, the courts' discretion under section 34 can neither be circumvented nor curtailed by the parties' agreement. Whenever the court felt that one of the parties might not have received a fair and just resolution or impartial treatment, it would have typically refused to stay its proceedings, even if such a decision violated the parties express choice of foreign-seated arbitration, with a view to preventing a miscarriage of justice.[298] Several cases provide ample precedent as to the use of such discretion. Fraud was not mentioned in section 34 as a ground for refusing the stay of proceedings. However, in a string of cases, it was clear that if fraud was alleged, the applicability of

294. *Cotton Export Corporation of Pakistan (Pvt.) Limited Karachi v. Karim Sons Cotton Ginners and others*, 1996 CLC 796; *Farid Virani v. Feroz Virani*, 2013 CLD 1361.
295. *Akbar Cotton Mills Ltd. v. VES/OJUANOJO Objedinenije Tech/Amesh Export and another*, 1984 CLC 1605.
296. *Uzin Export Import Foreign Trade Co. v. Macdonald Layton & Co. Ltd., Karachi*, 1996 SCMR 690.
297. The Supreme Court extracted this passage from *Bristol Corporation v. Aird (John) & Co.* (1913 A.C. 214 (260)).
298. *Akbar Cotton Mills Ltd. v. VES/OJUANOJO Objedinenije Tech/Amesh Export and another*, 1984 CLC 1605.

section 34 would be displaced, and as a result, the courts declined to grant a stay of proceedings.[299] However, it should be noted that the courts were inclined to stay proceedings in favour of arbitration on the application of a party against whom the allegations of fraud were directed, unless said party desired to resolve its dispute by the courts, or otherwise if a prima facie case of fraud was established before the courts.[300]

6.2.1.2. Forum Non Conveniens

Where Pakistani courts are of the opinion that the conduct of arbitration abroad was inconvenient for one of the parties, they have exercised their discretion to refuse stay of proceedings. It may fairly be said that such non-convenience ground is always against the will of parties as reflected in their arbitration agreement. Grounds invoked to prove the inconvenience have included the availability of evidence, witnesses, and subject matter of dispute in Pakistan, involvement of foreign exchange restrictions, the residence of the defendants and plaintiff in Pakistan and the prospective inability of a party to manage legal representatives for foreign arbitration.[301]

Apart from granting or declining the stay application, a third solution has also been adopted by the courts. In a case decided by the Pakistani courts, under the main construction contract containing a Paris-seated ICC arbitration clause, two subcontracts were concluded, both of which adopted all the provisions of the main contract along with its arbitration agreement. Under the first subcontract, the court granted the stay of its proceedings because the issue in question was covered by that arbitration clause. In addition, it also held that the ICC arbitration clause did not result in divesting the court of its jurisdiction and that the clause was tantamount to a domestic arbitration agreement. The court went on to say that because the arbitral process in Paris was far too expensive and inconvenient for the requesting party, it should not be allowed to take place there. Therefore, it ordered the parties to defer the arbitral proceedings to Karachi.[302] With respect to the second subcontract, the same court, this time constituted with a different set of judges, refused to stay the arbitration in Paris, and it held that owing to the expensive and inconvenient nature of arbitration, the stay could not possibly be granted. It further argued that to change the venue of arbitration would be

299. *Avari Hotels v. Hilton International Company*, PLD 1985 Karachi 445; On discretion, *see also ASLO Marines Ltd. v. M. T. Magda and another*, PLD 1985 Karachi 745; *Uzin Export Import Enterprises v. M. Iftikhar & Company Ltd.*, PLD 1986 Karachi 1.

300. *Haji Soomar Haji Hajjan v. Muhammad Amin Muhammad Bashir Ltd.*, 1981 SCMR 129.

301. *Akbar Cotton Mills Ltd. v. VES/OJUANOJO Objedinenije Tech/Amesh Export and another*, 1984 CLC 1605, wherein it was held that the availability of voluminous evidence in Karachi along with the involvement of foreign exchange restrictions, residence of defendant and his business in Karachi had made the conduct of Moscow arbitration impracticable and impossible. In *Ails. M.M. Yasin v. Irving R. Body & Co.*, PLD 1967 Karachi 756, stay was refused in favour of New York-seated arbitration on the ground that the plaintiff, resident in Pakistan, might not manage to find counsels for arbitration. For refusal of stay due to availability of evidence in Pakistan, *see also Muhammad Hanif v. Eckhard & Co. Marine Gmbh and others*, PLD 1983 Karachi 613; *Hasan Amin v. The Capital Development Authority, Islamabad through its Chairman*, 1979 CLC 565.

302. *Uzin Export & Import Enterprises for Foreign Trade v. M. Iftikhar & Company Limited*, 1993 SCMR 866.

like substituting the consent of the parties with the consent of the court, which was not permissible.[303] It may be noticed that in both cases, the arbitration agreement was not respected by the courts.

6.2.1.3. Steps Taken in the Proceedings

Section 34 stipulates that the defendant in a suit should apply for a stay of court proceedings 'before filing a written statement or taking any other steps in the proceedings'. The question as to whether the defendant has taken appropriate steps in the proceedings depends on the facts of each case. If the defendant's conduct manifests unequivocally that he or she has acquiesced to the court proceedings and wants to contest the matter before the court on the merits, his or her application for a stay under section 34 will not be granted. If this is not the case, the defendant should make his stance clear at the earliest opportunity 'before taking any steps in the proceedings', expressly opting for arbitration, because a delay on any pretext would estop him from seeking the stay of court proceedings.[304]

Steps disentitling a party from requesting a stay are only those taken prior to filing a section 34 application and which clearly and unambiguously manifest the intention of the defendant to waive the benefit of the arbitration agreement.[305] The word 'before' appearing in relation to 'filing a written statement or taking any other steps in proceedings' clearly indicates that the option to seek the stay of court proceedings should be exercised only before and not even simultaneously with the filing of the applicant's written statement.[306] Hence, a written statement, which constitutes a necessary step in the proceedings, if filed after a section 34 application, would not debar a defendant from seeking stay of court proceedings.[307]

The following actions are not considered as constituting 'steps' in court proceedings:

- Filing or defending an application for injunction.[308] This is so because, under the 1940 Act, an arbitrator does not have the power to deal with injunctions.[309]

303. *Uzin Export Import Foreign Trade Co. v. Macdonald Layton & Co. Ltd., Karachi and another*, 1996 SCMR 690.
304. *Island Textile Mills Ltd. Karachi v. V/O Technoexperts and others*, 1979 CLC 307; *Uzin Export Import Enterprises v. M. Iftikhar & Company Ltd.*, 1987 CLC 2205; *Badsha Meah Sowdagar v. Nurul Haq and others*, PLD 1967 Dacca 250; *Pakistan International Airlines Corporation v. Pak Saaf Dry Cleaners*, PLD 1981 SC 553; *Province of the Punjab v. Irfan & Co.*, PLD 1956 (W. P.) Lahore 442; *Muhammad Farooq v. Nazir Ahmad and others*, PLD 2006 SC 196; *Mac Donald Layton & Company v. Uzin Export Import Enterprises*, PLD 1989 Karachi 645.
305. *Danish Brothers Limited v. Cotton Export Corporation of Pakistan (Pvt.) Limited*, 1994 MLD 2227. Court extracted this from the judgment of Indian Supreme Court in *Rachappa Guruadappa, Bijapur v. Gurusiddappa Nuraniappa and others*, 1990 MLD 1383.
306. *Naseer and others v. Muhammad Hanif*, 2004 YLR 2154.
307. *MacDonald Layton & Company v. Uzin Export Import Enterprises*, PLD 1989 Karachi 645; *Royal Group v. Semos Pharmaceuticals (Pvt.) Ltd.*, 2011 CLC 235.
308. *Island Textile Mills Ltd. Karachi v. V/O Technoexperts and others*, 1979 CLC 307. *See also* PLD 1969 Dacca 719; *Uzin Export and Import Enterprises for Foreign Trade v. M. Iftikhar and Company Limited*, 1993 SCMR 866.
309. *Serulean (Pvt.) Ltd. Karachi v. Bhoja Airlines (Pvt.) Ltd.*, 2001 YLR 3150.

- Mere prayer from the defendant for additional time to file objections to the application for the receiver's appointment.[310]
- Filing *vakalatnama* (power of attorney from one's lawyer).[311]
- Unilateral withdrawal of the suit and application to seek time towards a compromise.[312]

While deciding the stay application, the court has to satisfy itself that the applicant has not relinquished its right to arbitrate.[313] This right is relinquished if a party takes, for instance, any of the following steps before the court:

- *Submission of a written statement in response to the plaint.*[314] In one case, the defendant filed an application under section 34 for stay of proceedings. Thereafter, he filed a written statement with preliminary objections, qualifying these as being 'without prejudice' to the preliminary objections or any application filed under section 34. The court held that with the use of such expression, the defendant made it clear that by filing the written statement, he had not waived his right to invoke section 34.[315] Although the submission of a written statement after the filing of a stay application does not prejudice the stay application, where a party proceeds with a suit, this may deprive the said party of the right to seek the stay.[316]
- *Request for additional time for the submission of a written statement.*[317] If the hearing is adjourned for the court to file a written statement *proprio motu*,

310. *Badsha Meah Sowdagar v. Nurul Haq and others*, PLD 1967 Dacca 250.
311. *Mac Donald Layton & Company Ltd. v. Uzin Export Import Enterprises and another*, PLD 1989 Karachi 645.
312. *Uzin Export & Import Enterprises v. M. Iftikhar & Company Limited*, 1993 SCMR 866.
313. *Ibid.*
314. *Ibid.*, *Pakistan and Brothers v. Faiz Ahmad*, 1983 CLC 1369. Written statement is a defence which is filed by the defendant in response to the pliant submitted by the plaintiff. For detail on plaint and written statement, *see* Order VII and VIII of Code of Civil Procedure 1908, and *G. M. Pfaff A. G. v. Sartaj Engineering Co. Ltd., Lahore and others*, PLD 1970 Lahore 184; *Anjuman Faizul Islam (Regd.), Rawalpindi v. Building Artisans Ltd, and another*, PLD 1994 Lahore 122; *Cotton Export Corporation of Pakistan (Pvt.) Limited Karachi v. Karim Sons Cotton Ginners and others*, 1996 CLC 796; *Friends Corporation Pesticides Dealers and another v. Granulars (Private) Limited*, 1993 CLC 583; *Water And Power Development Authority and others v. Mian Manzoor Ahmad*, 1988 CLC 1169; *Uzin Export Import Enterprises v. M. Iftikhar & Company Ltd.*, PLD 1986 Karachi 1; *Universal Business Equipment (Pvt.) Ltd. v. Kokusai Commerce Inc. and others*, 1995 MLD 384.
315. *Pakistan Refinery v. Shaihda Sultan*, 1988 MLD 1150.
316. *Mac Donald Layton & Company Ltd. v. Uzin Export Import Enterprises and another*, PLD 1989 Karachi 645.
317. *Board of Intermediate and Secondary Education Sargodha and another v. Akhtar Brothers*, 1981 CLC 221; *Muhammad Ilyas Khokhar v. Ihsan Ilahi Mughal*, 2000 CLC 206; *Muhammad Idris and others v. Tobarak Hussain*, PLD 1965 Dacca 260. *See also ASLO Marines Ltd. v. M. T. Magda and another*, PLD 1985 Karachi 745; *Pakistan International Airlines Corporation v. Pak Saaf Dry Cleaners*, PLD 1981 SC 553; *New Bengal Shipping Company v. Eric Lancaster Stump*, PLD 1952 Dacca 22. Frequent requests for adjournment to file written statement would be tantamount to steps into proceeding, *see Muhammad Farooq v. Nazir Ahmad and others*, PLD 2006 SC 196; *Shin Satellite Public Company Limited v. Kasb Technology Services Limited*, 2016 YLR 2322. For opposite view, *see, Al-Faridia Industries v. Alfa Insurance Company Ltd. and others*, 1993 MLD 1074.

without any request from the defendant, such adjournment will not be termed as a 'step' in the proceedings.[318] This is because the notion of a 'step in the proceedings' is unrelated to any action or omission by the court; it concerns only action or inaction undertaken by or attributable to the defendant.[319] In an equal manner, seeking a single adjournment would not amount to a step in the proceedings.[320]

6.2.1.4. The Condition of Being Willing and Ready for Arbitration

The other condition under section 34 is that the party applying for a stay should be ready and willing to arbitrate at the time of the filing of the civil suit.[321] To determine the willingness and readiness for arbitration, the actions taken before filing the section 34 application will be of no relevance in this respect. In one case, Y filed a suit against his partner X in July 1978 for the dissolution of their partnership and rendition of accounts, which he withdrew in November 1980. In January 1981, X filed a suit for dissolution of the partnership. Y sought the stay of this suit in favour of an arbitration agreement in the partnership deed. A stay was granted on the basis of the principle that the filing of a suit by Y in 1978 was irrelevant to judge his willingness and readiness for arbitration on the eve of the commencement of the proceedings in 1981.[322] Similarly, in *Dr. Muhammad Shafi v. Maj. (Retd.) M. Iqbal Hussain and others*,[323] which concerned a dispute arising from a construction contract, the appellant made several requests for arbitration to the respondent in accordance with an arbitration clause incorporated in the construction contract. Upon refusal, the appellant filed a suit in the court which was resisted by the respondent, who then proceeded to file a section 34 application. The court stated that he who relies on section 34 must prove that at the time of the suit, as well as when the application under section 34 was made, he is ready and willing for arbitral proceedings. In that case, the court held that the respondent's refusal to commence arbitration in response to the appellant's notices demonstrates his unwillingness to arbitrate, which in turn disqualifies him from the benefits of section 34. Nonetheless, the court went on to note that the mere silence of the applicant (respondent in this case) in response to a notice for arbitration before the suit is filed does not amount to an unwillingness to arbitrate. The court supported this conclusion by reference to the fact that the respondent had not clearly averred in its application that he was ready and willing for the arbitration; as a result, the stay was refused.[324]

318. *Province of Punjab v. Ehsan Fazal & Company*, 1986 CLC 2800.
319. *Naseer and others v. Muhammad Hanif*, 2004 YLR 2154.
320. *Pakistan Stone Development Company Limited v. Muhammad Yousaf*, 2018 CLC 877.
321. *Gulf Iran Co. and another v. Pakistan Refinery Ltd. and others*, PLD 1976 Karachi 1060.
322. *Muhammad Yousuf Burney v. S. Muahmmad Ali*, 1983 CLC 1498. *See also Central Insurance Co. Ltd., Karachi v. Khyber Textile Mills Ltd. and another*, PLD 1978 Karachi 908; *Muhammad Shafi v. Maj. (Retd.) M. Iqbal Hussain and others*, PLD 1996 Lahore 667; *Uzin Export Import Enterprises v. M. Iftikhar & Co. Ltd.*, PLD 1986 Karachi 1.
323. *Dr. Muhammad Shafi v. Maj. (Retd.) M. Iqbal Hussain and others*, PLD 1996 Lahore 667.
324. *Ibid.*, paras 10-12.

However, in *Province of East Pakistan v. Nurul Huda and others*, the court held that the applicant is not bound to state expressly in his application that he is willing to arbitrate because his application for the stay of civil proceedings would be sufficient to prove his willingness.[325] As to the point of time when the applicant should be ready and willing for arbitration, *Whitehorn International Limited v. M. V. Ghantout-I* provides a stricter view, in which the court held that the defendant should be ready and willing to go to arbitration at all relevant times. In this case, the defendant did not invoke the arbitration clause but instead took possession of the vessel and initiated criminal proceedings against the plaintiff in the courts of the UAE and was thus declared by the Pakistani court as having taken steps in the proceedings.[326]

6.2.1.5. *Existence of Dispute and Encompassment Thereof by Arbitration Agreement*

Where there is no arbitration agreement, no stay under section 34 would be granted.[327] Furthermore, the party requesting the stay has to establish the existence of a dispute, which itself must moreover fall within the ambit of the arbitration agreement.[328] For instance, a claim for damages arising from a hiring contract fell within the ambit of the arbitration agreement laid down in the hiring contract and hence the request for a stay was granted.[329] However, the defendant issued a cheque in favour of the plaintiff in a sequence of various bills and purchase orders. The payment for the cheque was stopped by the defendant. The plaintiff filed a suit for recovery that was resisted by the defendant, who went on to file a section 34 application on the basis of the arbitration clause in the purchase orders. It was contended by the defendant that the dispute over the cheque, in fact, arose from the purchase orders and, as a result, should have been resolved through arbitration. The court held that 'dishonoring of cheques being an independent cause of action, section 34 was not applicable' and subsequently refused to grant the stay.[330] If the suit for the recovery was filed by the plaintiff on the basis of a promissory note or other negotiable instruments, the court would be inclined to hold that the suit was not founded on any controversy encompassed under the arbitration clause; hence, it would not assume that any dispute thereunder fell under the terms of

325. *Province of East Pakistan v. Nurul Huda and others*, PLD 1970 Dacca 699.
326. *Whitehorn International Limited v. M. V. Ghantout-I (Ex-Bismillah)*, 1991 MLD 75.
327. *Diamond Food Industries Limited v. Werner & Pfleiderer Gmbh Germany*, 1992 MLD 926.
328. *Zohra Begum v. Abdul Razzak & Co. and others*, 1984 CLC 1643 Karachi; *Muhammad Yousuf Burney v. S. Muahmmad Ali*, 1983 CLC 1498; *Novelty Cinema, Lyallpur v. Firdous Mills and others*, PLD 1958 Lahore 208. A dispute means the assertion of right by one and its repudiation from the other. *See also Jamia Industries Ltd. v. Pakistan Refinery Ltd., Karachi*, PLD 1976 Karachi 644; *Indus Valley Construction Company Ltd. v. Comentation Intrafor Ltd.*, 1982 SCMR 1127; *Uzin Export Import Enterprises v. M. Iftikhar & Company Ltd.*, PLD 1986 Karachi 1; *Mac Donald Layton & Company Ltd. v. Uzin Export Import Enterprises and another*, PLD 1989 Karachi 645.
329. *Pakistan Telecommunication Corporation Ltd. v. Dr Waqar Hussain Chaudhary*, PLD 2007 Lahore 678.
330. *Nasir Ahmad v. Pakland Cement Limited*, 2001 CLC 1156.

the said arbitration agreement. Consequently, a request for a stay would have been refused.[331]

An application under section 34 should categorically state either in itself or through the affidavit in support of it that there is an arbitration agreement which covers the dispute in a suit, the applicant's response to the dispute without the need for further details, and an expression of willingness, at all material times, on the part of the applicant to go to arbitration in order that the dispute be resolved. Even so, the courts have held that in the event that such particulars are missing, the dismissal of the application on that score alone may, while technically correct, be inappropriate. Likewise, the obligation to elaborate the details of the dispute as a prerequisite for stay of proceedings on pains of refusal of relief may also be unwarranted in the language of section 34.[332]

6.2.1.6. Non-parties to the Arbitration

If one of the parties to the suit is not a party to the arbitration proceedings, the court may refuse to grant the stay of its proceedings.[333] For instance, in *A. Nawaz & Co. (Regd.) and others v. National Bank of Pakistan,*[334] the National Bank of Pakistan (Bank) filed a suit against petitioners for the recovery of PKR 2,08,795, which was due on an overdraft account of the petitioner with the Bank against a pledge of certain moveables and immovables which they insured with an insurance company (Company). These were subsequently destroyed by fire. The claim against the Company was referred to arbitration in accordance with an arbitration clause in the insurance policy. In a recovery suit by Bank, the petitioners filed a section 34 application by relying on the arbitration clause in the insurance policy. This application was rejected on the ground that the Bank was not liable for the loss sustained by the petitioner due to fire. Therefore, the Bank was not concerned with the claims of the petitioner in arbitration proceedings against the insurance company. Despite this judgment, in *Ovex Technologies (Private) Limited v. PCM PK (Private) Limited and others,*[335] the Islamabad High Court has pertinently stated that:

> Merely because a plaintiff has impleaded other parties (with whom the plaintiff does not have an arbitration agreement) as defendants in a suit and also sought relief against them does not deprive the defendant (with whom the plaintiff has entered into an arbitration agreement) of his right vested in him under Section 34 of the 1940 Act or Section 4 of the 2011 Act, as the case may be, to seek stay of the

331. *Shell Pakistan Ltd. v. Bhoja Air Pvt. Ltd.*, 2007 MLD 1424; *Suriya Waseem Usmani and others v. L & M International (Pvt.) Ltd.*, 2002 CLD 624; *Cotton Export Corporation of Pakistan (Pvt.) Ltd. v. Asif Cotton Ginners and others*, 995 CLC 1024.
332. *Hyderabad Municipal Corporation v. Columbia Enterprises*, 1990 CLC 47; *Cosmopolitan Development Company v. So Dime S.P.A. and another*, 1987 MLD 2832.
333. *Haji Muhammad Zafar v. Muhammad Sikandar and others*, 2000 YLR 2503.
334. *A. Nawaz & Co. (Regd.) and others v. National Bank of Pakistan*, 1970 SCMR 234.
335. *Ovex Technologies (Private) Limited v. PCM PK (Private) Limited and others*, 2020 CLD 15. *See also Lithuanian Airlines v. Bhoja Airlines (Pvt.) Ltd.*, 2004 CLC 544; *Haji Muhammad Ibrahim v. Karachi Municipal Corporation*, PLD 1960 Karachi 916.

> proceedings in the suit to his extent. It has become common place for unscrupulous litigants to rope in other parties in addition to the party with whom they have an arbitration agreement as defendants in a suit in order to avoid the proceedings in the suit being stayed on account of such an arbitration clause. More often than not, when proceedings in a suit are stayed under section 34 of the 1940 Act or section 4 of the 2011 Act to the extent of the defendant who is party to an arbitration agreement, the plaintiff loses interest in the suit against the other defendants or withdraws the suit. Courts ought to be vigilant as to such an abuse of its process and visit the dismissal or withdrawal of such cases with exemplary costs.

By stating that the court has discouraged the refusal to grant the stay of court proceedings on the impleadment of non-parties, the court seems to have effectively made the case that such suit against the co-defendants should be declared frivolous and vexatious.

6.2.1.7. Conflicting Judgments by Court and Arbitral Tribunal

If there is a possibility of conflicting decisions between the court and the arbitral tribunal, the application for a stay will be refused.[336] For instance, where there are several interlinked questions, some of which may be referred to arbitration while others are to be decided by the court, this will generate the possibility of conflicting decisions.[337] Similarly, where some of the parties to the suit were not parties to the arbitration agreement, there might well be a possibility of conflicting judgments, in which case the courts will be inclined to refuse an application for the stay of court proceedings.[338]

6.2.2. Stay of Proceedings Initiated under Section 33 of the 1940 Act

The authority to adjudge the existence and validity of an arbitration agreement rests only with the court.[339] The parties cannot confer such a power on the arbitrator even through a widely drafted arbitration agreement.[340] Pakistani courts have reasoned that the referral of the matter to an arbitrator is based on the arbitration agreement and the

336. *Gulf Iran Co. and another v. Pakistan Refinery Ltd. and others*, PLD 1976 Karachi 1060.
337. *Whitehorn International Limited v. M. V. Ghantout-I (Ex-Bismillah)*, 1991 MLD 75.
338. *Lithuanian Airlines v. Bhoja Airlines (Pvt.) Ltd.*, 2004 CLC 544; *Hidayatullah and others v. Shamimuddin and others*, 1993 MLD 993; *National Development Leasing Corporation Ltd. v. Chairman, Banking Tribunal/Court-Ii, Faisalabad and others*, 2000 YLR 176; *Gulf Iran Co. and another v. Pakistan Refinery Ltd. and others*, PLD 1976 Karachi 1060.
339. *Province of West Pakistan v. Fakir Spinning Mills Ltd and others*, PLD 1962 (W. P.) Karachi 386. In this case, court by quoting an Indian Judgment (*Ratnji Virpal & Co v. Dhirajlal Manilal*, AIR 1942 Bom. 101), held that if the question with regard to the existence and validity of arbitration agreement arises, that question will be decided by court. For challenge to arbitration agreement generally, *see also AGRICIDES (Pvt) Ltd. v. Ali Agro Supply Corporation Ltd.*, 1988 CLC 59. For challenge to arbitration agreement on the ground that there exists no parent contract in which the arbitration agreement is included, wherein the jurisdiction of arbitrator was denied by the court, *see Cosmopolitan Development Company Ltd. v. Alfred C. Toepfer International and others*, 1991 CLC 1087.
340. *WAPDA v. Abdur Razzaq*, PLD 1977 Lahore 5.

decision on its existence and validity involves very complex legal questions. Hence, these issues cannot be left to the arbitrator's sole consideration since it would be futile if the court, without having considered the matter, refers it to the arbitrator. The Pakistani courts' reasoning is further predicated on the risk that the tribunal may issue an award before the courts have a chance to declare the tribunal's jurisdiction as defective on the ground of the absence of a valid agreement to arbitrate.[341]

The power to declare the existence of a valid or effective arbitration agreement is conferred upon the courts by virtue of section 33 of the 1940 Act as follows:

> Arbitration agreement or award to be contested by application: Any party to an arbitration agreement or any person claiming under him desiring to challenge the existence or validity of an arbitration agreement or an award or to have the effect of either determined shall apply to the Court and the Court *shall* decide the question on affidavits.
>
> Provided that where the Court deems it just and expedient, it may set down the application for hearing on other evidence also, and it may pass such orders for the discovery and particulars as it may do in a suit.

In spite of the fact that the applicability of the 1940 Act is confined to domestic arbitration,[342] the power of the courts to rule on the existence and validity of arbitration agreements is extended to foreign arbitration.[343] Furthermore, the word 'shall' appearing in this provision has been interpreted as encompassing all applications to the courts under section 33, in which case the courts are obliged to determine the validity and effect of the arbitration agreement,[344] even if during the pendency of such application an award is issued by the tribunal. In this situation, the court will first decide the application filed under section 33 because the fate of the award will depend on the fate of that application. That is to say, if the arbitration agreement is non-existent, the award will be vitiated, and if the arbitration agreement is found valid, then the enforceability of the award will be checked against other applicable grounds.[345]

Proceedings initiated under section 33 of the 1940 Act will not be stayed by the application of section 34. In *Asian Mutual Insurance v. Pakistan Insurance Corporation*,[346] the Sindh High Court held that when the question of validity, existence or effectiveness of an arbitration agreement is raised before the court by an application filed under section 33, due to the mandatory wording of section 33, the court seized is bound to decide that question and the proceedings do not come to an end under section 34. It further elaborated that the stay of proceedings might be granted under section 34 only after the court has concluded that the arbitration agreement was valid, existent and effective. It is submitted that this interpretation may turn out to be cumbersome for

---

341. *Avari Hotels v. Hilton International Company*, PLD 1985 Karachi 445. For single bench decision from where appeal arose, *see Avari Hotels Ltd. v. Hilton International Company*, PLD 1984 Karachi 488.
342. Section 1(2) of the 1940 Act.
343. *Pakistan Chrome Mines Ltd. v. Phibro Asia Ltd. and others*, 1976 SCMR 93.
344. *Kashmir Corporation Ltd. v. PIA*, PLD 1995 Karachi 301.
345. *Hakimuddin Harmusji & Sons v. Ghafoor Textile Mills*, PLD 1978 Karachi 152.
346. *Asian Mutual Insurance Co. Ltd. v. Pakistan Insurance Corporation and others*, PLD 1982 Karachi 778.

arbitration. The general disposition of the courts is not in favour of staying their proceedings because numerous grounds are available to refuse the stay, thus encouraging the obstruction of arbitral proceedings. To add more melancholy, it appears likely that if the application is filed under section 33, its disposal will be mandatory on the courts before deciding the stay application submitted under section 34. It should also be noted that the word 'shall', appearing in section 3 of the 1937 Act, was interpreted to mean 'may' by giving the courts discretion instead of obliging them to grant the stay of their proceedings in favour of foreign-seated arbitration. However, the word 'shall', appearing in section 33 of the 1940 Act, was interpreted in a way that made it binding on the courts to refuse the stay until deciding the existence and effect of the arbitration agreement under that section. It is still not clear what indications the courts have used to provide two different interpretations of the same word. It does, however, seem clear that opposite interpretations were afforded to the word 'shall' in both sections in order to attain the one and same aim of preserving the jurisdiction of the courts and deny the jurisdiction of arbitrators.

Therefore, if the proceedings in court are launched under any provision of the 1940 Act, as for instance, relating to the competency of the arbitrator under sections 5 and 11 or the existence and validity of the arbitration agreement under section 33, there cannot be any stay under section 34. This is the reason, as elaborated by the courts, that the legality of an arbitrator's appointment or the existence and validity of an arbitration agreement is to be investigated under the 1940 Act before the arbitration proceedings set off. The courts must first decide the validity of the arbitration agreement prior to granting a stay under section 34. Section 33 also deals with the same question; hence, section 34 does not have any application upon proceedings subject to section 33.[347] Thus, a challenge against an application under section 33 does not qualify as a 'step' in the proceedings; rather, it would qualify as a step in the proceedings under section 34.[348]

6.3. ENFORCEMENT OF ARBITRATION AGREEMENTS AND THE RELATION BETWEEN SECTIONS 20 AND 34 OF THE 1940 ACT

Under section 34, a court can only stay its proceedings in favour of arbitration and has no power to issue directions to send the file to the arbitrator.[349] *Stricto sensu*, proceedings under sections 34 and 20 are not civil suits but are treated as civil suits. More specifically, an application under section 20 is treated as a civil suit and any direction under section 20 for filing the arbitration agreement and making reference to the arbitration would amount to a decree.[350]

347. *Asian Mutual Insurance Co. Ltd. v. Pakistan Insurance Corporation and others*, PLD 1982 Karachi 778.
348. *WAPDA v. Abdur Razzaq*, PLD 1977 Lahore 5. *See also AGRICIDES (Pvt) Ltd. v. Ali Agro Supply Corporation Ltd.*, 1988 CLC 59.
349. *S. M. Qasim & Co. v. Sh. Azimuddin*, PLD 1962 (W. P.) Lahore 95; *Muhammad Jaffar v. Municipal Committee, Hasilpur*, 1988 MLD 1345.
350. *Coca Cola Beverages Pakistan Limited v. Echo West International (Pvt.) Ltd.*, 2016 MLD 1077.

6.3.1. Conditions for Application under Section 20 of the 1940 Act

After the stay of court proceedings under section 34, the parties are free either to refer the dispute to arbitration without court intervention (under Chapter II of the 1940 Act) or with the intervention of the courts (under section 20 of the 1940 Act).[351] There are three essential conditions for the satisfaction of an application under section 20, namely: the existence of an arbitration agreement, the existence of a dispute between the parties and the non-invocation of Chapter II of the 1940 Act.[352]

6.3.1.1. Existence of an Arbitration Agreement

The parties must have entered into an arbitration agreement before the filing of a suit concerning the subject matter of the arbitration. To determine the existence of an arbitration agreement, the arbitration agreement is considered as a normal contract, and both are governed by the same principles of interpretation.[353] For instance, the arbitration agreement is perused in its entirety[354] and effective[355] and liberal interpretation[356] by applying the principle of good faith[357] is given to it.

6.3.1.2. Existence of a Dispute

There must be a real dispute falling within the scope of the parties' arbitration agreement over which the tribunal has not initiated proceedings because it constitutes the cause of action under section 20. The dispute implies the assertion of a right by one party and its repudiation by the other.[358] For instance, whether payment is due or whether a party has paid more than what was due,[359] or whether a party is entitled to appropriate the entire amount of a guarantee[360] was declared by the courts to constitute disputes. It should be noted that where the claim raised by one party was settled by the

351. *S. M. Qasim & Co. v. Sh. Azimuddin*, PLD 1962 (W. P.) Lahore 95; *BNP (Pvt.) Limited v. Collier International Pakistan (Pvt.) Limited*, 2016 CLC 1772; *Allied Engineering Consultants (Pvt.) Ltd., Lahore v. Sui Gas Transmission Company Ltd.*, 1989 CLC 1143.
352. *Project Director, Balochistan Minor Irrigation and Agricultural Development Project, Quetta Cantt. v. Murad Ali & Company*, 1999 SCMR 121; *Waseem Ahmed Usmani v. L. & M. International (Private) Ltd.*, 1998 CLC 256; *Commodities Trading International Corporation v. Trading Corporation of Pakistan Ltd and another*, 1987 CLC 2063; *Muhammad Umar v. Yar Muhammad*, 2009 CLC 348; *Mujtaba Hussain Siddiqui v. Sultan Ahmed*, 2005 YLR 2709.
353. *Yasmeen v. Beach Developers through Managing Director and another*, 2003 YLR 1109.
354. *Nawab Brothers Ltd. Karachi v. Project Director, Office of the Project Director, Special Projects, Planning and Development Department, Karachi and another*, 1981 CLC 638.
355. *Muhammad Akram and others v. Ch. Muhammad Salim*, PLD 1964 (W. P.) Lahore 490.
356. *Province of Punjab v. Malik Muhammad Ilyas and others*, 1994 MLD 476; *G.M.K. Enterprises v. Shaheen Builders*, 1999 CLC 1698.
357. *Zohra Begum v. Abdul Razak & Co. and others*, 1984 CLC 1643.
358. *Industrial Fabrication Company v. Managing Director, Pak American Fertilizer Limited*, 2015 PLD 154 SC; *Global Energy & Commodity Exchange Group Italy Spa (Gecx Group) v. Trading Corporation of Pakistan*, 2013 CLD 681; *Jamia Industries Ltd v. Pakistan Refinery Ltd., Karachi*, PLD 1976 Karachi 644.
359. *Arabtec Pakistan (Pvt) Ltd. v. Enshaanlc Developments*, 2011 CLC 323.
360. *Jamia Industries Ltd v. Pakistan Refinery Ltd., Karachi*, PLD 1976 Karachi 644.

parties by making payment, there would be no dispute.[361] However, the authority of the courts is limited to the determination of the dispute's existence and cannot go into the substantive claims of the dispute or prescribe the manner of resolution of such dispute, which befalls the authority of the tribunal.[362]

6.3.1.3. *Non-invocation of Chapter III of the 1940 Act*

The parties should not initiate proceedings under Chapter II (sections 3-19) of the 1940 Act. If the parties to an arbitration agreement have invoked the provisions of Chapter II (sections 3-19), the remedy under Chapter III (section 20) of the 1940 Act would not be available to them.[363] If a party opts for arbitration with the intervention of the court and its application under section 20 is successful, the court seized will order the arbitration either under the authority of the arbitrator appointed by the parties or 'where the parties cannot agree upon an arbitrator' the court may refer the dispute to be resolved by an arbitrator appointed by itself.[364]

Where the parties choose to proceed to arbitration without the intervention of the court, sections 3-19 provide a comprehensive procedure for the appointment of arbitrators. If the parties are unable to make an appointment according to these provisions, then they can approach the court under section 20 with a prayer for the appointment of an arbitrator. However, proceedings under Chapter II (sections 3-19) and Chapter III (section 20) cannot proceed simultaneously. Where an applicant has exercised its option under sections 3-19, he cannot file a section 20 application.[365] In one case, after achieving a stay of court proceedings under section 34, a party appointed its arbitrator and then sent notice to the other party by invoking section 8, by which it requested it to concur with its chosen arbitrator. The court held that the first party could not file the section 20 application because it had already invoked Chapter II.[366]

6.3.2. Procedure for Application under Section 20

The 1940 Act provides three modes of arbitration. First, arbitration without the intervention of the court, as covered by Chapter II (sections 3-19); second, arbitration with the intervention of the court where there is no suit pending before the court, as encompassed under Chapter III containing only one section, i.e., section 20 and; lastly,

---

361. *Industrial Fabrication Company v. Managing Director, Pak American Fertilizer Limited*, 2015 PLD 154.
362. *Global Energy & Commodity Exchange Group Italy Spa (Gecx Group) v. Trading Corporation of Pakistan*, 2013 CLD 681.
363. *Nasim Ahmad Vana v. State*, 2017 PLD 497 Karachi.
364. *Hafiz Abdul Aziz Cotton Ginning Factory v. Haji Ali Muhammad Abdullah & Co.*, PLD 1966 (W. P.) Karachi 197.
365. *Commodities Trading International Corporation v. Trading Corporation of Pakistan Ltd and another*, 1987 CLC 2063.
366. *Mujtaba Hussain Siddiqui v. Sultan Ahmed*, 2005 YLR 2709.

arbitration concerning an issue in a suit pending before a court, as covered by sections 21-25.

The procedure for a section 20 application is explained in *Mujtaba Hussain Siddiqui v. Sultan Ahmed.*[367] After the fulfilment of the three above-mentioned conditions, the applicant may file a section 20 application in writing to a court with jurisdiction, which will then register it as a suit. Notices will then be issued to the interested parties, whether as plaintiffs or defendants. The parties other than the plaintiff are issued notices so they may show cause as to why the arbitration agreement should not be filed in the court, and if they are unable to show any sufficient cause, the court will order that the arbitration agreement be filed and make a reference to the arbitrator appointed by the parties. If the parties cannot agree on the person of the arbitrator, then the court would make the appointment of the arbitrator. After the appointment of the arbitrator, the arbitration proceedings will commence and be governed by other provisions of the 1940 Act. After these conditions are fulfilled, the purpose of section 20 is achieved, and a section 20 application stands disposed of.

The limitation period to file a section 20 application is three years, which are computed from the point in time the dispute arose between the parties.[368] Any application after the expiry of this period would not be entertained. The question as to whether a section 20 application is filed within the limitation period will be decided by the courts and not be left to the arbitrator.[369] Only a party to the arbitration agreement can file an application under section 20.[370]

6.4. POST-2011 ACT REGIME: NEW REGIME

The 2011 Act was promulgated to incorporate the New York Convention into Pakistani domestic law. It is noteworthy that the provisions of the 2011 Act are similar to those when this instrument was promulgated as an Ordinance.[371] Hence, judgments handed down by the courts under the instrument when it was enacted as Ordinance are very much relevant for the interpretation of the 2011 Act. Section 4 of the 2011 Act stipulates that:

> (1) A party to an arbitration agreement against whom legal proceedings have been brought in respect of a matter which is covered by the arbitration agreement may, upon notice to the other party to the proceedings, apply to the court in which the proceedings have been brought to stay the proceedings insofar as they concern that matter.

367. *Ibid.*
368. *Macdonald Layton Costain Ltd., Karachi v. State Bank of Pakistan*, PLD 1980 Karachi 87.
369. *Oil and Gas Development Company Ltd. v. Agha Muhammad and Brothers*, 2015 MLD 1821.
370. *Pakistan Real Estate Investment and Management Company (Pvt) Ltd. v. Sohail A. Khan, Associates-Assign JV*, 2018 PLD 115 Islamabad; *K & N International v. Motorway Operations and Rehabilitation Engineering (Private) Limited*, 2019 CLC 1613.
371. Article 89 of the Constitution of Islamic Republic Pakistan says that when neither house of Parliament is in session, President can enact a law by issue Ordinance which will last for four months. If within these four months, if Parliament does not make it an Act of Parliament, then it will lapse and on such expiry, President can reissue as Ordinance. However, President of Pakistan cannot issue one Ordinance twice.

(2) On an application under subsection (1), the court shall refer the parties to arbitration, unless it finds that the arbitration agreement is null and void, inoperative or incapable of being performed.

6.4.1. Grounds to Refuse the Stay of Court Proceedings

In *Metropolitan Steel Corporation Ltd. v. Macsteel International Ltd,*[372] the Sindh High Court held that it could not refuse to stay its proceedings on the basis of public policy or *forum non conveniens* since no ground out of 'null and void, inoperative or incapable of being performed' had been proved by the plaintiff and as a result, it was left with no discretion to refuse the stay. It stated that:

> There is no doubt some expense is involved in litigation but that is true anywhere in the world. In the present suit, the plaintiff has filed a suit for more than US$ 1 million, and it is reasonable to expect to incur some expense in the event of a dispute. Further, there is no restriction imposed by the State Bank of Pakistan on remittance of foreign exchange for any lawful purpose at any time and with the availability of modern devices such as teleconferencing facilities, evidence may be recorded easily anywhere in the world under the supervision of the arbitral body.

Similarly, in *Travel Automation (Pvt.) Ltd. v. Abacus International (Pvt.) Ltd.,*[373] the plaintiff (distributor) and defendant entered into a distributorship agreement for the territory of Pakistan, which was subsequently renewed for three years. The agreement was terminated unilaterally by the defendant without affording any reason. The plaintiff filed suit for a declaration that the agreement was valid, binding and enforceable against the defendant for damages and mandatory and permanent injunctions. The defendant filed an application to stay the court proceedings under section 34 of the 1940 Act, read together with sections 3 and 4 of the Ordinance, pursuant to an arbitration clause in the distributorship agreement with its seat in Singapore under the Arbitration Rules of the Singapore International Arbitration Centre. The contract was governed by the law of Singapore and was subject to the exclusive jurisdiction of the courts of Singapore. The Sindh High Court reiterated that the discretion had been given to the court under section 34 by which to stay or not the suit proceedings. It further highlighted that under this section, despite the presence of an arbitration agreement between the parties, the court would stay only after being satisfied that its order would not cause a miscarriage of justice or inconvenience to the parties. The Sindh High Court further referred to Article II of the New York Convention, emphasizing that the discretion of the court on grounds such as inconvenience, etc. had been removed by subsection 2 of section 4 of the Ordinance, which articulated that in matters covered by the Ordinance the stay might be refused only if the arbitration agreement was 'null and void, inoperative or incapable of being performed'.[374]

372. PLD 2006 Karachi 664.
373. *Travel Automation (Pvt.) Ltd. v. Abacus International (Pvt.) Ltd. and others*, 2006 CLD 497.
374. *Ibid.*, pp. 505-507.

The same approach was consistently followed and applied in its letter and spirit in *Far Eastern Impex (Pvt.) Ltd v. Quest International Nederland*[375] and then *Cummins Sales and Service (Pakistan) Ltd v. Cummins Middle East FZE.*[376] In both cases, a stay was granted on the ground that the party resisting the stay could not prove the arbitration agreement as being null and void, inoperative, etc., and in this regard, the court did not accept the *forum non conveniens* ground.

6.4.2. Null and Void, Inoperable and Incapable of Being Performed: Meaning and Interpretation

In *Travel Automation (Pvt.) Ltd. v. Abacus International (Pvt.) Ltd.*,[377] the Sindh High Court stated that:

> The words null and void and inoperative or incapable of being performed should be read keeping in view the rule of *ejusdem generis* i.e. when a particular word pertaining to class, category or genus are followed by general words, the general words are construed as limited to things of the same kind as those specified.

In *Abid Associated Agencies International (Pvt.) Ltd. and others v. Areva and others*,[378] it was held that the meaning of 'null and void, inoperable and incapable of being performed' are to be determined in relation to the arbitration agreement, which is separable from the main contract. There, the court highlighted the fact that these terms are not defined in the 2011 Act. However, the fact that the arbitration agreement was a contract would attract the standard principles of contractual interpretation. The court further stated that:

> An 'arbitration agreement' may be null and void due to several factors recognised by the applicable law e.g. for lack of consent, capacity, fraud etc. The invalidity in the case of being 'null and void' is from the very inception. The arbitration agreement will be 'inoperative' if for some reason it ceases to have effect. It will, therefore, be inoperative if, for example, disputes have been settled, or a judicial order has been passed by a competent court of law restraining the parties from giving effect to the arbitration agreement. Likewise, 'incapable of being performed' relates to circumstances where the enforcement or performance of the 'arbitration agreement' becomes impossible e.g. the forum agreed for arbitration no more exists, or the conditions of the 'arbitration agreement' are such that they are not capable of being enforced.

---

375. *Far Eastern Impex (Pvt.) Ltd. v. Quest International Nederland Bv and others*, 2009 CLD 153. This case was decided under Recognition and Enforcement (Arbitration Agreements and Foreign Arbitral Awards) Ordinance, 2007. In this case the contract was governed by Dutch law, providing for an arbitration clause with its seat in Geneva, under the ICC Rules of Conciliation and Arbitration. Ultimately, the stay was granted.
376. *Cummins Sales and Service (Pakistan) Limited v. Cummins Middle East FZE and others*, 2013 CLD 291. English law was to govern the contract, which contained a London-seated UNCITRAL Arbitration Rules clause.
377. *Travel Automation (Pvt.) Ltd. v. Abacus International (Pvt.) Ltd. and others*, 2006 CLD 497.
378. *Abid Associated Agencies International (Pvt.) Ltd. and others v. Areva and others*, 2015 MLD 1646.

In *Travel Automation (Pvt.) Ltd. v. Abacus International (Pvt.) Ltd. and others,*[379] the court stated that a plain reading of section 20 of the Pakistani Contract Act 1872 (agreement void where both parties are under mistake as to the facts) along with section 56 of the Contract Act 1872, demonstrates that where at the time of execution of the arbitration agreement this was void or subsequently became void for whatever reason, such as an act of Government, or the performance of the contract became impossible, or by change of law the contract becomes incapable of being performed, the court can refuse stay of the proceedings.

6.4.3. Confusion Subsequent to this Interpretation

Even with the enactment of the 2011 Act and all the aforementioned judgments, consistency has yet to be achieved, as is clear from *Lakhra Power Generation Co. Ltd (LPGCL) v. Karadeniz Powership Kaya Bey.*[380] In this case, a contract was concluded between Karkey, a Turkish company (defendant) and LPGCL (plaintiff) for the generation and supply of electricity. The Supreme Court of Pakistan declared (Power Rental Decision) that the main contract was void due to the involvement of illegality and corrupt practices and ordered the rescission of this contract along with the reimbursement of a specific amount from Karkey to LPGCL.[381] The main contract contained a London-seated arbitration clause, subject to LCIA Rules. The main contract, as well as the 'procedure, effectiveness, interpretation, construction, performance and application of the arbitration', was to be governed by Pakistani law.[382] LPGCL filed a suit for the recovery of that amount from Karkey. Karkey, just after the Power Rental Decision from the Supreme Court, initiated arbitration before ICSID pursuant to the dispute resolution clause in the 1995 BIT between Pakistan and Turkey.[383] In the Sindh High Court, where the suit for recovery was pending, Karkey submitted an application under section 4 of the 2011 Act by seeking to stay the suit proceedings, requesting that LPGCL's claim be referred to arbitration before the LCIA. The court refused to stay the proceedings by considering that the arbitration clause was incapable of being performed. It held that 'incapable of being performed' refers to the practical incapability of the arbitration proceedings to commence or proceed. The court supported its conclusion by pointing out that Karkey had already initiated arbitration under the ICSID Convention. While admitting that ICSID arbitration proceedings were not against LPGCL but only against the Government of Pakistan, the court, nonetheless, held that the substantial overlap between the issues raised in the proceedings

379. *Travel Automation (Pvt.) Ltd. v. Abacus International (Pvt.) Ltd. and others*, 2006 CLD 497.
380. *Lakhra Power Generation Company Limited (LPGCL) v. Karadeniz Powership Kaya Bey and others*, 2014 CLD 337. On waiver to arbitrate, *see also Ovex Technologies (Private) Limited v. PCM PK (Private) Limited and others*, 2020 CLD 15.
381. 2012 SCMR 773.
382. *Lakhra Power Generation Company Limited (LPGCL) v. Karadeniz Powership Kaya Bey and others*, 2014 CLD 337, para. 14.
383. This BIT took effect in 1997.

under ICSID and those before the LCIA would be unavoidable.[384] The court held that this would become more evident if Pakistan submitted its counter claim against Karkey in the ICSID proceedings or if Karkey were to submit its claim in the LCIA proceedings. The court also assumed that if it ordered LPGCL to initiate or submit to LCIA proceedings, Karkey would certainly seek from the LCIA tribunal the stay of its own proceedings during the pendency of ICSID proceedings.[385] In order to demonstrate the hierarchy of ICSID arbitration over its LCIA counterpart, the court referred to Article 25 of the ICSID Convention, which reads that arbitration under ICSID is 'to the exclusion of any other remedy'. The court then extracted a passage from the Commentary by Schreuer,[386] as follows:

> One of the functions of Article 26 is to create a rule of priority vis-a-vis other systems of adjudication in order to avoid contradictory decisions and to preserve the principle of *ne bis in idem* ... Therefore, a non-ICSID arbitral tribunal should decline jurisdiction in the face of a valid submission to ICSID arbitration unless a contrary intention of the parties can be established.

In this regard, the Sindh High Court noted that due to the claim of Karkey against Pakistan in ICSID arbitration, its rights under the Pakistan-Turkey BIT had been infracted, and LPGCL's claims as submitted in the present suit were based on a judgment of the Supreme Court in the Power Rental Case.[387] The court also observed that such a situation was not rare where two sets of claims arose in ICSID arbitration – the claims emanating from the terms of the BIT and others arising from the terms of one or more contracts. After establishing the identity 'between the substantive bases of both claims', it stated that such situation, as was in the present case, would fall in the paragraph quoted from Schreuer Commentary on ICSID.[388] The Sindh High Court also held that Karkey itself had created a situation wherein resort to LCIA arbitration had become impossible because the arbitration agreement had become incapable of being performed. By referring to section 4(2) of the 2011 Act, it stated that when the arbitration agreement was incapable of being performed, the suit proceedings ought

384. *Lakhra Power Generation Company Limited (LPGCL) v. Karadeniz Powership Kaya Bey and others*, 2014 CLD 337, para. 37.
385. *Ibid.*
386. Christoph H. Schreuer, *The ICSID Convention: A Commentary* (2nd ed., Cambridge University Press, 2009), 381.
387. *Lakhra Power Generation Company Limited (LPGCL) v. Karadeniz Powership Kaya Bey and others*, 2014 CLD 337, para. 41.
388. The classic position has been expressed in *Wena Hotels v. Egypt*, ICSID Annulment Decision (5 February 2002), where the parties had entered into a contract to regulate private leases but at the same time a BIT existed between Egypt and the investor's country of nationality which extended several investment guarantees to all investors holding the nationality of both countries. The governing law of the contract was clearly Egyptian law, whereas the applicable law under the BIT was international law. At some point, the investor claimed that Egypt had breached the private leases contract and had additionally failed to afford an investment guarantee. Which law applied to these disputes – Egyptian or international law? The tribunal held that the applicable law of each dispute was to be determined according to the source of the obligation claimed. The dispute as to the private leases arose from the parties' contract and therefore the parties' choice of law (i.e., Egyptian law) was applicable. The dispute as to the investment guarantee arose from the BIT, an international treaty, where the applicable law was designated as being international law.

not to be stayed.[389] The court further held that 'there appears to be nothing in the New York Convention to suggest that the reason why the arbitration agreement is incapable of being performed must be of a permanent or irremediable nature. It may well be temporary or remediable'.[390] The court then concluded that 'if the reason or situation rendering the arbitration agreement incapable of being performed exists when the application for stay of proceedings under section 4 comes up for hearing before the court, then such application is to be dismissed. But if subsequently the situation changes and the reason ceases to exist (e.g., the impediment is removed)', the defendant could renew the application for stay if the proceedings are still pending.[391] In the case at hand, if ICSID arbitration did not succeed or was abandoned, Karkey, according to the Sindh High Court, would be able to renew its application of stay of suit proceedings under section 4(2) of the 2011 Act, which would be dealt on its own merits and by taking into consideration the facts and circumstances prevailing at that time. Not surprisingly, the court held that the arbitration agreement as contained in clause 28 of the main contract had been rendered incapable of being performed by the initiation of ICSID proceedings by Karkey. It declined to stay the suit under section 4(2) of the 2011 Act without any prejudice to the right of Karkey to file a new application if appropriate.

This decision is not satisfactory. It was not the jurisdiction of the High Court to decide whether there was some overlap between the subject matters covered by the proceedings under ICSID and LCIA arbitrations and then to give priority to one over the other, because in this way, it had stepped into the shoes of the LCIA and ICSID tribunals. The court should not have decided the nature of the claims, whether they were treaty-based claims or contractual claims, unless, of course, the contractual claim envisaged the jurisdiction of Pakistani courts. Whether or not ICSID arbitration proceedings have priority over non-ICSID arbitration proceedings in a specific case is a matter to be decided by the ICSID tribunal and not by domestic courts. By deciding the claims which were (either identical to) or similar to the subject matter of ICSID arbitration, the court was effectively violating the BIT obligations of Pakistan. Article 26 of the ICSID Convention clearly excluded the jurisdiction of domestic courts and equally ICSID jurisprudence which allows parallel proceedings on the basis of a treaty and contract claims before ICSID tribunal and other forums, respectively.[392]

Since the party requested a stay in favour of LCIA arbitration and not ICSID arbitration, an argument may be raised that the court could not *suo moto* enforce the ICSID arbitration clause. However, it is also well established that an application launched under a wrong legal basis is not null if the prayer is legal.[393] Thus, if the

---

389. *Lakhra Power Generation Company Limited (LPGCL) v. Karadeniz Powership Kaya Bey and others*, 2014 CLD 337, para. 42.
390. *Ibid.*
391. *Ibid.*
392. *SGS Societe Generate de Surveillance SA v. Islamic Republic of Pakistan*, (ICSID Case No. ARB/01/13), Decision on Objections to Jurisdiction, 6 August 2003, 8 ICSID Rep. 406; *SGS Societe Generate de Surveillance SA v. Republic of the Philippines*, (ICSID Case No. ARB/02/6), Decision on Objections to Jurisdiction, 29 January 2004, 8 ICSID Rep. 515.
393. *Travel Automation (Pvt.) Ltd. v. Abacus International (Pvt.) Ltd. and others*, 2006 CLD 497.

prayer under the 2011 Act could not be sustained on the ground that the LCIA arbitration clause was found by the court to be incapable of performance, the same prayer of stay could be granted under the Arbitration (International Investment Disputes) Act, 2011, which incorporated the ICSID Convention 1965 in the domestic law of Pakistan. Hence, the Sindh High Court could have stayed its proceeding against Karkey on the basis of the ICSID Convention. However, the suggestion to stay court proceedings when such remedy is not expressly requested seems highly idealistic following *Reko Diq*.[394]

It will be remembered that in *Reko Diq*, a joint venture containing an ICSID arbitration clause provided that where an ICSID arbitral tribunal did not assume jurisdiction, the parties would turn to ICC arbitration in London. While ICSID proceedings were in progress, the Supreme Court of Pakistan conducted an in-depth review of the JVA and declared it void due to the involvement of illegality, fraud and bribery. Thereafter, by negating the principle of separability, it was held that the voidness of the main contract made it impossible for the arbitration agreement to survive. The Supreme Court then referred to section 4 of the 2011 Act and Article 2(3) of the New York Convention in order to apply the criterion of 'null and void, inoperative or incapable of being performed' with a view to ensuring jurisdiction over matters otherwise to be decided under the ICSID Convention, despite the fact that the Convention did not provide any such grounds for domestic courts to preclude arbitration.[395] The Supreme Court omitted to appreciate the differentiation between international commercial arbitration under the auspices of the New York Convention and investor-state arbitration as regulated by BITs and the ICSID Convention.

6.5. RELEVANCE OF THE PRE-2011 ACT REGIME

In *Taisei Corporation v. A.M. Construction Co.*,[396] the Punjab High Court highlighted that the 2011 Act repealed the 1937 Act by leaving the 1940 Act untouched. It stated further that there are some rights and reliefs provided in the 1940 Act which have not been contemplated by the 2011 Act. With regard to these rights and remedies, the parties can benefit from the 1940 Act even in case of foreign-seated arbitrations. It is submitted that the right to challenge the validity and effect of arbitration agreements has not been provided in the 2011 Act, which might be contested by filing an application under section 33 of the 1940 Act if *Taisei Corporation* is followed.

Similarly, Pakistani courts are now relying on the concept of 'null and void, inoperative or incapable of being performed' to decide stay applications, which makes it very important to organize the principles established in Pakistani judgments under the *Pre-2011 Act* regime that may be relevant to define any or all of these grounds. Before turning to Pakistani judgments, it is noteworthy that while the concept of 'null and void' and 'incapable of being performed' is easy to grasp, the 'inoperative' dimension seems to be abstruse in its comprehension and neither the New York

394. *Maulana Abdul Haque Baloch v. Government of Balochistan*, PLD 2013 Supreme Court 641.
395. *Reko Diq*, paras 24, 105-106.
396. *Taisei Corporation v. A.M. Construction Company (Pvt.) Ltd.*, PLD 2012 Lahore 455.

Convention, UNCITRAL Model Law along with the domestic legislations adopting it nor their *travaux preparatoire*, enlightens us as to its precise scope and meaning. However, it does not seem unsafe to say that where an arbitration agreement is terminated by the parties with mutual consent, such agreement would be considered 'inoperative'. This termination, if not express, may be inferred from the conduct of the parties. For instance, English courts have accepted that where the first party expressly repudiated the arbitration agreement, this was considered as having been accepted by the other party who launched proceedings in court on the subject matter covered by the said arbitration agreement.[397] The arbitration agreement also turns into 'inoperative' or 'incapable of being performed' by mutual waiver of the parties or by operation of some statutory instruments. Whether the arbitration agreement is 'null and void', 'inoperative' or 'incapable of being performed' will make no real difference as, in case of the occurrence of any of these, the stay of court proceedings will not be granted.[398]

In a notable Pakistani case, the list of arbitrators set out by a professional association that the parties had chosen in their arbitration agreement had subsequently ceased to exist, and thus, the arbitration agreement was declared ineffective.[399] In another case, the post on which the person employed was to be appointed as arbitrator, was abolished and the mechanism of its appointment was also materially changed; the arbitration agreement was held to be infructuous.[400] An arbitration agreement entered on behalf of a minor without prior leave from the court has equally been declared null and void.[401] Where an unqualified and unfettered right to appoint the arbitrator was given by one party to the other, the arbitration agreement was declared unenforceable for lack of mutuality.[402] An arbitration agreement forming part of a contract that was illegal by law would equally be void.[403] If the department or office, whose head was agreed by parties to act as arbitrator, ceased to exist due to its reorganization, the arbitration agreement would not be enforceable. In the case at hand, the arbitration agreement provided for the submission of any controversy to the 'Secretary, Government of Punjab, Civil Supplies Department'. This arbitration agreement was held to be incapable of being performed because the office had ceased to exist after the reorganization of the department. Moreover, this arbitration clause was held to be void on account of uncertainty for the reason that it was not clear from the agreement whether the parties intended to appoint the Secretary acting at the time of conclusion of the

397. *Downing v. Al Tameer Establishment*, [2002] EWCA Civ 721; [2002] C.L.C 1291; *see also* Jonathan Turley, *Acceptance of the Repudiation of an Arbitration Agreement*, 5(4) Int'l Arb L. Rev. 46-47 (2002); Max Bonnell, *When is an Arbitration Agreement 'Inoperative'?*, 11(3) Int'l Arb. L. Rev. 111 (2008).
398. For a detailed description as to when an arbitration agreement becomes 'null and void', 'inoperative' or 'incapable of being performed', *see* Michael Pryles, *The Kaplan Lecture 2009, When Is an Arbitration Agreement Waived?*, 27(2) J. Int'l Arb. 105 (2010).
399. *Hafiz Abdul Aziz Cotton Ginning Factory v. Haji Ali Muhammad Abdullah & Co.*, PLD 1966 (W. P.) 197; *Hafiz Abdul Aziz Yousufani & Co. v. Haji Ali Muhammad Abdullah & Co.*, PLD 1967 Karachi 698; *Oil & Gas Development Corporation v. Karachi Builders*, 1978 SCMR 278.
400. *Taj Muhammad Khan v. NWFP Forest Development Corporation and another*, PLD 1984 Peshawar 64.
401. *Zarel Bibi and others v. Shamsuldin Khan and others*, PLD 1956 (W. P.) Karachi 150.
402. *Amin Agencies Ltd v. Haji Moosa Haji Oomar*, PLD 1953 Karachi 57.
403. *Karachi Development Authority and another v. Mst. Haseena Begum and others*, 1980 CLC 522.

contract or the person at the time when the dispute arose.[404] From these instances, one may not infer any presumption in favour of the arbitration agreement. It is submitted that the jurisprudence on this topic should evolve in accordance with the underlying intent of the New York Convention.

In *Taj Muhammad Khan v. NWFP Forest Development Corporation*, the parties in their arbitration agreement agreed to submit their future disputes to the Chairman of the NWFP Forest Development Corporation. This corporation was established under the NWFP Forest Development Corporation Act, 1977 (Act XI of 1977). Under this Act, one director from the board of directors used to be appointed as its Chairman. Subsequently, the NWFP Forest Development Corporation Ordinance 1980 was enacted, which changed the structure of the Corporation by abolishing the office of the occupier, who was to act as arbitrator. In view of this, the court held that the arbitration agreement had become inoperative and infructuous, and the stay of arbitral proceedings could not be granted.[405]

In another case, *Macdonald Layton Costain Ltd., Karachi v. State Bank of Pakistan,*[406] disputes were agreed to be referred to the 'Chief Accountant' of the State Bank of Pakistan. When a dispute arose, the defendant argued that due to the change in the Regulations of the State Bank, such office had been abolished, and hence the arbitration clause was frustrated. The court did not agree and emphasized that the intention of the parties as gleaned from the agreement would determine if the supervening event had the effect of frustrating the arbitration agreement. It was held that the parties could not be allowed to defeat the arbitration by merely changing the nomenclature of the office of the bearer. The court observed that the amendment in the Regulations had retained the functions and powers of 'Chief Account' unaltered, and only the name of 'Chief Accountant' was replaced by the name 'Director of Accounts'.[407] The court went on to state that the clear object and aim of the parties in designating the office of 'Chief Accountant' to become arbitrator was to appoint a person as an arbitrator who had knowledge of accounts and that this requirement was fulfilled by the appointment of Director of Accounts. In this way, the court had no problem finding that the arbitration was not incapable of being performed.[408]

In every case, the dispute should be covered by the arbitration agreement. The courts have held that the parties have the freedom to choose the disputes to be resolved by arbitration. If they have excluded some dispute from the ambit of their arbitration agreement expressly, that dispute would not be referred to arbitration and would be decided by the courts. Whether a dispute falls within the import of an arbitration agreement is to be interpreted and decided by the court.[409] However, in *Cummins Sales and Service (Pakistan) Limited v. Cummins Middle East FZE,*[410] the court held that this

404. *Province of The Punjab v. Irfan & Co.*, PLD 1956 (W. P.) Lahore 442.
405. *Taj Muhammad Khan v. NWFP Forest Development Corporation and another*, PLD 1984 Peshawar 64.
406. *Macdonald Layton Costain Ltd., Karachi v. State Bank of Pakistan*, PLD 1980 Karachi 87.
407. *Ibid.*, para. 4.
408. *Macdonald Layton Costain Ltd., Karachi v. State Bank of Pakistan*, PLD 1980 Karachi 87.
409. *Ovex Technologies (Private) Limited v. PCM PK (Private) Limited and others*, 2020 CLD 15.
410. *Cummins Sales and Service (Pakistan) Limited v. Cummins Middle East FZE*, 2015 CLD 1655.

is not the job of the court and distinguished between disputes falling within the scope of arbitral agreements and those that do not, noting that such determination befalls the authority of the tribunal.

6.6. CONCLUSION

With regard to foreign arbitration, apparently, the discretion of the court to refuse stay has been removed, but the negation of separability and *competence-competence*, along with an in-depth review of the main agreement to decide the fate of arbitration agreement on the basis of the ground of 'null and void, inoperative', etc., has failed the utility of this absence of discretion. Ironically, it implies that if the main contract is void, the arbitration agreement being void will justify the court in declining the stay of its proceedings. After the enactment of the 2011 Act, the discretion of the court respecting the stay of its proceedings for foreign arbitration has vanished. However, the situation with regard to domestic arbitration is still grim, wherein the arbitration agreement cannot oust the jurisdiction of the court, and the court has given a wide interpretation to the scope of its discretion under section 34. Under this section, the court invented a wide array of grounds to defeat the will of a party to opt for arbitration, even if the validity and existence of such an arbitration agreement were not challenged. It has become the need of the hour for the Pakistani courts to demonstrate deference to the domestic arbitration by honouring the parties' intention to arbitrate.

CHAPTER 7

Attitude of Pakistani Courts to Anti-suit and Anti-arbitration Injunctions

This chapter discusses the attitude of Pakistani courts to anti-suit injunctions and anti-arbitration injunctions. There is no law empowering Pakistani courts to issue such injunctions, but they seem inclined to issue anti-suit injunctions, although they have not yet done so. However, there are many instances of issuance of anti-arbitration injunctions from Pakistani courts that have not laid down tests such remedy. The preferable approach is to bar anti-arbitration injunctions, but if a regime chooses to grant this remedy, then the test to decide applications for anti-arbitration injunctions should take into consideration the consensual and international character of arbitration.

7.1. INTRODUCTION

When a party to an arbitration agreement (plaintiff) files a suit in a civil court for its decision on a dispute which the parties have already agreed to arbitrate, the other party to the arbitration agreement (defendant) may file a section 34 application for the stay of court proceedings in favour of arbitration. In this case, the court has two options: first, it may grant the stay of its proceedings, and second, it may refuse to stay its proceedings. If it opts to exercise the first option, the defendant may ask it further to compel the plaintiff from initiating similar proceedings before any other domestic or foreign judicial forum, or if he has already commenced such proceedings, from continuing such proceedings. In other words, after getting the remedy of a stay of court proceedings, the defendant is further praying for the relief of an anti-suit injunction. If a court opts for the second option and refuses to stay its proceedings, the plaintiff moves a step further, asking the court to stop the plaintiff from initiating arbitration proceedings, or if he has already set arbitration proceedings in motion, to discontinue those arbitration proceedings. This is the remedy of anti-arbitration injunctions. Although these two remedies seem to be a continuation of the court's decision to a section 34 application on stay of court proceedings, it seems, a prior application for stay of the court is not mandatory, and for this, an independent application can be made to a court where no application for stay of court proceedings is pending.

There is no provision in Pakistani law discussing these two reliefs. The principles governing the courts' power to impart these injunctions are extracted from court judgments. The first segment of this chapter discusses anti-suit injunctions to demonstrate that the author could not find any case where these were issued in relation to foreign court proceedings with a possibility that the Pakistani courts may do so in the future. The second part of this chapter discusses anti-arbitration injunctions, as well as the grounds used by the courts to decide the application for anti-arbitration injunctions in domestic and foreign arbitration. This part also analyses the intrusion of the courts through the issuance of anti-arbitration injunctions. In conclusion, this chapter furnishes a preferable approach for Pakistan.

7.2. ANTI-SUIT INJUNCTIONS

Where a party has covenanted in an arbitration agreement to resolve disputes in arbitration and then commences or is likely to start proceedings concerning those disputes in a forum other than arbitration, can Pakistani courts issue injunctions to restrain those proceedings initiated in violation of the arbitration agreement? What will be the attitude of Pakistani courts when such proceedings are initiated before a foreign court? The civil law approach regarding anti-suit injunctions is opposite to that of the common law, and this conflict is based on the difference in assumption as to the role of the legal system and the values to which it should give primacy.

Concerning dispute resolution, the dominant consideration in civil law is the doctrinal principle that the receiving court's authority to determine what suits may be brought before it should be unquestioned by foreign courts. Compared to this principle of sovereignty, the private rights and obligations of the parties, and the practical consequences of upholding the principle, are of relatively little importance. Due to this, the civil law approach is that the court where such proceedings in violation of arbitration agreement are initiated will have primary jurisdiction to decide its jurisdiction, and the anti-suit injunctions issued by a court of any other jurisdiction will have no value.

In contrast, in common law, in relation to jurisdictional conflicts, the question of primary significance, as a matter of justice, is where a dispute should be resolved in order to offer practical justice between the parties and according to their private law rights. Public law considerations as to the sovereignty of foreign courts, and relations between courts, encapsulated in the concept of comity, are second-order constraints to be deployed sparingly where they conflict with private justice.[411] According to this approach, anti-suit injunctions operate in personam only and not in rem, which means

411. Thomas Raphael, *The Anti-suit Injunctions* (1st ed., Oxford University Press, 2008), 15-17.

that such injunctions are directed to the impugned defendant and not the court to which they are addressed.[412]

The New York Convention does not give any explicit authority to the courts of member states to issue anti-suit injunctions to restrain proceedings in breach of agreements initiated in the courts of another member state, but confers the authority on the court first seized of the dispute to refer the dispute to arbitration if the arbitration agreement is not 'null and void, inoperative or incapable of being performed'.[413]

Pakistani courts never issued an anti-suit injunction against foreign court proceedings. Section 58(b) of the Specific Relief Act 1877 says that injunctions cannot be issued against a court that is not subordinate to the issuing court. Even so, a tendency and permissibility can be seen in the Pakistani judicial attitude that if it is needed in the future, they might issue anti-suit injunctions. The matter of anti-suit injunctions came to the fore in a revenue case where these were sought to restrain a landlord from initiating or continuing any litigation in any other Pakistani courts during the pendency of appeals in the High Court. These injunctions were granted and the court, without mentioning arbitration, specifically said that it had inherent jurisdiction to issue such injunctions against a foreign court if the outcome of those foreign proceedings would affect the decision of the issuing court.[414]

Later in the *HBCO* case,[415] injunctions were also issued by the Sindh High Court in arbitral proceedings to restrain other proceedings before a civil judge in Lahore on the ground that proceedings had been launched to deliberately hamper the exercise of jurisdiction of the Sindh High Court. It stated that in order to avoid further abuse of process and to prevent the mockery of the institution of the judiciary, the parties to the proceeding are restrained from initiating or continuing to pursue any proceedings before the Lahore Civil Judge.

Then, in *Nadeem Ghani v. United Bank Limited*,[416] the defendant brought an action in the English courts against the plaintiff, and the plaintiff filed a suit in Pakistani courts, praying for an injunction to stay the foreign proceedings. The Sindh High Court refused to issue injunctions against the English court on the ground that the defendant had lawfully commenced those proceedings there in accordance with a mutual agreement, whereunder, the plaintiff had surrendered himself to the jurisdiction of English courts. In this scenario, the court held that the application from the plaintiff to stay the English court's proceedings did not seem bona fide and hence ordering a stay the proceedings in England, especially since these had been initiated prior to those in Pakistan, would be an improper exercise of discretion available under section 56 of the Specific Relief Act 1877. Hence, the court held that the plaintiff could not make a prima facie case for an injunction; the balance of convenience was not in his favour, and he would not suffer irreparable loss if proceedings in English courts were not stayed.

412. *Turner v. Grovit & ors.*, [2002] C.L.C 463.
413. Article II(3) of the New York Convention.
414. *Ahmad Din and others v. Faiz Ali and others*, PLD 1954 Lahore 414.
415. *Hub Power Co. v. WAPDA*, 1999 CLC 1320.
416. *Nadeem Ghani v. United Bank Limited*, 2001 CLC 1904. *See also Jannana De Malucho Textile Mills Ltd., Kohat v. Waqar Ahmad Chaudhry*, PLD 1972 SC 34.

Thus, an application under Order 39, Rules 1 & 2 for the injunction to stay the English court proceeding was declined.[417]

7.3. ANTI-ARBITRATION INJUNCTIONS

As far as the compatibility of anti-arbitration injunctions with the New York Convention is concerned, the relevant provision is Article II(3), which provides that the court should refer the matter to arbitration unless the arbitration agreement is 'null and void, inoperative or incapable of being performed'. This provision mandates a court to enjoin its proceedings in case of validity of the arbitration agreement and, in the converse, allows the court to adjudicate the matter. However, this provision is silent on the matter of issuance of an anti-arbitration injunction by a court arriving at the conclusion that the arbitration agreement is 'null and void, inoperative or incapable of being performed'.

Anti-arbitration injunctions are one of the most controversial subjects of arbitration. This contentious nature is because of the test applied on the eve of their issuance without taking the culture and nature of arbitration into consideration. Pakistani courts have been issuing anti-arbitration injunctions without laying down a test to be applied when deciding such applications. In Pakistan, it seems that suits for anti-arbitration injunctions are either decided by the courts on a case-to-case basis or by applying the tests employed in civil litigation. There is a need for a test for anti-arbitration injunctions to be formulated by giving particular regard to the internationally accepted principles of arbitration. This segment explores the Pakistani regime's attitude on arbitration, with a view to investigating how applications for anti-arbitration injunctions are decided by the courts.

7.3.1. Source and Nature of Courts' Power to Issue Anti-arbitration Injunctions

It has been expressly pronounced by Pakistani courts that during the pendency of arbitration proceedings with a foreign seat, a Pakistani court cannot, in the exercise of its civil jurisdiction, control or regulate said proceedings.[418] The other fact relevant to this principle is that no provision empowering Pakistani courts to issue anti-arbitration injunctions against a foreign arbitration has been incorporated in the 1940 Act or any other statute dealing with arbitration generally. Despite this very explicit pronouncement, Pakistani courts have issued anti-arbitration injunctions without laying down standards to be followed on a consistent basis.

In *Hakimuddin Harmusji v. Ghafoor Textile Mills*, the Sindh High Court restrained the arbitrator from proceeding with the arbitration.[419] While issuing such orders, the

417. For an opposite view, *see, Riaz-Ur-Rehman Khan v. Lufthansa German Airlines, Quaid-e-Azam International Airport, Karachi*, PLD 2002 Karachi 434.
418. *Hasan Ali Rice Export Co. through Sole Proprietor v. Flame Maritime Limited and another*, 2004 CLD 334. *See also Hitachi Limited and another v. Rupali Polyester and others*, 1998 SCMR 1618.
419. *Hakimuddin Harmusji & Sons v. Ghafoor Textile Mills*, PLD 1978 Karachi 152.

court held that section 33[420] of the 1940 Act bestows jurisdiction on the court to declare an arbitration agreement invalid, non-existent or ineffective, and ancillary to the main relief, confers power on the court to debar the arbitration proceedings pending a decision by the courts. Thus, the court which deals with the application submitted under section 33 for a decision on the existence, validity or effect of an arbitration agreement enjoys the power to issue an order staying arbitral proceedings, and such order would be in the form of a 'stay' as distinguished from an 'injunction'.

In the Pakistani legal system, a stay order is directed to a subordinate court or tribunal in a manner that restrains it from continuing certain proceedings, while an injunction is addressed to a party enjoining it from committing or omitting particular acts. The former takes effect immediately when it is issued, even if it is not noticed or known by the directed court or tribunal, whereas an order for injunction becomes operative only after it is served on its addressee.[421] The court held that it had the power to issue a stay and an injunction.

The Sindh High Court's interpretation fulfils, to a very large extent, the desire of the Punjab High Court, which has considered the absence of any provision in the 1940 Act to empower a judge to revoke a valid submission altogether. It viewed this as a flaw in the 1940 Act and subsequently demanded the amendment of the 1940 Act to vest the judge with discretion to revoke the authority of an arbitrator, even in case of a valid reference when circumstances so justify.[422]

7.3.2. Grounds for the Issuance of Anti-arbitration Injunctions

The issuance of anti-arbitration injunctions cannot be supported, but if they are to be issued, certain constraints are imperative. As the power to issue an anti-arbitration injunction is ancillary to the power to adjudge the validity of an arbitration agreement, and since this power is granted by section 33, it must be used in matters covered by section 33, i.e., when the issues before the court concern the validity, effectiveness, and existence of an arbitration agreement. This was the case in *Cosmopolitan Development Co. Ltd. v. Alfred C. Toepfer International*. In this case, following the filing of a challenge against the arbitration proceedings, the court restrained the arbitrators from conducting the arbitration in Germany on the ground that the contract containing the arbitration agreement was never concluded and hence the arbitration agreement along

420. Section 33 reads as follows:

> Any party to an arbitration agreement or any person claiming under him desiring to challenge the existence or validity of an arbitration agreement or an award or to have the effect of either determined shall apply to the Court and the Court shall decide the question on affidavits:
>
> Provided that where the Court deems it just and expedient, it may set down the application for hearing on other evidence also, and it may pass such orders for the discovery and particulars as it may do in a suit.

421. It should be noted that despite the dichotomy in the nomenclature, the term 'injunction' is used for both kinds of orders, i.e., orders for injunction or orders of stay.
422. *M. A. Ghani Soofi & Sons v. The Federation of Pakistan*, PLD 1957 (W. P.) Lahore 363.

with the carrier contract was non-existent.[423] Similarly, in *HUBCO v. WAPDA*,[424] injunctions issued by the Sindh High Court were later confirmed by the Supreme Court of Pakistan on the basis that the contract containing a London-seated ICC arbitration clause was void because of the involvement of illegality and bribery. Also, in *SGS v. Pakistan*,[425] the Supreme Court of Pakistan attempted to restrain an ICSID arbitration on the ground that Pakistan was not bound by the applicable BIT. It merits mentioning that such injunctions issued by the Pakistani Supreme Court were disregarded by the ICSID tribunal.

7.3.2.1. Grounds Beyond Section 33 of the 1940 Act

Pakistani courts have been issuing anti-arbitration injunctions in cases where the matter in question before the court was not encompassed under section 33, without any apparently reasonable justification for the exercise of such power. In these cases, the Pakistani courts did not develop and apply any test particular to the character of arbitration to be used in the adjudication of applications contesting the issuance of anti-arbitration injunctions. For example, in *Pakistan Agro Forestry Co. Ltd. v. T.C. PAF Pakistan Pvt. Ltd*,[426] a case concerning the recovery of damages and compensation, anti-arbitration injunctions were issued on the ground that allowing arbitration proceedings abroad would cause huge expense and that the arbitration proceedings if allowed to continue in parallel to court proceedings, would result in conflicting judgments. Order 39 Rules 1 & 2 of the CPC were employed in support of the decision.

In that case, *T.C. PAF Pakistan Pvt. Ltd* ('PAF' hereinafter), a trading company, had invited tenders for the import of sugar from India. The company accepted a tender from Agro because it was the lowest. Agro submitted a bid bond equivalent to 2% of the total contract amount. PAF issued a letter of intent in favour of Agro by which Agro was required to furnish a performance bond for PAF equal to 5% of the contract price within seven days, and thereafter PAF was to furnish a letter of credit. Due to the monopoly of the Indian Sugar and General Industry Export Corporation Ltd. ('ISGIEC') in the Indian sugar market, Agro could not make the necessary arrangements with ISGIEC. Agro, however, made an offer to PAF to replace the sugar with sugar of Brazilian origin, and it was then that PAF declined the offer. Upon Agro's failure to supply the sugar as agreed, PAF contracted with another Indian company to purchase the sugar from ISGIEC at a higher price. Meanwhile, PAF also claimed on the 2% bid bond placed by Agro on the ground that Agro had failed to submit the performance bond. Agro challenged the collection of the bond in a writ petition submitted to the Lahore High Court in 1997. The court found in favour of Agro, and PAF's appeal petition was dismissed by the Supreme Court of Pakistan in 1999. Afterwards, PAF filed

423. *Cosmopolitan Development Company Ltd. v. Alfred C. Toepfer International and others*, 1991 CLC 1087.
424. *Hub Power Company Limited (HUBCO) v. WAPDA*, PLD 2000 SC 841.
425. *Societe Generale De Surveillance S.A. v. Pakistan through Secretary, Ministry of Finance Revenue Division, Islamabad*, 2002 SCMR 1694.
426. *Pakistan Agro Forestry Corporation Ltd. v. T.C. PAF Pakistan (Pvt.) Ltd. and others*, PLD 2003 Karachi 284.

a suit (Suit No. 1114) for the recovery of damages arising from the same contract for the supply of sugar. In 2002, while Suit No. 1114 was still pending in the court, PAF notified Agro that it would invoke the arbitration clause.

Agro commenced the lawsuit, praying to the court to issue a decree of a permanent injunction restraining PAF from commencing or continuing the arbitration proceedings. Agro based its petition on clause 12 of the agreement concluded between Agro and PAF. Agro contended that it had won a lawsuit in the Lahore High Court and that the court had ordered the amount of the bid bond, improperly collected by PAF, to be refunded to Agro. Agro also contended that PAF's appeal to the Supreme Court had been denied. Based on these arguments, Agro alleged that PAF could not initiate new arbitration proceedings on the same subject matter because PAF's claim before the arbitrator was also in respect of damages on which the High Court and then the Supreme Court had given their verdicts. The reopening of the same matter would lead the arbitrator to rule on the jurisdiction of these courts, which the arbitrator could not do. The court accepted these arguments and noted that PAF had already filed a suit that had a very close nexus with the subject matter of the instant suit. In the previous suit (filed by Agro in 1997), the High Court held that within one month, the parties were to refer their dispute to arbitration with mutual consent. However, PAF never obtained consent from Agro and instead invoked the arbitration clause very late in 2002.

With this context, the Punjab High Court held that 'the proceedings before the arbitrator cannot be allowed to be carried out to consider the effect of the judgment/order of our superior courts by a foreign tribunal'. The Punjab High Court further said that PAF had referred to arbitration matters relating to the bond money, which was the subject matter of a petition already decided by the Division Bench of the Lahore High Court, Rawalpindi Bench in 1997. It also reiterated the fact that the instant suit had been filed by Agro to enforce rights conferred upon it as a result of the 1997 judgment and to secure injunctions to restrain PAF from re-litigating before the arbitrator the same subject matter that had already been adjudicated by the High Court and the Supreme Court of Pakistan. On the basis of the foregoing, the Punjab High Court concluded that the matter could not be re-adjudicated afresh before the foreign tribunal.

The triple identity test was used by the Punjab High Court to decide the injunction application: the existence of a prima facie case for an injunction, the balance of convenience in favour of an injunction and the irreparable loss if the injunction was refused.

Expanding upon this test, the Punjab High Court expounded that Suit No. 1114 of 1998 for the recovery of damages arising from the same contract for the supply of sugar filed by PAF was pending before the court, which if resolved in favour of PAF, would entitle PAF to a satisfactory compensation for Agro's contractual breaches if any were found to have been committed by the plaintiff. The court also enunciated that if arbitration proceedings are allowed during the pendency of Suit No. 1114, both parties will incur significant expenses entailing an irreparable loss consequent to the participation in foreign arbitration. In addition, the court considered that it would be a futile exercise to allow the arbitration to proceed, which might result in conflicting decisions and enforcement problems. With regard to the balance of convenience, the court concluded that if at any stage PAF was declared to be entitled to have recourse to arbitration, PAF could commence arbitration without any difficulty, but Agro would face inconvenience if arbitration proceedings were permitted to proceed and then halted. The court held that it would be in the interests of both parties to be restrained from pursuing the arbitration until a final judgment was delivered in Suit No. 1114 to recover damages filed by PAF. Therefore, PAF was restrained from initiating or continuing the arbitration proceedings.

Similarly, in *Trading Corporation of Pakistan (Pvt.) Ltd v. Nidera Handelscompagnie B.V.*,[427] the Pakistani Supreme Court did not object to the tests applied by the trial court and afterwards, the High Court in deciding the application to issue a stay order restraining the other party from pursuing arbitration. It applied the prima facie case, irreparable loss and balance of convenience factors. It is noteworthy that the triple identity test is used by Pakistani civil courts to decide applications for injunctions in civil suits.[428]

In *Island Textile Mills v. V/O Technoexport*, the Pakistani Supreme Court dealt with anti-arbitration injunctions on different grounds. It issued injunctions to stay proceedings before an arbitrator in Moscow because the case involved questions of law, the arbitration agreement needed interpretation, the property in dispute and all the relevant evidence were situated in Karachi and fraud and misrepresentation were alleged, etc.

These grounds cannot justify the issuance of an injunction. These are the same grounds that have been used by Pakistani courts to refuse to stay their own proceedings initiated in disregard of arbitration agreements,[429] and nothing extra was offered here to support restraining arbitration proceedings; rather, the courts have gone one step further by using these contentious grounds to stop arbitration proceedings.[430]

7.3.2.2. Anti-arbitration Injunctions under the 2011 Act

With the promulgation of the 2011 Act, grounds like inconvenience and the location of arbitration outside Pakistan, as well as the apprehension of high expenditure in case of compliance with a foreign arbitration clause, have been discarded as grounds for

427. *Trading Corporation of Pakistan (Pvt.) Ltd, Karachi v. Nidera Handelscompagnie B.V. and another*, 2001 SCMR 646.
428. *Cooperative Housing Society, Rawalpindi v. Secretary, Cooperative Societies, Government of Punjab, Lahore etc.*, 2001 CLC 838; *Abid v. Nisar*, 2000 SCMR 780; *Generale Biscuit v. Diamond Food Industries*, 1999 YLR 305; *Income Tax Karachi v. Sham Muhammad* 1997 MLD 2801; *Karachi Catholic Cooperative Housing Society Ltd v. Daphne Mendonca*, 1993 SCMR 1510; *P. P. A. v. K.M.C.*, 1993 MLD 1681; 1991 CLC 694; Marghub *v. Hamid*, 1974 SCMR 519; *Asia Steel Industries v. Iftikar & Co.*, 1987 CLC 984.
429. For forum non-convenience as ground for the refusal to stay court proceedings, *see*, 1984 CLC 1605; PLD 1967 Karachi 756; PLD 1983 Karachi 613; 1979 CLC 565; 1986 SCMR 463; 1979 CLC 307; 1989 SCMR 225; 2004 CLC 544; 1993 SCMR 866.
430. *Island Textile Mills Ltd. v. V/O Technoexport and another*, 1986 SCMR 463.

determining the stay of court proceedings in favour of arbitration.[431] It may be expected that these grounds will also be rejected while deciding the application for anti-arbitration injunctions. This expectation is encouraged by the Supreme Court's decision in *Reko Diq.*[432] In this case, it did not issue an anti-arbitration injunction against an ICSID arbitration but only instructed the Government of Pakistan to request the ICSID tribunal to stop its proceedings until the decision of the Supreme Court was rendered.

7.3.3. Instances of Refusal to Issue Anti-arbitration Injunctions

Sometimes, the courts have refused to grant anti-arbitration injunctions on the condition that an award issued in the arbitration proceedings will not be enforced without the prior leave of the court. This was the case in *Pakistan Chrome Mines Ltd v. Phibro Asia Ltd* regarding an ICC arbitration in Paris.[433] Anti-arbitration injunctions have also been declined by applying section 35[434] of the 1940 Act. For instance, in *Muhammad Rafiq & Co. (Pvt.) Ltd v. International Construction Corp. (Pvt.) Ltd*, the claimant's prayer for an anti-arbitration injunction was denied because the subject matter referred to arbitration was broader than the subject matter before the court. Elaborating on the condition of section 35 to invalidate arbitration, the court said that judicial proceedings should include all the parties and comprise 'the whole of the subject matter' of the arbitration proceedings. It observed that in the instant case, the suit did not cover 'the whole of the subject matter of the reference'.[435]

7.3.4. Anti-arbitration Injunctions in Relation to Domestic Arbitration

The situation with regard to domestic arbitration is not promising. Under a lease agreement, the Capital Development Authority (CDA) of Islamabad leased a hotel to the lessee that was later terminated by the Martial Law Authority. Thereafter, the CDA demanded from the lessee a certain amount due from him in respect of the lease paid. This generated controversy, and the lessee appointed an arbitrator under the arbitration agreement in the lease agreement, albeit the CDA did not. The lessee's appointed

431. *Metropolitan Steel Corporation Ltd. v. Macsteel International U.K. Ltd.*, PLD 2006 Karachi 664; *Travel Automation (Pvt.) Ltd. v. Abacus International (Pvt.) Ltd.*, 2006 CLD 497; *Far Eastern Impex (Pvt.) Ltd. v. Quest International Nederland BV and others*, 2009 CLD 153.
432. *Maulana Abdul Haque Baloch v. Government of Balochistan*, PLD 2013 SC 641.
433. *Pakistan Chrome Mines Ltd. v. Phibro Asia Ltd. and others*, 1976 SCMR 93.
434. Section 35 of 1940 Act reads as follows:

> (1) No reference nor award shall be rendered invalid by reason only of the commencement of legal proceedings upon the subject-matter of the reference, but when legal proceedings upon the whole of the subject-matter of the reference have been commenced between all the parties to the reference and a notice thereof has been given to the arbitrators or umpire, all further proceedings in a pending reference shall, unless a stay of proceedings is granted under section 34, be invalid.
> (2) In this section the expression 'parties to the references' includes any person claiming under any of the parties and litigating under the same title.

435. *Muhammad Rafiq & Co. (Pvt.) Ltd. v. International Construction Corporation (Pvt.) Ltd. and others*, 1994 MLD 2282.

arbitrator proceeded with arbitration in Pakistan. On an application against arbitration from CDA, the court stated that the *locus standi* of Hasan Amin, who was taking legal action against CDA on behalf of the lessee, was challenged, and a large counterclaim was demanded by the lessee in response to the claim from the CDA, all of which are serious questions to be considered. The court said that 'the inconvenience to be caused to the parties in case the tribunal was ultimately found to be incompetent would be greater than the inconvenience to be caused on account of a stay of the proceedings'. Therefore, anti-arbitration injunctions were granted.[436]

7.3.5. Analysis of Anti-suit Injunctions and Grounds for Issuance

Arguments presented against anti-arbitration injunctions that normally emanate from less developed countries and are a manifestation of the protectionism of their courts seem correct if viewed from the Pakistani perspective.[437] Anti-arbitration injunctions have not gathered support, having been considered to 'violate conventional and customary international law, international public policy and the accepted principles of international arbitration' like *competence-competence* as well as separability.[438] This is so because the court is considered to be usurping the function of the arbitrator to decide the validity and continuity of the arbitration proceedings in response to an application challenging the validity of an arbitration agreement.

Moreover, the issuance of an anti-arbitration injunction is not justified to guard the court's own judicial proceedings because these injunctions constitute an intrusion into the jurisdiction of both the arbitrator and the court of the seat; protection of the integrity of court proceedings does not justify stopping all proceedings being conducted elsewhere in the world.[439] The fact of interference with the supervisory jurisdiction of foreign courts with the issuance of these injunctions was acknowledged in *A v. B.*[440] In this case, the parties chose a seat of arbitration and agreed and submitted to the supervisory jurisdiction of the court of seat. The court stated that there should be a strong reason for an English court to intervene by issuing arbitration injunctions in an arbitration seated in a foreign territory. In the same way, in *Weissfisch v. Anthony Julius*,[441] another English court maintained that the natural consequence of the parties'

436. *Hassan Amin v. Capital development authority Islamabad*, 1979 CLC 565.
437. Doak Bishop, *Combatting Arbitral Terrorism*. Available at: https://www.yumpu.com/en/document/read/23975713/combatting-arbitral-terrorism-anti-arbitration-king-spalding *See also* Stephen M. Schwebel, *Anti-suit Injunctions in International Arbitration – An Overview*, in *Anti-suit Injunctions in International Arbitration*, ed. Emmanuel Gaillard (Juris Publishing Inc, 2003), 5-14.
438. Doak Bishop, *Combatting Arbitral Terrorism*. Available at: https://www.yumpu.com/en/document/read/23975713/combatting-arbitral-terrorism-anti-arbitration-king-spalding. *See also* Stephen M. Schwebel, *Anti-suit Injunctions in International Arbitration – An Overview* in *Anti-suit Injunctions in International Arbitration*, ed. Emmanuel Gaillard (Juris Publishing Inc, 2003), 14.
439. *Nigel Peter Albon v. Naza Motor Trading SDN BHD*, [2007] EWHC 1879 (Ch).
440. *A v. B & Ors.*, [2006] EWHC 2006 (Comm), [2007] 2 C.L.C 157, at 112, 113, 124, 125.
441. *Amir Weissfisch v. Anthony Julius, Rami Weisfisch, Philip Davis*, [2006] EWCA Civ 218, para. 33; *See also* Thomas Raphael, *The Anti-Suit Injunction* (Oxford University Press, 2008).

express choice of Switzerland as a seat of arbitration is that any issue pertaining to the arbitration clause would fall in the jurisdiction of Swiss courts.

If a legal system chooses to allow the issuance of injunctions, it may be wise that the tests used by the courts in adjudicating anti-arbitration injunctions should recognize the consensual nature of arbitration. In addition, this test should also recognize the arbitrator's power attained through the evolution of *competence-competence* and separability principles because the test currently used for anti-suit injunctions or other similar remedies is not appropriate for arbitration.

Arbitration is the product of arbitration agreements, and there might be a case when, on an application challenging the existence or validity of an arbitration agreement, a court could develop an inkling that its declaration to the effect that the arbitration agreement is non-existent or invalid by leaving the arbitrator with no jurisdiction, would not be sufficient or effective and that it should move to issue an anti-arbitration injunction. However, where no such challenge is made as to whether the parties are subject to a valid arbitration agreement or the arbitration tribunal has jurisdiction, then the issuance of an anti-arbitration injunction is not justified. In other words, whether the arbitration proceedings should be continued is a matter to be decided only with a specific reference to the arbitration agreement and no other circumstance. Anti-arbitration injunctions should be completely barred, but even if their issuance is felt imperative, the test used by the court to decide the matter should be arbitration agreement-centric.

If the circumstances are such that the arbitration agreement does not survive, or if the arbitration agreement is valid but the arbitrator, for some reason, does not have the power to proceed (e.g., if the matter is non-arbitrable), then the court may, on a party's application, move to issue anti-arbitration injunctions. It may be said that the more liberal interpretation of these principles (*competence-competence* and separability), the more arbitration friendly the regime is, and subsequently, the more disinclined it would be to issue anti-arbitration injunctions.

The conclusion would be to expand the scope of *competence-competence* and reduce the grounds negating the severability of the arbitration agreement from its parent contract. For this, it is submitted that an arbitrator should be considered a judge, because like a judge, he would have inherent power not only to rule on his own jurisdiction, including the existence and validity of an arbitration agreement, but also on matters ancillary to it, like whether the arbitration proceedings should proceed or halt. The approach of arbitrators with judges was followed by English courts in *Elektrim v. Vivendi*,[442] where the court held that as per the policy inscribed in the 1996 Act, it is the arbitrator who has to decide jurisdictional as well as procedural questions, including if arbitration proceedings should be brought to a halt.

The same disposition of accepting the arbitrator as a judge is observed in French law, which is clear from Article 1474 of the Code of Civil Procedure. This provision explains the function of the arbitrator as: 'The arbitral tribunal shall decide the dispute in accordance with the law, unless the parties, in the arbitration agreement, have

442. *Elektrim S.A. v. Vivendi Universal S.A., Vivendi Telecommunication International S.A., Elektrim Telekomunikacja Sp. z.o.o, Carcom Warszawa Sp. z.o.o.*, [2007] EWHC 571 (Comm).

empowered such arbitrator to rule as *amiable compositeur.*'[443] Article 12 of the French Code of Civil Procedure speaks of the function of a judge as: 'The judge settles the dispute in accordance with the rules of law applicable thereto.'[444] Similarly, Article 21 of the Code of Civil Procedure gives the power to a judge to reconcile n the parties: 'To conciliate parties is part of the mandate of the judge.'[445]

To make a brief comparison between the functions of judge and arbitrator, it is patent that both decide a dispute according to the law, and both have the mandate to reconcile the parties. It is submitted that the similarity between the functions of arbitrator and judge is not unconscious; rather, the French legislature, as well as its English counterpart, have moved to accept the arbitrator as a judge. The same kind of judicial function is reposed in Pakistani jurisprudence on the arbitrator, which is actually the determinative feature to decide if the person performing adjudicative duties is an arbitrator or a referee. The arbitrator has been declared to be a person who decides the dispute after conducting an inquiry and essentially determines the dispute after following a 'judicial procedure keeping in view the principles of natural justice and the law of land'. And the person who decides a matter on the basis of his own knowledge and who is not authorized to make an inquiry cannot be termed an arbitrator, as he would be a referee whose decision is not binding on the parties unless the parties obligate themselves by mutual contract to follow the statement of the referee.[446]

With very limited grounds affecting the separability of the arbitration agreement, if an arbitrator is acknowledged to have inherent power to rule on his jurisdiction, the result would be the absence of anti-arbitration injunctions if the test to decide such injunctions is confined to the challenge of the validity and existence of an arbitration agreement.

7.3.5.1. Preferable Approach

The preferable approach is to bar the issuance of anti-arbitration injunctions in their entirety. The prescription of any kind of tests will be an infertile job because certainty and autonomy of arbitration will be damaged in the end. This suggestion is not impracticable as this approach is already being practised, and France may be quoted as

443. CODE CIVIL [C. CIV.] Article 1474 (Fr.). This provision was re-enacted by French Decree 2011 in two separate Articles. Article 1511 provides that 'the arbitral tribunal shall decide the dispute in accordance with the rules of law chosen by the parties,' whereas Article 1512 provides that '[t]he arbitral tribunal shall rule as *amiable compositeur* if the parties have empowered it to do so'. *See* Decree No. 2011-48 of 13 January 2011 Reforming the Law Governing Arbitration, Journal Officiel de la République Française [J.O.] [Official Gazette of France], 14 January 2011.
444. Article 12 of French Code Civil.
445. Article 21 of French Code Civil.
446. *Pakistan through Secretary, Ministry of Housing and Work, Government of Pakistan v. Gulnar Sher Muhammad and others,* 2002 YLR 2830; *Sher Zaman Khan v. Noor Zaman Khan and another,* PLD 1977 Lahore 672; *Muhammad Hanif Khan and another v. Ghulam Farid Khan and others,* PLD 1988 Lahore 25; *Ch. Muhammad Saleem v. Muhammad Akram and others,* PLD 1971 SC 516; *Zulifqar Ali Shah and 5 others v. Muhammad Hussain and others,* 2002 YLR 1560; *Abdullah and others v. Abdur Rehman and others,* 2004 YLR 295.

an example where the injunction was refused even when the arbitrator's jurisdiction and the validity and existence of an arbitration agreement were in dispute.[447]

In *S.A. Elf Aquitaine and Total v. Mattei*,[448] Elf Neftgaz (a subsidiary company of Elf Aquitaine) and entities from Russia entered into a cooperation agreement. The shareholders of Elf Neftgaz, in a meeting, resolved to liquidate the Elf Neftgaz Company. Arbitration commenced in Paris, and an ad hoc representative for Elf Neftgaz was appointed on the application from its Russian counterpart for the arbitration proceedings in Paris. However, this representative for Elf Neftgaz was later revoked on the order of a court on the plea from Elf Aquitaine. This decision was challenged on appeal by the Russian counterpart of the contract. Elf Aquitaine applied for an anti-arbitration injunction to restrain the arbitration on the ground of retraction of the representative of Elf Neftgaz as appointed by the court, and thus that the tribunal lacked power because the arbitrator appointed by such representative rendered the tribunal defective. The court held that once the tribunal is constituted, the jurisdiction to decide its own jurisdiction lies exclusively in that tribunal, whose decision on jurisdiction will be reviewed once it is given. In the instant case, the court held that the effect of the revocation of a representative appointed for the appointment of an arbitrator on the validity of the constitution of the tribunal has to be determined exclusively by the tribunal itself. The courts do not have the power to restrain such authority by summary proceedings.

Similarly, in *Republic of Equatorial Guinea v. Fitzpatrick Equatorial Guinea*,[449] a contract concluded between the Republic of Equatorial Guinea (REG) and Fitzpatrick Equatorial Guinea (FEG) to construct a highway, containing a Paris-seated arbitration agreement, gave birth to a dispute and FEG commenced arbitration, but the jurisdiction of the tribunal was challenged by the REG. It argued that arbitration could not start before the exhaustion of local remedies as mandated by the agreement to arbitrate and the laws of the REG. REG also raised an objection on the competence of FEG to plead its case due to the insolvency proceedings initiated against FEG, contending that FEG could only be represented by the receiver designated by the domestic court. The tribunal rendered an award in favour of its jurisdiction by moving to the merits phase of the proceedings. On the basis of a challenge against this partial award made before the Paris Court of Appeal, REG sought a stay of arbitration proceedings, which was refused. Thereafter REG commenced summary proceedings in the Tribunal de Grande Instance in order to achieve orders restraining the arbitrators from proceeding until the Paris Court of Appeal decided to set the award aside.[450] On the basis of lack of exhaustion of local remedies and insolvency proceedings, REG contended that if arbitration were not enjoined, it would suffer an irreparable loss. REG had filed a

447. *S.A. Elf Aquitaine and Total v. Mattei*, Judgment of 12 October 2011, n° de pourvoi: 11-11058 (French Cour de cassation, civ. 1e); *Republic of Equatorial Guinea v. Fitzpatrick Equatorial Guinea*, Judgment of 29 March 2010, No. 10-52825 (Paris First Instance Tribunal).
448. Judgment of 12 October 2011, n° de pourvoi: 11-11058 (French Cour de cassation, civ. 1e). Supreme by giving this judgment actually upheld the verdict decreed by Paris Cour d'appel on 5 November 2010, from where the matter was appealed to Supreme Court.
449. Judgment of 29 March 2010, No. 10-52825 (Paris First Instance Tribunal).
450. Judgment of 12 November 2013, No. 12/01857 (Paris Cour d'appel).

criminal suit for forgery against the FEG and prayed that arbitral proceedings be stayed. The court did not grant the application and reasoned that in order to repel imminent and irreparable harm and to bring the patently illegal controversy to an end, it could impart an order in summary proceedings under Article 809 of the French Code of Civil Procedure. This was so despite the subsequent constitution of the tribunal, which normally deprives courts of their power. The court added that such powers may only be used for the purpose of enforcement of arbitral awards and that the courts cannot issue orders to bring the arbitration proceedings to a halt. The court premised this conclusion on the argument that such orders would interfere with arbitral proceedings, for which there exists no authority even in summary proceedings.[451]

It is also interesting to note that the Paris Court of Appeals has categorically held that the courts do not possess the power to issue orders restraining arbitration proceedings in any circumstances and on any kind of legal grounds.[452]

7.4. CONCLUSION

In the face of section 58(b) of the Specific Relief Act prohibiting the issuance of injunctions against a court that is not subordinate, the Pakistani Supreme Court has stated that it can issue an anti-suit injunction. Similarly, Pakistani courts have issued anti-arbitration injunctions, despite the express absence of any provision empowering them to do so. Pakistani courts need to justify sound grounds for their interference with a foreign court's jurisdiction through anti-suit injunctions. One way to do so may be the declaration that these injunctions are not meant to restrain foreign courts but rather that such orders are in personam.

451. *Proceedings in both of above cases were based on Article 809 of the French Code of Civil Procedure*:

> The president [of the Tribunal of First Instance] may always, even if the request is subject to serious objections, order in summary proceedings such conservatory or protective measures that may be necessary to prevent imminent harm or to put an end to a manifestly illegal trouble.

452. Judgment of 24 June 2004, Rev. Arb. 2005, 1037 (Paris *Tribunal de Grande Instance*).

CHAPTER 8

Constitution of Arbitral Tribunal: Interplay between Power of Parties and Pakistani Courts

Pakistani law gives appreciable power to parties to appoint, remove and reappoint arbitrators in accordance with an arbitration agreement. The 1940 Act contemplates two situations: first, where a party can make the appointment of an arbitrator for another party without recourse to the courts, and second when it has to get help from the court. On this, the law gives the courts wide powers in support of arbitration and the parties thereto. However, the power given in this regard to the courts does not have extra-territorial extension due to the apparent inability of such orders to be enforced outside of Pakistan.

8.1. INTRODUCTION

Pakistani law has a domesticated approach on the issue of appointment, removal, and reappointment of the members of an arbitral tribunal. In line with arbitration's consensual nature, the parties have the powers to make such appointments. However, Pakistani courts have also been empowered to assist the arbitral process by making these appointments at the request of the parties. Pakistani courts were restrained from making appointments or removal of arbitrators when arbitration was seated abroad because Pakistani courts do not have territorial jurisdiction over such arbitrations.

This chapter discusses the parties' and courts' power to appoint, remove and reappoint arbitrators. The situation where a party can appoint an arbitrator on behalf of another party or its arbitrator as the sole arbitrator has also been discussed. This chapter also explores the point of time when a party has the right to resort to the court for assistance in such an appointment. There are times when the parties are not satisfied with the arbitrator and want to remove him or her. This chapter also discusses how the authority of arbitrators can be revoked. To facilitate the discussion on these points, the difference between chairman and umpire and then between arbitrator, referee and commission has also been explained.

8.2. SECTION 9:[453] POWER OF PARTY TO APPOINT ARBITRATORS OR, IN CERTAIN CASES, A SOLE ARBITRATOR

As is clear from the consensual nature of arbitration, it is primarily the parties who have the power to appoint arbitrators. In other words, the arbitrator should be appointed in accordance with the arbitration agreement between the parties. *Oil & Gas Development Corporation v. Karachi Builders* involved an arbitration agreement providing for the appointment of the Production Engineer of the Appellant Corporation as arbitrator. When the dispute arose, the Deputy Chief Engineer of the appellant corporation was performing additional duties as Production Manager, and he took up the task of the arbitrator and pronounced an award. The Supreme Court held that the parties intended to appoint the Production Manager as an arbitrator and not any other officer performing functions of Production Manager in addition to his own duties and so held the Deputy Chief Engineer to be incompetent to arbitrate and set aside the award.[454] Arbitration agreements authorizing one of the parties (sellers in this case) to appoint the sole arbitrator have been declared valid by the courts.[455] However, where the arbitration agreement is silent on the number of arbitrators to be appointed, then section 3 read with the First Schedule of the 1940 Act would be applicable, providing for the implied conditions of an arbitration agreement. The first of these implied conditions says that the matter in such situations would be decided by a sole

453. Section 9. Power to party to appoint new arbitrator or, in certain cases, a sole arbitrator:

> Where an arbitrations agreement provides that a reference shall be to two arbitrators, one to be appointed by each party, then, unless a different intention is expressed in the agreement
>
> (a) if either of the appointed arbitrators, neglects or refuses to act, or is incapable of acting or dies, the party who appointed him may appoint a new arbitrator in his place;
> (b) if one party fails to appoint an arbitrator, either originally or by way of substitution as aforesaid, for fifteen clear days after the service by the other party of a notice in writing to make the appointment, such other party having appointed his arbitrator before giving the notice, the party who has appointed an arbitrator may appoint that arbitrator to act as sole arbitrator in the reference, and his award shall be binding on both parties as if he had been appointed by consent.
>
> Provided that the Court may set aside any appointment as sole arbitrators made under clause (b) and either, on sufficient cause being shown, allow further time to the defaulting party to appoint an arbitrator or pas such other order as it thinks fit.
>
> Explanation. The fact that an arbitrator or umpire, after request by either party to proceed with the reference, and which does not within one month comply with the request, may constitute a neglect or refusal to act within the meaning of section 8 and this section.

454. *Oil & Gas Development Corporation v. Karachi Builders,* 1978 SCMR 278.
455. *Intertrade Ltd., Karachi v. Trading Corporation of Pakistan Ltd. and another,* PLD 1976 Karachi 496.

arbitrator,[456] and the courts are not allowed to go against the tribunal's award. For instance, in a case involving an arbitration agreement that was silent on the number of arbitrators, the appointment of two arbitrators by the court was declared as producing no effect.[457]

The parties can include in their arbitration agreement the name of a person to be appointed as arbitrator. In an arbitration agreement, they can also designate a third person who will appoint an arbitrator on their behalf. The party who appoints his arbitrator will also have the power to appoint a substitute arbitrator if his appointee dies, is incapable of acting as arbitrator, or neglects or omits to act as arbitrator.[458] This third person can be included by name or office.[459] *In University of The Punjab v. Perfect Electric Concern,*[460] under the arbitration agreement, the Vice-Chancellor (VC) of the University of Punjab was to act as sole arbitrator to decide any dispute arising in relation to an electrification agreement. The VC refused to act as arbitrator, and the matter was before the court as if the arbitration agreement became ineffective or as if some new sole arbitrator had been appointed by the court. The court held that there is no difference between the arbitrator who is named in the arbitration agreement by virtue of his office and the one who is specifically named in the arbitration agreement. The fact that the parties had not expressed their intentions as to if their named arbitrator declined his appointment, then no other arbitrator would be appointed, and in the absence of expression of such intention from the parties in their agreement, a new arbitrator could be appointed by the parties or the court. So the court held that the parties cannot be assumed to have never intended that only the VC will act as arbitrator, and no other person would be appointed. The court highlighted the fact that contracts with the government as a party normally choose some government official by his office as arbitrator, and it is also not uncommon for this official to be very busy at the time of arbitration and to decline to act as arbitrator. In this situation, if the arbitration becomes ineffective due to the declination of the arbitrator, the power to frustrate the arbitration agreement would vest in the named arbitrator rather than the principle of bilateralism in the parties.

However, if the first party fails to appoint an original arbitrator or substitute arbitrator, the other party may serve on the first party notice for the appointment of an arbitrator within fifteen days. If the first party fails to act in accordance with the notice, the other party may appoint his arbitrator as a sole arbitrator, and the award from this arbitrator shall be binding on both parties.[461] Where a party failed to appoint his arbitrator, and the other party appointed its arbitrator as sole arbitrator, such appointment of a sole arbitrator may be set aside by the court if the defaulting party can

456. *Government of Sindh and others v. Tausif Ali Khan,* 2003 CLC 180.
457. *Pakistan Real Estate Investment and Management Company (Pvt) Ltd. v. Sohail A. Khan, Associates-Assign JV,* PLD 2018 Islamabad 115.
458. Section 9 of the 1940 Act. *Abdul Hakim K. Khan v. Begum Khanum Jan and others,* 1989 MLD 1304.
459. Section 4 of the 1940 Act.
460. *University of The Punjab v. Perfect Electric Concern,* PLD 1980 Lahore 305.
461. Section 9 of the 1940 Act.

establish that his default was not deliberate and that he was acting under a misunderstanding or confusion or that non-appointment was negligent, evasive or obstructive.[462]

The aforementioned procedure is not mandatory and may be deviated if an arbitration clause inconsistent with this provision is drafted by the parties. In *Balgamwalla Cotton Ginning and Pressing Factory v. Elite Textile Mills and Pressing Factory Ltd.*, the by-laws of the corporation in question contained an arbitration clause whereby:

> If one of the parties fails to appoint its arbitrator after having received fifteen-day notice from other party to do so, that other party having appointed its own arbitrator, shall have power to appoint a second arbitrator on behalf of the defaulting party.

The petitioner appointed its arbitrator and served requisite notice on the respondent to appoint its own arbitrator. However, the respondent failed to make such an appointment, whereon the petitioner appointed the second arbitrator. Upon the second arbitrator's refusal to act as arbitrator, the petitioner appointed a substitute arbitrator. Both arbitrators pronounced the award. This award was set aside by the lower court on the ground that the petitioner should have given a fifteen-day notice before appointing the substitute. However, in revision, the High Court highlighted the fact that the arbitration clause was inconsistent with section 9 of the 1940 Act and held that neither section 9 nor the procedure and principle laid down in it would be applicable there. The court held that the appointment of the arbitrator would be complete only after he had accepted the office. Similarly, the power of a party to appoint an arbitrator on behalf of a recalcitrant party also includes appointing the substitute arbitrator in case of his incapability or refusal to act as arbitrator for any reason. Based on these principles, the court held that the petitioner was not bound to follow the procedure mandating for the service of fresh notice on the respondent before he could proceed with the appointment of a substitute.[463]

8.3. SECTION 8: POWER OF COURT TO APPOINT ARBITRATORS

Section 8 of the 1940 Act[464] gives power to the court to appoint an arbitrator or umpire and also provides situations in which such powers can be exercised. *First*, the court can

462. *Board of Trustees of Port of Karachi v. National Construction Co. (Pakistan) Ltd. and another*, PLD 1981 Karachi 377.
463. *Balgamwalla Cotton Ginning and Pressing Factory v. Elite Textile Mills and Pressing Factory Ltd.*, PLD 1968 Karachi 916.
464. Section 8. Power of Court to appoint arbitrator or umpire:

> (1) In any of the following cases:
> (a) where an arbitration agreement provides that the reference shall be to one or more arbitrators to be appointed by consent of the parties, and all the parties do not, after differences have arisen, concur in the appointment or appointments; or
> (b) if any appointed arbitrator or umpire neglects or refuses to act, or is incapable of acting, or dies, and the arbitration agreement does not show that it was intended

appoint an arbitrator if the arbitration agreement stipulates that the arbitrator or arbitrators are to be appointed with the consent of all parties. If the parties do not agree on the name of the arbitrator, then a party may approach the court for the appointment of an arbitrator after giving a fifteen-day notice to the other party.[465] If one party appoints his nominee as a sole arbitrator without the consent of the other party and without any recourse to the court, this would be in contravention of section 8, even if the other party failed to concur with such appointment. This outcome is justified because it is the exclusive jurisdiction of the court to appoint an arbitrator in such a case.[466]

To make the appointment of a new arbitrator under this provision, the party has to establish to the satisfaction of the court the 'death, incapacity, refusal or omission to act' of the arbitrator. In one case, the arbitrator was out of Karachi on the date of the arbitral hearing and could not perform his duties, which resulted in the delay in arbitration proceedings. On these facts, the court held that:

> There is a difference between neglecting or omitting to act and being careless or being fettered by incidents which are not one's own doings or being imprudent in applying one self to work. Neglecting to act is entirely different from acting negligently. In the latter sense there is an omission to act like a prudent or reasonable man, whereas neglecting to act means failing to act. I agree with the learned First Appellate Court that the arbitrator did not neglect to act. If he has acted negligently and caused delay, then the remedy open to the present applicant was to apply to the Court for his removal under section 11 (1) of the Act, or for leave, under section 5 of the Act, to revoke his authority. His substitute could not be appointed by the respondent under section 9 (a) of the Act. Thus, the appointment by the applicant of new arbitrator under section 9 (b) of the Act as the sole' arbitrator owing to the failure of the respondent to act under section 9 (a) was illegal. Consequently, the new arbitrator supposed had no authority to give an award as the sole arbitrator. His award has been rightly set aside.[467]

In another case, the umpire failed to proceed with the reference within the stipulated time. This failure constituted neglect and refusal to act on the part of the Umpire under section 8. The authority of the Umpire was revoked by the court. Thereafter, the Umpire was appointed by the arbitrators, and then two other umpires

---

that the vacancy should not be supplied, and the parties or the arbitrators, as the case may be, do not supply the vacancy; or

(c) where the parties or the arbitrators are required to appoint an umpire and do not appoint him;

any party may serve the other parties or the arbitrators, as the case may be, with a written notice to concur in the appointment or appointments or in supplying the vacancy.

(2) If the appointment is not made within fifteen clear days after the service of the said notice, the Court may, on the application of the party who gave notice and after giving the other parties an opportunity of being heard, appoint an arbitrator or arbitrators or umpire, as the case may be, who shall have like power to act in the reference and to make an award as if he or they had been appointed by consent of all parties.

465. Section 8(1)(a) of the 1940 Act. *Alpha Insurance Co. Limited v. Ch. Nizam Din & Sons and another*, 2001 CLC 289.
466. *Karachi Dock Labour Board v. Quality Builders Ltd.*, PLD 2016 SC 121.
467. *Haroon Oil Mills v. Kohinoor Cotton Ginning Factory,* PLD 1967 Karachi 175.

were appointed by the defendant on two other occasions. However, each of them failed to make the award, and their authority was revoked. The court concluded that this was a fit case for the court to appoint an umpire who would make an award with all dispatch.[468] Where the parties have agreed on an arbitrator and have included his name in the arbitration agreement, the court cannot substitute such an arbitrator. However, sections 8(1) and 20(4) do not put any restriction on the powers of the court to remove the arbitrator and appoint a fresh arbitrator.[469]

Second, the court also has the power to fill the vacancy created due to the death of an arbitrator or his incapability, refusal or omission to act, or removal of the arbitrator. The court will exercise such powers if the arbitration agreement does not suggest that such vacancy should not be filled and the parties or arbitrators fail to supply that vacancy.[470] Where a court removed an arbitrator, it is not bound to ask the party whose nominee was removed to nominate another person to be appointed as arbitrator, nor is it bound to appoint the nominee of another party. It may, however, ask the party whose nominee is removed to name some persons to help the court to choose an arbitrator to fill the vacancy. The court also has the power to appoint a sole arbitrator after the removal of an arbitral tribunal even if the arbitration agreement provides for the appointment of an arbitral tribunal. The final authority rests in the court to make an appointment.[471]

Third, the court has also been given powers where the parties or arbitrators are required to appoint an umpire, but they fail to do so.[472]

To have recourse to the court in any of these three situations, a party will first have to give a fifteen-day notice to the other party to concur with its appointment. If the other party fails to concur within these fifteen days, the first party may make an application to the court, and the court, after giving the other party an opportunity of a hearing, will appoint the arbitrator or umpire as the case may be. However, if such application to the court is made without serving a fifteen-day notice, such application would be considered premature and will be dismissed.[473] The purpose of issuing a notice to the other party under section 8(2) of the 1940 Act is to intimate to the other party that if it does not concur with the first party's decision on the arbitrator's appointment, it would invoke the jurisdiction of the court.[474]

The application of this section was elaborated by the Punjab High Court in *Taj Din and Other v. Muhammad Sharif and other*.[475] In this case, while the suit for dissolution of a partnership and rendition of accounts was pending, the parties agreed to refer the matter to arbitration. Both parties appointed their arbitrators and also agreed that in case of disagreement between the arbitrators, Karam Illahi would be

468. *Vaseem Construction Company v. Province of Sindh*, 1985 MLD 397.
469. *Design Group of Pakistan v. Clifton Cantonment Board*, 1990 MLD 2010.
470. Section 8(1)(b) of the 1940 Act. *Interhom (Pvt.) v. Pakistan Steel Mills Corporation*, PLD 1992 Karachi 99.
471. *Federation of Pakistan v. James Construction Company (Pvt) Ltd.*, PLD 2018 Islamabad 1.
472. Section 8(1)(c) of the 1940 Act.
473. *Province of Punjab and others v. Rana & Sons*, 1996 CLC 69.
474. *Abdul Salam v. Muhammad Yaqoob and another*, 1999 CLC 1005; *Transocean Asia Ltd., Karachi v. Rice Export Corporation of Pakistan Ltd.*, 1980 CLC 556.
475. PLD 1970 Lahore 840.

Sarpanch. After the matter was referred to arbitration, one arbitrator said after having perused the record that he was unable to make any findings. The civil judge referred the matter to a Sarpanch on the ground that there was a difference of opinion between the arbitrators. However, the Sarpanch was removed at the instance of the defendants, and a new Sarpanch was appointed, who went on to make an award.

The award was challenged before the court on the basis that the Sarpanch could not adjudicate the matter alone in the absence of one arbitrator because he was not the sole arbitrator. The court admitted that the Sarpanch was not a sole arbitrator. However, the main question for the court was whether the arbitrator had refused to act as an arbitrator or whether his inability to arrive at any conclusion would be tantamount to a difference of opinion between the two arbitrators. The court concluded that: 'he was incapable of acting as an arbitrator since he could not come to any finding. It can by no stretch of imagination be called a difference of opinion since no finding on merits contrary to the other arbitrator was given'.

The court further noted that the other question was if, in the absence of one of the arbitrators, the umpire could act as sole arbitrator. The court noted that nothing in the arbitration agreement indicated that the Sarpanch would act as sole arbitrator to determine the dispute. It further held that on account of the inability of the arbitrator to act as such, the Sarpanch did not have any power to make that award. Instead, he would have power only if there was a difference of opinion, which was not there in the present case. The court made the point that:

> A Division Bench in *Harriam Khiaram v. Gpbondram Rattan Chandd*, PLD 1949 Sindh 30, held that where one of the appointed arbitrators refused to act and no attempt was made to supply the vacancy through the assistance of the court as provided by section 8, the award vitiated and the dispute had to be determined by the civil court. In Yar Muhammad v. Ghulam Sarwar PLD 1952 Lah 563, it was held that it would be clear that the refusal of an arbitrator to act would not put an end to the agreement itself, but would enable the court in the last resort to supply the deficiency. Under section 8(1), it shall be presumed that it was intended that the vacancy shall be supplied and the burden to show other shall rest on the person objecting to it.

In *Interhom (Pvt.) Limited v. Pakistan Steel Mills Corporation*,[476] where the arbitrator was transferred to some other place and the parties could not agree on the new arbitrator, the court held that it had the power to appoint an arbitrator. However, where a court intended to appoint a nominee of the respondent as sole arbitrator due to the failure of the appellant to appoint their arbitrator, it would be incumbent on such court to give notice of fifteen clear days to the defaulting party (appellant) of its intention to appoint thereof. Violation of any legal requirements would render reference to the sole arbitrator invalid.[477] For instance, in *Province of Punjab v. Akhtar Saleem*, a dispute arose out of a construction contract under which the matter was to be sent to arbitration. The respondent filed an application for arbitration under sections 8 and 20 of the 1940 Act and called for the appointment of the arbitrator. The

---

476. PLD 1992 Karachi 99.
477. *Abdul Khaleq v. Province of East Pakistan*, PLD 1964 Dacca 166.

respondent nominated his arbitrator, but the appellant did not. The court gave three adjournments so that the appellant could nominate his arbitrator but all in vain. Then the court passed an order by appointing the arbitrator nominated by the respondent to be the sole arbitrator. At the request of the respondent, this sole arbitrator was substituted by the court by another sole arbitrator. Meanwhile, the appellant applied to the court, praying that he should be allowed to appoint a second arbitrator because the arbitration agreement spoke of the appointment of two arbitrators; one arbitrator to be appointed by each of the parties. This application was dismissed by the court. The award by the sole arbitrator was filed, which was certified by the court.

On appeal, the court noted that while appointing the arbitrator nominated by the respondent to be sole arbitrator, the court did not give any notice to the appellant of its intention of doing so. Although three adjournments were given by the court, the High Court held that the appellant failed to nominate their arbitrator. Nevertheless, this failure *ipso facto* did not empower the court to appoint the nominee of the respondent as the sole arbitrator.[478]

Where the agreement lays down some condition precedent to be fulfilled for going to arbitration, the court normally turns down the request for arbitration and the appointment of the arbitrator if a party seeks that remedy from the court. For instance, where the parties first agree to approach an engineer for the resolution of their dispute but fail to fully take advantage of this, none of the parties may approach the courts for the appointment of a new arbitrator.[479]

The identification of a court with jurisdiction to appoint an arbitrator is very important. The court in whose jurisdiction the agreement is executed would have jurisdiction. Similarly, the court in whose jurisdiction a party refused to make the appointment of an arbitrator will also have jurisdiction because the cause of action partially arose there.[480] The court in whose jurisdiction the contract was performed in whole or in part, and the price of goods was paid, would equally enjoy jurisdiction.[481]

8.4. RELATION BETWEEN SECTION 8 AND SECTION 9 OF THE 1940 ACT

The difference between section 8 and section 9 was discussed by the Sindh High Court in *Haroon Oil Mills v. Kohinoor Cotton Ginning Factory*.[482] In this case, by comparing sections 8 and 9, it stated that both sections 8(1)(b) and 9(a) provide that a party can appoint an arbitrator in the place of an arbitrator who neglects to act. If a party who is to concur in such an appointment or is to make the appointment of a substitute arbitrator fails to do so, then both these sections provide two different mechanisms. Section 8(2) says that the court should be approached, whereas section 9(b) says that the opposite party can appoint its arbitrator as a sole arbitrator, which means that this

478. 1986 MLD 1980.
479. *Federation of Pakistan v. James Construction Company (Pvt) Ltd.*, PLD 2018 Islamabad 1.
480. *Province of Punjab and others v. Rana & Sons*, 1996 CLC 69.
481. *Fauji Foundation and others v. Yousuf*, 1985 CLC 2799.
482. PLD 1967 Karachi 175.

section does not require recourse to the court. The Sindh High Court stated that phrases such as: 'by consent of the parties' and 'notice to concur', which occur in clause (a) and (c), respectively, of section 8(1), restrict the application of this section to arbitration in which the arbitrator(s) is to be appointed with the mutual consent of the parties. On the other hand, section 9 applies to those arbitrations in which two arbitrators are to be appointed by the parties, one by each of them, which is clear from the opening part of section 9. This difference was summarized by the Sindh High Court, in another case, as follows:

> It will at once be seen that whereas under section 8, for want of concurrence in the appointment of the arbitrator(s), aid and attention of the Court is necessary, the appointment, in terms of section 9 of the Act, by the party not in default can ipso facto, upon the requirements being met, becomes final and no recourse to Court needs to be made. This is what distinguishes sections 8 and 9.[483]

In *Karachi Dock Labour Board v. Quality Builders Ltd.*,[484] the Supreme Court enlisted the following conditions to be fulfilled to invoke its application:

- that the agreement itself provides that a reference shall be to two arbitrators;
- that the agreement further provides that, of the two arbitrators, one has to be appointed by each party;
- that one arbitrator has in fact been appointed by one of the parties, and the other party has failed to appoint an arbitrator;
- that the party who has appointed their arbitrator has served a notice in writing (after the appointment of their arbitrator) to the party who has failed to appoint their arbitrator; and
- that fifteen days have passed since a notice in writing to make the appointment was served to the party who has failed to appoint their arbitrator.

The Supreme Court held that the first two conditions form the basis of the last three ones, and those conditions constitute *sine qua non* for the application of section 9(b).

8.5. DIFFERENCE BETWEEN SECTION 8 AND SECTION 20 OF THE 1940 ACT

Section 8 and section 20 seems to be similar in their purpose and application, but there are points of differences between them. This difference was elaborated by the Sindh High Court in *Karachi Shipyard and Engineering Works Ltd. v. Muhammad Aslam Khan*. It stated that where parties entered into an arbitration agreement and a dispute arose to which such arbitration agreement was applicable, the parties could opt for any of two procedures available in the form of section 8 and section 20. Section 8 mandates that the applicant will first give a fifteen-day notice to the other party to concur in the appointment of the arbitrator or in filling the vacancy. Such a party can approach the

483. *Akbar Hussain v. Wadero Muhammad Tayyab*, PLD 1996 Karachi 545.
484. *Karachi Dock Labour Board v. Quality Builders Ltd.*, PLD 2016 SC 121.

court only after the expiration of fifteen days. On the other hand, section 20 does not require any notice prior to approaching the court. This section stipulates that when a controversy arises, that is encompassed by the arbitration agreement, the party can straightaway approach the court, enjoying jurisdiction over the matter with a prayer that the agreement be filed in the court. Under section 20, the right to approach the court accrues when 'a difference has arisen'. A difference arises when one party does not agree with its counterpart on a particular issue encompassed under the arbitration agreement,[485] as, for instance, when a party declines to make full payment of a bill to the contractor.[486] The right to approach the court, under section 8, arises on the expiry of a fifteen-day notice. In this regard, the Sindh High Court stated that the phrase 'after differences have arisen' as appears in section 8(1)(a) of the 1940 Act, has not been employed in relation to the application to the court because this has been dealt with by section 8(2). Rather, these words have been used in connection with the condition, as laid down in section 8(2), of service of notice to the other parties to concur in the appointment of the arbitrator. Such notice can be given only when all the concerned parties do not agree on the appointment of the arbitrator, and the difference in that regard arises. In the face of this difference, when one party serves a notice to the other party to concur in the appointment of the arbitrator within fifteen days and the other party fails to do so, the right to approach the court under section 8 will arise. Therefore, the right to apply to the court accrues at materially different points of time under sections 8 and 20. The limitation period under section 8 does not start from the point when a difference arose between the parties, but only when the fifteen-day notice expires.[487]

8.6. REMOVAL OF ARBITRATOR

Section 5 of the 1940 Act[488] says that after an arbitrator is appointed, his authority can be revoked in accordance with the terms of the arbitration agreement. If no mechanism is laid down in the arbitration agreement, then the party may have recourse to the court to secure its leave for revocation of authority of the arbitrator. Unless a contrary intention appears from the agreement of the parties, the authority of the arbitrator can be revoked only with the leave of the court. For this, the aggrieved party files an application to the court under section 5 of the 1940 Act, or if the arbitrator was

485. PLD 1979 Karachi 635.
486. The Sindh High Court extracted this from *Imam-ud-Din v. Thal Development Authority*, PLD 1972 SC 123.
487. *Karachi Shipyard and Engineering Works Ltd. v. Muhammad Aslam Khan* PLD 1979 Karachi 635. The Sindh High Court also relied on *West Pakistan, WAPDA v. Omar Sons Ltd.*, PLD 1970 Lahore 398.
488. Section 5. Authority of appointed arbitrator or umpire irrevocable except by leave of Court:

> The authority of an appointed arbitrator or umpire shall not be revocable except with the leave of the Court unless a contrary intention is expressed in the arbitration agreement.

appointed by the court, then the aggrieved party files an appeal against such order of the court to appoint the arbitrator.[489]

The application of section 5 of the 1940 Act is attracted to those cases in which the authority of arbitrator subsists and needs to be revoked. The court defined revocation to mean 'withdrawal, recall, annulment or repudiation', the need for which emerges when the arbitrator is living, is capable of acting, is willing to act and does not carry out the mandate. In other words, if he is dead, or incapable of acting as an arbitrator or is not willing to act or does not carry out his mandate, then there would be a vacancy, and that vacancy will be filled according to section 8(1)(b) & (c), due to the occurrence of the word 'vacancy' or as a result of section 9(a), due to the occurrence of the phrase 'may appoint a new arbitrator in his place'.

It should be noted that section 5 does not provide grounds on the basis of which the court should assess the application for the leave to revoke the authority of the arbitrator. However, section 11 of the same Act[490] provides three grounds and on the basis of any of them, an arbitrator can be removed. *First*, when the arbitrator 'fails to use all reasonable dispatch in entering on and proceeding with the reference and making an award'. *Second*, if he misconducts himself. *Third*, if he misconducts the proceedings. It is clear from the foregoing that apart from misconduct,[491] an arbitrator can be removed if he fails to use all his dispatch to start and conduct the arbitration proceedings.

The court will grant its leave to revoke the authority of an arbitrator only if sufficient grounds for doing so exist, and hence this is a discretionary relief. The removal of an arbitrator is a very serious matter and cannot be allowed on flimsy or ephemeral grounds. For instance, the termination of a contract containing an arbitration agreement on the ground that the main agreement is terminated or that the arbitrator is charging an exorbitant fee cannot become sufficient grounds for leave to revoke the authority of the arbitrator.[492] In *U. K. Construction Co., Karachi v. Chief Engineer, Highways Department, Hyderabad*, in order to resolve a dispute in relation to heavy construction work, a Superintending Engineer was appointed as arbitrator. However, he wrote a letter to the Head of Communication and Works Department, that given the heavy and complex work involved in the matter, it looked feasible to him that some senior officer should be appointed as arbitrator. After this letter and before any

489. *Mst. Salma Aftab v. Shaikh Muhammad Tufail and others*, 2009 CLC 56.
490. Section 11. Power of Court to remove arbitrators or umpire in certain circumstances:

> (1) The Court may, on the application of any party to a reference, remove an arbitrator or umpire who fails to use all reasonable dispatch in entering on and proceeding with the reference and making an award.
> (2) The Court may remove an arbitrator or umpire who has misconduct himself or the proceedings.
> (3) Where an arbitrator or umpire is removed under this section, he shall not be entitled to receive any remuneration in respect of his services.
> (4) For the purposes of this section the expression 'proceeding with the reference' includes, in a case where reference to the umpire becomes necessary, giving notice of that fact to the parties and to the umpire.

491. For misconduct, *see* Ch. 13 below.
492. *National Refinery Ltd. v. Anaud Power Generation Ltd and others*, 1999 YLR 1673.

action was taken by the Head, the Superintending Engineer started the arbitration and issued notice to the parties. The court held that by sending this letter to the Head, he neither resigned nor declined to work as an arbitrator and did not show any negligence or carelessness in entering on the reference.[493] In that respect, 'entering on the reference' means that the reference has been made to the arbitrator and he has accepted it. It does not mean that parties should be present before the arbitrator because following this approach would, in most cases, frustrate the purpose of the 1940 Act, which aims at the speedy disposal of disputes through arbitration.[494]

In *Perma Construction (Pvt) Ltd. v. Oberoi Textiles Ltd*, the arbitration agreement provided that the dispute between the parties would be referred to a sole arbitrator to be appointed by the respondent from 'amongst a retired judge of the Supreme Court or High Court or an Advocate of the Supreme Court or High Court having not less than ten years standing'. The respondent appointed a sole arbitrator who was an advocate with ten years standing. The petitioner challenged such an appointment on the ground that the respondent had first to appoint a retired judge, and it was only in case of unavailability that he could resort to an advocate. The court, however, held that the authority of the arbitrator could not be revoked as he was not disqualified for being an advocate. The court further said that unless a contrary intention is expressed in the arbitration agreement, the appointment of an arbitrator can be revoked only by leave of the court under sections 5 and 11 of the 1940 Act.[495]

In cases not involving failure on the part of the arbitrator to initiate and conduct the arbitration proceedings vigilantly, the courts are reluctant to revoke their authority. For instance, in one case, the parties entered into an arbitration agreement to refer their controversy to arbitrators holding the office of Superintending Engineers in the petitioner's department. Upon appointment, the petitioners applied to the court to revoke their authority on the ground that they were retired from that department and that they could not act as arbitrators. The court held that their retirement from the office of Superintending Engineers did not have any impact on their authority to act as arbitrators because they were validly appointed in accordance with the arbitration agreement.[496] However, where an arbitrator was called upon to act on 22 June 1966, and he did not enter on the reference until 18 October 1966, the court held that he had failed to use 'all reasonable dispatch in entering on reference for the purpose of making an award within the prescribed time of four months and therefore was liable to be removed'.[497] Similarly, in another case, the sole arbitrator did not take any step from the date of his appointment as arbitrator until only four days before the expiry of the four months as laid down in the Act for making an award. The Supreme Court stated that he was rightly removed.[498]

493. *U. K. Construction Co., Karachi v. Chief Engineer, Highways Department, Hyderabad*, PLD 1976 Karachi 1152.
494. *M. M. Ispahani Ltd v. Pakistan Trading Company*, PLD 1966 Dacca 54.
495. *Perma Construction (Pvt) Ltd. v. Oberoi Textiles Ltd.*, 2002 YLR 2687.
496. *Punjab Province v. Hussain Construction Company Ltd*, 1993 CLC 2082.
497. *Province of East Pakistan v. Abdur Rashid*, PLD 1970 Dacca 69.
498. *Province of East Pakistan v. Abdur Rashid*, 1970 SCMR 319.

The courts have also considered other grounds to revoke the authority of an arbitrator, such as where proceedings are conducted without the involvement of a necessary party to the arbitration, in which case the authority of the arbitrator may be terminated or revoked by the court.[499] Where one party secures the appointment of an arbitrator by fraud, such appointment can be cancelled by the court.[500]

For the revocation of the authority of an arbitrator, the conferment of valid authority upon him is necessary. Where he was appointed in contravention of the arbitration agreement, there would be no need for the revocation of his authority. Conferment of jurisdiction and appointment of an arbitrator must strictly be in line with the letter and spirit of the arbitration agreement and express provisions of the law.[501] By the same token, the authority of an arbitrator cannot be revoked before a reference is made to him. Although the revocation of an arbitrator's authority by a court before a reference is made to him would be wrong, that does not mean that the order of the court to refer the dispute to an arbitrator other than the named arbitrator would be without jurisdiction and an award pronounced by this second arbitrator would not be vitiated.[502]

Section 5 does not confer any power on the courts to revoke the authority of arbitrators; rather, such power is conferred on any party who can use it by leave of the court.[503] When the authority of an arbitrator is revoked by leave of the court or the arbitrator is otherwise removed, the court, by proceeding under section 12 of the 1940 Act,[504] either supersedes the arbitration agreement or substitutes such outgoing arbitrator with a new arbitrator. In this regard, unless otherwise expressed, the court is not bound by the provisions of the arbitration agreement to leave the appointment of such arbitrator to any authority designated in the arbitration agreement because the power conferred on a third person to make an appointment does not permit the exercise of such powers again and again.[505] Section 12 says that where the court

499. *Aj-Bag Corporation v. Pakistan through the Secretary, Ministry of Defence, Islamabad and others,* 1973 SCMR 98.

500. *Ch. Ghulam Qadir v. Province of the Punjab and another,* 1980 CLC 1854.

501. *Karachi Dock Labour Board v. Quality Builders Ltd.*, PLD 2016 SC 121.

502. *Azad J & K Government v. Khawaja Muhammad Usman & Co.*, PLD 1966 Azad J & K 19.

503. *Ahmad Khan v. Naziran Bibi*, 2003 YLR 1028.

504. Section 2. Power of Court where arbitrator is removed or his authority revoked:

> (1) Where the Court removes an umpire who has not entered on the reference or one or more arbitrators (not being all the arbitrators), the Court may, on the application of any party to the arbitration agreement, appoint persons to fill the vacancies.
>
> (2) Where the authority of an arbitrator or arbitrators or an umpire is revoked by leave of the Court, or where the Court removes an umpire who has entered on the reference or a sole arbitrator or all the arbitrators, the Court may, on the application of any party to the arbitration agreement, either
>
> (a) appoint a person to act as sole arbitrator in the place of the person or persons displaced, or
>
> (b) order that the arbitration agreement shall cease to have effect with respect to the difference referred.
>
> (3) A person appointed under this section as an arbitrator or umpire shall have the like power to act in the reference and to make an award as if he had been appointed in accordance with the arbitration agreement.

505. *WAPDA v. Naeem Trading Co.* 1982 CLC 353.

removes the arbitrator or grants its leave to a party to revoke the authority of said arbitrator, it would have the power to appoint a sole arbitrator even if the arbitration agreement spoke of the reference to more than one arbitrator; the court may further order that the arbitration agreement cease to have any effect in relation to the dispute referred to arbitration. If the proceedings for the revocation of authority of an arbitrator are still pending and not disposed of and the award is filed in the same court, the former proceedings would become dormant and will be revived if the award is set aside.[506]

8.7. POWER OF ARBITRATOR

After the award is pronounced by the arbitrator, he becomes *functus officio*. He can act as arbitrator only under section 13(b)[507] or in case of remission of the award to him by the court. If the court sets aside the award, it has the power to supersede the reference. But, if it does not supersede the reference, the arbitration agreement exists, and the same arbitrator can be reappointed, provided the terms of arbitration agreement so permit. However, the court has ample power to substitute the arbitrator with another one.[508] In *Abdul Sattar Mandokhal v. Port Qasim Authority*, some of the claims arising out of the contract were already decided by the arbitrators. Some other disputes arose from the same contract. To resolve those disputes, the court appointed the same arbitrators, which decided conflicts arising from the contract before. The court did so in order to avoid a divergent decision under similar circumstances.[509]

The arbitrator thus did not possess any power to fill any vacancy unless such power was conferred on him by the arbitration agreement. Where, however, the parties had submitted themselves to the jurisdiction of an umpire who was subsequently appointed by the arbitrators – following the demise of the previous umpire and having appeared along with their counsel in the proceedings before him without any objection to his jurisdiction – said parties would be estopped from questioning the jurisdiction of such umpire to enter into reference. Active participation of objectors before the umpire would be tantamount to their acquiescence.[510]

Where the petitioner has appointed the arbitrator unconditionally and participated in the proceedings before him, his application to revoke the authority of the

506. *Design Group of Pakistan v. Clifton Cantonment Board*, 1990 MLD 261.
507. Section 13 Powers of arbitrator:

> The arbitrators or umpire shall, unless a different intention is expressed in the agreement, have power to
>
> ...
>
> (b) state a special case for the opinion of the Court on any question of law involved, or state the award, wholly or in part, in the form of a special case of such question for the opinion of the Court.

508. *Design Group of Pakistan v. Clifton Cantonment Board*, 1990 MLD 2010.
509. *Abdul Sattar Mandokhal v. Port Qasim Authority*, 2001 YLR 758.
510. *Reliance Construction Co. v. Agha Khan Medical College Foundation Karachi*, 1994 MLD 248.

arbitrator would not succeed due to the application of the principle of estoppel.[511] In *Mian Fazal Muhammad (Deceased) through his Legal Heirs v. Province of West Pakistan and others,* the arbitrator gave his award, and the issuance of such award was also in the notice of the parties. During the pendency of the arbitration proceedings, no step was taken by the parties to stop the arbitrator from giving the said award. After the award, the arbitrator had become *functus officio,* and no application under section 11 could be filed, or if it had already been filed, it would become infructuous.[512] After the removal of an arbitrator, the newly appointed arbitrator may conduct de novo arbitration proceedings because no embargo exists in the 1940 Act on this.[513]

8.8. ACCRUAL OF RIGHT TO APPLY TO COURT FOR THE APPOINTMENT OF ARBITRATOR AND LIMITATION PERIOD

A party can move to the court for the appointment of an arbitrator after the expiration of the fifteen-day notice served on the other party, and it is at this point of time when the limitation period starts and not from the time when the cause of action arises. In *West Pakistan Water and Development Authority v. Omar Sons Ltd.,*[514] WAPDA engaged a contractor for the construction of the Gujranwala Hydel Project by an agreement containing an arbitration agreement that spoke of the appointment of a sole arbitrator. The contractor alleged that after the completion of works by him, the consideration for work was outstanding, and for that reason, he proposed a panel of three arbitrators to WAPDA to choose a sole arbitrator. It gave first notice to WAPDA under section 8(1) to appoint a sole arbitrator, but WAPDA suggested resolving the matter through negotiation. However, the negotiation proved abortive. The contractor gave a second notice to WAPDA and then filed an application to the court for the appointment of the arbitrator. WAPDA took the plea that the matter of appointment of the arbitrator was then time-barred because the Contractor completed the works in 1961 and filed the application for the appointment of the arbitrator in 1965, which was far beyond the three-year limitation period stipulated under Article 181 of the Limitation Act. Such claim from WAPDA was premised on the argument that the 'right to claim arbitration like the right to sue arises, as soon as the claim becomes due and payable but refused'. The court held that:

> It is important to bear in mind the distinction between 'cause or action' giving rise to a claim and 'the right to sue' on the basis of that claim. 'Cause of action' has been generally defined as covering every fact, which if traversed, it would be necessary for the plaintiff to prove in order to support his right to the judgment of the Court. This is clearly different from 'right to sue'. For instance, a person may have cause of action against the Government or the Railway Administration but

511. *Communication and Works Department v. Pavital/Pivato Joint Venture and others,* 2003 CLC 1798, *See also Travel Agents Association of Pakistan v. Pak Travel Agency (Pvt) Ltd.,* 1999 CLC 1962.
512. *Mian Fazal Muhammad (Deceased) through his Legal Heirs v. Province of West Pakistan and others,* 1975 SCMR 312.
513. *Adaptive Solutions (Pvt.) Ltd. v. Utility Stores Corporation, Islamabad,* 2010 YLR 1618.
514. PLD 1970 Lahore 398.

> will have no right to sue unless gives a notice of suit under section 50. C. P. C. or 177 of the Railways Act, 1890, as the case may be. Strictly speaking, notice does not form part of the cause of action though it is necessary preliminary for the suit. Similarly Order XXII, rules 1 and 2, C. P. C. speak of survival of 'right to sue' in contradistinction with 'cause of action' in section 80 of the Code upon which the 'right to sue' is based. In the instant case, it is true that the contractor's claim rests on the plea that he completed the execution of works and therefore performed his part of the contract on the 1st of June 1961, but this is not to say that simultaneously with the completion of works, the right to apply for the appointment of the arbitrator under section 8 of the, Arbitration Act also accrued in his favour. The date when the 'right to apply' for the arbitrators' appointment accrued that the contractor will have to be determined with reference to the provisions of the section 8.[515]

The case of *Government of Pakistan v. Shafsal Enterprises Government* is even more elaborative in which a contract was terminated in 1977. The respondent gave legal notice to the petitioner on 20 February 1990, and an application for the appointment of an arbitrator was filed in the same year. The petitioner contended that the three-year period for filing the application expired in 1980; therefore, the said application was time-barred. The High Court concluded that under Article 181 of the Limitation Act 1908, read with section 8 of the 1940 Act, allowed a party to make an application for the appointment of an arbitrator when the time period mentioned in the notice lapsed and not at any time before that. Therefore, the application was held to be within time.[516]

8.9. UMPIRE AND CHAIRMAN

Both umpire and chairman perform the function of arbitrator, but they are different from each other. A chairman (also Sarpanch or panch in Urdu) works with other arbitrators without any distinct and separable office from other arbitrators.[517] Chairmen are not required to record independent reasons of their own in the award, and they could agree with the reasons of any of the other arbitrators.[518] A chairman is like other members of the tribunal but different from the umpire.

The ordinary meaning of umpire is a person who settles disagreements. In the sense in which this term is used in the 1940 Act, the term 'umpire' denotes a person who is to settle any difference that may arise between the arbitrators 'which cannot be settled without having gone through the entire record with independent and diligent application of mind'.[519] In this way, an umpire is separate and superimposed over the other arbitrators and acts only when the two arbitrators have a difference of opinion and the decision of the umpire would play a final role. Where the arbitrators have

515. *The West Pakistan Water and Development Authority v. Omar Sons Ltd.*, PLD 1970 Lahore 398.
516. *Government of Pakistan v. Shafsal Enterprises Government Contractors*, 2002 YLR 2528.
517. *Lahore Improvement Trust v. Al-Azam Limited*, 1991 CLC 1307.
518. *Lahore Development Authority and another v. Alicon Limited, Lahore*, PLD 2014 SC 494; *Lahore Development Authority v. Alicon Limited*, 2001 MLD 925.
519. *Muhammad Farooq Shah v. Shakirullah*, 2006 SCMR 1657. *See also Saeed Ahmad v. Niaz Ahmad and others*, 2012 CLC 1015.

agreed, then there would be no need for the appointment of an umpire. Therefore, normally it is stipulated in the arbitration agreement that in case of difference between the two arbitrators, an umpire will be appointed. However, where the arbitration clause speaks of the appointment of a third arbitrator by the two arbitrators, for instance, a third arbitrator would not be considered an umpire.[520]

The umpire is not an arbitrator but functions in lieu of an arbitrator. On the other hand, the Sarpanch or Chairman is like other arbitrators (panches) of the arbitral tribunal with the duty to sit with the tribunal as its Chairman. In one case instance, there was an agreement providing the names of three persons – the appointment of two panches and one Sarpanch – stating that the decision given by these three would be binding on the parties. This agreement did not say that the Sarpanch would act only in case of difference between the panches; therefore, the Sarpanch would not be an umpire.[521]

8.10. ARBITRATOR, REFEREE AND LOCAL COMMISSION

The terms arbitrator, referee and local commission were elaborated in *Nazir Ahmad and others v. Muhammad Qasim and others*.[522] The law contemplates different persons to whom a matter may be referred. First, the matter is referred to an arbitrator who decides a matter through judicial proceedings. Second, a local commission may be appointed under Order 26 Rule 9 of the Civil Procedure Code[523] to conduct local investigations. The local commission is appointed to only obtain explanations and clarifications with regard to matters in confusion because there may be occasions when the evidence on record does not furnish a clear picture. In this situation, the court has been given the power to appoint a local commission that elucidates, clarifies and explains the matter for the court. Third, a referee may be appointed under Article 33[524] of the Qanun-e-Shahadat Order 1984 in order to make statements on the basis of individual knowledge. Sometimes the parties rely on the statement of a third party in their litigation. The law says that if the matter is left or referred to the statement of a third party, such a statement would be considered as an admission by the parties to litigation. The illustration attached to Article 33 clears this point, which says: 'Go and ask C. C knows all about it'. The status of the referee is more of a witness than a local commission or arbitrator. Article 33 has four ingredients, as was explained by the court:

520. *Lahore Improvement Trust v. Al-Azam Limited*, 1991 CLC 1307.
521. *Abdul Hamid v. H. M. Qureshi*, PLD 1957 SC 145. This case was followed in *Abdul Ghani v. Inayat Karim and others*, PLD 1960 SC 98. *See also Oudh Judicial Commissioner's Court in the case of Lala Abdus Samad* (17 IC 320).
522. *Nazir Ahmad and others v. Muhammad Qasim and others*, 2004 SCMR 1292.
523. Order 26, rule 9 of the C.P.C. provides that 'in any suit in which the Court deems a local investigation to be requisite or proper for the purpose of elucidating any matter in dispute, or of ascertaining the market value of any property, or the amount or any mesne profits or damages or annual net profits, the Court may issue a commission to such person as it thinks fit directing him to make such investigation and to report thereon to the Court'.
524. Article 33 entitled as 'admission by persons expressly referred to by party to suit' reads as 'statements made by persons to whom a party to the suit has expressly referred for information in reference to matter in dispute are admissions'.

> First that some party must have referred the matter to a third person. Second, that the reference must be for information and third, that the referee must make a statement qua such information and lastly that such statement shall be deemed to be an admission by the party who expressly referred to such third person for information.

Controversies normally arise as to whether the third person to whom a matter is referred is an arbitrator or referee. It becomes important to elaborate on this point. The referee makes the statement on the basis of his knowledge or belief and is not allowed to record evidence or conduct an inquiry by inspecting the site and speak with people to verify his belief or knowledge. The court then pronounces a decree on the basis of the referee's statement.[525] In *Muhammad Ashraf v. Abdur Rehman*, in order to give a statement on a property dispute between the parties, the referee visited the site, examined the witnesses, called for the settlement record and examined it. The court held that with these functions, he was no longer a referee, and his statement was, in fact, an award which he was not authorized to make.[526] However, it is not forbidden for a referee to acquire further information from any corner while preparing his report to augment and supplement his knowledge.[527]

To ascertain the nature of the appointment so that the relevant law should be applied to his actions, the conduct of the parties (agreement) and the order of the court are important.[528] In *Ghulam Farid Khan v. Muhammad Hanif Khan and others*,[529] the Supreme Court held that where the task assigned to the referee was not to provide personal expertise, but rather a 'faisala' (decision) in respect of the difference between the parties, he would not be considered a referee despite the use of the term 'referee' in the agreement. This is so because Article 33 of the Qanun-e-Shahadat Order 1984 refers to statements affording information and not to a decision entailing judicial determination of the conflicts between the parties.

8.11. CONCLUSION

The inapplicability of Pakistani courts' power in respect of the appointment, removal, and reappointment in case of foreign-seated arbitration is conceivable, for which the primary reason may be the inability of the courts to enforce their decision abroad. So far as arbitration seated in Pakistan is concerned, it is assumed that the parties have been given due power and autonomy to appoint and remove arbitrators, and section 5 (revocation of authority of arbitrator) and section 9 serve as very good examples in this regard. However, when they fail to make such an appointment, the court's support is available for them. This is important for parties to bear in mind the type of person – arbitrator, referee or commission – they are going to appoint.

525. *Tariq Aslam Sheikh Tooni v. Haq Nawaz*, 2005 CLC 1949.
526. *Muhammad Ashraf v. Abdur Rehman*, 1993 CLC 1875.
527. *Muhammad Aslam and others v. Muhammad Ajmal and others*, 2011 MLD 285.
528. *Zulifqar Ali Shah and others v. Muhammad Hussain and others*, 2002 YLR 1560; *Mirza Muhammad Siddique v. Muhammad Abdullah*, 1989 MLD 54.
529. *Ghulam Farid Khan v. Muhammad Hanif Khan and others*, 1990 SCMR 763.

CHAPTER 9

Pakistani Legal Regime on Interim Measures in Arbitration

One of the reasons for the failure of arbitration in Pakistan is the inefficacious law on interim measures. A party can get these measures from the court only through a technical procedure in an environment where the courts have a tendency to go into the merits of a dispute at this preliminary stage. Pakistan should give the arbitrator power to issue interim measures, including ex parte, enforceable against non-parties. Since the conferral of such powers to a private person, not appointed as a judge by the state, is not new in Pakistan, it is suggested to incorporate this approach either as a precedential or statutory law, which is not only in line with the amendments in the UNCITRAL Model Law regarding interim measures as were made in 2006 but is also compatible with Pakistani legal culture.

9.1. INTRODUCTION

Courts frequently issue interim measures to maintain the status quo between the parties until the final adjudication of the dispute, or to preserve the assets forming the subject matter of the dispute, or for some other purposes under relevant domestic laws. Commercial arbitration as a parallel and a comprehensive dispute resolution mechanism contains almost all the dimensions present in litigation. For that reason, it is reasonable for a party, desiring to resolve its dispute more expeditiously through arbitration, to expect the remedy of these measures from the arbitrator.[530] To meet this

530. Jason Fry, *Interim Measures of Protection: Recent Developments and the Way Ahead* 6(5) Int'l Arb. L. Rev. 153-160 (2003).

prospect, the arbitrator's authority to issue interim measures has been accepted by most jurisdictions,[531] which is evident from pertinent laws[532] and arbitration rules.[533]

Unfortunately, the 1940 Act of Pakistan does not confer this power on the arbitrator as only the court is vested with it. Moreover, the procedure to get interim measures from the court is riddled with formalities and complexities. In this chapter, the problems in the 1940 Act with regard to interim measures and their effects on the arbitration process in Pakistan are elaborated in the light of Pakistani judgments, and some recommendations are made so that the expectation to bring Pakistani law in conformity with international practices is met.

9.2. LEGAL REGIME ON INTERIM MEASURES

The scheme of power conferred on a court to issue interim measures in support of arbitration being conducted in Pakistan is laid down in section 41 of the 1940 Act, read with its Second Schedule and Order 39, Rules 1 & 2 of the CPC. If the court refuses to grant the interim order, there is no appeal; only revision is allowed.[534]

Section 41 reads as follows:

> Subject to the provisions of this Act and of rules made thereunder:
>
> (a) the provisions of the Code of Civil Procedure, 1908, shall apply to all proceedings, before the Court, to all appeals, under this Act, and
> (b) the Court shall have, for the purpose of, and in relation to, **arbitration proceedings**, the same power of making orders in respect of any of the matters set out in the Second Schedule[535] as it has for the purpose of, and in relation to, any proceedings before the Court:

531. Italian Code of Civil Procedure, Article 818 and Greek Code of Civil Procedure, Article 889 are exceptions in that regard.
532. UNCITRAL Model Law Ch. IV A. Interim Measures and Preliminary Orders; section 1014 of the German Code of Civil Procedure, Ch. 10; Article 183 of the Swiss Private International Law Act 1987; Article 1051(1) of the Netherlands Arbitration Act 1986; sections 38-39 of the 1996 English Arbitration Act 1996; section 2GB of the Hong Kong Arbitration Ordinance, 1990; the countries like Australia, Mexico, Russian Federation, Peru, India, Hungry and Bulgaria also incorporated Article 17 of UNCITRAL Model Law empowering the arbitrator. For more detail *see* Tijana Kojovic, *Court Enforcement of Arbitral Decision on Provisional Relief*, 18(5) J. Int'l Arb. 511-532 (2001).
533. Article 25 of LCIA Arbitration Rules; Article 23(1) of ICC Arbitration Rules; Article 21 of AAA International Rules of 1997. *See also* Tijana Kojovic, *Court Enforcement of Arbitral Decision on Provisional Relief*, 18(5) J. Int'l Arb. 511-532 (2001).
534. *Petrosin Products (Pvt.) Limited v. Government of Pakistan*, 2000 MLD 785 Lahore; NLR 1980 AC 542. In the following cases the decision of the trial court was challenged through revision in the High Court. *Attock Industrial Products Limited v. Heavy Mechanical Complex (Pvt.) Limited*, 1999 MLD 1876 Lahore; *Al-Khan Construction Company (Pvt.) Ltd. v. Pak American Fertilizers Limited, Sikandarabad, District Mianwali*, 2000 CLC 1053 Lahore; *Lahore Stock Exchange Ltd. v. Hassan Associates*, 2010 MLD 800 Lahore; *Syed Muddasar Shah v. Managing Director, N. W. F. P. Forest Development Corporation, Peshawar* etc., 1999 MLD 736 Peshawar; *Sunrise Textiles Limited v. Tomen Corporation and others*, 1994 CLC 2000 Lahore; *Saeeda Bang and others v. Mian Muhammad Amin*, 1995 MLD 187 Lahore; *Hatta Construction Company (Pvt.) Ltd v. Faisalabad Development Authority, Faisalabad*, 1995 CLC 1877 Lahore; *Fareed Yaqub Ali v. Haji Muhammad Tahir*, PLD 1989 Quetta 16.
535. The Second Schedule – Power of Court:

> Provided that nothing in clause (b) shall be taken to prejudice any power which may be vested in an arbitrator or umpire for making orders with respect to any of such matters.[536]

9.2.1. Time When Power of Court to Issue Interim Measures Accrues

Though section 41(b) of the 1940 Act confers powers on the court to pass measures as specified in the Second Schedule of the 1940 Act for the purpose of and in relation to arbitration proceedings,[537] two interpretations of section 41(b) may be observed as to what point of time the court is granted the power to award these measures.

9.2.1.1. First Interpretation of 'Arbitration Proceedings'

The first likely interpretation of section 41(b) may be made by discerning the judgment of the Punjab High Court along with other relevant authorities. In *Muhammad Akbar v. The Province of Punjab*, the Punjab High Court said that:

> Clause (a) specifies the procedure which a Court acting under the Arbitration Act 1940 may follow while clause (b) speaks of the powers of the Court with respect to

---

1 The preservation, interim custody or sale of any goods which are subject matter of the reference.
2 Securing the amount in difference in the reference.
3 The detention, preservation or inspection of any property or thing which is the subject of the reference or as to which any question may arise therein and authorizing for any of the aforesaid purposes any person to enter upon or into any land or building in the possession or any party to the reference, or authorizing any samples to be taken or any observation to be made, or experiment to be tried, which may be necessary or expedient for the purpose of obtaining full information or evidence.
4 Interim in junction or the appointment of a receiver.
5 The appointment of a guardian for a minor or person of unsound mind for the purposes of arbitration proceedings.

536. Section 41 of the 1940 Act.
537. *Jamia Industries Ltd. v. Pakistan Refinery Ltd., Karachi,* PLD 1976 Karachi 644; *Attock Industrial Products Limited v. Heavy Mechanical Complex (Pvt.) Limited,* 1999 MLD 1876 Lahore; *Pakistan Water and Power Development Authority, Hyderabad v. China International Water and Electric Corporation, Karachi,* PLD 1999 Karachi 235; *Engineer Khalid Rashid Qureshi v. Institution of Engineers, Pakistan,* 1999 CLC 288 Karachi; Mrs *Rubby Hameedullah etc. v. Dr Arif etc.,* 2010 YLR 3331 Karachi; *Province of Punjab v. Mian Fakhar And Company,* 2007 YLR 3181 Lahore; *Shoukat and Raza Limited Karachi v. Karachi Development Authority etc.,* 1980 CLC 346; *Asadullah Khan v. Karachi Shipyard Engineering Works,* 1979 CLC 625; *Commodities Trading International Corporation v. Trading Corporation of Pakistan Ltd.,* 1987 CLC 2063 Karachi; *Abdur Rauf v. Mrs Zubeda Kaleem etc.,* 2001 CLC 664 Lahore; *Sunrise Textiles Limited v. Tomen Corporation etc.* 1994 CLC 2000 Lahore; *Hatta Construction Company (Pvt.) Ltd. v. Faisalabad Development Authority, Faisalabad,* 1995 CLC 1877 Lahore; Civil Revision No. 113 of 1988 *Fareed Yaqub Ali v. Haji Muhammad Tahir* – Civil Revision No. 103 of 1988 *Haji Muhammad Tahir v. Fareed Yaqub,* PLD 1989 Quetta 16; *Muhammad Akbar v. The Province of Punjab,* PLD 1974 Lahore 231; *Island Textile Mills Ltd., Karachi v. V/O Technoexpert,* 1979 CLC 307 Karachi.

> arbitration proceedings. There are no words in clause (b) or in the entire section which may be taken as limiting the expression 'arbitration proceedings' occurring in clause (b) to such proceedings to have been initiated through the intervention of a Court. The words 'the same power' as occurring in clause (b), when read in conjunction with the words 'as it has', make it abundantly clear that clause (b) has reference to *proceedings other than those which may be pending before a Court.* Otherwise clause (b) will be entirely redundant as clause (a) has already provided for the procedure which a Court is to follow while exercising its functions under the Act. In the presence of clause (a) it is entirely unnecessary to confer some specific powers on a Court under clause (b), for these are already available to it under clause (a).[538]

This means that the term '*arbitration proceedings*' as employed in section 41(b) does not include proceedings pending before the court. Therefore, when an arbitrator is appointed either by the parties or by the court and some action is taken before that arbitrator, for example, a statement of claim is made to him, only then are arbitration proceedings deemed to have commenced.[539] The time of commencement of these proceedings is at the point in time a court acquires the authority to afford interim measures under section 41(b) and not prior to that. For this reason, in *Shaukat and Raza Limited Karachi v. Karachi Development Authority*,[540] the Sindh High Court rejected the contention taken by the applicant that, under section 37(2), arbitration proceedings commence when a party serves a notice on the other party for the appointment of an arbitrator and hence the court gets the power to issue interim measures on the eve of serving of such notice by one party to the other.[541] In this case,[542] the applicant sent a letter on 18 September 1979 to the respondents' Superintending Engineer requiring him to refer the dispute according to the arbitration agreement to one of the four persons named in the arbitration agreement within fifteen days after the dispute arose. But before the expiry of fifteen days for such appointment, on 2 October 1979, the applicant filed an application under section 41(b), read with the Second Schedule of the 1940 Act, and Order 39, Rules 1 & 2 of CPC, praying that the Respondent or any of his employees and agents should be restrained from the encashment of the guarantees. When the respondent raised a preliminary point regarding the maintainability of the application by arguing that no arbitration proceedings had started so as to attract the applicability of section 41(b), the applicant replied that the arbitration proceedings had been initiated under section 37(3) as soon as the notice for the appointment of the arbitrator was served on the respondent. Section 37(3) says:

> For the purposes of this section and of the Limitation Act, 1908, an arbitration shall be deemed to be commenced when one party to the arbitration agreement serves

538. *Muhammad Akbar v. The Province of Punjab*, PLD 1974 Lahore 231.
539. *Commodities Trading International Corporation v. Trading Corporation of Pakistan Ltd.*, 1987 CLC 2063 Karachi; *Asadullah Khan v. Karachi Shipyard Engineering Works*, 1979 CLC 625; *Ab Sukab v. M/S. Ghee Corporation of Pakistan*, PLD 1993 Karachi 508; *Shaukat and Raza Limited Karachi v. Karachi Development Authority*, 1980 CLC 346.
540. *Shaukat and Raza Limited Karachi v. Karachi Development Authority*, 1980 CLC 346.
541. *Ibid. See also Ab Sukab v. Ghee Corporation of Pakistan*, PLD 1993 Karachi 508.
542. *Shaukat and Raza Limited Karachi v. Karachi Development Authority*, 1980 CLC 346.

> on the other parties thereto a notice requiring the appointment of an arbitrator, or where the arbitration agreement provides that the reference shall be to a person named or designated in the agreement, requiring that the difference be submitted to the person so named or designated.[543]

The court rejected the submission of the applicant. It held that the applicant had ignored the controlling words of '*For the purposes of this section and of the Limitation Act, 1908*' given at the inception of section 37(3), which spells out that the commencement of proceedings by serving a notice to the other party would be only for the purposes of this section given in subsections 2, 4 and 5 and for the purpose of the Limitation Act 1908.[544] But if the respondent had not appointed the arbitrator even after the expiry of fifteen days, the applicant would have access to the remedy of filing an application under section 8 or 20 of the 1940 Act for the appointment of an arbitrator or for the filing of an arbitration agreement respectively.

The procedure for filing the arbitration agreement under section 20 was discussed in *Mujtaba Hussain Siddiqui v. Sultan Ahmed.*[545] Under this procedure, the application is registered as a suit in the court with a prayer that the agreement should be filed there. Then, the court issues the notices to all the parties to the agreement other than the applicants, requiring them to show cause as to why the agreement should not be filed. If the parties fail to show any sufficient or valid cause, the court orders the filing of the

543. Section 37(3) of the 1940 Act.
544. The provisions regarding the time for the commencement of arbitral proceedings have been inserted in the arbitration laws of various jurisdictions but these concern the start of the limitation period. For example, *see* the Swiss Private International Law Act 1987, Ch. 12, Article 182, which states: 'The arbitration proceeding shall be pending from the moment one of the parties files a claim before the sole arbitrator or the arbitrators designated in the arbitration agreement or, in the absence of such designation, if one of the parties institutes the procedure for the appointment of the arbitral tribunal.' Similarly, English Arbitration Act 1996, section 14 says: Commencement of arbitral proceedings:

    (1) The parties are free to agree when arbitral proceedings are to be regarded as commenced for the purposes of this Part and for the purposes of the Limitation Acts.
    (2) If there is no such agreement the following provisions apply.
    (3) Where the arbitrator is named or designated in the arbitration agreement, arbitral proceedings are commenced in respect of a matter when one party serves on the other party or parties a notice in writing requiring him or them to submit that matter to the person so named or designated.
    (4) Where the arbitrator or arbitrators are to be appointed by the parties, arbitral proceedings are commenced in respect of a matter when one party serves on the other party or parties notice in writing requiring him or them to appoint an arbitrator or to agree to the appointment of an arbitrator in respect of that matter.
    (5) Where the arbitrator or arbitrators are to be appointed by a person other than a party to the proceedings, arbitral proceedings are commenced in respect of a matter when one party gives notice in writing to that person requesting him to make the appointment in respect of that matter.

    But it should be noted that these provisions are regarding the time for limitation and not for the ascertainment of point of time where a court is empowered to issue the interim orders. The corresponding provision in the 1940 Act is section 37 which is for the purpose of Limitation Act.
545. *Mujtaba Hussain Siddiqui v. Sultan Ahmed* 2005 YLR 2709 Karachi. *See also Commodities Trading International Corporation v. Trading Corporation of Pakistan Ltd.*, 1987 CLC 2063 Karachi; *Province of Baluchistan v. Sardar Muhammad Usman Khan*, PLD 1987 Quetta 33.

agreement and refers the parties to arbitration. Afterwards, if the parties to an arbitration agreement fail to appoint the arbitrator, the court by itself passes the orders for the appointment of the arbitrator. Once the arbitrator is appointed, the arbitration proceedings commence under the provisions of the 1940 Act and with this, the application under section 20 is disposed of. According to the first interpretation, at this point in time, the court should acquire the power to issue interim measures.

Although the procedure for interim measures is problematic and lengthy, this interpretation of section 41(b) seems to be correct when considering these decisions. This construction explains that if a party wants interim measures from a court, it should first fulfil the condition precedent for empowering the court, i.e., the commencement of '*arbitration proceedings*' in relation to which the court has to issue the measures; and to commence the '*arbitration proceedings*', the parties should appoint the arbitrators either by themselves or by the court. The dilemmas in procedure are not only due to problems with appropriate interpretations but also because of the wording of section 41(b).

9.2.1.2. Second Interpretation of 'Arbitration Proceedings'

To reduce the trouble of procedure, the second interpretation, which is flexible and prevalent, was forwarded by the Sindh High Court in *Commodities Trading International Corporation v. Trading Corporation of Pakistan Ltd.*[546] The court said that if proceedings are pending neither before the arbitrator nor before the court, the court will not have the power to issue interim measures. But if proceedings are pending before the arbitrator, the application under section 41(b) is maintainable. Similarly, if no proceedings are pending before the arbitrator but the proceedings under any provision of the 1940 Act are pending before the court, where for instance, a party filed an application or petition under any provision of the 1940 Act, such as under sections 8,[547] 9,[548] 11[549] or 20,[550] then also the application under section 41(b) is maintainable, and the court will acquire authority to issue the orders enumerated in the Second Schedule of the 1940 Act. In this way, the court seems to have concluded that at the time of commencement of '*proceedings*' before the court under any provision of the 1940 Act, it is granted the power to issue the measures. It may be inferred from this conclusion that any order issued in proceedings initiated before the court under any provision of the 1940 Act would be '*for the purpose of, and in relation to, arbitration proceedings*', even if these '*arbitration proceedings*' are not in existence at the time of making of such provisional measures.

546. *Commodities Trading International Corporation v. Trading Corporation of Pakistan Ltd.*, 1987 CLC 2063 Karachi.
547. Section 8 speaks about the power of courts to appoint arbitrators or umpires.
548. Section 9 concerns the power of parties to appoint new arbitrators or, in certain cases, a sole arbitrator. *Commodities Trading International Corporation v. Trading Corporation of Pakistan Ltd.*, 1987 CLC 2063 Karachi.
549. Section 11 is about power of courts to remove arbitrators or umpires in certain circumstances.
550. Section 20 is about the application to file the arbitration agreement.

In *Ovex Technologies (Pvt.) Ltd. v. CM Pak (Pvt.) Ltd. and others,*[551] the Islamabad High Court held that the jurisdiction of the court for interim measures can be invoked before the commencement of arbitration proceedings, during the pendency of such proceedings, or after the award is made.

9.2.1.3. *A Flawed Interpretation?*

Although this interpretation is practically preferable for arbitration, it seems to be flawed. The court, relying on *Shaukat and Raza Limited case,*[552] first explained the meaning of '*proceedings*' generally by saying:

> There cannot be any proceedings without there being an arbitrator or court or authority being in existence to decide the claim or dispute and proceedings can be said to have commenced only when some action is taken before an arbitrator or court or authority for example filing a statement of claim or dispute before an arbitrator or a plaint before a court.

By explaining '*arbitration proceedings*' specifically, and the time for their commencement, the court said that '*in the instant case no arbitrator has yet been appointed and no reference has been made and therefore, it cannot be said that arbitration proceedings have commenced*'. From these statements, it is clear that '*proceedings*' is not a relevant term for the interpretation of section 41(b) of the 1940 Act, but it is the term '*arbitration proceedings*' that is relevant, and their commencement time should have been relied upon to define the time of attainment of powers because powers conferred on a court for interim measures is to be utilized for the purpose of and in relation to '*arbitration proceedings*' and not in respect of mere '*proceedings*'. But the court seems to have extended the ambit of '*for the purpose of, and in relation to, arbitration proceedings*' by including in it the range of '*proceedings*' being conducted in the courts under any provision of the 1940 Act, which is seemingly not appropriate.

Thus, where the two applications are filed, for instance, one under section 20 and the other under section 41(b), an application for interim orders will be entertained if the application under section 20 is proved to be maintainable. Ironically, the procedure to be followed to ascertain the maintainability of applications under section 20 is too lengthy, which is evident from the discussion in *Jamia Industries Ltd. v. Pakistan Refineries Ltd., Karachi,*[553] although not as lengthy as the procedure given in respect of the first interpretation.

9.2.2. Tendency of Courts to Ascertain Merits

While deciding an application for interim measures, a court should not express its opinion on all issues involved or virtually decide the suit.[554] All such assessments are

551. *Ovex Technologies (Pvt.) Ltd. v. CM Pak (Pvt.) Ltd. and others*, 2020 CLD 15.
552. *Shaukat and Raza Limited Karachi v. Karachi Development Authority*, 1980 CLC 346.
553. *Jamia Industries Ltd. v. Pakistan Refineries Ltd., Karachi* PLD 1976 Kar. 644.
554. *Government of Sindh and others v. Saiful Haq Hashmi and others*, 1993 SCMR 956; *Mehr Muhammad Tariq v. Muhammad Shafi and others*, 1986 SCMR 1976; *The National Electric Fans*

of a temporary nature and do not bind the court trying the suit.[555] However, the courts sometimes show a tendency to go into the merits of the dispute and into the interpretation of the agreement while deciding preliminary matters. It is the settled position in Pakistani case law that the court does not have authority to discuss or conclude matters relating to the contract or dispute and questions of facts because this would amount to the usurpation of the arbitrator's jurisdiction.[556]

However, infractions of this principle can be seen from the courts. For example, in *Attock Industrial Products Ltd v. Heavy Mechanical Complex (Pvt.) Ltd*,[557] the Punjab High Court refused to issue injunctions to restrain the petitioner from the encashment of bank guarantees placed at his disposal by the respondent. The court held that the terms of guarantees made it clear that the guarantees should be construed independent of the primary contract, and so the petitioner should not be obligated to hold himself off from such encashment until the arbitral resolution of the dispute. The court went further, and in respect of the allegations of default in fulfilling the contractual obligations and of the breach thereof by the parties, it concluded that the fault was on the side of the respondent. The same propensity was exhibited by the High Court in another case, although it was remedied by the Supreme Court in *Standard Construction Co. (Pvt.) Ltd v. Pakistan Through Secretary M/O Communications*.[558] In this case, the dispute was again regarding the encashment of guarantees. The Supreme Court did not agree with the approach taken by the High Court and said that:

Manufacturers (Regd.), Gujrat v. S. Muhammad Din & Sons Ltd., Lahore, 1980 SCMR 97; *Marghub Siddiqi v. Hamid Ahmad Khan and others*, 1974 SCMR 519; *Farid Ahmad v. Ghiasuddin Chowdhury and others*, 1968 SCMR 88; *Shah Jehan Khan v. Fazal-ur-Rehman Khan and another*, 2001 CLC 1695; *Islamic Republic of Pakistan through Secretary, Ministry of Defence v. Messrs Masood Enterprises through Managing Director*, 2001 YLR 327; *M/S. International Trade and Marketing through Proprietor v. Integra Trade And Marketing and others*, 1993 CLC 2223; *The Karachi Catholic Cooperative Housing Society Ltd. v. Mrs. Daphne Mary Mendonca and others*, 1990 MLD 2232; *Syed Muhammad Khurshid Abbas Gardezi and others v. Province of Punjab and others*, 1988 CLC 362; *Sub-Divisional Canal Officer v. Fazal Ahmed*, 1982 CLC 59; *Ata Ullah Khan and Another v. Mst. Ghulam Zohran and another*, 1970 SCMR 654; *Mst. Khurshid Begum and others v. Inam Rabbani and another*, 1979 CLC 570; *Abdur Rahman Mobashir and others v. Syed Amir Ali Shah Bokhari and others*, PLD 1978 Lahore 113; *Aboo Noor Muhammad v. General Iron & Steel Works Ltd., Karachi*, PLD 1973 Karachi 234; *Dr. Md. Mobarak Ali v. Prop. Md. Allarakha*, PLD 1971 Dacca 293; *Oil And Gas Development Corporation v. Lt.-Col. Shujauddin Ahmed*, PLD 1970 Karachi 332; *Messrs Sui Northern Gas Pipelines Company Limited v. Messrs Pakistan Cement Industries*, PLD 1968 Lahore 876.

555. *Abdul Hamid Khan and others v. Mst. Rajo Bibi and others*, 1990 SCMR 911; *Mehr Muhammad Tariq v. Muhammad Shafi and others*, 1986 SCMR 1976; *Safdar Ahmad v. Malik Ahmad Khan and others*, 2003 MLD 1337; *The Karachi Catholic Cooperative Housing Society Ltd. v. Mrs. Daphne Mary Mendonca and others*, 1990 MLD 2232; *Messrs Karachi Gas Co. Laid., Karachi v. Messrs Fancy Foundation*, PLD 1977 Karachi 191.

556. *Project Director, Balochistan Minor Irrigation and Agricultural Development Project, Quetta Cantt v. Murad Ali & Company*, 1999 SCMR 121; *Jamia Industries Ltd. v. Messrs Pakistan Refineries Ltd., Karachi*, PLD 1976 Karachi 644.

557. *Attock Industrial Products Ltd. v. Heavy Mechanical Complex (Pvt.) Ltd.*, 1999 MLD 1876 Lahore.

558. *Standard Construction Company (Pvt.) Limited v. Pakistan Through Secretary M/O Communications*, 2010 SCMR 524.

> High Court while referring matter to arbitrator, had gone deep and discussed minutely various clauses, terms and conditions of agreement and other relevant documents and their effect for arriving at its conclusion ... (because) ... after referring dispute to arbitrator it was not appropriate and was uncalled for High Court to discuss the agreement as such findings of High Court would influence proceedings before Arbitrator.[559]

While disapproving the findings of the High Court, the Supreme Court declined to affirm or disaffirm the findings of the High Court because it was not possible to comment without interpreting the terms of the agreement.

9.2.3. Three Conclusions on the Pakistani Regime of Interim Measures

From the above discussion, three points may be concluded. *First*, according to the first interpretation, the court does not have the power to issue interim orders before the commencement of requisite arbitration proceedings. This is problematic because the main argument in support of the conferral of power on the court to issue interim orders is that the arbitral tribunal may not have been constituted and that any of the parties to the agreement may be in dire need of interim orders. Therefore, the applicant party should have at least one resort to court so that the arbitral process may not be undermined by the other party. But the 1940 Act overlooks this justification and leaves the party remediless where interim measures are sought before the appointment of arbitrators. *Second*, according to the second interpretation, if a party resorts to the court to secure interim measures, it will also have to pursue a very lengthy and technical procedure to initiate the requisite proceedings under any provision of the 1940 Act to entitle itself as well as to empower the court for awarding such measures. A party may urgently need the interim orders to maintain the status quo or to preserve the subject matter of arbitration, or to preserve the evidence with an apprehension in its mind that the other party may destroy it or change it as soon as possible. But these objectives of exigency cannot be fulfilled if the protracted procedure under the 1940 Act is followed. *Third*, after the commencement of requisite proceedings, if a party asks the court for interim orders, there is a strong fear that the court will go into the substance of the dispute. This may influence the opinion of the arbitrator, which will impair the arbitral process ultimately.

When all the three points are deliberated collectively, it becomes patent that interim measures may be obtained only by following a long-drawn-out and technical procedure. This is against the objectives of the 1940 Act as outlined in various judgments of the courts, whereby the 1940 Act is to save the parties from formalities, delay, technicalities, expense and the ordeal of litigation and to resolve their disputes through arbitration speedily.[560]

---

559. *Ibid.*
560. *Abdul Salam v. Muhammad Yaqoob* 1999 CLC 1005; *Shafi Corporation Ltd. v. Government of Pakistan Through Director-General of Defence Purchase, Ministry of Defence, Karachi*, PLD 1994 Karachi 127; *Khalid Rasheed Qureshi v. Institution of Engineers Pakistan*, 1999 CLC 288 Karachi.

9.2.4. Powerlessness of Arbitrator to Issue Interim Measure

This predicament could have been remedied to a great extent if the arbitrator had been accorded the powers to issue the interim measures, but this is unfortunately not the case. This is clear from the absence of any such provision in the 1940 Act and also from the judgment[561] of the Sindh High Court, which pronounced expressly that the arbitrator does not have any power to issue such orders. However, the arbitrator has been empowered to make an interim award under section 27 as follows:

> (1) Unless a different intention appears in the arbitration agreement, the arbitrators or umpire may, if they think fit, make an interim award.
> (2) All references in this Act to an award shall include references to an interim award made under subsection (1).

Interim awards are different from interim measures, and to get an interim award, the party will have to follow the same procedure as is followed for the final award.[562] So, it is lucid that the interim award is not an effective remedy for the party who wants it on an urgent basis. Due to these reasons, the 1940 Act proved to be ineffective and outdated for arbitration in general and for interim measures in particular.

9.3. PRINCIPLES GOVERNING THE GRANT OF INTERIM MEASURE BY COURTS

The principles governing the issuance of interim measures in relation to arbitration are the same as those which are applied by the court in litigation matters under Order 39, Rules 1 & 2.[563] Therefore, to get interim measures from the court, the applicant has to prove that he has a prima facie case, the balance of convenience lies in his favour, and he will suffer an irreparable loss if the interim measures are refused.[564]

For instance, in *Omv Maurice Energy Limited v. Ocean Pakistan Limited*, the petitioner contended that it could not carry out the exploration work without the joint decision of the parties, which had working interests in the operations, whereas the respondents' non-participation in the meeting intended to halt the operations. This contention was further supported by the fact that due to the non-attendance of such a meeting by the respondent, the government's representative equally did not attend the meetings. Hence, the petitioner prayed for permission to carry out the exploration and

561. *Island Textile Mills Ltd. Karachi v. Technoexpert*, 1979 CLC 307 Karachi.
562. *Burjorjee Cowasjee & Co v. New Hampshire Insurance Company*, 1992 CLC 1269 Karachi.
563. *Dewan Petroleum (Pvt.) Ltd. v. Oil and Gas Investment Ltd.*, 2019 CLC 1486; *Omv Maurice Energy Limited v. Ocean Pakistan Limited*, 2012 CLD 619.
564. *Dewan Petroleum (Pvt.) Ltd. v. Oil and Gas Investment Ltd.*, 2019 CLC 1486; *Puri Terminal Ltd. v. Government of Pakistan*, 2004 SCMR 1092; *Imtiaz Ahmad v. Muhammad Shoaib Shah*, 2015 CLC 1121; *Mst. Azra Parvez v. Sheikh Ashfaq Hussain*, 2015 CLC 1695; *M.Y. Corporation (Private) Ltd. v. Erum Developers*, PLD 2003 Karachi 222; *Managing Committee, Revenue Employees Cooperative Housing Society v. Secretary, Cooperative Societies, Government of Punjab*, 2001 CLC 838; *Zakaria Dada v. Maneck Byramji Javat*, 1992 CLC 345; *Haji Khan v. Government of Sindh*, 1990 MLD 155.

development work at its own risk and cost. The court noted that the petitioner and respondents possessed 75% and 20% interests respectively in the operations, which proved a prima facie case in favour of the petitioner. The loss which would have been caused to the petitioner due to the halting of operations shifted the balance of convenience in his favour, and this loss would have been irreparable not only for the petitioner but also the public at large who are directly involved. Therefore, the High Court held that the petitioner was at liberty to carry out the work even if the respondents did not participate in the meetings.[565]

Where the civil judge does not mention these three grounds, the order will be set aside.[566] In *Pakistan Railways v. Four Brothers International (Pvt.) Ltd. and others,*[567] the Supreme Court set aside the order of courts because they did not apply the three limbed test. In this case, a company entered into an agreement with Pakistan Railways to operate the business on a particular route for which the company was to pay PKR 1.5 million per journey and was to invest PKR 225 million for value-added services. The latter amount was also to be considered a performance guarantee. Disputes emerged, and the company could not pay these amounts for the commencement of the venture. The company approached the civil court for referral of the dispute to arbitration and prayed for injunctions restraining Pakistan Railway from the recovery of this amount from it. The court granted both applications. When the appeal came to the Supreme Court, it held that the court below it had granted injunctions without applying the three limbed, the balance of convenience and the assessment of potential irreparable loss. It held further that:

> Unrestricted permission to Respondent No.1 (Company) for plying the Business Train without discharging their obligations of payment of amounts agreed to in the Agreement cannot be termed as justifiable grounds for grant of injunction. In the case in hand, prima facie, Respondent No.1 (Company) has defaulted in paying the agreed amounts towards fares besides the investment, as is evident from the record; therefore, grant of injunction of nature to the disadvantage of the Petitioner was not justified.

The Supreme Court vacated the injunctions issued in favour of the Company.

It is to note that courts have also gone beyond the three limbed test to decide the issuance of interim measures like they will impart this remedy if injunctions are against the public interest.[568]

9.3.1. Prima Facie Case

The prima facie existence of the right claimed and its infringement should be proved by the applicant.[569] For that, it would be sufficient if he is successful in proving the

565. *Omv Maurice Energy Limited v. Ocean Pakistan Limited,* 2012 CLD 619.
566. *Dewan Petroleum (Pvt.) Ltd. v. Oil and Gas Investment Ltd.,* 2019 CLC 1486; *Omv Maurice Energy Limited v. Ocean Pakistan Limited,* 2012 CLD 619.
567. *Pakistan Railways v. Four Brothers International (Pvt.) Ltd. and others,* PLD 2016 SC 199.
568. *Al-Rahim Trading Co. (Pvt.) Ltd. through Chief Executive v. Pakistan through Ministry of Petroleum and Natural Resources, Islamabad and others,* PLD 2002 Karachi 147.
569. *Pakistan Railways and others v. Ittefao Foundries (Pvt.) Ltd. and another,* 1990 SCMR 355; *Shahzada Muhammad Umar Beg v. Sultan Mahmood Khan and another,* PLD 1970 SC 139;

existence of a serious question to be tried[570] or an arguable case[571] or that there is a likelihood of his winning the case if the evidence remains the same.[572] To ascertain the validity of these grounds, the court need not examine the merits of the case;[573] rather, to dispose of the application for an interim measure, the court will examine pleadings, affidavits and other documents present on the record.[574] Hence, while deciding the application for an interim measure, the court will not virtually decide the case of the applicant.[575]

Asian Construction Co. (Pvt.) Ltd. v. Government of the Punjab through Secretary, Communications and Works Department Civil Secretariat, Lahore and others, 2000 CLC 1543; *Mrs. Shamim Ara Omrao through her Attorney v. Qazi Saeed Akbar and another,* 1999 CLC 1826; *Balagamwala Oil Mills v. Messrs Shakarchi Trading A.G. and others,* 1991 CLC 2071; *M. Aobool Ahmad and others v. Syed Farzand Ali Shah and others,* 1990 CLC 1756; *Mian Muhammad Latif v. Province of West Pakistan through the Deputy Commissioner, Khairpur and another,* PLD 1970 SC 180; *Feroze Din v. Abdul Hamid and others,* PLD 1969 Lahore 89; *H. M. Saya &. Co. v. Wazir Ali Industries and another,* PLD 1965 (W. P.) Karachi 603; *Perveen Begum v. Mohammad Sarwat Khan,* PLD 1956 Sindh 521.

570. *Sakhawat Ali and another v. Mst. Shui Khelay,* PLD 1981 SC 454; *Mian Muhammad Latif v. Province of West Pakistan through the Deputy Commissioner, Khairpur and another,* PLD 1970 SC 180.
571. *Muhammad Yaqoob v. Mohsin,* 2000 CLC 1546; *Rizwan Ahmad and others v. University of Agriculture and others,* 1998 CLC 2045; *Mrs. Shazadi Baber v. Htna Housing Project (Pvt.) Ltd. and others,* 1994 CLC 1601; *M/S. International Trade and Marketing through Proprietor v. Integra Trade and Marketing and others,* 1993 CLC 2223; *Mrs. Naz Shaukat Khan and others v. Mrs. Yasmin R. Minhas and another,* 1992 CLC 2540; *Fida Ahmed and others v. Amir Masood Khan and others,* 1989 MLD 920; *Motsons v. Trustees of the Port of Karachi,* 1988 CLC 1261; *Syed Muhammad Khurshid Abbas Gardezi and others v. Province of Punjab and others,* 1988 CLC 362; *Mst. Kaneez Fatima and another v. Ghulam Hussain and others,* 1985 CLC 217; *Muhammad Matin v. Mrs. Dino Maneck Chenoy and others,* PLD 1983 Karachi 387; *Mst. Khurshid Begum and others v. Inam Rabbani and another,* 1979 CLC 570; *Carrier Telephone Industries Ltd., Islamabad v. Messrs Sohail Brothers and others,* PLD 1978 Lahore 1116; *Karachi Gas Co. Laid., Karachi v. Fancy Foundation,* PLD 1977 Karachi 191; *Iqbal Fatima v. Kaiser Tanveer,* PLD 1976 Karachi 734; *S. N. Gupta v. Sardar Nanda Ghosh,* PLD 1960 Dacca 153; *Mansur Ahmed v. Kalipada Chattopadhya,* PLD 1959 Dacca 498.
572. *Shah Nook Studios v. W. Z. Studios,* 1980 CLC 433.
573. *Muhammad Arif and another v. Subedar Muhammad Rafique and others,* 2001 YLR 132; *Muhammad Rasab and another v. Muhammad Siddiquie Chaudhry,* 1998 MLD 2045; *Muhammad Matin v. Mrs. Dino Manekji Chinoy and others,* PLD 1983 Karachi 387; *Abdur Rahman Mobashir and others v. Syed Amir Ali Shah Bokhari and others,* PLD 1978 Lahore 113; *Feroze Din v. Abdul Hamid and others,* PLD 1969 Lahore 89; *H. M. Saya &. Co. v. Wazir,* PLD 1965 (W. P.) Karachi 603; *Ghazi Nasiruddin v. Seth Hashim Dawood Divan and others,* PLD 1962 (W. P.) Karachi 59.
574. *M/S. International Trade and Marketing through Proprietor v. Integra Trade and Marketing and others,* 1993 CLC 2223; *Karachi Development Authority v. Hadi Bux Memon and another,* 1992 CLC 1036; *Syed Muhammad Khurshid Abbas Gardezi and others v. Province of Punjab and others,* 1988 CLC 362; *The Chairman, Karachi Water and Sewerage Board and another v. S. Wazir Hyder and others,* 1988 CLC 308; *Motsons v. Trustees of the Port of Karachi,* PLD 1988 Karachi; *The Hotel Metropole Ltd. v. The Federation of Pakistan and others,* PLD 1954 Sindh 61.
575. *Islamic Republic of Pakistan through Secretary, Ministry of Defence v. Masood Enterprises through Managing Director,* 2001 YLR 327; *Iftikhar Siddiqui v. Clifton Cantonment Board and others,* PLD 1998 Karachi 373; *Administrator, Karachi Public School v. Dawood Ahmed Salar and others,* 1998 MLD 234; *Sardar Muhammad Abdullah Khan v. Sahibzada Muhammad Usman Khan Abbasi and others,* 1997 MLD 2983.

However, interim relief will not be imparted in a suit which itself is not maintainable.[576] Along with the proof of prima facie case, the applicant has to prove the other two factors.[577]

9.3.2. Balance of Inconvenience

The court will examine whether the inconvenience to be suffered by the applicant by the refusal of interim relief is more than that to be suffered by the defendant if it is granted[578] and will impart this remedy only if the balance tilts in favour of the plaintiff.[579] It is to note that the balance generally lies in favour of the maintenance of the status quo,[580] but a court will not injunct a person from undertaking lawful acts.[581] For instance, injunctions will not be issued to restrain the payment under an irrevocable letter of credit,[582] bank guarantee,[583] or a bill of exchange.[584] For the same reason,

576. *Concentrate Manufacturing Company of Ireland and others v. Seven-Up Bottling Company (Private) Limited and others*, 2002 CLD 77.
577. *Asia Steel Industries Aid Ltd v. Iftikar & Co. Ltd. and others*, 1987 CLC 984; *Abdul Shakoor v. Haji Shaukat and others*, 1983 CLC 351; *G. M. Pfaff A. G. v. Sartaj Engineeering Co. Ltd., Lahore and others*, PLD 1970 Lahore 184; *Oil and Gas Development Corporation v. Lt.-Col. Shujauddin Ahmed*, PLD 1970 Karachi 332; *Sui Northern Gas Pipelines Company Limited v. Pakistan Cement Industries*, PLD 1968 Lahore 876.
578. *Qamar Ali Shah v. Waryam Ali others*, 1976 SCMR 393; *Noorali Bana and others v. The Province of Sindh through the Chief Secretary, Government of Sindh & Baluchistan, Karachi and another*, 1972 SCMR 100; *Rizwan Ahmad and others v. University of Agriculture and others*, 1998 CLC 2045; *Haji Sher Muhammad v. WAPDA through its Chairman and others*, PLD 1988 Lahore 511; *Mst. Kaneez Fatima and another v. Ghulam Hussain and others*, 1985 CLC 217; S. A. *Abbasi v. Chairman; District Council Gulshan-e-Iqbal, Karachi*, PLD 1985 Karachi 400; *Jamil Anmad v. Provincial Government of West Pakistan and others*, PLD 1982 Lahore 49; *Associated Mining Corporation v. Squadron Leader. G. R Sipra and others*, PLD 1968 Karachi 771; *Mian Nur Hussain and others v. Khalifa Muhammad Sultan and others*, PLD 1956 Lahore 893.
579. *Mrs. Shazadi Baber v. Htna Housing Project (Pvt.) Ltd. and others*, 1994 CLC 1601; *Nooruddin and others v. M/S. Sindh Industrial Trading Estate Ltd. and others*, 1993 CLC 2204; *The Burmah Oil PLC and another v. Pakistan State Oil Company Limited and another*, 1992 CLC 1028; *Nazeer Ahmad v. Muhammad Murad Ali*, PLD 1978 Lahore 930; *Carrier Telephone Industries Ltd., Islamabad v. Messrs Sohail Brothers and others*, PLD 1978 Lahore 1116; *Sardar Walt Muhammad v. Sardar Muhammad Iqbal Khan Mokal and others*, PLD 1975 Lahore 492; *Mian Nur Hussain and others v. Khalifa Muhammad Sultan and others*, PLD 1956 Lahore 893.
580. *Haji Feroze Din v. The District Magistrate, Lahore and another*, 1995 SCMR 705; *Major (Retd.) Shaikh A. Naeem v. Lt.-Col. Asif Burhan Malik and others*, 1989 CLC 2178.
581. *Aligarh Muslim University Old Boys Cooperative Housing Society Limited v. Muhammad Yousaf Qureshi and another*, 1997 CLC 918; *Senator Sultan Ali Lakhani v. Mir Shakil Ur Rahman and others*, PLD 1997 Karachi 41; *Karachi Bus Owners Association and others v. Karachi Yellow Mini Coach Owners Association and others*, 1994 CLC 606; *Muhammad Yasin Tahir v. Agricultural Development Bank of Pakistan, Islamabad another*, 1993 CLC 1316.
582. *Shipyard K. Damen International v. Karachi Shipyard and Engineering Works Ltd.*, PLD 2003 SC 191; *Shaheen Woollen Mills v. President, Allied Bank of Pakistan and others*, PLD 2001 Lahore 406; *Ijaz Anis v. Tariq Isa and others*, 2000 MLD 1337; *Progressive Fibres Ltd. v. Hyusung Corporation and others*, 1999 YLR 478; *Ajaz Anis v. Tariq Isa and others*, 1999 CLC 259; *Banque Indosuez Belgium and others v. Haral Textile Ltd.*, 1998 CLC 582; *U.D.L. Industries Ltd. v. Hongguang Electron Tube Plant and others*, PLD 1997 Karachi 553; *Manzoor Textile Mills Ltd. v. Special Judge Banking, Lahore and others*, 1996 CLC 422; *M/S. Ab Sukab v. M/S. Ghee Corporation of Pakistan*, PLD 1993 Karachi 508; *Printpac (Pvt.) Limited v. Rice Export Corporation of Pakistan Ltd.*, 1992 MLD 1161; *Kohinoor Trading (Pvt.) Ltd. v. Mangrani Trading Co. and others*, 1987 CLC 1533.

recovery of the amount which became due under a contract[585] and the encashment of performance bond[586] will not be normally restrained. Similarly, in relation to contracts, they will not be issued to stop the violation of a contract when such breach has already occurred[587], nor will they be issued to extend the time for performance of a contract that has already lapsed[588] or to enforce an agreement of personal services.[589] The court will also not issue an injunction to prevent the conduct of lawful affairs, like the organization of a meeting of a company's management[590] or the act to which the defendant is entitled under a contract to do.[591]

9.3.3. Irreparable Damage or Injury

After the proof of the other two grounds, the plaintiff also has to convince the court that he will incur an irreparable injury with the non-issuance of injunctions[592] and that no relief is there to avoid such apprehended damage.[593] In this respect, it is to note that damage will not become irreparable when it is merely not physically repairable; rather, for damage to become irreparable, its compensation should not be an adequate remedy for such injury.[594] In other words, the damage will not be irreparable if it can be ascertained in monetary terms.[595] It has been stated that:

---

583. *Shipyard K. Damen International v. Karachi Shipyard and Engineering Works Ltd.* PLD 2003 SC 191; *Heavy Mechanical Complex (Pvt.) Ltd., Taxila v. Attock Industrial Products Ltd. Rawalpindi,* PLD 2003 SC 295; *Shipyard K. Damen International v. Karachi Shipyard and Engineering Works Ltd.*, 2003 CLD 1; *Pak Consulting & Engineering (Pvt.) Ltd. v. Pakistan Steel Mills and another,* 2002 SCMR 1781.
584. *Chemi Viscofibre Ltd. v. Ing. A. Maurer S.A. and others,* 2003 CLD 420.
585. *The Agricultural Development Bank of Pakistan, Islamabad v. M/S. Chaudhry Harvesting Company, Lahore,* PLD 1993 Lahore 328; *Muhammad Yasin Tahir v. Agricultural Development Bank of Pakistan, Islamabad another,* 1993 CLC 1316.
586. *M/S. Ab Sukab v. M/S. Ghee Corporation of Pakistan,* PLD 1993 Karachi 508.
587. *World Wide Trading Co. v. Santo Electric Trading Co. Ltd. and another,* PLD 1986 Karachi 234.
588. *Hafiz Muhammad Ishaque and others v. Inspector-General Prisons, Sindh and another,* PLD 1994 SC 733; *Airport Limousine Services v. The Airport Manager, Civil Aviation Authority, Quaid-e-Azam International Airport, Karachi and another,* 2000 YLR 1277; *Zaidi's Enterprises and others v. Civil Aviation Authority and others,* PLD 1999 Karachi 181.
589. *Marghub Siddiqi v. Hamid Ahmad Khan and others,* 1974 SCMR 519; *Syed Aziz Ahmad v. Bolan Bank Limited,* 2002 CLC 857.
590. *Syed Hasan Masroor Zaidi and others v. Syed Ghayoor Zaidi and others,* 1988 CLC 1347.
591. *Royal Foreign Currency v. The Civil Aviation Authority and another,* 1998 CLC 374; *Abdul Rehmat Abbasi v. Malik Muhammad Asadullah and another,* 1993 MLD 1272.
592. *Mian Muhammad Latif v. Province of West Pakistan through the Deputy Commissioner, Khairpur and another,* PLD 1970 SC 180.
593. AIR 1946 Pat. 177; AIR 1920 Lahore 436.
594. *Tauseef Corporation (Pvt.) Ltd. v. Lahore Development Authority and others,* 2002 SCMR 1269; *Puri Terminals Ltd. v. Port Qasim Authority and others,* 2003 CLD 153; *Col. (Retd.) Dr. Sharifullah Khan v. Superintending Engineer (Pesco). Peshawar Electric Supply Corporation, Peshawar and others,* PLD 2000 Peshawar 4; *Mrs. Shazadi Baber v. Htna Housing Project (Pvt.) Ltd. and others,* 1994 CLC 1601; *Haji Khan and another v. Government of Sindh and others,* 1990 MLD 155; *Hussain Nasser v. Syed Shamim Yaoub,* 1989 CLC 2125; *Syed Muhammad Khurshid Abbas Gardezi and others v. Province of Punjab and others,* 1988 CLC 362; *Kohistan Travel Service and another v. Province of Punjab through Collector, Lyallpur and others,* PLD 1977 Lahore 85; *N. K. Gandhy v. D. P. Edulji & Company Ltd.*, PLD 1951 Lahore 262.
595. *Bolan Beverages (Pvt.) Limited v. Pepsi Co. Inc. and others,* PLD 2004 SC 860; *Friends Associates (Recd.) through Managing Partner, Lahore and others v. Binn Bak Industries (Pvt.) Limited*

> Manifestly, contracts involving collection of monetary benefits, which themselves have been obtained on specific monetary considerations, on principle, cannot involve irreparable loss because such loss, inherently, means and implies only such loss as is incapable of being calculated on the yardstick of money.[596]

However, the fact that the plaintiff's loss can be compensated in case of his success on the merits will disentitle him of the remedy of injunction.[597] Where the plaintiff, along with financial loss, will also suffer from the loss of his customers, the court may issue injunctions.[598]

9.3.4. Effect of Injunction

An injunction only acts in personam.[599] Injunction becomes effective only when it comes to the knowledge of its addressee[600] and not when it is issued by the court.[601] Although an injunction comes to an end with the termination of the suit in which it is issued,[602] the courts have sometimes issued injunctions after the final disposal of the case, and in such instance, the effect of the injunction was to continue even after the disposal of the matter before the court.[603]

Parties to a suit are bound to obey the orders (injunctions) of the court[604] unless such orders were issued by a court without any jurisdiction to that effect.[605] Disobedience to these orders will amount to contempt of court irrespective of the fact that the

through Chief Executive, Faisalabad and others, PLD 2003 Lahore 17; *Fawad Rehman v. Shakira Nawaz,* PLD 2003 Karachi 57; *Mian Muhammad Shah and another v. Ghee Corporation of Pakistan (Pvt.) Ltd. and others,* 2003 CLD 729.

596. *Dewan Petroleum (Pvt.) Ltd. v. Oil and Gas Investment Ltd.,* 2019 CLC 1486. In this case, for this principle, court relied on these judgments: *Tauseef Corporation (Pvt.) Ltd. v. Lahore Development Authority,* 2002 SCMR 1269; *Al-Tamash Medical Society v. Dr. Anwar Ye Bin Ju,* 2019 CLC 1; *Maxim Advertising Company (Pvt.) Ltd. v. Province of Sindh,* 2007 MLD 2019; *Haji Khan v. Government of Sindh,* 1990 MLD 155.
597. *Molasses Export Co. Ltd. v. Consolidated Sugar Mills Ltd.,* 1990 CLC 609.
598. *Ibid.*
599. *Abdul Majid and another v. Bashir Ahmad,* 1988 CLC 1370.
600. *Mrs. Rashida v. Mrs. Shahzad Khanem and others,* 1999 YLR 910; *Haydari Construction Co. Ltd. v. Bank of Credit and Commerce International Overseas, Limited and another,* 1991 CLC 149.
601. *Din Muhammad and others v. Abdul Rehman Khan,* 1992 SCMR 127; *Syed Ahmad Shah and Feroze Din v. The State and Malik Abdul Aziz,* PLD 1967 SC 42; *Abdul Rashid Khan and others v. Mst. Nasim Akhtar,* 1974 SCMR 509; *Karam Ali and others v. Raja and others,* PLD 1949 Lahore 100; *Fazal Karim v. Fateh Begum and others,* 2004 CLC 365; *Mst. Hamida Akhtar v. Nazir Muhammad and others,* 1995 CLC 2020; *Municipal Committee, Pasrur v. Compensation Commissioner and others,* 1991 PLC 488; *Haydari Construction Co. Ltd. v. Bank of Credit and Commerce International Overseas, Limited and another,* 1991 CLC 149.
602. *Gul Baran and others v. Abdul Zahir and another,* 1988 CLC 65.
603. *Anjuman-e-Ahmadiya, Sargodha v. The Deputy Commissioner, Sargodha and the Government of West Pakistan, through the Secretary Colonies, Board of Revenue, West Pakistan, Lahore,* PLD 1966 SC 639.
604. *Iftikhar Ali v. Javid Dastgir Mirza and others,* PLD 1975 Lahore 126; *Dr. A. N. M. Mahmood v. Dr. M. O. Ghani, Vice-Chancellor and others,* PLD 1967 Dacca 67.
605. *Muhammed Siddiq and others v. Haji Ahmed & Co.* PLD 1967 KARACHI 468; *Muhammad Swaleh and another v. Messrs United Grain & Fodder Agencies,* PLD 1964 SC 97; *Mian Sultan Ali Nanghiana v. Mian Nur Hussain,* PLD 1949 Lahore 301.

parties came to know of these orders officially or unofficially[606] and regardless of whether the suit in relation to which injunction was issued was later withdrawn.[607] If the injunction is addressed to a non-party to the suit, he will commit contempt of court by disobeying it.[608] While punishing contempt, the penalties enshrined under Order 39, Rule 2(3) are to be imposed.[609] The court, in an appropriate circumstance, allows the contemnor to retract.[610]

9.3.5. Breach of Contract

An injunction can be granted restraining breach of contract,[611] provided it is a completed contract.[612] The granting of an injunction under Rule 2 of Order 39 is also governed by the principles regulating the granting of perpetual injunctions. In accordance with section 56(f)[613] of the Specific Relief Act, no injunction can be issued to prevent the breach of a contract that cannot be ordered to be specifically enforced.[614] By virtue of section 21(a)[615] of the Specific Relief Act, a contract will not be specifically

606. *Syed Ahmad Shah and Feroze Din v. The State and Malik Abdul Aziz,* PLD 1967 SC 42; *Karam Ali and others v. Raja and others,* PLD 1949 Lahore 100; *Sadaruddin v. K. Moinuddin and others,* PLD 1969 Dacca 147; *Dr. A. N. M. Mahmood v. Dr. M. O. Ghani, Vice-Chancellor and others,* PLD 1967 Dacca 67.
607. *Naveed Nawazish Malik v. Ghulam Rasool Bhatti and another,* 1997 SCMR 193; *Iftikhar Ali v. Javid Dastgir Mirza and others,* PLD 1975 Lahore 126.
608. *Dr. A. N. M. Mahmood v. Dr. M. O. Ghani, Vice-Chancellor and others,* PLD 1967 Dacca 67.
609. Order 39, Rule 2(3) says 'in case of disobedience, or of breach of any such terms, the court granting an injunction may order the property of the person guilty of such disobedience or breach to be attached and may also order such person to be detained in the prison for a term no exceeding six months unless in the meantime the court directs his release'. *Muhammad Rahim v. Surayya Rahim,* 1999 CLC 1392.
610. *Saleem-ud-Din v. Municipal Committee, Tando Allahyar,* 2000 SCMR 460; *Muhammad Riaz v. Federation of Pakistan,* PLD 1992 SC 204; *M. Adil Hayat Khan v. Government of Sindh,* PLD 2002 Karachi 131.
611. *A.M. Fabric (Pvt.) Ltd. v. I.D.B.P. and others,* 2003 CLD 1321; *Hafeezullah Khan and others v. Al-Haj Chaudhri Barkat Ali and others,* PLD 1998 Karachi 274; *Syed Waqar Hussain and another v. Messrs National Refinery Ltd. through Managing Director,* 1993 CLC 2497; *Kohinoor Trading (Pvt.) Ltd. v. Mangrani Trading Co. and others,* 1992 CLC 1559.
612. *Umer Farooque and others v. Province of Sindh through Deputy Commissioner, Hyderabad to be served through the District Attorney, Hyderabad and others,* 1998 CLC 760; *Salahuddin Khan and others v. Sultan-e-Romf and others,* PLD 1973 Peshawar 95.
613. 56. Injunction when refused. An injunction cannot be granted:

    (f)to prevent the breach of a contract the performance of which would not be specifically enforced.

614. *Petrocommodities (Pvt.) Ltd. v. Rice Export Corporation of Pakistan,* PLD 1998 Karachi 1; *Qasimabad Enterprises v. Province Of Sindh Through Secretary, Housing and Town Planning Department, Government of Sindh, Karachi and others,* 1998 CLC 441; *Karachi Gas Co. Laid., Karachi v. Fancy Foundation,* PLD 1977 Karachi 191.
615. Section 21. Contracts not specifically enforceable. The following contracts cannot be specifically enforced:

    (a) a contract for the non-performance of which compensation in money is an adequate relief.

enforced where its non-performance can be adequately compensated by an award of damages.[616]

9.4. RECOMMENDATIONS

The 1940 Act is silent on Pakistani courts' power to issue interim injunctions in support of arbitration seated abroad. It may be said that Pakistani courts should interpret the 1940 Act in favour of conferment of such power because to restrict their powers to arbitration seated only in Pakistan is not desirable for a country striving to modernize its laws and to make them compatible with international practices.

The other suggestion is to clarify the interface between the interim measures ordered by the court and those by the arbitral tribunal.[617] Where there is a strong fear that the courts may usurp the jurisdiction of the arbitrator by going into the substance of disputes, it becomes imperative to clarify whether the applicant, following the constitution of the arbitral tribunal, will first have to go to the court or to the tribunal. For example, Swiss law has made it clear that the applicant will first make the application to the tribunal for interim orders and if successful but the other party fails to comply, then the first party will resort to the court for its assistance.[618]

The State of Ohio's law is even clearer on the issue by adopting the UNCITRAL Model Law.[619] It states that a party can approach the court to secure the interim measure. However, it adds further that the court would not issue any interim measure unless:

> The party shows that an application to the arbitral tribunal for the measure of protection would prejudice the party's rights and that an interim measure of protection from the court is necessary to protect those rights.[620]

---

616. *Syed Aziz Ahmad v. Bolan Bank Limited*, 2002 CLC 857; *Petrocommodities (Pvt.) Ltd. v. Rice Export Corporation of Pakistan*, PLD 1998 Karachi 1; *Qasimabad Enterprises v. Province of Sindh Through Secretary, Housing and Town Planning Department, Government of Sindh, Karachi and others*, 1998 CLC 441; *Naeemuddin v. Federation of Pakistan and others*, 1994 CLC 625.
617. *See* Alan Redfern, Martin Hunter, Nigel Blackaby, Constantine Partasides, *Law and Practice of International Commercial Arbitration* (4th ed., Thomson, 2004), 399-401 wherein Redfern and Hunter pointed to the laws of Switzerland, the state of Ohio and England to clarify where an application for interim measures should first be made, whether to the court or the arbitrator.
618. The Swiss Private International Law Act 1987, Article 183 – Provisional and protective measures:

    > 1 Unless the parties have agreed otherwise, the arbitral tribunal may enter provisional or protective measures at the request of one party.
    >
    > If the party concerned does not comply voluntarily, the arbitral tribunal may request the assistance of the judge with jurisdiction who shall apply his own law.

619. Adopting Article 17 of UNCITRAL Model Law, Ohio Code, International Commercial Arbitration states in section 2712.14(A) that 'It is not incompatible with an arbitration agreement for a party to request a court of common pleas, before or during arbitral proceedings, to issue an interim measure of protection, or for the court to grant such a measure.'
620. Ohio Code, International Commercial Arbitration, section 2712.36.

The English Arbitration Act has dealt with this matter very carefully by conferring power on the court to issue interim measures listed in section 44, which it can use only if the applicant proves that the case is urgent, and if that is not the case, then the court will only grant these measures either with the permission of the tribunal or with the written agreement between the parties to that effect. Similarly, in any other instance, the court will act to issue or not to issue the measures only in cases where the tribunal has not been vested with powers in that regard.[621]

The approach adopted by these jurisdictions is arbitration-friendly. This attitude depicts the evolution of arbitration towards an autonomous, comprehensive and effective system of dispute resolution. Therein, the arbitrators have all the powers required to resolve the *lis* being independent of any assistance from the court. This approach has also created clarity in the procedure for interim measures in which the court's domain and powers of the tribunal have been demarcated incontrovertibly to avoid any kind of ambiguity. Hence, it is suggested to benefit from the experiences of these jurisdictions because it would be advantageous for arbitration if the arbitrator is granted priority over the court for the issuance of interim measures. In this way, the apprehension of courts' going into the substance of disputes at the stage of interim measures may also be minimized.

Along with giving priority to the arbitrator over the court in deciding the issuance of measures, the power should also be given to arbitrators to issue ex parte interim measures enforceable even against third parties. Such an approach will put arbitration in Pakistan on the track of being completely autonomous and free from the intervention

621. Section 44 of the Arbitration Act 1996. Court powers exercisable in support of arbitral proceedings:

(1) Unless otherwise agreed by the parties, the court has for the purposes of and in relation to arbitral proceedings the same power of making orders about the matters listed below as it has for the purposes of and in relation to legal proceedings.
(2) Those matters are—
(a) the taking of the evidence of witnesses;
(b) the preservation of evidence;
(c) making orders relating to property which is the subject of the proceedings or as to which any question arises in the proceedings—
(i) for the inspection, photographing, preservation, custody or detention of the property, or
(ii) ordering that samples be taken from, or any observation be made of or experiment conducted upon, the property;
and for that purpose authorizing any person to enter any premises in the possession or control of a party to the arbitration;
(d) the sale of any goods the subject of the proceedings;
(e) the granting of an interim injunction or the appointment of a receiver.
(3) If the case is one of urgency, the court may, on the application of a party or proposed party to the arbitral proceedings, make such orders as it thinks necessary for the purpose of preserving evidence or assets.
(4) If the case is not one of urgency, the court shall act only on the application of a party to the arbitral proceedings (upon notice to the other parties and to the tribunal) made with the permission of the tribunal or the agreement in writing of the other parties.
(5) In any case the court shall act only if or to the extent that the arbitral tribunal, and any arbitral or other institution or person vested by the parties with power in that regard, has no power or is unable for the time being to act effectively.

of the courts. The arguments forwarded in support of empowering courts are as follows:

- The arbitrator's interim measures are not enforceable.
- Arbitrators cannot issue measures against third parties.
- Arbitrators cannot issue ex parte measures.
- A party may need interim measures before the constitution of an arbitral tribunal.

The solution for these issues can be discussed if the subject of appointment of the Commission, their powers and functions, under the CPC is first discussed. The Commission is appointed by the courts under section 75 and order 26 of the CPC. Section 75 of the CPC stipulates that:

> Subject to such conditions and limitations as may be prescribed, the Court may issue a Commission
>
> (a) to examine any person;
> (b) to make a local investigation;
> (c) to examine or adjust accounts; or
> (d) to make a partition.

Conditions, purposes and powers of the Commission are enunciated in Order 26[622] of the CPC. Order 26, Rule 16 of the CPC gives the Commissioner the power to examine any person who he thinks fit, and this may be a person other than the parties or the parties' chosen person.[623] Rule 18(2) empowers the Commissioner to proceed ex parte if any of the parties do not appear before him.[624] Similarly, the Commissioner's order regarding summoning of witnesses can be enforced under Order 26, Rule 17 of the CPC, which says that '*for purposes of this rule the Commissioner shall be deemed to be a Civil Court*'. For the enforcement of directions of a Commissioner, the Punjab High Court held in *Muhammad Abid v. Mst. Nasreen Yousuf*[625] that the Commissioner performs the function of the court and enjoys the same powers as possessed by the court for all intents and purposes. The court further held that non-compliance with the

622. In Order 26, Rules 1-8 relate examination of witnesses, Rules 9-10 relate to local investigation, Rules 11-12 relate to examination and adjustments of accounts, and Rules 13-14 relate to making of partition.
623. Order 26, Rule 16 says:

> Any Commissioner appointed under this Order may, unless otherwise directed by the order of appointment:
>
> (a) examine the parties themselves and any witness whom they or any of them may produce, and any other person whom the Commissioner thinks proper to call upon to give evidence in the matter referred to him;
> (b) call for and examine documents and other things relevant to the subject of inquiry;
> (c) at any reasonable time enter upon or into any land or building mentioned in the order.

624. The CPC, Order 26, Rule 18(2) says 'where all or any of the parties do not so appear, the Commissioner may proceed in their absence'.
625. 2002 CLC 655 Lahore.

direction of the Commissioner amounts to disobedience of the orders of the courts, and all consequences attached thereto follow. It also merits mentioning that one of the consequences for disobedience of the court's order is also contempt of court.[626]

The court cannot appoint one of its officials as Commissioner,[627] which means that this private person who is not a judge nor a court official possesses all the powers of a judge with regard to the specific task assigned to him. This is so because, for that specific task, his selection and appointment is made by the court and is vested the Commissioner with these powers. All this signifies that the phenomenon of bestowing these powers on a private person by selecting him in a special way is not new to Pakistan. And if a similar process of appointment for arbitrators is followed just as is followed for the appointment of the Commissioner, the powers conferred on the Commissioner for the conduct of the specific task assigned to him may also be conferred on the arbitrator for matters relating to the adjudication process. The court cannot delegate the powers of adjudication to a Commissioner.[628] So, the scope of the task assigned to the Commissioner is very narrow, but the powers conferred on him regarding this task are very wide. On the other hand, the arbitrator has been given the very important and wide task of adjudication, but for the conduct of this adjudication process (arbitration proceedings), he does not have powers as wide as the powers granted to Commissioners, i.e., to issue enforceable interim measures, to pass ex parte interim measures and to bind third a party against these measures. This difference in powers conferred on both is due to the difference in the powers of their appointers. An arbitrator is appointed privately, but the Commissioner is appointed by the entity possessing coercive powers, i.e., the court. The possession and utilization of these vast powers by the Commissioner is justified because his appointment is made by the judge.

The solution for the above-mentioned issues is to strengthen the process of institutionalization of arbitration in Pakistan. An arbitral institution should be established in Pakistan, which like national institutions in other jurisdictions, would also have its arbitration rules a list of qualified and specialized arbitrators. There should be a process for their selection and inclusion of their names in the list of arbitrators maintained by this institution. This selection process may be done transparently with the help of, or participation of, the authority that selects and appoints judges at the district level in Pakistani courts. In that regard, this institution may have access to the Selection Commission, which will finalize the names of arbitrators in the list of specialized arbitrators, and this Selection Commission may have, along with other elements, some representation by the High Courts. In this way, the origin of arbitrators in the list of this institution will emanate somewhat from the coercive authority. It may be declared by the legislature through legislation, by-laws or institutional arbitration rules that if institutional arbitration is conducted under the rules and supervision of this institution by the arbitrators selected from that list and appointed by this institution,

626. Section 3 of the Contempt of Court Ordinance 2004.
627. *Mehr Lal Khan v. Haji Ahmad,* 1991 MLD 663 Lahore.
628. *Faqirullah v. Khadim Hussain,* 2003 CLC 122 Lahore; *Muhammad Bakhsh v. Nizam Din,* PLD 1978 Lahore 31; *Mirza Muhammad Saeed v. Muhammad Akram Munir etc.,* 2001 YLR 919 Lahore; *Masroor Ali Khan v. Jamshed Alam,* 1999 MLD 2583 Lahore; *Khatoon Begum v. Hyesons Commercial and Industrial Corporation Ltd., Karachi,* 1980 CLC 1666 Karachi.

these arbitrators will have the power to issue interim and ex parte measures and to issue the measures enforceable against parties as well as against non-parties. Now, if arbitration is subjected to this institution and its rules, the said institution will appoint arbitrators from the list, and the ambit of the powers of the arbitrators will be manifest to the parties who will subject them to this institution.

Once it is established in principal terms that the arbitrators should be given these powers, the guidance to draft provisions to that effect may be taken from the UNICTRAL Model Law as amended in 2006 regarding interim measures.[629] It is strongly suggested that Pakistan should incorporate these amendments either in the 1940 Act or any new law on arbitration because it will make Pakistani law arbitration-friendly, and also, these amendments are in line with the Pakistani legal culture. For example, discussing the conditions that a party has to prove for the approval of interim measures, the Model Law as amended in 2006 says:

> (1) The party requesting an interim measure under Article 17(2)(a), (b) and (c) shall satisfy the arbitral tribunal that:
> (a) Harm not adequately reparable by an award of damages is likely to result if the measure is not ordered, and such harm substantially outweighs the harm that is likely to result to the party against whom the measure is directed if the measure is granted.
> (b) There is a reasonable possibility that the requesting party will succeed on the merits of the claim. The determination on this possibility shall not affect the discretion of the arbitral tribunal in making any subsequent determination.[630]

These conditions also apply if the arbitrator is to issue ex parte orders.[631] Pakistani lawyers and courts are quite familiar with these grounds. Pakistani courts consider factors similar to those given in the Model Law when deciding whether or not to issue interim measures under Order 39, Rules 1 & 2 of the CPC, as discussed above.

As far as why a party may need interim measures before the constitution of an arbitral tribunal, as is the case with the Netherlands Arbitration Institution's rules,[632] a sole arbitrator may be appointed by the Pakistani arbitral institution on the receipt of an application by a party for the initiation of arbitration. This arbitrator will only act to

629. UNCITRAL Model Law on International Commercial Arbitration 1985 with amendments as adopted in 2006, Ch. IV.
630. UNCITRAL Model Law, Ch. IV A, section 1, Article 17A.
631. *Ibid.* Ch. IV A, section 2, Article 17B. The issue of ex parte orders was discussed in very much detail in the Working Group. *See* UN Doc A/CN.9/468, para. 70; UN Doc A/CN.9/485, paras 89-94; UN Doc A/CN.9/487, paras 69-76; UN Doc A/CN.9/508, paras 77-79; UN Doc A/CN.9/523, paras 15-76; UN Doc A/CN.9/545, paras 49-92; UN Doc A/CN.9/547, paras 109-116; UN Doc A/CN.9/569, paras 13-72; UN Doc A/CN.9/573, paras 12-69; UN Doc A/CN.9/589, paras 49-75.
632. Arbitration Rules of the Netherlands Arbitration Institute, Article 42; *See also* A Redfern, M Hunter, N Blackaby, C Partasides, *Law and Practice of International Commercial Arbitration* (4th ed., Thomson, 2004), 395-396.

decide about the issuance of the interim measures, and once the arbitral tribunal is constituted, this sole arbitrator will become *functus officio*.

9.5. CONCLUSION

Since the 1940 Act is outdated and bad law for interim measures, this flaw may preferably be removed by legislative amendment rather than leaving it for judicial surgery. As far as arbitrator's lack of power to issue enforceable interim measures against the party to arbitration as well as non-party and ex parte interim measures are concerned, this may be resolved through strengthening the arbitral institute by benefitting from the UNCITRAL amendments and legislation from other jurisdictions. Otherwise, the poor legal regime on interim measures will hinder the materialization of a wish to have a modern, arbitration-friendly and effective law on arbitration in Pakistan.

CHAPTER 10

Intensity of Judicial Review of Arbitral Awards by Pakistani Courts

This chapter enquires into the standards employed by Pakistani courts to review arbitral awards. Although domestic and foreign awards are administered by two discrete legal regimes, the question is how the nationality of the award is best determined. This differentiation in the nationality of arbitral awards, in turn, calls forth the application of distinct rules for domestic and foreign awards in case the award debtor wants to impeach the validity or enforceability of awards where the award creditor has not yet committed the award for enforcement. Similarly, different limitation periods bear on domestic and foreign awards in order to delve if their enforcement is time-barred. But this divergence in treatment based on the foreign and domestic nature of awards does not lead to a differentiation in judicial review of awards since Pakistani courts review both kinds of awards with the same intensity.

10.1. INTRODUCTION

The consideration of justice and fairness in the review of arbitral awards is no less important than their finality. However, the review of the merits of a dispute is not permitted, which means that the set-aside or enforcement court should not act as a court of appeal. This assertion is valid because parties enter into the arbitration bargain to exclude the jurisdiction of courts. Therefore, the role of a court as an appellate forum will render this exercise futile. Whether Pakistani courts cherish this expectation from parties has not, hitherto, been explored, and this is precisely the subject of this chapter.

Before undertaking a discussion on the review of awards, the procedural closely relevant to judicial review are highlighted. For instance, the Pakistani legal regime differentiates between domestic and foreign awards. The grounds on the basis of which the nationality of an award is decided will be investigated. Determination of the nationality of arbitral awards (domestic or foreign) is important because different laws are applicable; that is, the 1940 Act governs domestic awards while the Recognition and Enforcement (Arbitration Agreements and Foreign Arbitral Awards) Act 2011 regulates foreign awards. Along with the fact that different limitation periods pertain to domestic and foreign awards, this differential treatment on the basis of nationality affects the respective consequences. If the award debtor desires to challenge the enforceability of an arbitral award at a time when the award creditor has not yet presented or filed that award in Pakistani courts, the law distinguishes between and foreign awards. Ironically, despite the bifurcation in the regime for domestic and foreign awards, the extent and intensity of review to be applied by Pakistani courts are the same for both domestic as well as foreign awards. This will be discussed below in detail.

10.2. NATIONALITY OF AWARDS: FOREIGN AND DOMESTIC AWARDS

The view prevailing before the enactment of the 2011 Act was that if the parties to arbitration were Pakistani nationals,[633] or if Pakistani law governed the arbitration agreement,[634] Pakistani courts would assume exclusive jurisdiction over the arbitration. This, in turn, would render both the arbitral proceedings and ensuing award domestic in nature. These principles were established under the repealed Arbitration (Protocol and Convention) Act, 1937. This was the prevalent view, although several judgments to the contrary could also be observed. For instance, in *Petrocon (Pvt.) Ltd. v. Hyderabad Development Authority,*[635] both petitioner and respondent were Pakistani companies and entered into a contract for the execution of some works in Pakistan. Thereafter, disputes ensued and, in accordance with the agreement, were referred to the sole arbitrator under the ICC Rules in Paris. An award was issued in favour of the petitioner, who demanded the respondent to pay him the awarded sum. The respondent reimbursed only part of that sum. An application under section 5 of the 1937 Act was then lodged to enforce the award in its entirety due to the non-payment of the outstanding amount.

The application was resisted on the grounds, *inter alia,* that the award was not foreign because both parties to arbitration were resident in Pakistan, along with the fact that the subject matter of the agreement was also performed in Pakistan. Therefore, being a domestic award, it was governed by the provisions of the 1940 Act instead of the 1937 Act.

The Sindh High Court agreed with the assertion that for an award to be foreign under Article 2 of the 1937 Act, one of the parties 'must be subject to the jurisdiction of one of the powers or territories ... ' However, it also took the view that, for an award

633. *The Hub Power Co. v. WAPDA,* 1999 CLC 1320; *Hitachi Limited v. Rupali Polyester,* 1998 SCMR 1618.
634. *Rupali Polyester Ltd v. Dr. Nael G Bunni,* PLD 1994 Lahore 525 which was upheld by Supreme Court in *Hitachi Limited v. Rupali Polyester,* 1998 SCMR 1618.
635. *Petrocon (Pvt.) Ltd. v. Hyderabad Development Authority, Hyderabad,* 1990 MLD 1675.

to be foreign, this provision did not stipulate that one of the parties must be resident outside the territories of Pakistan. Therefore, the Sindh High Court decreed that the arbitral award might be foreign, despite the fact that both parties to arbitration were residents or nationals of Pakistan. Applying this approach to the instant case, wherein Pakistani nationals consensually subjected themselves to foreign arbitration, the court declared the award thereunder as foreign and amenable to the provisions of the 1937 Act instead of the 1940 Act. However, this judgment was an isolated decision, which was never relied on in other cases.

At present, section 2(e) of the new law, i.e., the 2011 Act, defines a foreign arbitral award as an 'award made in a Contracting State and such other State as may be notified by the Federal Government, in the official Gazette'.[636] Section 2(b) of the same Act explicates that a 'Contracting State means a State which is a party to the Convention'. However, it is to note that despite the seat criterion to determine the nationality of awards, an arbitral award was declared domestic for the reason that Pakistani law governed the arbitration clause.[637] Therefore, it seems that Pakistani courts have not used the seat criterion as an exclusive ground to designate the nationality of awards in order to attract the applicability of the New York Convention. As a result, the effect of *ratio decidendi* of the old judgments given under the 1937 Act and the 1940 Act could not be discarded, which should have disappeared with the repeal of the 1937 Act by the 2011 Act.

Pronouncing arbitral proceedings and ensuing awards as be domestic on these grounds appears to be much unwarranted when compared to other jurisdictions. In France, for instance, the arbitration and ensuing award would be international 'when it involves the interests of international trade'.[638] In this respect, the seat of arbitration or applicable laws[639] are of no relevance. English law renders a unified approach towards both domestic as well as international arbitration,[640] although most provisions in the English Arbitration Act 1996 apply only to arbitrations seated within England.[641] While it is not an inappropriate time for a jurisdiction like Pakistan to modernize its legal regime on these lines, at the present time, sticking to the seat criterion in its letter and spirit may also give rise to very good outcomes. Further, Pakistani courts should keep away from the old interpretation and instead evolve a new jurisprudence under the new 2011 Act in line with the arbitration-friendly disposition of the New York Convention.

636. 'Made' usually refers to the seat of arbitration but it would be more preferable if instead of 'made', the term 'seat of arbitration' was used.
637. *Taisei Corporation v. A.M. Construction Company (Pvt.) Ltd.*, PLD 2012 Lahore 455.
638. Article 1492 of the French Code of Civil Procedure.
639. Judgment of 1 July 1997, XXIVa Y.B. Comm. Arb. 281 (Paris Cour d'appel) (1999).
640. DAC Report paras 317-331, DAC Supplementary Report, January 1997, paras 47-50. *See also* Steven Friel, *Arbitration in Context*, in *Arbitration in England*, eds Julian D.M. Lew, QC and others (Kluwer Law International, 2013), 3-7, 3-8.
641. *See* section 2 of English Arbitration Act 1996.

10.3. LAW AND PROCEDURE TO GOVERN THE ARBITRAL AWARD

10.3.1. Which Law Should Be Applied to Foreign Arbitral Awards?

After the nationality of awards (whether it is foreign or domestic) is established, the next step to consider is what is the legal regime regulating such an award. In this respect, the judgments rendered before the enactment of the 2011 Act are still relevant to predict the tendency of Pakistani courts after the promulgation of the new law. The old judgments have interpreted consistently that the 1940 Act would not apply to foreign awards. In *Nan Fung Textiles Ltd. v. Sadiq Traders Ltd.*,[642] the Sindh High Court held that the inapplicability of the 1940 Act to foreign awards was very well established, in which case, these would be exclusively governed by the provisions of the 1937 Act.[643] In other words, any non-observance of the 1940 Act would not render a foreign award void, nor would such award be set aside by applying the provisions of the 1940 Act. This is because of the fact that the validity of foreign awards as defined in section 2 of the 1937 Act could be contested only by utilizing the grounds enumerated in section 7 of the 1937 Act.[644]

Similar findings may be observed in *Nan Fling Textiles Ltd. v. Pir Muhammad Shamasuddin*,[645] with regard to awards rendered in favour of the petitioner (a company registered in Hong Kong) in an arbitration conducted in England under the rules of the Liverpool Cotton Association. The Sindh High Court held that the grounds listed in section 30 of the 1940 Act to set aside domestic awards were different from those given in section 7 of the 1937 Act for foreign awards. For example, under section 30, an award would be refused enforcement if it was pronounced subsequent to the issuance of a decree from the court to supersede the arbitration proceedings or to declare such proceedings invalid under section 35 of the 1940 Act, whereas such ground was absent in section 7 of the 1937 Act.[646]

However, there has been an inconsistent view under the 1937 Act as to whether Pakistani courts were to apply Pakistani law to determine the validity of agreements in order to adjudge the enforceability of foreign awards. For instance, in *Quinn Corporation v. Cotton Export Corporation*,[647] the Sindh High Court declined to apply Pakistani

642. *Nan Fung. Textiles Ltd. v. Sadiq Traders Ltd.*, PLD 1982 Karachi 619.
643. *See also Pfaff & Co. v. Sartaj Engineer Co. Ltd.*, PLD 1970 Lahore 184, wherein it was ruled that all arbitration proceedings, with the exception of those excepted by section 47 are to be regulated by the 1940 Act as one of the exceptions is 'save in so far as is otherwise provided by any law for the time being in force'. The Arbitration (Protocol and Convention) Act, 1937 is one such law. The 1940 Act far from prohibiting an arbitration covered by the Act of 1937, recognizes it by the force of section 47. *See, Hassan Ali & Co. Cotton (Private) Limited v. Poly Cotton, S.A., 2-Rue, Andrien Vallin, 1201 Geneva, Switzerland and others*, PLD 1996 Karachi 416, wherein the court highlighted the practice of the courts to treat the award as foreign, which begot in arbitration under the Rules of the Liverpool Cotton Association.
644. *Nan Fung. Textiles Ltd. v. Sadiq Traders Ltd*, PLD 1982 Karachi 619. *See also Marines Limited v. Aegus Shipping Co. Ltd and others*, 1987 CLC 1299.
645. *Nan Fling Textiles Ltd., Hong Kong v. H. Pir Muhammad Shamasuddin*, PLD 1979 Karachi 762.
646. The same approach was followed in its letter and spirit in *European Grain & Shipping Ltd v. Polychem Company Ltd.*, PLD 1990 Karachi 254.
647. *Quinn Corporation and others v. Cotton Export Corporation and others*, 2004 CLD 1040.

law to interpret the validity of a contract on the application of an award debtor who asserted the invalidity of an award rendered under the rules of the Liverpool Cotton Association on that ground. The award debtor contended that the governmental ban on the import of raw cotton incapacitated him from importing the cotton. This inability had thus frustrated the contract (under section 56 of Pakistani Contract Act 1872) by activating the force majeure clause embedded therein. Hence, he asserted that the arbitrators had pronounced the award without any jurisdiction. In this respect, he also placed reliance on two Pakistani cases reported as PLD 1978 Karachi 585 and PLD 1980 Supreme Court 122.

The force majeure ground and these judgments referred to by the award debtor were rejected by the court, observing that they pertained to the award given under the 1940 Act, whereas the award sought for enforcement in the instant case was a foreign award to be governed by the provisions of the 1937 Act. Therefore, the applicability of Pakistani law was completely excluded since the contract was to be governed by the Rules of the Liverpool Cotton Association.

There are instances where the courts have applied Pakistani law to adjudge the validity of agreements to decide the enforceability of an award, as was the case in *Ralli Brothers & Coney Ltd. v. Muhammad Amin Muhammad Bashir Ltd.*[648] In this case, it was contested that, as the correspondence between the parties occurred through cables, the contract was not concluded so as to become a valid basis for arbitration. The court was at variance with this plea. It was an admitted fact that the contract, as well as arbitration, was governed by the Rules of the Liverpool Cotton Association. However, when the enforceability of the foreign award was contested by the defendant on the ground of absence or non-conclusion of the contract, including the arbitration agreement, by applying Pakistani law, the court held that there was no need of the parties' signature; rather, what was mandatory under section 2(a) of the 1940 Act was that the agreement should be in writing. Hence, the court maintained the arbitration agreement to be valid. It is noteworthy that although Pakistani law was applied, the same approach proved to be advantageous for arbitration.

To sum, the approach developed from the above-mentioned judgments is that when the award is established to be foreign, it would be governed by the provisions of the 1937 Act to the exclusion of the 1940 Act. Now, when the 1937 Act was repealed by the 2011 Act, it may fairly be inferred that foreign awards will be governed only by the 2011 Act. The general statement asserting the exclusion of the jurisprudence under the 1940 and 1937 Acts in relation to foreign awards may be qualified by the fact that although the 1940 Act is not relevant to foreign arbitral awards, yet the principles evolved under this instrument are very much relevant to the basic purpose of arbitration even now. The principles concerning the judicial review of awards, public policy, due process and arbitrator bias, judicial review, etc., may be mentioned here, in particular.

---

648. *Ralli Brothers & Coney Ltd. v. Muhammad Amin Muhammad Bashir Ltd.*, 1987 CLC 83.

10.3.2. Suit Cannot Be Filed to Adjudge the Validity of Award

When the award creditor seeks the enforcement of an award in Pakistan, statutory provisions to that effect exist. For domestic awards, section 30 of the 1940 Act is relevant, and before the enactment of the 2011 Act, sections 6 and 7 of the 1937 Act were applicable to the enforcement of foreign awards and now sections 6 and 7 of the 2011 Act are relevant. But the confusion, at present, prevails where the award has not yet been presented in Pakistani courts by the award creditor for its enforcement and the award debtor desires to challenge the validity, effect or enforceability of that award. This segment will dilate upon this issue.

Before elucidating the current law (the 2011 Act), the old jurisprudence will be explored, which is again very much enlightening due to its relevance to the present analysis. In the case of domestic awards, section 32 and section 33 of the 1940 Act emphasize that any party interested in challenging the award may do so by filing an application and for that purpose, a suit is not allowed. A similar provision, that is, section 5, was inserted in the 1937 Act with regard to foreign awards. Both sections were interpreted to the effect that suits cannot be brought for both domestic and foreign awards.

In *Marines Limited v. Aegus Shipping Co. Ltd*,[649] the Sindh High Court stated that if a party wanted to challenge the enforceability of a foreign award at a time when the award creditor had not yet filed said award in the courts, the former could not do so by filing an independent declaratory suit for a declaration to that effect. In that regard, the Sindh High Court relied on section 5 of the 1937 Act, which enunciated that 'any person interested in a foreign award may apply to any court having jurisdiction over the subject-matter of the award that the award be filed in court'. The court further held that a court thus approached under this section would require the parties to demonstrate the cause as to why such award should not be filed in that court. If the court decides in favour of filing the award, the next phase would be to submit objections against the enforcement of such an award. The Sindh High Court highlighted that the grounds on which the enforcement of awards might be challenged or resisted were enshrined in section 7 of the 1937 Act, which did not contain the filing of declaratory suits in court to render the already declared award unenforceable. The court held expressly that in the case of foreign arbitral awards, sections 30 and 33 of the 1940 Act were inapplicable because the mechanism for the enforcement of foreign arbitral awards was laid down in the 1937 Act. Similarly, in *Ali & Co. Cotton (Private) Limited v. Poly Cotton, S.A.*,[650] the Sindh High Court held that all the legal or factual controversies had to be raised in proceedings filed under section 5 of the 1937 Act because prior to filing those proceedings, civil courts had no jurisdiction to halt the operation of foreign arbitral award nor to impart a verdict declaring the award valid and legal or otherwise.

---

649. *Marines Limited v. Aegus Shipping Co. Ltd and others*, 1987 CLC 1299.
650. *Hassan Ali & Co. Cotton (Private) Limited v. Poly Coton, S.A., 2-Rue, Andrien Vallin, 1201 Geneva, Switzerland and others*, PLD 1996 Karachi 416.

This would be a case where the award was allegedly procured through fraud or misrepresentation. In *Government of Sindh v. Fazal Muhammad*,[651] it was held that if an award was induced through misrepresentation or fraud, the other party could challenge it on those grounds, but for that purpose, a suit under section 12(2) of CPC would not be maintainable. However, in *Hassan Ali & Co. (Pvt.) Ltd. v. Poly Cotton S.A.*,[652] the court referred to section 32 of the 1940 Act with regard to an award rendered in England under the rules of the Liverpool Cotton Association, holding that for the determination as to the effect, existence or validity of awards, no suit could be filed in Pakistani courts, nor could an arbitral award be 'set aside, amended, modified or in any way affected otherwise than as provided under the Law of arbitration'.[653]

Judgments are prescribing the same principle to the extent that suits under the CPC cannot be filed in respect of awards but are inconsistent as to the applicability of sections 32 and 33 of the 1940 Act to foreign arbitral awards. In *Marines Limited v. Aegus Shipping Co. Ltd*, these two provisions were explicitly held to be irrelevant to foreign awards, whereas in *Co. Cotton (Private) Limited v. Poly Cotton, S.A*, the maintainability of suits in respect of foreign arbitral awards was determined in light of these provisions. It is submitted that to hold sections 32 and 33 of the 1940 Act to be irrelevant with respect to foreign awards in a case where the award debtor desires to challenge it does not make any difference. The reason is that both section 5 of the 1937 Act and sections 32 and 33 of the 1940 Act were speaking the same thing, that is, that award debtors cannot file a suit to declare an award ineffective or unenforceable and that such remedy might be sought only by filing an application. This obscurity has ramifications after the enactment of the 2011 Act.

This ambiguity as to the true scope of sections 32 and 33 of the 1940 Act could not be clarified even by the enactment of the 2011 Act because, after the promulgation of the latter instrument, the relevance of these two sections was reaffirmed in *Taisei Corporation v. A.M. Construction Co.*[654] In this case, the Punjab High Court held that there were some remedies and rights provided in the 1940 Act which were not available under the 2011 Act. It further held that in order to avail those rights and remedies in respect of foreign arbitral awards, which were otherwise governed by the 2011 Act, the relevant provisions of the 1940 Act could be invoked. For example, under sections 32 and 33 of the 1940 Act, a party might solicit the court for the validity and effect of an award. This has not been contemplated under the 2011 Act. Therefore, the Sindh High Court held that sections 33 and 32 and the rights thereunder might be invoked in regard to foreign arbitral awards.

---

651. *Government of Sindh and another v. Ch. Fazal Muhammad and another*, PLD 1991 SC 197.
652. *Hassan Ali & Co. (Pvt.) Ltd. v. Poly Cotton S.A. and others*, 1996 CLC 1812.
653. The phrase in the quotations marks was extracted from section 32 of the 1940 Act. The complete section is reproduced as follows:

    Section 32. Bar to suit contesting arbitration agreement or award:

    Notwithstanding any law for the time being in force, no suit shall lie on any ground for a decision upon the existence, effect or validity of an arbitration agreement or award, nor shall any arbitration agreement or *award be set aside, amended, modified or in any way affected otherwise than as provided in this Act.*

654. *Taisei Corporation v. A.M. Construction Company (Pvt.) Ltd*, PLD 2012 Lahore 455.

This judgment has done nothing except inflating confusion by eliminating what the 2011 Act was enacted for. It is evident that, like the 1937 Act, the 2011 Act does not equally embody any provision entitling the parties to file declaratory suits for the validity or invalidity of foreign arbitral awards. Under the old law, requiring a party to file an application instead of a suit for challenging the validity or enforcement of an award seems to be a commendable job considering the fact that the processes and phases involved in the application are lesser in number and complication as compared to those involved in a full-fledged suit under CPC. But with the incorporation of the New York Convention into Pakistani domestic law through the 2011 Act, it was unnecessary in *Taisei Corporation v. A.M. Construction Co.*[655] to extend sections 32 and 33 to foreign awards banking on the assumption that if an award debtor wants to challenge the arbitral award, the courts of the seat were the proper forum. This intent of the New York Convention is evident from Article V(1)(e), which categorically provides that an award set aside by the courts of the seat may be refused recognition and enforcement on this basis. Therefore, the extension of sections 32 and 33 to foreign awards by conferring on Pakistani courts' jurisdiction to entertain applications from the award debtor praying for the remedy of checking the validity of foreign awards is tantamount to bestowing the enforcement courts with powers of setting aside foreign awards. It should be, however, in principle exclusive to the courts of the seat of arbitration.[656]

10.3.3. Limitation Period to File the Award in the Court

In *Riyasat Begum v. Ejaz Ahmad*,[657] the public policy objective behind the prescription of limitation periods was stated by the Peshawar High Court as follows:

> The object of law of limitation is to regulate the course and manner for providing relief or remedy, where substantive rights are pressed in litigation. The restriction of time limit is an outcome of public policy. Public policy to limit the time for bringing an action or claim before the court of law is adopted in the legal system of all civilized States. No doubt, the superior courts had time and again held and encouraged the decision on merits instead of technicalities but it does not mean that in every case the law of limitation is ignored, which will put the law redundant. The law of limitation itself has provided an inbuilt remedy for that purpose in the shape of section-5 thus, an application for condonation of delay[658]

655. *Ibid.*
656. For a discussion on the allocation of 'primary' and 'secondary' jurisdiction to the court of the seat and enforcement by the New York Convention, *see* W. Michael Reisman and Heide Iravani, *Symposium: Arbitration and National Courts: Conflict and Cooperation: The Changing Relation of National Courts and International Commercial Arbitration*, 21 Am. Rev. Int'l Arb. 5 (2010).
657. *Riyasat Begum v. Ejaz Ahmad and another*, 2013 CLC 597.
658. An application for condonation of delay is given under Article 5 of the Limitation Act 1908, which speaks as follows:

> 5. Extension of period in certain cases. Any appeal or application for a revision or a review or judgment or for leave to appeal or any other application to which this section may be made applicable by or under any enactment for the time being in force may be

is mandatory whenever, any application or appeal etc., has been filed after prescribed period.

It should be taken into consideration that the limitation period for filing an award to the court is ninety days, as stipulated by Article 178 of the Limitation Act 1908. However, Pakistani courts have very prudently interpreted that this provision is confined to domestic awards to the exclusion of foreign awards. For instance, in *Nan Fung Textiles Ltd. v. Sadiq Traders Ltd,*[659] the enforcement of awards, filed in court two years after their pronouncement, was resisted on the basis of Article 178 of the Limitation Act 1908. However, the Sindh High Court, by holding the applicability of this provision, was limited only to domestic awards and concluded that the lapse of the ninety-day period had no effect on the enforcement of foreign awards. A similar view was followed in *Petrocon (Pvt.) Ltd. v. Hyderabad Development Authority, Hyderabad,*[660] where the Sindh High Court declined to extend Article 178 to a foreign award.

However, *Cogetex v. Mayfair Spinning Mills Ltd*[661] deviates from this view. In this case, arbitration under the Liverpool Cotton Association Rules culminated in an award in favour of the plaintiff (a Swiss Company) and against a Pakistani defendant, which was appealed by the defendant before the Technical Appeal Committee of the Liverpool Cotton Association. The appeal was dismissed on account of the defendant's failure to pay the appropriate fee. The plaintiff, thereafter, filed the award with the Pakistani courts for enforcement, which was resisted by the defendant on the grounds, *inter alia*, that the limitation period for filing awards had expired. The defendant averred that the suit came in the ambit of Article 181 of the First Schedule to the Limitation Act, which prescribed the maximum limit of three years from the date of announcement of the award, or more flexibly from the date when an appeal against the award had been disposed of. The court did not share this objection. By relying on *Frederick E. Rose (Commodities) Limited v. Munsoor Ali Tanning Co.,*[662] it held that the application for the enforcement of foreign awards under section 5 of the 1937 Act was registered as a suit in the court. The court further stated that since no time limit had been specified for filing such suit under the First Schedule to the Limitation Act, it was Article 120 of the Limitation Act which would govern that suit, i.e., a period of six years.

It may be opined that this judgment seems to be inconsistent as opposed to *Riyasat Begum v. Ejaz Ahmad,*[663] which might be said to have freed the foreign award

admitted after the period of limitation prescribed therefor, when the appellant or applicant satisfies the Court that he had sufficient cause for not preferring the appeal or making the application within such period.

Explanation. The fact that the appellant or applicant was misled by any order, practice or judgment of the High Court in ascertaining or computing the prescribed period of limitation may be sufficient cause within the meaning of this section.

659. *Nan Fung. Textiles Ltd. v. Sadiq Traders Ltd.*, PLD 1982 Karachi 619.
660. *Petrocon (Pvt.) Ltd. v. Hyderabad Development Authority, Hyderabad,* 1990 MLD 1675.
661. *Cogetex S.A., A Company Duly Incorporated under the Laws of Switzerland v. Mayfair Spinning Mills Limited, a Public Limited Company Incorporated under the Pakistan Companies Ordinance, 1984*, 2004 CLD 1023.
662. NLR 1981 UC 175 Karachi.
663. *Riyasat Begum v. Ejaz Ahmad and another,* 2013 CLC 597.

from all kinds of limitation periods. Although, as compared to three years, the period of six years is friendlier, when compared with a complete absence of any limitation period, this judgment might seem cumbersome.

10.4. INTENSITY OF JUDICIAL REVIEW OF ARBITRAL AWARDS

The scope of judicial review of awards exercised by Pakistani courts is not easy to define, but they can, most often, be termed as conducting in-depth reviews.

10.4.1. Review by the Court of Arbitral Award: Fundamental Principles

The principles governing the judicial review of arbitral awards are the same for both kinds of awards, i.e., foreign and domestic. Therefore, the judgments rendered in respect of foreign as well as domestic awards are relevant and are looked upon to ascertain the judicial approach in more detail. Similarities concerning the standard of review make the survey of judgments on domestic awards more appropriate because every aspect of judicial review has not been discussed in judgments concerning foreign awards due to the dearth of foreign awards presented in Pakistani courts.

While reviewing the award, the courts will intervene only if the error is apparent on the face of the award and should be discoverable from the award itself.[664] The

664. For foreign award, *see Conticotton S.A. Co. v. Farooq Corporation and others*, 1999 CLC 1018. For domestic award, *see Premier Insurance Co. (Pakistan) Ltd., Karachi v. Ejaz Ahmed Khawaja and others*, 1981 CLC 311; *Gandhara Consultants (Pvt.) Ltd. v. Pakistan Defence Officer's Housing Authority, Karachi*, 2010 CLC 506; *Al-Abdullah Constructors (Pvt.) Ltd. v. Pakistan Water and Power Development Authority*, 2008 CLC 798; *Award in Dispute Between Mrs. Sunble Zareen Khan and D.C.A.S. (Admn.)*, 2008 CLC 426; *Falcon Enterprises v. National Refinery Ltd.*, 2006 CLC 888; *Abdullah Traders through Partner Mukhtar Ahmad v. Trading Corporation of Pakistan Ltd.*, 1999 CLC 2047; *Khan Brothers and Associates v. Director-General Food, Government of Pakistan*, 1998 CLC 1671; *Sainjee Cargo Service v. Cargo Movers and others*, 1989 CLC 2229; *Ascon Engineers (Pvt.) Ltd. v. Province of Punjab through Secretary, Housing and Physical Planning Department*, 2002 SCMR 1662; *S. Altaf Hussain v. Duty Free Shops (Pvt.) Limited*, 2000 YLR 2021; *Iftikhar Zaidi Associates v. Pakistan Steel Mills Corporation*, 2003 YLR 2596; *Rais Chiragh-Ud-Din v. Muhammad Aslam*, 2001 YLR 2162; *Mian Corporation v. Lever Brothers of Pakistan Ltd*, PLD 2006 SC 169; *National Fibers Ltd. and another v. Pakistan*, PLD 2004 Lahore 722; *Ghee Corporation of Pakistan (Pvt.) Limited v. Broken Hill Proprietary Company Limited*, PLD 1999 Karachi 112; *Azra Ali v. Arif Ali*, PLD 1993 Karachi 683; *Crescent Jute Products Ltd., Karachi v. Government of Pakistan*, PLD 1976 Karachi 31; *Chairman, WAPDA and another v. Syed Bhais (Pvt.) Ltd. and another*, 2011 CLC 841; *S.M.I. Brothers through Managing Partner v. Municipal Committee, Murree through Administrator*, 2003 CLC 419; *Premier Insurance Company and others v. Attock Textile Mills Ltd.*, PLD 2006 Lahore 534; *Tracon Services (Pvt.) Ltd. v. Sui Southern Gas Co. Ltd.*, PLD 2009 Karachi 54; *Water and Power Development Authority, WAPDA House, Lahore v. Ghulam Rasul and Company (Pvt.) Ltd.*, PLD 2006 Lahore 314; *Aer Rianta International Pakistan (Pvt.) Ltd. v. Civil Aviation Authority*, PLD 2006 Karachi 216; *Ashfaq Ali Qureshi v. Municipal Corporation, Multan and another.* 1985 SCMR 597; *National Fibers Ltd. and another v. Pakistan*, PLD 2004 Lahore 722; *Pakistan Steel Mills Corporation, Karachi v. Mustafa Sons (Pvt.) Ltd., Karachi*, PLD 2003 SC 301. In this judgment along with other things stated in the above paragraph, the Supreme Court held that if some contractual clause had been wrongly interpreted by the arbitrator, he was not obliged to give specific reasons, nor was he bound to give the reasons for the award so far as his award is within the purview of the terms of reference. *Adamjee*

courts, while hearing the objections against an award, will not act as a court of appeal to conduct a reappraisal of evidence produced before the arbitrator in order to explore infirmities in the award and to assess whether the arbitral tribunal had made the judgment in accordance with this evidence or not. Rather, the assessment of the court would be restricted to the award itself and the material put on record. The court cannot take a look into the material used by arbitrators to compare the reasoning furnished by the tribunal to discover the error in the award.[665]

Hence, the courts will act merely in an executing fashion, which means they cannot travel beyond the award, nor can they re-examine the award.[666] This is also the case even if the opinion of the court would have been at odds with that of the arbitrator or where the arbitrator has made an error. In other words, an award will not be set aside merely on the ground that when examining the record and evidence, the

Construction Co. Ltd. v. Islamic Republic of Pakistan and others, PLD 2003 Karachi 180. For instance, in *Province of Sindh and others v. Waseem Construction Co.*, 1991 CLC 66, it was held that the failure of the arbitrator to appreciate and consider the contract properly would amount to an error patent on the face of the award.

665. *Trustees of the Port of Karachi v. Iftikhar Brothers,* 1993 CLC 1491; *Fazal Textile Mills Ltd. v. Sattar Cotton Ginning Factory Ltd.*, 1982 CLC 97.

666. For Foreign award, *see Conticotton S.A. Co. v. Farooq Corporation and others,* 1999 CLC 1018; *A. Merdith Janes Co. Ltd. v. Crescent Board Ltd.*, 1999 CLC 437; *Quinn Corporation and others v. Cotton Export Corporation and others,* 2004 CLD 1040; *Cogetex S.A., A Company Duly Incorporated under the Laws of Switzerland v. Mayfair Spinning Mills Limited, A Public Limited Company Incorporated under the Pakistan Companies Ordinance, 1984,* 2004 CLD 1023; *Alfred C. Toepfer International Gmbh v. Pakistan Molasses Company and another,* 2003 CLD 1666. For domestic award, *see Gandhara Consultants (Pvt.) Ltd v. Pakistan Defence Officer's Housing Authority, Karachi,* 2010 CLC 506; *Al-Abdullah Constructors (Pvt.) Ltd. v. Pakistan Water and Power Development Authority through Chief Engineer,* 2008 CLC 798; *Award in Dispute Between Mrs. Sunble Zareen Khan and D.C.A.S. (Admn.),* 2008 CLC 426; *Falcon Enterprises v. National Refinery Ltd.,* 2006 CLC 888; *Adamjee Construction Company Ltd. v. Islamic Republic of Pakistan through Secretary, Ministry of Communications & Works, Islamabad and others,* 2004 CLC 1977; *S.G. Rayon Mills (Pvt.) Limited v. Fida Hussain & Associates* 2002 CLC 353 (If court is allowed to act as court of appeal, the very objective of arbitration will be ruined.); *Sezai Turkes Feyzi Akkaya Construction Company v. Board of Trustees of Karachi Port Trust, Karachi,* 2007 CLC 879; *Privatization Commission of Pakistan Constitution Avenue, Islamabad v. Petrosin Products (Pvt.) Limited and others,* 2001 CLC 1878; *G.M.K. Enterprises v. Shaheen Builders,* 1999 CLC 1698; *Abdullah Traders through Partner Mukhtar Ahmad v. Trading Corporation of Pakistan Ltd.*, 1999 CLC 2047; *Khan Brothers and Associates v. Director-General Food, Government of Pakistan,* 1998 CLC 1671; *Sainjee Cargo Services v. Cargo Movers and other,* 1989 CLC 2229; *Ascon Engineers (Pvt.) Ltd. v. Province of Punjab,* 2002 SCMR 1662; *S. Altaf Hussain v. Duty Free Shops (Pvt.) Limited,* 2000 YLR 2021; *Ghee Corporation of Pakistan Ltd. and others v. Multan Chemicals Ltd. and others,* 2000 YLR 253; *Ghee Corporation of Pakistan Ltd. v. Kuok Oils And Grains (Pvt.) Ltd.*, 1999 MLD 2617; *Haji Abdul Hameed & Co. v. Insurance Company of North America and others,* 1999 YLR 1213; *Waseem Construction Co. v. Province of Sindh,* 1997 MLD 2370; *Iftikhar Zaidi Associates v. Pakistan Steel Mills Corporation,* 2003 YLR 2596; *Rais Chiragh-Ud-Din v. Muhammad Aslam,* 2001 YLR 2162; *Mian v. Lever Brothers of Pakistan Ltd.*, PLD 2006 SC 169; *Ghee Corporation of Pakistan (Pvt.) Limited v. Broken Hill Proprietary Company Limited,* PLD 1999 Karachi 112; *Turner Morrison Garahams Group of Companies, London v. Rice Export Corporation Pakistan Ltd.*, PLD 1998 Karachi 79; *Azra Ali v. Arif Ali,* PLD 1993 Karachi 683; *Crescent Jute Products Ltd., Karachi v. Government of Pakistan,* PLD 1976 Karachi 31; *Chairman, WAPDA and another v. Syed Bhais (Pvt.) Ltd. and another,* 2011 CLC 841; *S.M.I. Brothers v. Municipal Committee, Murree,* 2003 CLC 419.

conclusion other than that derived by the arbitrator was possible.[667] It is the duty of the court to give every reasonable intendment to the enforcement of awards rather than their vitiation. Awards should be interpreted liberally in keeping with common sense.[668]

This approach of judicial review is equally apt to all the grounds utilized in order to resist the enforcement of awards. However, if a Pakistani court is convinced of the necessity of conducting a review of the award on any ground (enumerated in Article V of New York Convention for foreign awards and section 30 of the 1940 Act for domestic award), as discussed *infra*, it may be viewed as conducting a review which is far more detailed than a prima facie review.

10.4.2. Review of Arbitrator's Jurisdiction

While reviewing an award on the basis of the arbitrator's jurisdiction, the courts can examine the parent contract as well as the arbitration agreement, even if the error is not patent on the face of the award. In *Pakistan v. M. A. Aziz & Sons*,[669] it was held that if the case is to be decided on the basis of errors patent on the face of the award, the court will not look at anything extraneous to the award. But this principle will be of no relevance to the case where the controversy concerns the arbitrator's jurisdiction to adjudge a matter, which as a dispute could not be referred to him. In this case, the evidence extraneous to the award can be pressed into service to prove that the award bears upon the matter, which does not fall within the ambit of the arbitrator's jurisdiction. In the instant case, one of the controversies was that 'some matters

667. For foreign award, *see Quinn Corporation and others v. Cotton Export Corporation and others*, 2004 CLD 1040; *Alfred C. Toepfer International Gmbh v. Pakistan Molasses Company and another*, 2003 CLD 1666. For domestic award, *see Premier Insurance Co. (Pakistan) Ltd., Karachi v. Ejaz Ahmed Khawaja and others*, 1981 CLC 311; *Gandhara Consultants (Pvt.) Ltd. v. Pakistan Defence Officer's Housing Authority, Karachi*, 2010 CLC 506; *Al-Abdullah Constructors (Pvt.) Ltd. v. Pakistan Water and Power Development Authority*, 2008 CLC 798; *Award in Dispute Between Mrs. Sunble Zareen Khan and D.C.A.S. (Admn.)* 2008 CLC 426; *Falcon Enterprises v. National Refinery Ltd.*, 2006 CLC 888; *Sezai Turkes Feyzi Akkaya Construction Company v. Board of Trustees of Karachi Port Trust, Karachi*, 2007 CLC 879; *Azra Ali v. Arif Ali*, PLD 1993 Karachi 683; *Ibad & Co. v. Province of Sindh*, PLD 1980 Karachi 207; *Chairman, WAPDA and another v. Syed Bhais (Pvt.) Ltd. and another*, 2011 CLC 841; *S.M.I. v. Municipal Committee, Murree*, 2003 CLC 419; *Moinuddin Siddiqui v. Saleem Siodiqui*, 1984 CLC 2568.

668. For foreign awards, *see Alfred C. Toepfer International Gmbh v. Pakistan Molasses Company and another*, 2003 CLD 1666. For domestic award, *see Award in Dispute Between Mrs. Sunble Zareen Khan and D.C.A.S. (Admn.)*, 2008 CLC 426; *Falcon Enterprises v. National Refinery Ltd.*, 2006 CLC 888; *Adamjee Construction Company Ltd. v. Islamic Republic of Pakistan*, 2004 CLC 1977; *Province of Punjab v. Sh. Fazalul Hussain*, 2003 CLC 1780; *Sezai Turkes Feyzi Akkaya Construction Company v. Board of Trustees of Karachi Port Trust, Karachi*, 2007 CLC 879; *Ascon Engineers (Pvt.) Ltd. v. Province of Punjab*, 2002 SCMR 1662; *S. Altaf Hussain v. Duty Free Shops (Pvt.) Limited*, 2000 YLR 2021; *Rais Chiragh-Ud-Din v. Muhammad Aslam*, 2001 YLR 2162; *Aer Rianta International Pakistan (Pvt.) Ltd. v. Civil Aviation Authority*, PLD 2006 Karachi 216; *Ashfaq Ali Qureshi v. Municipal Corporation, Multan and another*, 1985 SCMR 597; *Zakaullah Khan v. Government of Pakistan*, PLD 1998 Lahore 132; *Turner Morrison Garahams Group of Companies, London v. Rice Export Corporation Pakistan Ltd.*, PLD 1998 Karachi 79; *S.M.I. Brothers v. Municipal Committee, Murree through Administrator*, 2003 CLC 419.

669. *Pakistan v. M. A. Aziz & Sons*, PLD 1980 Lahore 422.

including the question of supply of steel racks were not the subject-matter of the dispute and consequently were never referred to the arbitrator'. The court held that in this situation, it would not only read the award but would also peruse the contract. On the basis of those documents, if it was established that:

> The supply of the steel racks was included in the lump sum contract, it will follow that this was not matter of dispute between the parties and was not referred since the only matters referred were disputes arising out of the contract. The supply of the material contracted upon and paid for as a part of the lump sum contract cannot be a subject-matter of dispute between the parties unless the case of the contractor be based upon the liability of the Government to pay some extra costs or damages.

Hence, the court will not go behind something extraneous to the award, except in three situations. First, if the matter fell outside the jurisdiction of the arbitrator; second, if the award was procured through fraud; and finally, if the award was not complete and unambiguous in a way that it cannot be trusted as an exhaustive document to explore the error on the face of it.[670]

With regard to the challenge of an award lacking arbitral jurisdiction, the case of *A. Merdith Janes Co. Ltd. v. Crescent Board Ltd*[671] is also pertinent. There, the enforcement of an award emanating from the rules and by-laws of the Liverpool Cotton Association was refused by the award debtor on the basis that the arbitrators did not have a sight of the Agreement Form on which both parties had signed and hence they did not have jurisdiction to give an award, which was *void ab initio*. Regarding this objection, the court reproduced paragraph 8 of the award, which stipulated that:

> Neither the Buyers nor the Sellers dispute the existence of this contract, in spite of the Arbitrators having no sight of the contract form signed by both parties.

From this, the court came to a conclusion that the defendant seemed to have relied merely on the later part of this statement while objecting to this award, whereas in the arbitration proceedings, they had actually accepted the existence of the contract. Thus, a perusal of the whole paragraph suggests that they, in fact, had waived the fact that the arbitrators did not have sight of the contract.[672]

10.4.3. Procedural Fairness or Due Process

In the perspective of domestic awards, it was held in *Mian Corporation v. Lever Brothers of Pakistan Ltd.*[673] that to challenge an award on the basis of misconduct from the

670. *See also Muhammad Sadiq Muhammad Afzal v. Ministry of Industries (Department of Supplies and Development), Government of Pakistan*, PLD 1962 (W. P.) Karachi 113, where it was held under the 1940 Act, where it is patent from the award that the arbitrator decided questions not actually referred to him, such an award will be set aside.
671. *A. Merdith Janes Co. Ltd. v. Crescent Board Ltd.*, 1999 CLC 437.
672. *See also China International Water v. Pakistan Water and Power Development Authority*, PLD 2005 Karachi 670 where the court held that the award rendered on the basis of an invalid reference (or arbitration agreement) would not be enforced.
673. *Mian Corporation v. Lever Brothers of Pakistan Ltd*, PLD 2006 Supreme Court 169.

arbitrator, such misconduct should be proved to the satisfaction of the court.[674] An award cannot be set aside merely on account of some irregularity that occurred in the arbitration proceedings but could only be vacated if some illegality or error is floating on the surface of the award.[675] However, when the allegation concerns the misconduct of the arbitrator,[676] the court will necessarily take into account the intrinsic evidence as well as evidence extraneous to the award to pass judgment on such misconduct.[677]

In *European Grain & Shipping Ltd* case,[678] concerning the enforcement of a foreign award, one of the issues framed was whether the arbitrators had committed misconduct. For that purpose, the trial court gave permission to examine two witnesses residing outside Pakistan. The question of whether such permission should be granted reached the Supreme Court of Pakistan, which granted leave to appeal in order to consider, among others, the following.

Whether in such a case, the only evidence that can be recorded against the enforcement of the foreign award are that which relate to proving all or any of the grounds mentioned in section 7(1) and (2) of the Act, 1937, and whether evidence relating to misconduct in such proceedings can only be confined to that kind of misconduct which is also regarded as a breach of rules of natural justice and not 'misconduct' of general nature.

However, the Supreme Court did not feel it necessary to resolve this question because by that time, it had not been decided by the trial court, and the High Court had not come to any decision over the questions of law and jurisdiction relating to that case. Thereafter, on the issues of law and jurisdiction, the matter was remanded to the trial court by the Supreme Court. Hence, no authority exists on the subject of recording the evidence in foreign awards enforceable under the 1937 Act. Due to the absence of such authority, it may be inferred that the courts could apply the principles developed under domestic law while reviewing due process infringements in foreign arbitrations, which, it is submitted, might not be a preferable approach.

10.5. WAIVER OF REVIEW BY PARTIES AND EX OFFICIO EXAMINATION BY COURT OF OBJECTIONS

It is established that arbitral bias is a subcategory of misconduct; therefore, the principles applicable to arbitral misconduct will also govern those cases of arbitral bias.[679] In that regard, it has been held by Pakistani courts that even if no objection was filed against the award on the basis of misconduct, it was the duty of the court under

674. Court approved the decision in *Pakistan Steel Mills Corporation v. Mustafa Sons (Pvt.) Ltd.*, PLD 2003 SC 301. *See also Water and Power Development Authority, WAPDA House v. Ghulam Rasul and Company (Pvt.) Ltd., Lahore,* PLD 2006 Lahore 314.
675. *Province of Punjab v. Muhammad Anwar & Co.*, 2002 YLR 3796.
676. For the topic as to how an arbitrator misconducts himself or the arbitration proceedings, *see* Ch. 13 below.
677. For intrinsic evidence, *see Mow Ansari Enterprises v. Trading Corporation of Pakistan Ltd.*, PLD 1980 Karachi 226. For extraneous evidence, *see Abdullah Contractors v. Water and Power Development Authority,* 2006 YLR 589.
678. PLD 1982 SC 407.
679. For a detailed discussion, *see* Ch. 13 below.

section 16 of the 1940 Act to scrutinize if the award suffered from any procedural infirmity.[680] Awards valid on their face may be set aside on the ground of misconduct by the arbitrator.[681] The reason for such non-waiver could be inferred from the judgment of the Supreme Court of Pakistan in *Director Housing, A.G'S Branch, Rawalpindi v. Makhdum Consultants Engineers and Architects*,[682] which reiterated the significance of an arbitrator's impartiality by asserting that he must act honestly and fairly while adjudging the controversy between the parties, stating further that while choosing arbitration over litigation, the parties cannot be considered to have sacrificed 'the paramount and most avowed objective of seeking adjudication of their disputes in a just, fair and impartial manner'.

In *Adamjee Construction Co. Ltd. v. Islamic Republic of Pakistan*,[683] the court held that if no objections were filed against the award, it was the duty of the court to check ex officio whether there was any patent illegality or infirmity in the award necessitating the remission of the award or its setting aside. The absence of any objection from the parties did not absolve the court from such a duty to determine if the award was valid

680. *Province of Baluchistan through Secretary, Government of Baluchistan, Communication and Works Department, Quetta and another v. Haji Muhammad Hassan and another*, 1988 CLC 1583. *See also Saleem Ali v. Akhtar Ali and others*, PLD 2004 Lahore 404. Some elements which are considered to constitute legal misconduct by the arbitrator have also been summarized by the Punjab High Court in *Khalid Abbas v. Hafiz Muhammad Farooq and another*, 2004 YLR 274 as follows:

(a) Neglect of duties and responsibilities by arbitrators;
(b) something contrary to what Courts of justice expect from them before allowing finality to their award;
(c) if arbitrator has refused to postpone a meeting for the purpose of allowing a party to engage a counsel, when the other party unexpectedly turns up with a counsel;
(d) if award is made without having heard all the evidence;
(e) if evidence of witnesses is recorded behind the back of a party;
(f) if a party has not been allowed reasonable opportunity of proving his case;
(g) if arbitrator has not brought to the notice of opposite-party a document received by him from his adversary or not given him an opportunity of meeting the inferences deducible from them;
(h) if irregularities in the proceedings are proved, which amount to improper hearing of the matter in dispute;
(i) if a finding is perverse or unsupported by evidence before him;
(j) if arbitrator decides a disputed question without going into evidence as in such a case he would be said to have decided blindly;
(k) if there is indication of gross negligence or recklessness on the face of the record;
(l) if there is some mistake of fact, provided it is either admitted or at least clearly beyond reasonable doubt.

These points were followed in: *Kashmir Corporation Ltd. v. Pakistan International Airlines*, PLD 1995 Karachi 301; *Pakistan Steel Mills Corporation, Karachi v. Mustafa Sons (Pvt.) Ltd., Karachi*, PLD 2003 SC 301. For specific instances of misconduct, *see West Pakistan Small Industries Corporation, Lahore v. Haji Bashir Ahmad*, PLD 1977 Lahore; *Maqbool Associates Ltd. v. Sindh Sugar Corporation Ltd.*, 1990 CLC 55.

681. *Abdullah Contractors v. Water and Power Development Authority*, 2006 YLR 589.

682. *Director Housing, A.G's Branch, Rawalpindi v. Makhdum Consultants Engineers and Architects*, 1997 SCMR 988.

683. *Adamjee Construction Co. Ltd. v. Islamic Republic of Pakistan and others*, PLD 2003 Karachi 180.

on the face of it or not.[684] In this case, when a court examines an award and finds that the arbitrator had admitted that no witnesses were presented to submit details regarding the method of calculation and formula which it adopted to ascertain the claims of the plaintiff (in whose favour award was given) it must set it aside. In another case, the arbitrator also acknowledged the absence of a record to instruct about the market value of property or the tool to determine the operational cost. Such admission from the arbitrator in the award was taken by the court as patent illegality which the court could not be overlooked, even if the objections were not submitted by the defendant against the award. This award was not made a rule of court.[685] If, however, this were to be viewed as an expert opinion regarding the market evaluation of the property that was not binding on the arbitrator, this should not have been counted as patent illegality by the court, for these grounds do not look very important.

10.6. QUESTION OF LAW SPECIFICALLY SUBMITTED TO ARBITRATOR OR INCIDENTALLY ARISEN

In *Muhammad Sadiq Muhammad Afzal v. Ministry of Industries Pakistan,*[686] it was held that if a question of law was specifically submitted to the arbitrator and it was patent that the parties wished to secure the verdict of the arbitrator on it and not from the court, the court would not interfere. However, in a case where the question of law was material incidentally for the purpose of deciding the question actually entrusted to the arbitral tribunal, it was open to the court to intervene to set aside the award if the error of law was apparent on the surface of the award or the record. For instance, in this case, the only issue submitted for arbitral consideration was whether the government had unjustly cancelled the contract and, if so, whether it was bound to make a compensation on account of its default in performing the contract. It was held by the court that the matter of construction of contract emerged incidentally before the arbitral tribunal, which was material for the decision on the issue referred. The matter of interpretation of the contract, which would have been the question of law, was not specifically referred to the arbitrator so as to cloth himself with exclusive authority to decide it and that the issue of contractual interpretation was incidental to the main issue of finding the liability of the government. The court held that this was an error of law apparent on the face of the record, and it would intervene to set the award aside.[687]

684. On this point with same approach, *see also Ascon Engineers (Pvt.) Ltd. v. Province of Punjab,* 2002 SCMR 1662; *Wajid Ali and others v. Liaqat Ali and others,* 2000 YLR 2484; *Meer Muhammad Sharif v. Mirza Muhammad Ashraf and others,* 1980 CLC 1984.

685. Court referred to Dacca High Court in *Abdul Khaliq v. Province of East Pakistan and another,* PLD 1964 Dacca 166; *Province of Balochistan v. M/S. Tribal Friends Company, Loralai,* PLD 1986 Quetta 321; *see also Iftikhar & Company (Pvt.) Ltd. v. Pakistan Steel Mills Ltd.*, 2002 YLR 1494.

686. *Shaikh Muhammad Sadiq Muhammad Afzal v. Ministry of Industries, Department of Supply and Development, Government of Pakistan, Karachi,* PLD 1966 (W. P.) Karachi 412.

687. *See also Transocean Asia v. Secretary to Government of Pakistan, Ministry of Agriculture Auto Works,* PLD 1967 Karachi 445. *See also Umar Bibi and Others v. Bashir Ahmad and others,* PLD

An even more objectionable view on judicial review can be seen in *Pakistan Television Corporation Limited v. Interconstruct (Pvt.) Limited*,[688] wherein a lower court's judgment making the award a rule of the court was turned down on appeal by the Peshawar High Court because, *inter alia*, the lower court had not evaluated the award and failed to discuss in detail the findings of the arbitrator. It was held that such a 'tentative, shallow and cursory glance of assaying the award was not permissible under the law'. Instead, in the words of the Peshawar High Court, the court was obliged to evaluate each and every aspect of the award minutely. The Peshawar High Court also held that a court should analyse the evidence employed by the arbitrator to assess if such evidence has properly been sifted and utilized by the arbitrator according to the law. It further underscored that a court should concern itself with the findings of the award as well as the facts to figure out if the award complied with the terms of reference, etc. The High Court also laid down a principle that while making an award a rule of court, the court should not mechanically stamp the award because the court was not expected to be a passive consenter but rather must be an active dissenter. On the basis that the lower court could not perform all these functions, the judgment was set aside by the High Court.[689]

10.7. CONCLUSION

The point of concern is the 'error patent on the face of an award', and as has very frequently been held by Pakistani courts, they will not intervene unless the error is patent on the face of the award. The first facet is that the court will step in if the dispute is about the jurisdiction of an arbitrator to decide a case, even if the error was not patent on the face of the award.[690] The same principle of 'patent error' will not apply if the allegations are linked to the 'misconduct' of the arbitrator, either attributed to himself personally or related to the arbitration proceedings he undertakes. The reason given by the courts is that it cannot discover the evidence or reasons for such misconduct, if any, on the face of an arbitral award because the arbitrator does not make an account of all the happenings before him during the course of arbitration proceedings. So, the court has to go beyond the award.[691]

Second, the definition and the way to discover the patent error justifying a judicial intervention in the award is a matter of concern as well. In *Azra Ali v. Arif Ali*,[692] the court held that 'error apparent on the face of record' means that 'such error must be discoverable by reading the award itself and not by reference to other

1968 Lahore 629; *Gandhara Consultants (Pvt.) Ltd. v. Pakistan Defence Officer's Housing Authority, Karachi*, 2010 CLC 506; *Sainjee Cargo Services v. Cargo Movers and others*, 1989 CLC 2229.

688. *Pakistan Television Corporation Limited v. Interconstruct (Pvt.) Limited*, PLD 2010 Peshawar 34.
689. *See also Government of NWFP v. Shahin Shah and others*, 2009 MLD 1418.
690. *Pakistan v. M. A. Aziz & Sons*, PLD 1980 Lahore 422.
691. For intrinsic evidence *see*, *Mow Ansari Enterprises v. Trading Corporation of Pakistan Ltd.*, PLD 1980 Karachi 226. For extraneous evidence, *see Abdullah Contractors v. Water and Power Development Authority*, 2006 YLR 589.
692. *Azra Ali v. Arif Ali*, PLD 1993 Karachi 683.

materials, namely the record and proceedings before the arbitrators or umpire'. In spite of this commendable statement from the court, the ambit of 'patent error floating on the face of an award' has been interpreted widely to include an array of matters that cannot be discovered without first intruding into the merits. For instance, in *Province of Sindh and others v. Waseem Construction*,[693] it was held that failure to appreciate and consider the contract properly would amount to an error patent on the face of the award. Similarly, if the question of law decided by the arbitrator was not specifically referred by the parties but arose incidentally to the main issue, then the award on such incidental question of law would be counted as an error of law on the face of an award, justifying a court's intervention.[694] The question may be raised here as to how it may be apparent on the face of an award if the contract has not been interpreted properly by the arbitrator or if he has decided issues not specifically referred to him. In this way, it may be submitted that the hurdle in the way of the courts to exercise an in-depth review of awards is if an error is apparent on the face of the award. Such an obstacle has been interpreted by the courts in a way that has lost its utility. That is to say, first, this condition does not apply if the award is to be reviewed from an arbitrator's jurisdictional ground or procedural fairness ground, and then so many matters are included into its ambit that their determination actually demands an intrusion into the merits.

The Pakistani approach to the standard of judicial review is obscure. A conclusion that can be inferred is that Pakistani courts review the merits of the case. This attitude is worthy of criticism. The parties' expectations in arbitration, *inter alia*, of a one-shot mechanism free from appeals and court interventions would be compromised if the judicial review of merits is allowed. These expectations can be fulfilled only if awards are considered final. The presumption of finality also strengthens the arbitral system as a dispute resolution mechanism for international trade disputes.[695] Allowing judicial review for weak reasons will undermine arbitration by introducing a new instance in addition to the three already available.[696] Therefore, the standard of review should be reasonably limited and clear beyond uncertainty so that after the award creditor is successful in repelling the challenges to the award, he should not have to suffer from the dilatory and costly justice.[697]

693. *Province of Sindh and others v. Waseem Construction Co.*, 1991 CLC 66.
694. *Shaikh Muhammad Sadiq Muhammad Afzal v. Ministry of Industries, Department of Supply and Development, Government of Pakistan, Karachi*, PLD 1966 (W. P.) Karachi 412 (Wahiduddin and H.T. Raymond, JJ); *Ghee Corporation of Pakistan (Pvt.) Limited v. Broken Hill Proprietary Company Limited through their Local Agents*, PLD 1999 Karachi 112.
695. Alexis Mourre and Luca G. Radicati Di Brozolo, *Towards Finality of Arbitral Award: Two Steps Forward and One Step Back*, 23(2) J. Int'l Arb. 171 (2006).
696. Hans Smit, *Contractual Modification of the Scope of Judicial Review of Arbitral Awards*, 8 Am. Rev. Int'l Arb. 147.
697. Amokura Kawharu, *The Public Policy Ground for Setting Aside and Refusing Enforcement of Arbitral Awards: Comments on the New Zealand Approach*, 24(5) J. Int'l Arb. 491 (2007).

CHAPTER 11

Challenge of Domestic Award Before Pakistani Courts

In Pakistan, the provisions of the 1940 Act, along with judicial interpretations thereon provide a comprehensive account of domestic arbitral awards, including their making, filing and enforcement. In relation to each of these stages, the conditions pertaining to the limitation periods for various matters, such as notices, registration, and stamp duty, are laid down by adopting a flexible approach thereon. The problematic area may be the wide powers of Pakistan courts on the points of remission, modification and setting aside. Although the appellate and revisional remedies on the decision of arbitrators and the courts are provided under the 1940 Act and the CPC, the utility of these remedies seems to be compromised by the lengthy and complex procedure followed by the Pakistani courts.

11.1. INTRODUCTION

An award constitutes the final determination and decision of an arbitrator upon the matter submitted to him in accordance with the arbitration agreement between the parties who consensually and with their free will authorize the arbitrator to settle their controversy through arbitration.[698] It is important to understand the difference between the award and a referee's report. Arbitrators adjudge a controversy by following a procedure, bearing in mind the principles of natural justice and the law. The outcome of this exercise is termed an award, which is made a rule of the court after the court follows the mechanism laid down in arbitration laws. On the other hand, the statement of the referee is his opinion and not a decision and is not binding on the parties. He has

698. *Khalida Malik v. Farida Malik*, 1994 MLD 2348.

to make this statement on the basis of his knowledge or belief.[699] In one case, the parties consensually appointed a referee agreeing to be bound by his decision. The referee submitted his report to the court after recording evidence and examining the record called by him and submitted by the parties. The Punjab High Court declared this report to be an arbitral award and did not agree with the lower court, which treated it as a piece of information from the referee.[700]

With respect to domestic arbitration and awards, Pakistani law prescribes a set time for the arbitrator to conclude the arbitration proceedings, as well as the conditions regarding the stamping and registration of the award. This award is then filed to the court so that it may be rendered a rule of court. Before it is made a rule of the court, the other party may file objections against the award. After hearing these objections, the court can either modify the award or remit it to the arbitrator. The court also has the power to set it aside if certain conditions are fulfilled. This chapter discusses these issues along with the limitation periods prescribed.

11.2. TIME LIMITS TO CONCLUDE THE ARBITRATION PROCEEDINGS

Arbitrators are bound to conclude the arbitration proceedings and give the award within 120 days. A four-month period has been stipulated by the 1940 Act in its section 3, read with the First Schedule annexed thereto. Section 3 stipulates that unless a different intention appears from the arbitration agreement, the provisions postulated in the First Schedule pertain to the arbitration agreement so far as they are applicable. The third paragraph of the First Schedule, which is invoked to ascertain the period of arbitration, reads as follows:

> The arbitrators shall make their award within four months after entering on the reference or after having been called upon to act by notice in writing from any party to the arbitration agreement or within such extended time as the Court may allow.

The condition of making an award in four months is statutorily incorporated in every arbitration agreement as an integral part thereof, whereby the award shall be made in four months by the arbitrator after entering upon the reference.[701] For the calculation of this period, the first day is to be excluded, but the last day will be included.[702] The 1940 Act does not define the phrase 'after entering on the reference'. It was held that the arbitrator enters on the reference:

> When he first applies his mind to dispute or controversy before him and exercises any judicial function in furtherance of the work of arbitration. Where an arbitrator holds a preliminary meeting and gives directions to the parties as to the progress

699. *Abdullah and others v. Abdur Rehman and others*, 2004 YLR 295.
700. *Province of Punjab v. Khalid Hussain and Company Government Contractors*, 2007 MLD 1366.
701. *WAPDA and another v. Khanzada Muhammad Abdul Haque Khan Khattak and Company*, PLD 1990 SC 359.
702. *Khan Brothers and Associates v. Director-General Food, Government of Pakistan*, 1998 CLC 1671.

of the arbitration proceedings before him, he assumes the office of an arbitrator and exercises the functions of an arbitrator.[703]

In case of delay by an arbitrator in making the award, the court has power, under section 28 of the 1940 Act,[704] to extend the time for making the award, following a written as well as oral application, unless the delay in making the award is material, detrimental or unconscionable. The court can extend the time even *ex post facto* after the award has been made.[705] Such power of the court is permissive and discretionary. This discretion should be used by the court when 'cogent reasons are available, including all circumstances surrounding the making of awards'.[706] The phrase 'from time to time' as appearing in section 28 of the 1940 Act implies that the court has the power to extend the time on more than one occasion.[707]

Since section 3 and the First Schedule are not mandatory and just like any other non-mandatory legal provisions, the parties can alter these with their mutual consent. In this regard, the parties can either, upon mutual consent, extend the time for making an award or confer such power on the arbitrator.[708] If the parties have waived the delay by the arbitrator to make an award and have submitted themselves to the jurisdiction of the arbitrator by participating in the arbitration proceedings, leading evidence and taking the chance of getting a favourable award even after the expiry of the prescribed period, they later cannot challenge the award on the ground that it was not declared within time,[709] because in this case, the principles of estoppel and waiver apply in full force.[710] Therefore, the objection that the award was made beyond the period of four

---

703. *Telecom Foundation v. Asko Enterprises*, 2020 CLC 1605. *See also Muhammad Shafi v. Muhammad Sabir*, PLD 1960 Lahore (W. P.) 591; *Haji Abdullah v. S. Iqbal Naseem*, 1987 CLC 166.
704. Section 28. Power of court to enlarge time for making award:

> (1) the court may if it thinks fit whether the time for making the award has expired or not and whether the award has been made or not, enlarge from time to time the time for making the award.
> (2) any provisions in an arbitration agreement whereby the arbitrators or umpire may, except with the consent of all the parties to the agreement, enlarge the time for making the award, shall be void and of no effect.

705. *Civil Aviation Authority, Karachi v. Kist Consultants (Pvt.) Ltd. Lahore*, 1998 SCMR 2393; 2001 MLD 1444; *Khan Brothers and Associates v. Director-General Food, Government of Pakistan*, 1998 CLC 1671. The appellate court also has power to extend the time for making of an award because the appellate court is a 'court' under section 28 of the 1940 Act. *See, Telecom Foundation v. Asko Enterprises*, 2020 CLC 1605.
706. *Khan Brothers and Associates v. Director-General Food, Government of Pakistan*, 1998 CLC 1671. *See also Province of Sindh v. Haji Khan*, PLD 1983 Karachi 621; *Elite Builders and Developers v. Nooruddin Hemani*, 1988 CLC 564; *Tayab Sharif v. Kasam Adamji*, PLD 1955 Sindh 224; *Ghulam Mohyuddin v. Federation of Pakistan*, PLD 1967 Lahore 204; *Engro Chemical Pak. Limited v. Trading Corporation of Pakistan*, 1996 CLC 344.
707. *Engro Chemicals Pakistan v. Trading Corporation of Pakistan*, 1996 CLC 344.
708. *WAPDA and another v. Khanzada Muhammad Abdul Haque Khan Khattak and Company*, PLD 1990 SC 359; *Khan Brothers and Associates v. Director-General Food, Government of Pakistan*, 1998 CLC 1671; *Maj. (Retd.) Humayun Akhtar v. Pakistan Defence Officers Housing Authority*, PLD 2002 Karachi 427.
709. *Quality Builders Ltd. v. Karachi Metropolitan Corporation*, 1999 CLC 1777.
710. *Khan Brothers and Associates v. Director-General Food, Government of Pakistan*, 1998 CLC 1671.

months should first be raised before the arbitrator within this period. Otherwise, such objection before the court will not be entertained.[711]

11.3. MAKING OF AN AWARD

It is not imperative for an arbitrator to frame issues for making an award or to give his findings on each issue in the award. Any omission will not render the award invalid.[712] Similarly, the law does not cast any duty on an arbitrator to record evidence on oath if the parties did not require him to do so. Therefore, he can decide by relying on the documents presented before him by the parties.[713] While making an award, the arbitrator is not bound to record evidence in detail. It would be sufficient if the arbitrator makes an award after hearing both parties and considering their points of view.[714]

An arbitrator does not need to provide his findings on each issue framed by him because an award settling the controversy between the parties would be sufficient in law.[715] However, under section 26-A of the 1940 Act, an arbitrator should give reasons to support his decision in an award so that, while making that award a rule of court, the court should be able to consider any question of law emerging from the award and to appreciate if the arbitrator's conclusion was not suffering from any error of law or misconduct of arbitrators. The reasons given in the award are not required to be in as much detail as mandated in a civil court's judgment. The force of section 26-A is not equal to that of sections 30 and 33 of the 1940 Act because an award cannot be set aside by the court merely on the ground of the absence of a sufficient reason. The award would become void only if, on account of the absence of sufficient reasons, it was remitted by the court to the arbitrator with a direction to resubmit the award within the stipulated time and the arbitrator failed to comply with the directions of the court.[716] An oral award cannot be enforced because an award should be reasoned and registered under the Registration Act 1908, which cannot happen with an oral award.[717]

The non-participation of the arbitrator in the finalization of awards vitiates the award unless such non-participation has been waived by the parties.[718] In one case, the matter was to be decided by three arbitrators, but ultimately only two were appointed. The court held that the forum of the arbitral tribunal was *coram non judice*, and hence,

711. *Hakim Muhammad Ibrahim v. Muhammad Ibrahim and others*, 1999 MLD 1738; *Pakistan Swedish Institute of Technology Garment Production Unit v. The Karachi Port Trust*, 1997 MLD 2034; *Water and Power Development Authority v. Ghulam Rasul and Company (Pvt.) Ltd Lahore*, PLD 2006 Lahore 314.
712. *China International Water v. Pakistan Water and Power Development Authority*, PLD 2005 Karachi 670.
713. *Akhtar Trading Co. v. Food Department and others*, 1991 CLC 258.
714. *Saeeda Bang and others v. Mian Muhammad Amin*, 1995 MLD 187.
715. *Associated Constructors Ltd. v. Karachi Municipal Corporation*, 1982 CLC 1984.
716. *Abdullah Traders v. Trading Corporation of Pakistan Ltd.*, 1999 CLC 2047; *Province of Punjab v. Tarmic Construction (Pvt) Limited*, 1999 CLC 946; *Gandhara Industries Ltd., Karachi. v. Government of Pakistan*, PLD 1532 Kar. 262; *Karachi Electric Supply Corporation Ltd. v. Consortium 2000 P.E.C.H. Society, Karachi*, 1985 CLC 1350.
717. *Abdul Hussain Darugar and another v. Gul Muhammad and others*, 2015 MLD 488.
718. *Haji Nawab Din v. Sh. Ghulam Haider and another*, 1988 SCMR 1623.

the award could be made a rule of court.[719] Similarly, where the award was made by two arbitrators, the submission thereto by one party was of no legal value.[720]

The award should be dated and signed by the arbitrators; otherwise, it would not be made a rule of court.[721] After having signed the award and authorized one of them to get it registered, the arbitrators are considered to have completed their task. Except for any clarification on any clause of the award or correction of typographical errors, the arbitrator cannot modify, reverse or change the award. These tasks can only be performed by the court under sections 15, 16, 17 of the 1940 Act.[722]

Section 14(1) of the 1940 Act says that: 'when the arbitrators have their award, they shall sign it and shall give notice in writing to the parties of the making and signing thereof'. However, the Supreme Court has held in *Farida Malik and others v. Khalid Malik*[723] that awards will not be set aside on the ground that the arbitrator did not give notice to the parties before making the award or affixing his signatures on it. It stated further that although 'shall' has been used in section 14 of the 1940 Act to stipulate the provision of notice of making and signing of the award, this condition is not mandatory, and the omission thereof has no effect on the foundation of the proceedings. It said that:

> In order to invoke penalty of dismissal under Article 178 of the Limitation Act, the factum of service of notice of making and signing the award assumes importance but omission to give notice does not vitiate the award, though such omission gives rise to a controversy as to when the party is posted with the knowledge of making of the award.

However, there is another line of judgments declaring the notice mandatory, but this seems to have been repealed in the face of the Supreme Court's judgment. In these judgments, the issuance of a notice by the arbitrator to the parties has been declared mandatory. The objective was to intimate to the parties the completion of the award so they may approach the court to contest it or make it a rule of court.[724] In any case, under Article 178 of the Limitation Act 1908, the parties have to file such an application

719. *A.M. Associates v. Government of Khyber Pakhtunkhwa and others*, PLD 2015 SC 21.
720. *Raja Karam Dad Khan v. Faiz Ahmad*, 2017 CLC 1720.
721. *Syed Abdul Manan and others v. Malik Asmatullah and others*, 2019 CLC 1096; *Muhammad Sharif v. Roze Deen and others*, 2015 MLD 1804.
722. *Farida Malik and others v. Khalid Malik*, 1998 SCMR 816; *Muhammad Iqbal v. P. I. D. C.*, 2000 CLC 876. *See also Khalida Malik v. Farida Malik*, 1994 MLD 2348. In this case, it was held that the award would be vitiated if on the day of its making one of the arbitrators did not participate or was absent. The court will ignore such vitiation only where the conduct of a party amounts to a waiver or estoppel. An arbitrator is not obligated to give detailed reasons for his findings. Although the award need not be a reasoned judicial decision, it should be an intelligible decision which 'defines rights of parties, in relation to the subject matter of reference'.
723. *Farida Malik and others v. Khalid Malik*, 1998 SCMR 816.
724. *Abdul Hussain Darugar and another v. Gul Muhammad and others*, 2015 MLD 488; *Dil Muhammad v. Additional District Judge, Sahiwal and others*, 1991 MLD 2068; *Muhammad Vasi Saigal v. Shaikh Rashid Ahmad and others*, 1988 CLC 267. Some courts have not considered this notice as mandatory by saying that the object of a section 14(1) notice is to inform the parties of the making of an award so that they may request the arbitrator to file the award to which they then raise objections. This need is fulfilled when an arbitrator, without giving a section 14(1) notice, files an award under section 14(2) and the court gives them notice thereof to file objections. Therefore, an omission by the arbitrator to give a section 14(1) notice

within ninety days of the service of the making of the award.[725] In the absence of such notice, Article 181 would apply, which provides a three-year limitation period.[726]

If any party, arbitrator or umpire sends a notice otherwise than through the courts, such notice should be served in a manner agreed by the parties in the arbitration agreement. If an arbitration agreement is silent on the mode of service, then the notice should be delivered to the person on whom it was to be served or by dispatching such notice in a letter to such person at his usual or last known address.[727] A notice is sent in strict compliance with section 42 of the 1940 Act.[728] The phrase 'date of service of notice of the making of award' has to be interpreted in their technical sense, which means the written notice to the parties of the fact of making and signing of the award. Therefore, the fact that the parties had knowledge of the making of the award or that they had signed the award would not fulfil the requirement of service of notice under Article 178 of the Limitation Act 1908.[729]

In *Chaudhary Sardar Muhammad Khan v. Muhammad Jafar Khan and others,*[730] an arbitrator made the award on 13 August 1995 in the presence of the parties who also signed the award. An application to file the award was made on 25 January 2000, five years after the making of the award. Under Article 178 of the Limitation Act, the award is to be filed within ninety days after the arbitrator gives notice of such award to the parties under section 14(1) of the 1940 Act. The court held that in this case, no notice was given to the parties, and therefore, Article 178 was not applicable; rather, Article 181 of the Limitation Act was applicable.[731] Delivery of a copy of the award by the arbitrator to each party would fulfil the requirement of notice under section 42 of the 1940 Act[732], and the limitation period under Article 178 of the Limitation Act would run

to the parties will not vitiate the arbitral proceedings or award. *See* for this, *Saeeda Bang and others v. Mian Muhammad Amin,* 1995 MLD 187.

725. *Chief Resident Representative WAPDA v. Transglobe Shipping Services,* 2013 CLD 1213; *Besrock (Pvt.) Ltd. v. Pakistan Steel Mills Corporation,* 2013 CLD 719.
726. *Telecom Foundation v. Asko Enterprises,* 2020 CLC 1605; *Besrock (Pvt.) Ltd. v. Pakistan Steel Mills Corporation,* 2013 CLD 719.
727. *Muhammad Wasi Saigal v. Shaikh Rashid Ahmad and others,* 1994 CLC 1406.
728. *Telecom Foundation v. Asko Enterprises,* 2020 CLC 1605; *Besrock (Pvt.) Ltd. v. Pakistan Steel Mills Corporation,* 2013 CLD 719.
729. *Besrock (Pvt.) Ltd. v. Pakistan Steel Mills Corporation,* 2013 CLD 719; *Telecom Foundation v. Asko Enterprises,* 2020 CLC 1605; *Muhammad Shafi and others v. Muhammad Sabir and others,* PLD 1960 (W. P) Lahore 591; *Sh. Maboob Alam v. Sh. Mumtaz Ahmad,* PLD 1960 (W. P) Lahore 601.
730. *Chaudhary Sardar Muhammad Khan v. Muhammad Jafar Khan and others,* 2010 YLR 164.
731. *Ibid.*
732. Section 42. Service of notice by party or arbitrator:

> Any notice required by this Act to be served otherwise than through the Court by a party to an arbitration agreement or by an arbitrator or umpire shall be served in the manner provided in the arbitration agreement, or if there is no such provision, either (a) by delivering it to the person on whom it is to be served, or (b) by sending it by the post in a letter addressed to that person at his usual or last known place of abode or business in [Pakistan] and registered under Chapter VI of the Post Officer Act, 1898 (VI of 1898).

from the date of delivery of the copy by the arbitrator to the parties.[733] In *Mushtaq Ahmad Alias Mastay Khan and another v. Ahmad Yar and others*,[734] the court stated:

> It is clear from the provisions of Article 178 that the period of limitation has to start from 'the date of service of the notice of the making of the award'. This provision has to be read with reference to and in the context of the provisions of section 14(1) of the Arbitration Act which provides inter alia that the arbitrator 'shall give notice in writing to the parties, of the making and signing' of the award. The words contained in Article 178 of the Limitation Act and section 14 of the Arbitration Act have a technical meaning and can only be construed as requiring a separate notice in writing by the arbitrator notwithstanding the fact that the parties had knowledge of the arbitration award ... the period of limitation is not intended to start from the date on which the parties had knowledge of the award but is to commence from the date on which a written notice of the making of the award is given to the parties pursuant to section 14 (11 of the Arbitration Act ... It is to be noted that a notice in writing of the making of the award cannot, for the purposes of Article 178 of the Limitation Act, be equated with the handing over of copies of award to the parties.[735]

An arbitrator becomes *functus officio* after making an award and may serve as arbitrator only as provided under section 13 of the 1940 Act or after the remission of the award to him by the court. He can be reappointed as arbitrator so far as the reference is not superseded by the court, provided the arbitration agreement so permits. After setting aside the award, the court has the power to supersede the reference. The supersession of a reference by the court brings the arbitration agreement to an end. If the court does not supersede the reference, the arbitration agreement survives, provided no intention to the contrary exists, in which case the court has the power to reappoint the same arbitrator to resolve the dispute or substitute him with some other arbitrator.[736]

11.4. STAMPING THE AWARD

The objection that the award was not produced on the proper stamp paper and that it was written and signed on plain paper has been rejected by the Supreme Court. The Supreme Court highlighted the fact that the award, although drawn on plain paper, was signed by all three arbitrators, and the stamp duty was duly supplied later. On the point of law, the Supreme Court stated that Article 3 of the Stamp Act, read with its Article 12, prescribes the levy of stamp on an arbitral award. Therefore, an unstamped award violates Article 12 of the Stamp Act. However, because the award was drawn on an unstamped paper will not invalidate the award within the meaning of section 30 of the 1940 Act. Therefore, in the event of an unstamped award, the parties can remedy the deficiency of awards on unstamped papers. The Supreme Court stated that section 33 of the Stamp Act furnishes the mechanism of impounding the document, which is

733. *Maqbool Elahi v. Muhammad Iqbal and others*, 2002 YLR 3159.
734. *Mushtaq Ahmad Alias Mastay Khan and another v. Ahmad Yar and others*, 2000 CLC 1518.
735. *Ibid.*
736. *Design Group of Pakistan v. Clifton Cantonment Board*, 1990 MLD 2010.

chargeable with a duty and which has been filed before the court. The Supreme Court said that under this procedure, the discrepancy can be rectified. If such deficiency is not cured, as a result of section 35 of the Stamp Act, the award would not be admissible in evidence because it was chargeable with said duty under Article 12 of the Stamp Act.[737] The court gave two opportunities to the appellant to affix the stamp on the arbitral award, but he neither complied with the orders of the court nor did he provide good reasons for non-compliance. The High Court noticed that sections 35[738] and 38[739] of the Stamp Act 1899 clearly mandate that an unstamped instrument, an award, in this case, is not admissible as evidence, and if such instrument is to be accepted as evidence, then it is subject to the penalty provided in section 35. In this case, the award was not made a rule of the court.[740]

The matter of stamping an award was again discussed by the Supreme Court in detail in *James Construction Company (Pvt.) Ltd v. Province of Punjab*.[741] After the

737. *Farida Malik and others v. Khalid Malk*, 1998 SCMR 816.
738. Section 35. Instruments not duly stamped inadmissible in evidence, etc.:

> No instrument chargeable with duty shall be admitted in evidence for any purpose by any person having by law or consent of parties authority to receive evidence, or shall be acted upon, registered or authenticated by any such person or by any public officer, unless such instrument is duly stamped. Provided that–(a) any such instrument not being an instrument chargeable with a duty 7 [not exceeding twenty-five paisa] only, or a bill of exchange or promissory note, shall, subject to all just exceptions, be admitted in evidence on payment of the duty with which the same is chargeable, or, in the case of an instrument insufficiently stamped, of the amount required to make up such duty, together with a penalty of five rupees, or, when ten times the amount of the proper duty or deficient portion thereof exceeds five rupees, of a sum equal to ten times such duty or portion; (b) where any person from whom a stamped receipt could have been demanded, has given an unstamped receipt and such receipt, if stamped, would be admissible in evidence against him, then such receipt shall be admitted in evidence against him on payment of a penalty of one rupee by the person tendering it; (c) where a contract or agreement of any kind is effected by correspondence consisting of two or more letters, and any one of the letters bears the proper stamp, the contract or agreement shall be deemed to be duly stamped; (d) nothing herein contained shall prevent the admission of any instrument in evidence in any proceeding in a Criminal Court, other than a proceeding under Chapter XII or Chapter XXXVI of the Code of Criminal Procedure, 1898; (e) nothing herein contained shall prevent the admission of any instrument in any Court when such instrument has been executed by or on behalf of [the Government], or where it bears the certificate of the Collector as provided by section 32 or any other provision of this Act.

739. Section 38. Instruments impounded how dealt with:

> (1) When the person impounding an instrument under section 33 has by law or consent of parties authority to receive evidence and admits such instrument in evidence upon payment of a penalty as provided by section 35 or of duty as provided by section 37, he shall send to the Collector an authenticated copy of such instrument, together with a certificate in writing, stating the amount of duty and penalty levied in respect thereof, and shall send such amount to the Collector, or to such person as he may appoint in this behalf. (2) In every other case, the person so impounding an instrument shall send it in original to the Collector.

740. *Malik Muhammad Aslam v. Sh. Muhammad Amjad and others*, 2008 CLC 429. *See also Haji Ashraf Ali and others v. Haji Mushtaq Ali and others*, 2013 CLD 604.
741. PLD 2002 SC 310.

award was filed to the court, the respondent submitted an application to de-exhibit the award and impound the same because it was unstamped. The trial court, by accepting this application, directed the appellant to pay ten times stamp duty at a rate of 3% of the value of the subject matter. The appellant filed a revision petition to the High Court, which was dismissed. When the matter reached the Supreme Court, it observed that the matter was sent to arbitration by the court under section 20. Therefore, the entire proceedings from the point of institution until conclusion remained under the control of the court. Under these circumstances, the award was supposed to have arisen 'by an order of the court in the course of a suit'. The Supreme Court further held that the award pronounced with the intervention of the court is materially and substantially different from an award emanating from the parties' private reference. Awards rendered with the intervention of courts need not be stamped. Since this award was not subject to stamp duty, therefore no question of its being impounded arose, nor could any penalty be imposed upon the appellant. The Supreme Court highlighted the legislature's wisdom for not imposing stamp duty on awards made with the intervention of courts and stated that:

> Rationale behind not imposing stamp duty on such award is that arbitrators perform the functions entrusted to them under supervision of the court. Arbitrators are paid their fee separately which is paid by contesting parties who are not obliged to pay stamp duty. Additional liability on parties to pay stamp duty, under such circumstances would not be justified ... Stamp duty is to be charged on any decision in writing b an arbitrator or umpire on a reference made, otherwise than by order of the court in the course of suit. Expression 'otherwise than by an order of the court' as used in article 12 of stamp act 1899 is of extreme importance for determining the nature of award as it curtails the scope of its earlier part of definition of 'award'. In absence of such expression, any decision in writing by an arbitrator or umpire would have been subjected to stamp duty.

11.5. FILING OF AWARD TO THE COURT

After the award is made, any party may request the arbitrator to file the award together with the disposition or documents in the court, but there is no limitation period for a party to make this request to the arbitrator, nor is there any limitation period prescribed for an arbitrator or umpire to file awards in the courts.[742] After the award is pronounced, only the arbitrator or umpire can file the award in court. Any party to an arbitration agreement may request the arbitrator to file an original award to the court.[743] If the arbitrator fails to file the award at the request of parties, the court may direct the arbitrator to file the same. To seek such directions from the court, the party

---

742. *Besrock (Pvt.) Ltd. v. Pakistan Steel Mills Corporation*, 2013 CLD 719. *See also Telecom Foundation v. Asko Enterprises*, 2020 CLC 1605; *Muhammad Shafi and others v. Muhammad Sabir and others*, PLD 1960 (W. P) Lahore 591; *Sh. Maboob Alam v. Sh. Mumtaz Ahmad*, PLD 1960 (W. P) Lahore 601.
743. *Nazir Ahmad v. Haji Nazir Ali and others*, 2006 MLD 907.

can file an application under section 14 of the 1940 Act.[744] The responsibility of the arbitrator comes to an end after he files the award in court.[745]

The Peshawar High Court held that filing of an award to the court is a ministerial job, and the arbitrator is competent to file the award *suo moto*.[746] This decision was appealed in *Inayatullah Khan v. Obaidullah Khan and others*, in which the Supreme Court held that if the arbitrator files an award to the court to make it a rule of the court without a request from the parties or an order from the court, the award would not be enforced. If the court refuses to make the award a rule of the court, the arbitrator cannot appeal such a decision.[747] The fact that the award has been acted upon by the parties would render the pronouncement of a rule of court inconsequential.[748]

However, the parties to arbitration can also file awards to the court but only after they are specifically authorized by the arbitrators in that regard.[749] It is mention-worthy that mere delivery of a signed copy of an award by the arbitrator to the party would not amount to the conferment of implied authority on the party to file the award to the court on behalf of the arbitrator.[750] When the arbitrator files awards in the court, they should be accompanied by all depositions and documents produced and proven before the arbitrator. However, these documents are not required to be filed when the award is filed by a party,[751] in which case the court will call arbitrators to submit depositions and documents.[752]

Permission is needed to file photocopies of arbitral awards because photocopies are not admissible as evidence.[753] Where the arbitrator did not file an award in court,

744. *Syed Ziauddin v. Syed Rose ud Din and others*, 1999 YLR 978; *Farida Malik and others v. Khalid Malik*, 1998 SCMR 816.
745. *Pak Gulf Construction Private Limited and another v. Abdul Hamid Baig and another*, 2019 MLD 1178.
746. *Obaidullah Khan v. Inayatullah Khan*, 1998 MLD 1718.
747. *Inayatullah Khan v. Obaidullah Khan and others*, 1999 SCMR 2702.
748. *Haji Abdul Rashid Arif v. Aziz Rehman and others*, 2010 CLC 1014; *Asghar Ali Khan and others v. Janan and others*, 2017 YLR 301.
749. *Obaidullah Khan v. Inayatullah Khan*, 1998 MLD 1718.
750. *National Logistic Cell v. Hakas (Pvt) Ltd.*, 2010 YLR 1448.
751. Rules framed by Lahore High Court, R. 10(a) & (b) under section 44 of the 1940 Act reads as follows:

    (b) When the award is filed by the arbitrator or umpire he shall together with the award send to the court any depositions and documents which have been taken and proved before him and the opinion pronounced by the court on the special case submitted by him, if any in accordance with section 14 of the act by forwarding the same under a sealed cover addressed to the court. He shall also send together with the award a copy of the notice given to the parties concerned and affidavit of service of such notice and of attestation of his signature on the award.
    (c) When the award is filed by any of the parties to the arbitration under clause (a) the party may move the court for directing the arbitrator to produce in original such of the documents as were produced before him together with the record of the arbitration.

752. *Province of the Punjab v. M. A. Rashid Said Alam Khan*, PLD 1990 Lahore 25; Reference was made to *MA Rashid and Company v. The Punjab Small Industries Corporation and another*, PLD 1986 Lahore 254; *Province of The Punjab v. M.A. Rashid Said Alam Khan*, PLD 1990 Lahore 25.
753. *Nazar Hussain and others v. Fazal Ellahi and others*, 2010 CLC 1018. In *Faqir Spinning Mills Ltd. v. Government of West Pakistan*, 1970 SCMR 186, the arbitrator dispatched two copies of

despite such directions from the court, the true copy of the award can be taken as secondary evidence and acted upon.[754]

11.5.1. Notice of Filing of Award

After the award is filed in the court, section 14(2) stipulates that a notice of that fact must be served to the respective parties or their counsels so that they should file objections if they are so minded.[755] Given the concept of 'due process' and 'fair trial' as enshrined in Article 10-A of the Constitution, read with section 14(2) of the 1940 Act, notice in writing is a mandatory requirement for each and every proceeding.[756] It is only after the submission of documents and depositions that the court will give notice to the parties of the filing of the award.[757]

When a party has knowledge of the filing of the award in the court, no further notice is required to be served on such party.[758] This is so because the purpose of giving notice to the party is to bring to his knowledge that the award has been filed. If such filing is already in his notice, then there is no need for further action.[759] In one case, an award was initially filed in the court, and the court remitted it to the arbitrator for resubmission on a specified date. The arbitrator complied by filing the same on the stipulated date in the presence of the counsels for the parties. The court then adjourned four times so that the parties could file their objections but counsel for the appellate states that he did not want to submit objections. As a result, the court held that there was no need to serve a notice under section 14(2) of the 1940 Act.[760] Where the award was filed in the court in the presence of both parties, the notice contemplated under this provision will be assumed to have been complied with. This is so because insistence on the issuance of a notice under Order XXIX of the CPC would only be a technicality.[761]

---

the award to the parties retaining the original for himself. The Supreme Court held that a party could challenge the arbitral award on the basis of such copy of the award.

754. *Muhammad Vasi Saigal v. Shaikh Rashid Ahmad and others*, 1988 CLC 267.
755. *Chief Resident Representative WAPDA v. Transglobe Shipping Services*, 2013 CLD 1213; *Province of West Pakistan (Punjab) v. Mian Abdul Hamid & CO*, 1985 CLC 1170; *Besrock (Pvt.) Ltd. v. Pakistan Steel Mills Corporation*, 2013 CLD 719. In *Province of West Pakistan v. Mian Abdul Hamid*, 1985 CLC 1170, the court also considered the expressions 'notice in writing' as used in section 14(1) and 'thereupon give notice to the party' as stipulated in section 14(2). It held that these expressions were not synonymous because 'they connote that where a party had knowledge of filing an award in court, further notice need not be issued to such party by the court informing him about the filing of award'.
756. *Muhammad Ather Hafeez Khan v. Sangyong and Usmani J.V.*, 2016 YLR 214.
757. *M. A. Rashid and Company v. The Punjab Small Industries Corporation and another*, PLD 1986 Lahore 254.
758. *Shafi Corporation Ltd. v. Government of Pakistan*, PLD 1994 Karachi 127.
759. *Maj. (Retd.) Humayun Akhtar v. Pakistan Defence Officers Housing Authority*, PLD 2002 Karachi 427.
760. *Province of Punjab and others v. Mirza Muhammad Latif*, 1996 MLD 1115. *See also Saeeda Bang and others v. Mian Muhammad Amin*, 1995 MLD 187.
761. *Mian Asmat Shah and another v. Mian Faiq Shah and others*, PLD 2012 Peshawar 181; *Pak Gulf Construction Private Limited and another v. Abdul Hamid Baig and another*, 2019 MLD 1178; *Ashfaq Ali Qureshi v. Municipal Corporation, Multan and another*, 1984 SCMR 597; *S. H. Malik v. Additional District Judge*, 1990 MLD 1924.

Notice will be served on the party through a mode of service, or manner, provided in the arbitration agreement. If an arbitration agreement gives no mode of service, then the service of notice must be made either on the party to whom it was to be served or dispatched in a letter by registered post to the party at his usual or known address.[762] In this regard, a notice on the pleader of a party would be as effective as the delivery of such notice on the party himself.[763]

For filing objections against awards, Article 158 of the Limitation Act 1908 has prescribed the limitation period of thirty days from the service of such notice of award on the parties.[764] The time for filing the objections against the award starts from the time of furnishing the notice on the objector and not from the date of the order from a court to file the objections.[765] If the filing of an award is in the knowledge of the parties, then the limitation period will start upon the filing of the award.[766] The court will not take objections into consideration if they are filed beyond the thirty-day period.[767] This would be the case where no application to condone the delay has been made or no reason to justify such delay in filing objections exists.[768] Similarly, if the defendant failed to submit objections against the award at the time of submission of the award, he would be considered to have accepted the award and will not be allowed to submit objections at some belated stage.[769] The court is bound to examine *suo motu* if objections against the award are filed within the limitation period.[770]

11.6. OBJECTIONS AGAINST THE AWARD

Objections against the award must be clear and unambiguous. They must state with precision, clarity and certainty why the court should interfere with the award.[771] Objections should be filed either by the party itself or the person authorized. The objections filed by an unauthorized person will be considered non-existent. In one case, the power of attorney executed in favour of a person raising objections against the award was neither registered nor notarized by a notary public. The executant was alive at the stage of recording the evidence before the court but did not appear, nor was the original power of attorney produced before the court. The copy of the power of attorney

762. *Muhammad Wasi Saigal v. Shaikh Rashid Ahmad*, 1994 CLC 1406.
763. *Province of West Pakistan v. Mian Abdul Hamid*, 1985 CLC 1170.
764. *Airports Developments Agency Limited v. M. Y. Corporation*, PLD 2001 Karachi 158; *Ascon Engineers (Pvt.) Ltd v. Province of Punjab*, 2002 SCMR 1662; *Chief Resident Representative WAPDA v. Transglobe Shipping Services*, 2013 CLD 1213; *Besrock (Pvt.) Ltd. v. Pakistan Steel Mills Corporation*, 2013 CLD 719.
765. 1988 MLD 659; *Col. (Retd.) Muhammad Aslam v. Haji Muhammad Shafi and other*, PLD 1993 Lahore 11; *Amir v. Rajab Ali and others*, 1988 MLD 659; *Pak Gulf Construction Private Limited and another v. Abdul Hamid Baig and another*, 2019 MLD 1178.
766. *Shafi Corporation Ltd. v. Government of Pakistan*, PLD 1994 Karachi 127.
767. *Province of Punjab v. Mirza Bashir Ahmad*, 1987 CLC 651; *Province of Punjab v. Ilam Din*, 1998 SCMR 110; *Elite Builders and Developers Ltd. and others v. Nooruddin Moosa Hemani and another*, 1988 CLC 564.
768. *Airports Developments Agency Limited v. M. Y. Corporation*, PLD 2001 Karachi 158.
769. *Haji Ghulam Muhammad v. Tahir Mehmood and others*, 2016 YLR 198.
770. *Province of Punjab v. Mirza Bashir Ahmad*, 1987 CLC 651.
771. *Federation of Pakistan v. Joint Venture Kocks K.G. /Rist*, PLD 2011 SC 506.

was contested in accordance with Articles 75[772] and 76[773] of the Qanun-e-Shahadat Order 1984. Therefore, the authorization of the attorney could not be proven, and hence, his objections were considered invalid by the court.[774]

The power of the court to make an award a rule of court is not ministerial but judicial in nature. The absence of objections from a party would not, therefore, absolve the court from its duty to examine the award and can even set aside, modify or remit the award if it considers it null or prima facie illegal or determines that it suffers from invalidity floating on the face of the record, or if there is some other reason rendering the award unfit.[775] The court, while deciding the enforcement of arbitral awards, is bound to decide each and every objection raised by the parties against the award.[776] If the court makes the award a rule of the court hastily and in a summary manner without entertaining the objections filed by the defendant or without adjudging them in a judicial manner, the appellate court will remand the case to the trial court to decide those objections according to law and after hearing the parties properly.[777]

772. Article 75. Proof of documents by primary evidence:

> Documents must be proved by primary evidence except in the cases hereinafter mentioned.

773. Article 76. Cases in which secondary evidence relating to documents may be given:

> Secondary evidence may be given of the existence, condition or contents of a document in the following cases: – (a) when the original is shown or appears to be in the possession or power of the person against whom the document is sought to be proved, or of any person out of reach of, or not subject to, the process of the Court, or of any person legally bound to produce it, and when after the notice mentioned in Article 77 such person does not produce it; (b) when the existence, condition or contents of the original have been proved to be admitted in writing by the person against whom it is proved or by his representative-interest; (c) when the original has been destroyed or lost, or when the party offering evidence of its contents cannot, for any other reason not arising from his own default or neglect, produce it in reasonable time; (d) when, due to the volume or bulk of the original, copies thereof have been made by means of microfilming or other modern devices; (e) when the original is of such a nature as not to be easily movable; (f) when the original is public document within the meaning of Article 85; (g) when the original is a document of which a certified copy is permitted by this Order, or by any other law in force in Pakistan, to be given in evidence; (h) when the originals consist of numerous accounts or other documents which cannot conveniently be examined in Court, and the fact to be proved is the general result of the whole collection; (i) when an original document forming part of a judicial record is not available and only a certified copy thereof is available, certified copy of that certified copy shall also be admissible as a secondary evidence.
>
> In cases (a), (c), (d) and (e), any secondary evidence of the contents of the document is admissible. In case (b), the written admission is admissible. In case (f) or (g), certified copy of the document, but no other kind of secondary evidence, is admissible. In case (h), evidence may be given as to the general result of the documents by any person who has examined them and who is skilled in the examination of such document.

774. *Alpha Insurance Co. Limited v. Ch. Nizam Din & Sons and another,* 2001 CLC 289.
775. *A. Qutubuddin Khan v. Chec Millwala Dredging Co. (Pvt.) Limited,* 2014 CLD 824.
776. *Pepsi Cola International (Pvt.) Limited v. Maxim International (Pvt.) Limited,* 2017 CLC Note 176.
777. *Khalid Hussain v. Muhammad Sabir Javed,* 2003 CLC 1018.

11.7. EFFECT OF AWARD

The award is not a decree, even if the arbitrator uses the word 'decree' to describe it. This is on the basis that the decree comes only from the court after the award is filed to it.[778] Regarding the award not filed and not made a rule of the court, the Punjab High Court has held that such award will:

> Not operate to create, declare, assign, limit or extinguish, whether in present or in future, any right, title or interest whether vested or contingent in the property in dispute. Award which had not been made rule of court, also would not require registration because it would not create any right or title. Such award could, however, be used as piece of evidence during proceedings. When such an award was made rule of court, it was only then that its registration would become compulsory.[779]

The dispute was referred to the arbitrator who made an award, but neither party tried to make that award a rule of the court. On the same matter, the plaintiff filed a suit, and the judge issued interim measures that were resisted on the basis of the award. The court held that an award not made a rule of the court was of no value and did not 'create, extinguish or pass any right, title or interest and no party could be prejudiced by the mere existence of the award. The award could only become effective when it was made a rule of the court. Till the decree was passed, the award had no status in the eyes of the law'.[780] However, where an award was not challenged before the court that made it a rule of court, the decision of the arbitrator would become final and conclusive between the parties and no party can reopen that matter again by agitating a suit.[781]

An arbitral award is executed only after it is made a rule of the court by following the procedure laid down in sections 14 and 17 of the 1940 Act,[782] and only then it becomes legally effective and operates as res judicata on the cause of action decided therein by the arbitrators. Otherwise, on the cause of action arising between the parties to such arbitration and decided by the arbitrators in their award, it can be reagitated between the same parties before the court in a suit filed under section 11 of the CPC within the limitation period.[783]

Controversies referred to an arbitrator cannot become the subject of another reference due to the application of the principle of res judicata. However, the disputes which could have been raised and referred to the arbitrator but were not raised or referred to arbitration do not constitute res judicata and can become the subject of a new reference. The latter situation may occur where successive claims arise from the

778. *Maj. (Retd.) Humayun Akhtar v. Pakistan Defence Officers Housing Authority*, PLD 2002 Karachi 427.
779. *Haji Muhammad v. Syed Manzoor Hussain Shah*, PLD 2003 Lahore 208. In *Muhammad Khalil v. Shabina Shehzadi and others*, 2007 YLR 2689, the court, however, held that an award not made a rule of the court has no evidentiary value.
780. *Itehad Cargo Services, National Hotel Lahore v. Rana Rafaqar Ali and others*, PLD 2002 Karachi 420.
781. *Post Service Company Ltd. v. Port Services Pvt. Ltd*, 2006 CLC 303.
782. *Federation of Pakistan and others v. Captain Nawar Khan and another*, 1986 MLD 1800.
783. *Abdul Hussain Shall v. Allah Ditta*, PLD 2009 Lahore 442.

same transactions and, subject to agreement between parties, are referred to an arbitrator whose decision would then be enforced.[784]

11.8. REMISSION, MODIFICATION AND SETTING ASIDE OF AWARDS

An arbitral award generally ousts the jurisdiction of the court. Still, the court would have jurisdiction to control arbitrators and their misconduct and regulate procedures after the award. However, the court would not have any right to review the evidence examined by the arbitrators on the merits. Where the parties agree to arbitration, they are bound by the arbitrator's findings on facts and law, and the court has no power to modify or remit the award, even if such findings are erroneous.[785] Circumstances in which the court can resort to set aside, modify or remit an arbitral award are given in sections 14, 15 and 16 of the 1940 Act, respectively.

In this regard, no suit can be filed for the remission, modification or setting aside of an award, even if the circumstances enlisted in these sections are existent. The aggrieved party can either challenge the validity or existence of an award by filing an application under section 33 or raise grounds for setting it aside under section 30 of the 1940 Act.[786] In *Rehmat Ali Khan v. Nasim Jan and another*,[787] the court said that the 'first part of section 32 of the 1940 Act precludes the filing of a suit for a decision upon the existence, effect or validity of an arbitration agreement or award, while the second part of the section prevents the setting aside of an arbitration agreement or award or modifying the same except as provided in the Act'.[788]

On the point of impeachment of the validity of an arbitral award, sections 33 and 30 of the 1940 Act provide different and independent regimes. To decide the validity of an arbitral award with reference to the question of its existence, an application accompanied with affidavits under section 33 must be filed. Counter affidavits can be filed by the contesting party to rebut the pleas and contentions raised in such section 33 application. This application would be decided on the basis of affidavits. The proviso empowers the court to examine witnesses if the section 33 application cannot be decided on the sole basis of affidavits. For instance, an award arising from an invalid or non-existent arbitration agreement may be challenged through a section 33 application. Under section 30, an arbitral award has nothing to do with the arbitration agreement being disputed on the basis of it being invalid or non-existent; rather, it deals with the arbitral award arising from an arbitration agreement that is not disputed.[789]

784. *Abdul Sattar Mandokhal v. Port Qasim Authority*, 2001 YLR 758.
785. *Turner Morrison Garahams Group of Companies, London v. Rice Export Corporation Pakistan Ltd.*, PLD 1998 Karachi 79.
786. *Khuda Bukhsh and others v. Hamza and another*, 2015 YLR 1621.
787. *Rehmat Ali Khan v. Nasim Jan and another*, 1999 CLC 2082.
788. *See*, *Awan Industries Ltd. v. The Executive Engineer, Lined Channel Division and another*, 1992 SCMR 65.
789. *Kashmir Corporation Ltd. v. Pakistan International Airlines*, PLD 1995 Karachi 301. An award can be challenged on the basis of fraud, misrepresentation and want of jurisdiction under

The court will make an award a rule of the court only if it sees no reason to remit the award or set it aside. Therefore, it is mandatory for the court to satisfy itself that there is no illegality or other defect justifying the remission or setting aside of the award. To this end, the court will not act mechanically.[790] This court must examine *suo moto* if there is any reason to remit, modify or set aside the award despite the fact that no objections were filed by the parties against it.[791] The appellate court is vested with the powers of the trial court in this regard.[792] More specifically, although section 39 of the 1940 Act has given limited powers to the appellate court to interfere with the award, it can also use this jurisdiction to modify or remit the award, even if the objections from the party are time-barred.[793]

Despite the presumption of correctness that is attached to the award,[794] neither the courts nor arbitrators should presume that every arbitral award is free from all kinds of defects. While considering the objections of the parties against an award, the court is not meant to function as a court of appeal and cannot substitute its opinion with that of the arbitrators because its authority is confined within the parameters of section 30 of the 1940 Act. The court's function is to see if the arbitrator has answered all the questions referred to him by the parties and whether the substantial justice which could appeal to conscience has been done. If the arbitrator has appreciated the evidence adduced by the parties to the arbitration, the court would not interfere with the award.[795]

11.8.1. Modification of Award

The court has the power to modify or correct the award. That power can be used by the court in specific circumstances enumerated in section 15 of the 1940 Act.[796] For

---

sections 30 and 33, but these grounds cannot be reagitated after an award becomes a rule of the court. *See Zafarul Islam v. Mrs. Azra Malik*, PLD 1991 Karachi 377.

790. *Faisalabad Development Authority and another v. Orient Associates Architects and Contractors (Pvt.) Limited, Faisalabad*, 2013 CLC 820; *Government of N. W. F. P. and others v. Jan Construction Co.*, 2012 CLD 502; *Muhammad Yousuf v. Gul Zaman*, 2004 MLD 735. But, where the arbitrator has framed every issue and decided it, then it is not mandatory for the court to frame again the same issues. *See Oil & Gas Development Company Limited v. Marathon Construction Company and another*, 2013 CLD 1483.
791. *Pakistan through GM Pakistan Railway v. O.M.R. Export Consultants*, PLD 1990 SC 800; *Noor Nabuwwat v. Moulvi Muhammad Noor Ali Khan*, 1999 CLC 1685; *Awan Industries Limited v. Executive Engineers. Lined Channel Division and another*, 1992 SCMR 65.
792. *Maulvi Muhammad Zufran and others v. Malik Nehmat and others*, 1996 MLD 1576.
793. *Ascon Engineers (Pvt.) Ltd v. Province of Punjab*, 2002 SCMR 1662.
794. *Aer Rianta International Pakistan (Pvt.) Ltd. v. Civil Aviation Authority*, PLD 2006 Karachi 216.
795. *Kashmir Corporation Ltd. v. Pakistan International Airlines*, PLD 1995 Karachi 301.
796. Section 15. Power of Court to modify award:

> The Court may by order modify or correct an award
>
> (a) Where it appears that a part of the award is upon a matter not referred to arbitration and such part can be separated from the other part and does not affect the decision on the matter referred; or
>
> (b) Where the award is imperfect in form, or contains any obvious error which can be amended without effecting such decision; or

instance, it has such power where it appears that the award determined a matter not referred to the arbitrator. If such part is separable from the part dealing with the matter referred to arbitration, the court will modify or correct the award accordingly.[797] In other words, when a court concludes that part of an award is valid while the other part is invalid, and both are severable, it can uphold that part that is valid by vitiating the invalid part.[798] An arbitrator cannot award interest for the period the matter remains pending before him. However, he could award interest after the date of the award. Pakistani courts have declared the portion of an award awarding interest for the period the matter remained before the arbitrator, which was separable from the valid part of the award, that is to say, interest awarded by the arbitrator after the award.[799]

The court can also correct the award containing some clerical mistakes or errors which arose from an accidental omission.[800] Similarly, in one case, the miscalculation of damages by the arbitrator was modified, and the award was made a rule of the court.[801] The court has the power to modify the award if, in its form, the award is imperfect or some patent error is floating on its surface, and an amendment thereto will not have any effect on the decision of the arbitrator;[802] otherwise, such modification will be set aside.[803] Under a contract, the plaintiff was to transport certain pipes to the defendant, but the defendant disputed that because of the non-provision of the agreed number of pipes by the plaintiff, he had suffered a loss. The award was in favour of the plaintiff and awarded charges on account of the transportation of the lower number of pipes. At the same time, the award provided for man-month charges and interest but without referring to any specific provision in the contract. The court modified the award to the extent the plaintiff was entitled to only man-months for the period between 1 January 1996 to 30 June 1996 because there was no evidence on record to demonstrate that arrangements were in place for the transportation of pipes and also because the plaintiff himself had admitted that he had not transported the pipes in August 1996. The court modified the award by reducing the amount and directing the defendant to pay with interest within two months.[804] An arbitrator awarded damages more than 200% over the amount prayed from him, which was modified by the court.[805]

(c) Where the award contains clerical mistake or an error arising from an accidental slip or omission.

Lahore Development Authority v. Faisal International Construction Corporation Limited, 2004 CLC 594.

797. Section 15(a) of the 1940 Act.
798. 1988 CLC 430.
799. *Trading Engineers (International) (Pvt.) Ltd. v. Water and Sanitation Agency of the Lahore Development Authority*, 2001 MLD 868.
800. Section 15(c) of the 1940 Act.
801. *Pakistan through GM Pakistan Railway v. O.M.R. Export Consultants*, PLD 1990 SC 800; *Noor Nabuwwat v. Moulvi Muhammad Noor Ali Khan*, 1999 CLC 1685.
802. Section 15(b) of the 1940 Act.
803. *National Highway Authority v. Hakas (Private) Limited*, PLD 2011 Islamabad 43.
804. *Tracon Services (Pvt.) Ltd. v. Sui Southern Gas Co. Ltd.*, PLD 2009 Karachi 54.
805. *Pakistan through GM Pakistan Railway v. O.M.R. Export Consultants*, PLD 1990 SC 800 *See also Noor Nabuwwat v. Moulvi Muhammad Noor Ali Khan*, 1999 CLC 1685.

11.8.2. Remission of Award to Arbitrator

The law confers enough powers on the courts to remit the award for arbitral reconsideration.[806] Such remission would, however, be done if the conditions enumerated in section 16 are fulfilled. The Sindh High Court summarized the grounds on the basis of which a court may remit an award. It stated that:

> Award may be remitted under section 16 if the award leaves any of the matter which were referred to arbitration, undetermined; a part of the award is upon a matter which was not referred to arbitration and that part cannot be separated from the remaining part without affecting the decision of the matter which was referred to arbitration. The award is so indefinite as to be capable of execution and there is an objection to the legality of the award and such objection is apparent upon the face of it.[807]

In one case, the arbitrator awarded the costs and admitted that no witnesses were presented to elaborate the mechanism for the calculation and formula adopted to ascertain the plaintiff's claim. The award also admitted that there was no evidence on the record as to the market value or how the operational costs were determined. The defendant did not file objections on these facts, and the court checked these infirmities in the award *suo motu*. The court refused to make the award a rule of the court and remitted it to the arbitrator for reconsideration.[808] Similarly, an arbitrator committed an arithmetical error in the award. He awarded an amount of retention money separately in addition to the total figure arrived by him. In this case, the court remitted the case to the arbitrator.[809]

When the arbitrator does not give reasons in the award, or these are insufficient, the court will remit the award.[810] In this regard, the appellate court would also have the power to remit the award to the arbitrator for reconsideration, even if it was already merged into a decree by making it a rule of court.[811]

11.8.3. Setting Aside or Refusal to Set Aside an Award

Where an award is filed to a court to make it a rule of the court, the court would be obligated to deal with this matter.[812] An award can be made a rule of the court only after the limitation period prescribed for making an application to set aside the award expires, or if such application was made but the same was declined. The law prescribes no form for an application to set aside the award. If an application contains objections

806. Section 16 of the 1940 Act.
807. *Maj. (Retd.) Humayun Akhtar v. Pakistan Defence Officers Housing Authority*, PLD 2002 Karachi 427. *See also Al-Abdullah Constructors (Pvt.) Ltd., Karachi v. Pakistan Water and Power Development Authority*, 2003 YLR 3321.
808. *Adamjee Construction Co Ltd v. Islamic Republic of Pakistan*, PLD 2003 Karachi 180.
809. *Pakistan Steel Mills Corporation Ltd. v. Progressive Engineers Alliance Ltd.*, 1988 CLC 1709.
810. *All Pakistan CNG Association v. Pakistan State Oil Company Ltd.*, 2015 YLR 1813. For discussion on reasoned awards, *see* Ch. 12 below.
811. *Province of Punjab v. Industrial Machines tools Government Contractors*, 1986 MLD 501.
812. *Muhammad Yasin v. Muhammad Farooq*, 1989 MLD 2010.

against the arbitral award and prayer for setting it aside, such application would be taken as objections to the award.[813]

The arbitrator is the final judge of facts and law with regard to the controversy before him. Under section 30, the court does not reopen the issues already decided by the arbitrator[814] because the nature of the jurisdiction of the court to set aside the award is supervisory and not appellate. However, in supervisory jurisdiction, the court is empowered to examine the matters, including whether sufficient opportunity was afforded to the parties to present their case and the arbitrator based his decision on the material placed before him.[815] It is to note that the court's preference should be to uphold the award.[816]

An award will be set aside if, *inter alia*, it is procured illegally or the arbitrator misconducted in making the arbitral award or exercised improper jurisdiction;[817] the award is not based on evidence;[818] the arbitration proceedings had been superseded or invalidated by the court under section 35;[819] or the arbitration agreement or appointment of arbitrators was made without any notice to the other party.[820] In order to set aside an award, the illegality must be patent on the face of the award.[821]

The court cannot set aside an award on the ground that on the basis of the evidence adduced before the arbitrator, the court would have reached a different conclusion,[822] or that arbitrator gave the wrong interpretation to the agreement, or that he did not give specific findings on each issue.[823] If the court concludes that the award is partly invalid and partly valid, it can uphold the award to the extent of its valid part and set aside its invalid part.[824] Similarly, where an award is challenged partially, the undisputed part of the award will straightaway be made a rule of the court, and the court will hear and decide the disputed portion of the award according to the law.[825]

813. *Mirza Muhammad Siddique v. Muhammad Abdullah*, 1989 MLD 54.
814. *Dr. Mrs. Azra Ali v. Arif Ali*, PLD 1993 Karachi 683.
815. *Abdullah Contractors v. WAPDA*, 2006 YLR 589. In *Quality Builders Ltd. v. Karachi Metropolitan Corporation*, 1999 CLC 1777, the court held that under section 30, only questions of law can be agitated and awards cannot be impeached on the ground that the arbitrator has assessed the damages wrongly, as this is a question of fact.
816. *Mian Moazzam ud Din and others v. Haji Sadiq Jilani and others*, 2002 MLD 185; *Syed Faqir Shah v. Haji Inayatullah Khan and another*, 2013 MLD 689.
817. *Dr. Mrs. Azra Ali v. Arif Ali*, PLD 1993 Karchi 683; *S.M.I. Brothers v. Municipal Committee, Murree*, 2003 CLC 419.
818. *M. Aslam Amin v. Muhammad Ali Khan and another*, 1995 CLC 1795.
819. *Sainjee Cargo Services v. Cargo Movers and others*, 1989 CLC 2229; *Communication and Works Department, Azad Government of the State of Jammu and Kashmir v. Design and Engineering System and others*, 2013 CLD 1438.
820. *Awan Industries Limited v. Executive Engineers. Lined Channel Division and another*, 1992 SCMR 65.
821. *Gandhara Consultants (Pvt.) Ltd. v. Pakistan Defence Officer's Housing Authority, Karachi*, 2010 CLC 506.
822. *Ibad & Co. v. Government of Sindh*, PLD 1981 Karachi 236.
823. *Gandhara Consultants (Pvt.) Ltd. v. Pakistan Defence Officer's Housing Authority, Karachi*, 2010 CLC 506.
824. *Orient Builders v. The Chief Engineer Highways and another*, 1988 CLC 430.
825. *Engro Fertilizers Limited v. Federation of Pakistan*, 2014 CLD 132.

Where an award is found to be null or illegal on the face of it, the court has the power under section 17 to set it aside, even without waiting for the objections from the party against such award.[826]

11.8.3.1. Improperly Procured Award

Section 30(c) of the 1940 Act says that the award will be set aside if it has been improperly procured. For instance, an award procured by fraud and misrepresentation would be considered to have been procured improperly, and the aggrieved party can challenge the award by an application either under section 30 or 33 of the 1940 Act. The application under section 12(2) of the CPC for this purpose will not be maintainable because its aim is to challenge a decree procured improperly.[827] In that case, the plaintiff contested the award on the basis of fraud without successfully stating the stage when the fraud was committed. The award was made a rule of the court, and a decree was adopted concerning the allegations of the award. The plaintiff challenged the award in a declaratory suit, and the court set aside the award along with the decree pronounced on the basis of the award. The court also declared that the arbitration agreement was never concluded. On appeal, the Punjab High Court held that the award could be challenged under sections 30 and 33 of the 1940 Act. The decree passed on the basis of the award could be challenged under section 12(2) of the Civil Procedure Code. After elaborating these principles, the High Court highlighted the fact that the plaintiff failed to establish the stage (before or after the decree) at which fraud was committed. The High Court also held that the lower courts did not have the power to declare an arbitration agreement non-existent in a declaratory suit. The judgment passed by the lower court was set aside.[828]

11.8.3.2. Misconduct from Arbitrators

Arbitral awards will be set aside if the arbitrator misconducts himself or the proceedings. Some elements constituting misconduct on the part of arbitrators were enlisted by courts[829] as follows:

- Neglect of duties and responsibilities by arbitrators.
- Actions contrary to what courts of justice expect from them before allowing finality of award.
- If the arbitrator has refused to postpone a meeting for the purpose of allowing a party to engage a counsel when the other party unexpectedly turns up with a counsel.

826. *Pakistan v. Rajastan Alloy and Steel (Pvt.) Limited*, 2002 CLD 61.
827. *Government of Sindh v. Fazal Muhammad*, PLD 1991 SC 197; *Sardar Muhammad v. Mst. Hashmat Bibi alias Hashmatee and others*, 2004 YLR 626.
828. *Ahmed Khan and another v. Malka and others*, 2002 YLR 3109.
829. *Khalid Abbas v. Hafiz Muhammad Farooq*, 2004 YLR 274. For further discussion on misconduct, *see* Ch. 13 below.

- If an award is made without having heard all the evidence.
- If evidence of witnesses is recorded behind the back of a party.
- If a party has not been allowed the reasonable opportunity of proving its case.
- If the arbitrator has not brought to the notice of the opposite party a document received from its adversary or failed to provide an opportunity of meeting the inferences deducible from said evidence.
- If irregularities in the proceedings are proved as amounting to an improper hearing.
- If a finding is perverse or unsupported by evidence.
- If the arbitrator decides a disputed question without recourse to the evidence and hence decides blindly.
- If there is an indication of gross negligence or recklessness on the face of the record.
- If there is some mistake of fact, provided it is either admitted or at least clearly beyond a reasonable doubt.

In one case, the arbitrator gave an award in respect of the property left by a deceased person. The Supreme Court noticed that the arbitration agreement and the award were signed on the same day and that no explanation was furnished as to how the notices were issued to the parties. It thus concluded that the arbitration agreement and award on the same day was a device engineered between the arbitrator and petitioner to obtain the property by getting an award from the arbitrator.[830]

The consent of the parties giving authority to the arbitrator to decide their dispute does not confer an unbridled authority on him to make an award at his whim and conjecture without hearing the parties. Therefore, an award made at the back of the parties would be in flagrant breach of natural justice.[831] That does not mean that the arbitrator should record evidence in detail. It would be sufficient if the arbitrator makes an award after hearing both parties and considering their points of view.[832]

11.8.3.3. Invalidation of Arbitration Proceedings under Section 35 of the 1940 Act

For suppression of arbitration proceedings, section 35 lays down three conditions: namely, the subject matter of the civil suit should cover the whole of the subject matter of reference before the arbitrator; the parties should be the same in proceedings before the court and arbitrator and; the notice of the filing of the suit should have been given to the arbitrator. If any of these conditions are not fulfilled, the court will not declare the proceedings invalid. For instance, in *Sh. Saleem Ali v. Sh. Akhtar Ali and others,*[833]

830. *Mst. Wilayat Bibi and others v. Mst. Hayat Bevi and others*, 2005 SCMR 1697. In *Raza Muhammad v. Muhammad Khan*, 2012 CLD 488, the arbitrator added new lines at the end of an award, which were again not supported by reasons and were clearly the afterthought and tantamount to glaring misconduct.
831. *Abdul Razaq and another v. Sharif Khan and others*, 1986 CLC 281.
832. *Saeeda Bang and others v. Mian Muhammad Amin*, 1995 MLD 187.
833. *Sh. Saleem Ali v. Sh. Akhtar Ali and others*, PLD 2004 Lahore 404.

the properties involved in arbitration proceedings and civil suits and the parties to both proceedings were different. The court held section 35 to be inapplicable. It held that in order to attract the applicability of section 35, the term 'whole' means 'entire, complete, not less than, a thing complete in itself', and for that reason, the subject matter in the civil suit should cover the whole of the subject matter before the arbitrator.[834]

11.9. APPEALING THE DECREE ON AWARD

Section 39 of the 1940 Act gives a right of appeal on the decree on the award. But the nature of section 39 of the 1940 Act is different from that of section 17 of the 1940 Act, and both sections are independent in their nature and deal with two distinct situations. Under section 39, the order of the court on the award is appealed, whereas, under section 17, it is the decree which follows such an order that is appealed.[835]

The decree of the court based on an arbitral award can be assailed through a petition filed under section 12 of the CPC considering the factors mentioned in this section, namely fraud or misrepresentation to procure the decree or the defect of jurisdiction. On this, no provision or procedure is provided in the 1940 Act. The non-submission of objections or non-availing of any other relief does not create any bar in this respect. This is so because there is no provision in the 1940 Act to challenge a decree that has been procured by fraud or misrepresentation. For that reason, section 12(2) of the CPC has not been excluded, and the bar in sections 32 and 33 of the 1940 Act would not apply. Rather, 'the question would be connected with the proceedings of the court independently and in order to seek, setting aside of the same on the ground enunciated in section 12(2) of the CPC only such application would be competent'. In this way, an award can be set aside through an application under section 12(2) of the CPC, and it would be wrong to confine the remedy of setting aside an arbitral award only to sections 30 and 33 of the 1940 Act.[836] The limitation period to seek vitiation of an arbitration agreement, award or court proceedings on the basis of fraud under section 12(2) is three years, starting on the day the discovery of fraud was made.[837]

11.10. REGISTRATION OF AWARDS

An award that is not yet made a rule of the court will not require registration. The Registration Act was amended by Ordinance No. 445 of 1962. This amendment has

834. For a detailed discussion, *see* Ch. 4 above.
835. *Rashida Begum v. Ch. Muhammad Anwar and others*, PLD 2003 Lahore 522. For detailed discussion on appeal and difference between sections 39 and 17, *see* Ch. 14 below.
836. *Shamail Masud v. Malik Manzoor Ahmad and others*, 2007 CLC 1507. *See also Muhammad Yasin v. Sh. Hanif Ahmad and others*, 1993 SCMR 437; *Mst. Afroz Jahan v. Mst. Noor Jahan and others*, 1988 CLC 1318; *Dr. Izhar Fatima v. Aftab Ahmad Khan and others*, NLR 1993 A.C. (Civil) 551: *Mrs. Anis Haider and 3 others v. Additional District Judge and others*, 2003 CLC 462; *Abdul Basit and another v. Muhammad Ashraf Dar and another*, 2000 CLC 920; *Mian Moazzam ud Din and others v. Haji Sadiq Jilani and others*, 2002 MLD 185.
837. Article 181 and section 18 of the Limitation Act 1908. *Wazir Ali v. Allah Ditta and others*, 1994 CLC 1135.

made an unregistered award receivable in evidence. However, such awards will not operate to create, declare, assign, limit or extinguish, whether in the present or the future, any right, title or interest, whether contingent to or in respect of the immovable property. However, such awards may be used as evidence during proceedings. Its registration would become mandatory only after it became a rule of court.[838] In one case, an award related to the delivery of land worth more than PKR 100, which should have been registered under section 49 of the Registration Act, as otherwise it would not be made the rule of the court.[839] Awards made without the intervention of the court must be registered under section 49 of the Registration Act 1908.[840] The Supreme Court stated that:

> The award admittedly having been made without intervention of the court was compulsorily registerable under section 49 of the Registration Act. Such an award, though in view of the amendment in section 49 of the Registration Act by Ordinance XLV of 1962, is receivable in evidence because it does not operate to create, declare, assign limit or extinguish whether in present or in future any right title or interest whether vested or contingent to or in the immovable property.[841]

The Supreme Court, in another case, held that:

> Arbitration award, even if not registered, is receivable in evidence but by itself will not operate to create, declare, assign, limit or extinguish, whether in present or in future, any right, title or interest, whether vested or contingent to or in the immovable property.[842]

11.11. CONCLUSION

Regarding domestic awards, the 1940 Act gives a comprehensive procedure for making, filing and enforcing an award. To make an award, the arbitrator has to follow timelines and then file the award. Mandatory conditions of notices have been prescribed for arbitrators as well as the court on various points in the life cycle of awards. In response to such notice, if the objections are not filed to the court, the court is bound to ascertain *suo motu* the award in order to ascertain if there is any illegality floating on the face of the award. The remedies against the award and the decree on the award are provided in the form of appeal as well as an application under section 12 of the CPC. With all this, the flexible approach on limitation periods, registration and stamp duty makes the regime on domestic arbitral awards very conducive to arbitration. Problems may arise concerning the wide powers of courts with regard to remission, modification and setting aside of the award. Section 30 concerning misconduct has been interpreted very widely to include almost all kinds of irregularities to strike down the arbitral award.

838. *Haji Nawab Din v. Sh. Ghulam Haider and another*, 1988 SCMR 1623; *Haji Muhammad v. Syed Manzoor Hussain Shah*, PLD 2003 Lahore 208; *Haji Ashraf Ali and others v. Haji Mushtaq Ali and others*, 2013 CLD 604.
839. *Noor Nabuwwat v. Moulvi Muhammad Noor Ali Khan*, 1999 CLC 1685.
840. *Ghulam Muhammad v. Ghulam Abbas and others*, 2007 YLR 1608.
841. *Farida Malik and others v. Khalid Malik*, 1998 SCMR 816. *See also Ghulam Muhammad v. Ghulam Abbas and others*, 2007 YLR 1608.
842. *Haji Nawab din v. Ghulam Haider*, 1988 SCMR 1623.

CHAPTER 12

Public Policy in Arbitration in Pakistan

The public policy concept that thrived in contract law and domestic arbitration has been applied to international arbitrations. Statutory law in Pakistan does not spell out the notion of 'public policy', which has then been loosely and broadly defined by the courts, thereby setting up unobstructed roads to invent a new head of public policy. After exploring the origin and contents of public policy, this chapter differentiates matters of public policy concern from those that cannot assume that significance. To accomplish this task, this chapter also conducts an inquiry into the provision relevant to this concept on the basis of judgments from Pakistani courts.

12.1. INTRODUCTION

The public policy exception, as enshrined in Article V(II)(2) of the New York Convention, is very frequently relied on by award debtors to resist the enforcement of arbitral awards. This provision, by referring to the public policy of the enforcement/forum court, provides enough discretion to the enforcement/forum court with regard to enforcement.[843] The New York Convention also restrains itself by mentioning public policy without furnishing any definition of it. The adverse result of this state of affairs may be observed in the Pakistani regime, where the term has been defined very loosely and broadly by state courts by making the invention of the new head of public policy easier. In Pakistan, the public policy conception evolved primarily from the law of contracts with exclusive regard to domestic matters, and then this domestic notion of public policy was (or is expected to be) applied to international awards.

843. This discretion, available to states signatories to the New York Convention, is manifest from the different interpretations afforded to this term by different jurisdictions with regard to foreign awards. *See generally* Fifi Junita, *Public Policy Exception in International Commercial Arbitration – Promoting Uniform Model Reforms*, 5 Contemp. Asia Arb. J. 45 (2012).

Pakistani law does not define the term 'public policy'. Section 7 of the 2011 Act incorporates the grounds enshrined in Article V of the New York Convention by stating that 'the recognition and enforcement of a foreign arbitral award shall not be refused except in accordance with Article V of the Convention'. The term 'foreign arbitral award' has been defined by Article 2(e) of the 2011 Act as an award made in a state signatory to the New York Convention.

This chapter deals with the way of interpretation and application of the public policy conception by Pakistani courts at different stages of arbitration. It is important to consider how the term public policy is used in this chapter, according to the points in arbitration upon which it assumes its relevance. In Pakistan, public policy is relevant on two junctures. First, at the referral stage, when a party in disregard of the arbitration agreement initiates proceedings in court and the other party prays from the same court to stay its proceedings, and the recalcitrant party resists such application by asserting that the agreement is against public policy or that the matter cannot be arbitrated due to the involvement of public policy. Second, it becomes pertinent after the award is rendered, i.e., at the annulment and enforcement stages. As to the second stage, the term 'public policy ground' is used when an award debtor seeks annulment of the domestic award by contesting that such award is against the public policy conception of enforcing courts. With regard to the enforcement stage, the term 'public policy exception' is used. When a Pakistani court faces the contention of 'public policy ground' or 'public policy exception', it applies its own 'conception of public policy'. The reason for using the same term of 'public policy' or 'public policy conception' from the state court's perspective is that Pakistani courts apply the same conception of public policy at all stages of arbitration.

This chapter explores the public policy conception prevailing in Pakistan along with the elements subsumed as its subcategories. The discussion becomes more meaningful when the cradle from where this conception originated is researched. This analysis is coupled with discourse as to the stages when Pakistani courts face public policy questions and the way they treat them. This chapter also classifies those matters that are of public policy concern and those which have not been afforded that importance.

12.2. FRAUD, MISREPRESENTATION, ILLEGALITY AND BRIBERY AS GROUNDS OF PUBLIC POLICY

Fraud, misrepresentation, bribery and illegality have been considered to be of public policy concern at two stages. Pakistani courts encounter the public policy question first at the referral stage, at which point they normally decline to stay their proceedings in favour of arbitration, both domestic and foreign. They also repulse the principles of separability and *competence-competence* if the contract embodying the arbitration agreement is alleged to have been procured by fraud, misrepresentation, etc.[844]

844. *Hub Power Company Limited (HUBCO) v. WAPDA*, PLD 2000 SC 841; *Maulana Abdul Haque Baloch v. Government of Balochistan*, PLD 2013 SC 641.

Second, at the annulment or enforcement stage, public policy on the basis of these concepts is embroiled in three manners, namely: *first,* if the contract being enforced by the arbitral award was induced by the employment of any of these grounds; *second,* the award itself was obtained through the utilization of any of these elements or; *third,* the enforcement of the solution given by the award is repugnant to public policy. It is submitted that Pakistani courts apply the same conception of public policy in all of these stages when a party relies on fraud, bribery or illegality as a public policy ground or public policy exception, aimed at either annulling the arbitration agreement or obtaining an arbitral award.

In other words, if public policy is followed through the spectacles of the New York Convention, it is relevant under Article V(1)(a) and then Article V(2)(b) of the New York Convention. Under Article V(1)(a), the award may be refused recognition and enforcement if the arbitration agreement is not valid. In the Pakistani context, this is pertinent in two ways. First, the principles developed for general contracts under the Pakistani Contract Act 1872 are pressed into service to adjudge the validity of arbitration agreements.[845] One of the main principles puts across that the contract in conflict with the public policy will be void and invalid.[846] Second, in Pakistani case law, it is well settled that the arbitration agreement shares the fate of the main contract. Therefore, if the main contract is void, the supplementary arbitration agreement will also be void. In other words, if a parent contract is void for failing to observe Pakistan's public policy conception, then the arbitration agreement as one of the provisions of that contract would also be void for its departure from the well-settled principle of separability of the arbitration agreement.[847] This signifies that the notion of public policy of section 23 of the Contract Act 1872[848] is, strictly speaking, applicable.

The public policy conception that evolved under section 23 is also relevant to arbitral awards to be dealt with under Article V(2)(b) of the New York Convention. First, courts normally bring into use the national conception of public policy while adjudging the enforceability of an award on the basis of public policy exception, coupled with the certitude that the Pakistani conception of public policy primarily came about under section 23 of the Contract Act 1872. Second, even if Pakistani courts do not mention en passant section 23 while applying the public policy conception to

845. *Yasmeen v. Beach Developers,* 2003 YLR 110.
846. Section 23 of the Contract Act 1872.
847. *Hub Power Company Limited (HUBCO) v. WAPDA,* PLD 2000 SC 841; *Maulana Abdul Haque Baloch v. Government of Balochistan,* PLD 2013 SC 641.
848. Section 23. What considerations and objects are lawful or what not:

The consideration or object of an agreement is lawful, unless-

it is forbidden by law; or
is of such a nature that, permitted it would defeat the provisions of any law; or
is fraudulent; or
Involves or implies injury to the person or property of another; or
the Court regards it as immoral, or opposed to public policy.

In each of these cases, the consideration or object or of an agreement is said to be unlawful. Every agreement of which the object or consideration is unlawful is void.

foreign awards, they work over the compatibility of a foreign award with the Pakistani public policy conception against the same indexes provisioned in or deliberated under section 23, such as immorality, fraudulent or illegal consideration or objective, illegality, bribery, corruption, etc. Therefore, if section 23 is not directly applicable, it is relevant indirectly.

Under the 1937 Act, which incorporated the 1927 Geneva Convention on the Execution of Foreign Arbitral Award into Pakistani law, a foreign award was bound to conform to the public policy and principles of the law of Pakistan in order to be enforceable.[849] However, the New York Convention and the 2011 Act have dispensed with 'principles of law'. But it seems that the relevancy of 'principles of law' did not wither away as section 23 of the Contract Act 1872 sets out that contracts whose enforcement would ensue to 'defeat the provisions of any law' would be void. Some judicial verdicts have construed such contracts to be repugnant to public policy.[850] In this way, public policy may also encompass 'the principles of law'. It is plain to see that the conception of public policy metamorphosed for domestic as well as foreign arbitrations and awards are germane in the public policy exception under Article V(2)(b).

The certainty that the same conception of public policy is carried out on referral and enforcement (or annulment) stages for both domestic and foreign arbitrations affords a strong impression of consistency in the application of this notion. It nevertheless appears that this consistency has been pulled off by the misapplication of the law by Pakistani courts.

At the enforcement stage, awards enforcing a contract occasioned by fraud and misrepresentation would be at odds with public policy. However, it is submitted that under Pakistani law, the enforcement of such contracts at the referral stage by halting court proceedings and consigning the matter to an arbitrator should not be a subject of public policy. At the referral stage, the refusal by a court to bring its proceedings to a halt for arbitration is based, among others, on the fact that the procurement of the contract was induced by fraud and misrepresentation and hence was contradictory to public policy, under section 23. It is to note that under section 23, the court has been empowered to determine which contract is 'opposed to public policy' and hence void. But, section 19 of the Contract Act 1872,[851] which is different from section 23, provides

849. Section 7 of the Arbitration (Protocol and Convention) Act, 1937 reads in relevant part as follows:

> Conditions for enforcement of foreign awards
> (1) In order that a foreign award may be enforceable under this Act it must have
> (e) been in respect of a matter which may lawfully be referred to arbitration under the law of Pakistan, and the enforcement thereof must not be contrary to the public policy or the law, of Pakistan.

850. *Anayat Ali Shah v. Anwar Hussain and others*, 1995 MLD 1714, wherein Punjab High Court held that when agreement is found to be against the law, it would be deemed to be against public policy. In this case, agreement defeating the provisions of Pre-emption Act 1913 was declared to be against public policy. *See also Habib Bank v. Qayyum Spinning Ltd.*, 2001 MLD 1351; *Fauji Sugar Mills v. Mehmood Ahmad*, 2006 PLC 630.

851. Section 19. When consent to an agreement is caused by coercion, fraud or misrepresentation:

that contracts caused by fraud and misrepresentation would be voidable at the discretion of a party that was misrepresented or defrauded, who after being cognizant of the fraud and misrepresentation, can opt for the contract by designating the bargain valid. It implies that the fraud and misrepresentation perpetrated for the procurement of contracts fall in the purview of section 19 instead of section 23 by rendering these matters, at this stage, a non-public policy concern. In other words, the inducement of consent by fraud and misrepresentation (voidable contract) should be differentiated from the fraudulent consideration or fraudulent object (void contract). This is because section 23 does not speak of the commission of fraud or misrepresentation in the procurement of a contract. Rather it is bespeaking of the fraudulent consideration or objective of the contract, which is viewed at variance with public policy.[852]

While the procurement of a contract through fraud and misrepresentation is not difficult to comprehend, the phenomenon of fraudulent object and consideration is also self-evident in *Muhammad Yousuf v. Badruddin Ahmed,*[853] wherein the parties concluded two contracts over the same property - one with the actual price, and the second with a lower price. The intention of the parties to reach the second agreement was to part with the slashed sum of taxes and registration fee. The Sindh High Court effectuated the first agreement by pronouncing the second one void because it was contradictory to public policy for the reason that the object of the second agreement was fraudulent, i.e., to defraud the collection of public revenues. The second contract was deemed void in spite of the fact that the court could not find any intent among the parties to delude each other.[854]

Apart from relying on the stipulations laid down in section 23 of the Contract Act 1872, Pakistani courts, in order to define the public policy conception, also gave specific regard to the public interest or good or, in other words, any injury to the public. For example, in *Yasin Khan v. Feroze Khan*, the court reasoned as follows:

> The principle of the law which holds that no subject can lawfully do that which has a tendency to be injurious to the public or against the public good.[855]

> The agreement is a contract voidable at the option of the party whose consent was so caused.
>
> A party to a contract, whose consent was caused by fraud or misrepresentation may, if he thinks fit insist that the contract shall be performed and that he shall be put in the position in which, he would have been if the representations made had been true.
>
> *Explanation.* If such consent was caused by misrepresentation or by silence, fraudulent within the meaning of section 17, the contract, nevertheless, is not voidable, if the party whose consent was so caused had the means of discovering the truth with ordinary diligence.
>
> *Explanation.* A fraud or misrepresentation which did not cause the consent to a contract of the party on whom such fraud was practised or to whom such misrepresentation was made, does not render a contract voidable.

852. *Lahore Stock Exchange Limited v. Fredrick J. Whyte Group (Pakistan) Ltd.*, PLD 1990 SC 48.
853. *Muhammad Yousuf v. Badruddin Ahmed,* 2007 CLC 427.
854. *See, Pro Booh Chandra Barman v. Abdul Rehman,* PLD 1960 Decca 983; *Qasim Khan v. Jalal,* PLD 1987 Lahore 398, wherein it was held that a contract will be void where it is concluded for consideration that the criminal proceedings initiated for non-compoundable offences will be withdrawn. In this case, the consideration of contract was declared to be unlawful.
855. *Sardar Muhammad Yasin Khan v. Raja Feroze Khan*, PLD 1972 A J & K 46.

The court further elaborated the conception of public policy by asserting that it means:

> Any act the allowing of which would be against the general interests of the community. This policy has evolved itself with the growth of organised society. Certain standards in the domain of morality, used in its widest sense, have assumed sanctity on account of their acceptance by the general community. Therefore, any agreement which would destroy these standards or adversely affect the development of society or its organisation have to be viewed from this angle and it is here that the principle of public policy is born.[856]

The issue of public policy also transpired in *Nan Fung. Textiles Ltd. v. Sadiq Traders Ltd.*[857] In this case, in a dispute between a Pakistani party (respondent) and a party from Hong Kong (petitioner), an award was decreed by the arbitrator against the respondent under the Rules of the Liverpool Cotton Association. The Sindh High Court was to resolve if such award was unenforceable due to violation of public policy, as it did not contain any reasons from the arbitrator to support his findings. Whether such a non-speaking award infringes Pakistani public policy will be analysed *infra*. It suffices to mention the statement of the Sindh High Court here, which, by referring to *Sultan Textile Mills Ltd. v. Muhammad Yousuf Shamim*,[858] stated that: 'the problem in respect of illegality at common law on the ground of public policy is the discovery of injuriousness to society'. It also approvingly referred to AIR 1947 Sindh 94, which contained the following observation:

> The general head of 'public policy' covers a wide range of topics, such as, for example, trading with enemy in time of war, stifling prosecution, champerty and maintenance and various other matters.

The Sindh High Court also affirmatively extracted a paragraph from Chitty on Contracts describing the scope of public policy[859] as follows:

> *Scope of Public* Policy – Objects which on grounds of public policy invalidate contracts may, for convenience, be generally classified into *five* groups first, objects which are illegal by common law or by legislation; secondly, objects injurious to good government either in the field of domestic or foreign affairs; thirdly, objects which interfere with the proper working of the machinery of justice; fourthly, objects injurious to family life; and fifthly, objects economically against the public interest.

But the Sindh High Court did not seem to be content with the classification of public policy into five categories when it said that:

> This statement is not exhaustive as certain cases may not fit clearly into any of these five categories. However the aforestated classifications cover almost all conceivable cases except such cases which may arise in peculiar circumstances because in the words of Danckwert L. J. in *Nagle v. Feilden* (1966) 2 Q B 633, the

856. *Sardar Muhammad Yasin Khan v. Raja Feroze Khan*, PLD 1972 A J & K 46.
857. *Nan Fung Textiles Ltd. v. Sadiq Traders Ltd.*, PLD 1982 Karachi 619.
858. PLD 1972 Karachi 226.
859. 24th edition, para. 904.

law relating to public policy cannot remain immutable. It must change with the passage of time. The wind of change blows upon it.

It concluded that the respondent, who was relying on the public policy exception, could make his case of violation by any of the ingredients mentioned above so that the enforcement of the foreign award might be declined. The court arrived at the decision that the enforcement of the present award was not against public policy.

It is patent that the conception of public policy enshrined in the above-mentioned judgments is similar to the one encapsulated in section 23 of the Contract Act 1872. Immorality and illegality of consideration of an agreement have been regarded as injurious to the public and hence have been declared to be against public policy. For example, agreements of wagering, gambling or betting were held to be immoral, illegal and against public policy for their object and consideration were deemed unlawful.[860] Thus, the enforcement of an award recognizing or enforcing these agreements would also be interpreted as being against the public policy of Pakistan. The non-enforcement of such awards will not come off on the ground laid down in Article V(I)(a), because this provision stipulates that an agreement 'is not valid under the law to which the parties have subjected it; or failing any indication thereon, under the law of the country where the award was made'. On the other hand, in a situation where the award is declined enforcement on the basis that the agreement is void for it being repugnant to the notion of public policy of the enforcing state, the court or forum of enforcement is, in fact, applying its own law and not the law governing the agreement or the law of the seat of arbitration. In this way, it may be submitted that if the agreement is against the public policy of the enforcing state, the non-enforcement of the award in such case would also come under the public policy exception as articulated in Article V(2)(b) of the New York Convention.

The public policy limitation (both as an exception and a ground) has sometimes been conceived useful for it prohibits private parties in international contracts from overstepping policy limitations.[861] However, defining it so imprecisely or introducing new heads of public policy may amount to undermining international efforts to reduce the grounds thwarting the enforcement of arbitral awards.[862] It may be suggested that Pakistani courts should interpret the public policy exception to respect the enforcement of foreign arbitral awards by engulfing it with the pro-enforcement bias of the New York Convention. Such bias is evident from the fact that no grounds other than those provided in Article V of the New York Convention may be used by enforcing courts to refuse enforcement. On the other hand, the enforcing court has discretion in recognizing and enforcing the award, even if any of the Article V grounds are met.[863] In this regard, it is submitted that Pakistani courts should adopt a narrow interpretation of the

860. *Anjuman Prize Bond Dealers v. Province of Punjab and others*, PLD 2001 Lahore 129; *See also Abdul Razzak v. Karachi Development Authority*, 1991 CLC 1591.
861. Allen B. Green and Josh Weiss, *Public Policy and International Arbitration in the European Union*, 22 Am. Rev. Int'l Arb. 661 (2011).
862. Homayoon Arfazadeh, *In the Shadow of the Unruly Horse: International Arbitration and the Public Policy Exception*, 13 Am. Rev. Int'l Arb. 43 (2003).
863. *IPCO (Nigeria) Ltd v. Nigerian National Petroleum Corp.*, [2005] EWHC 726 (Comm).

public policy exception by shunning the tendency to employ this exception to protect the so-called interests of Pakistan or its nationals.[864]

The other facet of public policy is that the award should not have been obtained in a manner antagonistic towards the public policy conception of the enforcing court. The res judicata effect of an award may be called into question on the grounds that it was attained through collusion, fraud, misrepresentation, etc.[865] An identical view was re-established in *Government of Sindh v. Fazal Muhammad.*[866] In this case, the Supreme Court stated, in the context of domestic awards, that if the award was clinched through misrepresentation and fraud, the other party could contest it on public policy grounds. The same approach will be followed where a decree was secured on the enforcement of an award, as was held by the Supreme Court in *Government of Sindh v. Khalil Ahmed.*[867] In this case, it stated that if a decree enforcing an award was realized through fraud, the entire case would be considered to have not been adjudged in the correct perspective. This would amount to a miscarriage of justice. Similarly, the Punjab High Court stated that: 'fraud vitiates even the most solemn proceedings and courts of general jurisdiction are competent to *suo motu* recall decrees obtained from it by fraud'.[868] Briefly, an award can be challenged on the ground that it has been made through fraud or misrepresentation.[869]

To conclude, at the referral stage, Pakistani courts will negate the separability of an arbitration agreement and will also declare that these matters cannot be arbitrated in cases that involve fraud, bribery and illegality, which are matters of public policy.[870] Similarly, at the annulment or enforcement stage, no recognition or enforcement will be granted to an award if it was procured through any of these elements.

12.3. ABSENCE OF REASONS AS A GROUND OF PUBLIC POLICY

The arbitrator is bound to give sufficient but not detailed reasons in an award[871] so that the court may examine that such reasons are not inconsistent or contradictory to the

864. Vesselina Shaleva, *The 'Public Policy' Exception to the Recognition and Enforcement of Arbitral Awards in the Theory and Jurisprudence of the Central and East European States and Russia*, 19(1) (2003) Arb. Int'l. 67-93.
865. *Shahul Hamid v. Tahir Ali*, 1980 SCMR 469.
866. *Government of Sindh and another v. Ch. Fazal Muhammad and another*, PLD 1991 SC 197.
867. *Government of Sindh and others v. Khalil Ahmed and others*, 1994 SCMR 782.
868. *See also Chief Settlement Commissioner v. Muhammad Fazil*, PLD 1975 SC 331.
869. *Sardar Muhammad v. Hasmat Bibi alias Hasmatee and others*, 2004 YLR 626.
870. *Hub Power Company Limited (HUBCO) v. WAPDA*, PLD 2000 SC 841, at 868; *Maulana Abdul Haque Baloch v. Government of Balochistan*, PLD 2013 SC 641, para. 24.
871. *Wazir Khan and others v. Sardar Ali and others*, 2001 SCMR 750; *Raja Karam Dad Khan v. Faiz Ahmad*, 2017 CLC 1720; *Hassan Bakhsh v. Sultan and others*, 2016 MLD 1157; *Arshad Mehmood Anwar and others v. Muhammad Iqbal and others*, 2015 YLR 952; *All Pakistan CNG Association v. Pakistan State Oil Company Ltd.*, 2015 YLR 1813; *Muhammad Farooq Shah v. Shakirullah*, 2006 SCMR 1657; *Allah Din & Company v. Trading Corporation of Pakistan and others*, 2006 SCMR 614; *Mst. Zaib-Un-Nisa and others v. Muhammad Salim Akhtar and others*, 2005 YLR 2877; *Muhammad Gulzar v. Rana Abdul Jabbar and others*, 2004 MLD 667; *Tribal Friends Co. v. Province of Balochistan*, 2002 SCMR 1903; *Province of Punjab v. Tramic Construction (Pvt.) Ltd.*, 1999 CLC 946; *Noor Nabuwwat v. Moulvi Muhammad Noor Ali Khan*, 1999 CLC 1685; *J.F.C. Gollaher v. Samad Khan*, 1993 MLD 726.

material on the record. The sufficiency of reasons depends on the facts of each case,[872] but the reasoning in awards need not be in such details as required in judgment in civil suits.[873]

In Pakistan, neither the enforcement of a foreign arbitral award can be refused on the premise of a public policy exception, nor the enforcement of a domestic arbitral award on the basis of the public policy ground, if the award is non-speaking, i.e., without reasons or with insufficient reasons. Pakistani courts will not declare the enforcement of a non-speaking award to be against the public policy conception. In *Nan Fung Textiles Ltd. v. Sadiq Traders Ltd.*,[874] a case over a discord between a Pakistani party (respondent) and a party from Hong Kong (petitioner), an arbitral award was rendered under the Rules of the Liverpool Cotton Association, as was accorded by the arbitration agreement. At the enforcement stage, the Sindh High Court was faced with the contention, among others, that the arbitral award should not be enforced for being repugnant to public policy as it was a non-speaking award.

The Sindh High Court extracted section 26-A of the 1940 Act, which was inserted through the Arbitration (Amendment) Ordinance, 1981 (Order XV of 1981) as follows:

> 26-A – Award to set out reasons:
>
> (1) The arbitrator or umpire shall state in the award the reasons for the award in sufficient detail to enable the Court to consider, any question of law arising out of the award.
>
> (2) Where the award not state the reasons in sufficient detail, the Court shall remit the award to the arbitrators or umpire and fix the time within which the arbitrator or umpire shall submit the award together with the reasons in sufficient detail:
>
> Provided that any time so fixed may be extended by subsequent order of the Court.
>
> (3) An award remitted under sub-section (2) shall become void on the failure of the arbitrator or umpire to submit it in accordance with the direction of the Court.

The Sindh High Court underscored the clarity of this provision by making it obligatory on arbitrators or umpires to include sufficiently detailed reasons in an arbitral award[875] so as to put the judge in a position to determine any question of law emanating from such award. The Court acknowledged that in case of non-observance by the arbitrator of this provision, a court shall not straightaway set aside the award but

872. *Gerry's International (Pvt.) Ltd. v. Aeroflot Russian International Airlines*, 2018 SCMR 662; *Indhara Industries Ltd. Karachi v. Government of Pakistan*, PLD 1982 Karachi 260; *Umar Din v. Mst. Shakeela Bibi and others*, 2009 SCMR 29.
873. *Abdullah Traders v. Trading Corporation of Pakistan Ltd*, 1999 CLC 2047; *Associated Constructors Ltd. v. Karachi Municipal Corporation*, 1987 CLC 383.
874. *Nan Fung Textiles Ltd. v. Sadiq Traders Ltd.*, PLD 1982 Karachi 619. *See also Abdullah Traders v. Trading Corporation of Pakistan Ltd*, 1999 CLC 2047; *Muhammad Yousuf v. Gul Zaman*, 2004 MLD 735; *Karachi Metropolitan Corporation v. Associated Constructors Ltd.*, 1984 CLC 1077; *Water and Power Development Authority v. Ice Pak International Consulting Engineers of Pakistan*, 2003 YLR 2494.
875. *See also Associated Constructors Ltd v. Karachi Municipal Corporation*, 1987 CLC 383.

will remit the award to the arbitrator[876] and instruct him to transcribe the reasons in the award in sufficient detail within the time granted by the court. It also held that it was the court's discretion to either remit the award or abstain from doing so on account of the insufficiency or absence of reasons in the award. However, the court is not entrusted with any discretion to refuse the enforcement on the basis of insufficiency or absence of reasons. On such grounds, the enforcement shall be declined only if the non-speaking award was remitted to the arbitrator with a direction to resubmit it to the court within the time set by it and the arbitrator failed to do so without furnishing sufficient reasons.

In addition, the Sindh High Court re-established an important principle by holding that the provisions of the 1981 Ordinance enacting section 26-A were not applicable to the 1937 Act (foreign awards) for, had the legislature intended so, it would have interposed such provision in the 1937 Act. The Court further stated that it is well settled that the provisions laid down in the 1940 Act were of no relevance to foreign awards. Hence, both section 26-A of the 1940 Act and section 3 of the 1981 Ordinance can only be brought into play to resist a domestic award on the ground of absence of reasons. Since the 1937 Act did not comprehend any clause stipulating for a reasoned award, the enforcement of non-speaking foreign awards would not be in defiance of public policy. Since the 1937 Act was repealed by the 2011 Act, and the latter instrument does not include any provision mandating a reasoned award either, the principle would also extend to the 2011 Act, and the enforcement of an unreasoned foreign award regulated under the 2011 Act would not be against public policy.

Where the agreement itself or through incorporating the rules of an organization requires a reasoned award, the case of *European Grain & Shipping Ltd. v. Polychem Company Ltd.*[877] is instructive. In this case, under a contract between the appellant and respondent, the latter was to supply a specific amount of Guar Protein Extract to the appellant within a specific time. However, the respondent could not honour this commitment, for he could deliver only a quarter of the total quantity. The matter was referred, according to the agreement, to arbitration in London under the Grain and Feed Trade Association (hereinafter 'GAFTA') Rules. In this arbitration, an award was ordained in favour of the appellant. The award was brought to a Pakistani court for enforcement under section 5 of the 1937 Act. The enforcement of this award was resisted on many grounds, including the absence of reasons in the award.

Although it was not spelled out expressly, it might fairly be inferred from the wording of the court that if the rules governing the arbitration obligated the arbitrator to annex sufficient reasons and he failed to do so, this might become a ground for refusal of the enforcement of the award. For example, in this case, Rule 7:7 of the GAFTA Rules reads as follows:

---

876. On remand of domestic award to arbitrator for the absence of reasons, *see Sezai Turkes Feyzi Akkaya Construction Company v. Board of Trustees of Karachi Port Trust, Karachi*, 2007 CLC 879; *Pak Malik Constructors Ltd. v. Government of Pakistan*, PLD 1982 Lahore 57; *Muhammad Farooq Shah v. Shakirullah*, 2006 SCMR 1657; *Muhammad Gulzar v. Rana Abdul Jabbar and others*, 2004 MLD 667; *Tribal Friends Co. v. Province of Balochistan*, 2002 SCMR 1903; *Noor Nabuwwat v. Moulvi Muhammad Noor Ali Khan*, 1999 CLC 1685.
877. *European Grain & Shipping Ltd. v. Polychem Company Ltd.*, PLD 1990 Karachi 254.

> If reasons for the award are not evident from the wording of the award then the arbitrator(s) shall issue separate document containing in writing reasons for the award, which said reasons shall not form part of the award nor be referred to in the award and shall be stated to be issued for information only and on the basis that the contents of the document containing the reasons will not be used or referred to in any proceedings in the Courts of the United Kingdom.

The Court stated that the Rule obliged the arbitrator to put the reasons for the award in writing and that such reasons 'shall not form part of the award and ... will not be used or referred to in any proceedings in the Courts of the United Kingdom'. However, no further provision of the GAFTA Rules clarifies the repercussions in case of non-observance by the arbitrator of the condition to furnish reasons. Hence, the court concluded that such provisions were not of a mandatory nature but of a directory nature and thus could not render an award invalid.[878] It may be inferred that if some ramification had been provided by the Rules in case of the pronouncement of a non-speaking award, such as non-enforcement, the court might have executed that consequence.

12.4. INTEREST AS GROUND OF PUBLIC POLICY

The enforcement of arbitral awards, both foreign and domestic, by mandating a party to pay interest is not against the public policy conception of Pakistan and cannot be resisted on the basis or grounds of public policy exceptions. More recently,[879] the Supreme Court maintained that *Riba* (interest) is permissible, which means that the previous judgment of the Supreme Court prohibiting interest in its totality stands abolished.[880] However, as this issue has raised so much discussion in Pakistani jurisprudence, specifically regarding arbitration, it needs an in-depth survey and analysis of judgments on this matter.

Article 38(f) of the Constitution of Pakistan enunciates that 'the state shall ... eliminate *Riba* as early as possible'. Article 227 of the Constitution states that:

> (1) All existing laws shall be brought in conformity with the Injunctions of Islam as laid down in the Holy Quran and Sunnah, in this Part referred to as the Injunctions of Islam, and no law shall be enacted which is repugnant to such Injunctions.
>
> [Explanation: In the application of this clause to the personal law of any Muslim sect, the expression 'Quran and Sunnah' shall mean the Quran and Sunnah as interpreted by that sect.]
>
> (2) Effect shall be given to the provisions of clause (1) only in the manner provided in this Part.

878. Whereas the 1940 Act is not applicable to foreign awards, some principles laid thereunder are noteworthy, like the obligation on the arbitrator to give sufficient reason is not met by summary or sketchy reason in the award, rather they should be in detail and should be in the award itself. *See Karachi Metropolitan Corporation v. Associated Constructors Ltd.*, 1984 CLC 1077; *Wazir Khan and others v. Sardar Ali and others*, 2001 SCMR 750; *Muhammad Gulzar v. Rana Abdul Jabbar and others*, 2004 MLD 667.
879. Judgment of 6 October 2015.
880. *Aslam Khaki v. Muhammad Hashim*, PLD 2000 SC 225.

(3) Nothing in this Part shall affect the personal laws of non- Muslim citizens or their status as citizens.

It may be an extension of these constitutional provisions when *Riba* was proscribed in its entirety by the Supreme Court in *Aslam Khaki v. Muhammad Hashim*.[881] In this case, the Supreme Court held that all forms of interest prevailing at the moment were included in the definition of *Riba* and *Riba* was outlawed by the injunctions of Islam as laid down in the Quran and the Sunnah, no matter if the amount of interest was colossal or trivial. The Supreme Court of Pakistan thus adjured the government to transform the Pakistani system in consonance with the *Shariah* by subjecting it to radical changes. The Supreme Court acknowledged that the alternatives of *Riba* were within easy reach, and on account of such availability, the continuance of *Riba* on a permanent basis could not be accepted, not even on the ground of necessity. However, it held that the interest-based system might be allowed for a limited period until the groundwork already done by Islamic scholars and economists has materialized and concretized.

This judgment was observed in many subsequent judgments pertaining to arbitration matters.[882] In *Alpha Insurance Co. Ltd v. Ch. Nizam Din*,[883] the arbitrator granted interest at a rate of 15%. But the Punjab High Court invalidated it by holding that in its judgment *Aslam Khaki v. Syed Muhammad Hashim*, the Supreme Court of Pakistan had termed interest to be against the injunctions of the Quran and Sunnah. So, no interest could be granted.

In *Flame Maritime Ltd. v. Hassan Ali Rice Export*,[884] the Sindh High Court adhered to the same approach. In this case, the plaintiff chartered a ship for the carriage of goods from Karachi to Moroni (Comoros Islands). In this charterparty contract, the parties concurred that if the cargo could not be discharged in Moroni in accordance with the addendum annexed to the contract, alternative arrangements would be executed. The charterparty also set forth the referral of disputes to arbitration in London under English law. The delay and subsequent failure to deliver the cargo in Moroni sparked off disputes which were handed to the arbitrator accordingly. The arbitrator issued an award against the charterer, who was ordered to discharge a certain amount under the heads of damages and expenses for arbitration along with 7.5% of interest per year until the payment of these amounts was disbursed.

The award was filed under the 1937 Act. The Sindh High Court pronounced judgment in terms of the award having become a rule of court to the exclusion of the interest awarded. Keeping to the same determination as to the Supreme Court in *Aslam Khaki v. Muhammad Hashim*, the court maintained that:

> The enforcement of interest in Pakistan is repugnant to the injunction of Islam, therefore, the enforcement of interest as awarded would be against the law prevalent in Pakistan. For the reasons discussed above, since award has become

881. *Ibid.*
882. This judgment was relied and followed in *Habib Bank v. Qayyum Spinning Ltd.*, 2001 MLD 1351.
883. *Alpha Insurance Co. Limited v. Nizam Din & Sons and another*, 2001 CLC 289.
884. *Flame Maritime Limited v. Hassan Ali Rice Export*, 2006 CLD 697.

> final in England, where it was made enforceable under the Act, 1937, the defendant had failed to make out any ground to nullify the award, the objection raised by the defendants are hereby rejected. The award is made rule of the Court excluding the interest. The decree shall follow in terms thereof. The suit is hereby decreed in above terms with no order as to costs.

Despite the aforementioned rulings, it is submitted that the pervasive view had been in favour of upholding interest in arbitration cases, and it seems that the ruling from the Supreme Court[885] did not have any effect on the past trend of judgments on this subject. In this regard, the rule was very perspicuously established in *Pervez Industrial Corporation v. Messrs New Lahore Transport Corporation.*[886] In this case, the Sindh High Court held that the arbitrator could award interest if the rules applicable to arbitration authorized him to do so.

In an arbitration conducted in England under English law, interest was awarded, and the Sindh High Court held that interest awarded by the arbitrator was valid because the arbitration was administered in England, and hence, the arbitrator applied English law.[887] The same view was adhered to in *Sheikh Hussain Bux & Co. v. Zaib Tun Textile Mills Ltd.*[888] In this case, in an arbitration administered under the rules of the Karachi Cotton Association, the arbitrator decreed an award in which he granted the amount of PKR 330,581, which was held to be the balance amount on the sale of cotton and PKR 32,554 was rendered as interest on that sum. The arbitrator also awarded a 14% interest from the date of the award on the amount of interest. When *Pervez Industrial Corp. v. New Lahore Transport Corp.*[889] case was cited by the award creditor to demonstrate that the arbitrator could award interest, the Sindh High Court said that in that case, the Rules of the Karachi Cotton Association governing the arbitration authorized the arbitrator to award interest to the extent of 9%, and no more, but that in this case, the arbitrator awarded interest on interest, which was impermissible.

Sh. Mahboob Alam v. Sh. Mumtaz Ahmad[890] involved a dispute between partners. The arbitrator found that the partnership had earned profits, but those profits could not be ascertained exactly because the appellant had a responsibility to maintain the accounts, which he was not regularly keeping. The accounts actually produced were untrue. The arbitrator held that the respondent was entitled to half of the profits which could have been made. This was so because that partnership had made some profits, the determination of which was not possible for the arbitrator. Therefore, he granted interest at a rate of 5% per annum in lieu of such profits. In this way, the interest was included in the total amount awarded by the arbitrator. The court held that this was a just method for the calculation of profits.

885. *Aslam Khaki v. Muhammad Hashim*, PLD 2000 SC 225.
886. *Pervez Industrial Corporation v. New Lahore Transport Corporation and others*, PLD 1977 Karachi 37.
887. *Dampskibsselskabet Nordon Aktieselskale v. Ahmed Shipping Lines Limited*, PLD 1983 Karachi 247.
888. *Sheikh Hussain Bux & Co. v. Zaib Tun Textile Mills Ltd.*, PLD 1981 Karachi 28.
889. *Pervez Industrial Corporation v. New Lahore Transport Corporation and others*, PLD 1977 Karachi 37.
890. *Sh. Mahboob Alam v. Sh. Mumtaz Ahmad*, PLD 1960 (W. P.) Lahore 601.

It merits mentioning that the court is also empowered to award interest on the principal amount of award, under section 29 of the 1940 Act, for the post-decree period. This provision, however, does not prevent an arbitrator from awarding interest in his finding upon the reference before him. Rather, he is not vested with the power to award interest for a period starting at the date of the award until the payment of the principal sum declared in the award (*pendente lite* interest), except where there exists:

- an agreement, express or implied between the parties, empowering the arbitrator; or
- some substantive law provision or mercantile usage allowing the arbitrator to award interest; or,
- some equitable principle to that effect.

In the absence of such conditions, the arbitrator is powerless[891] and can vouch-safe the interest only up to the date of the arbitral award. Beyond that time, these powers lie within the exclusive domain of the court. Such powers of the court may be said to be a combined effect of section 29 of the 1940 Act and section 34[892] of the CPC.[893] Although the arbitrator lacks such powers, if he grants interest beyond the award and on which then judgment is entered by the court, it would be considered that the court had adopted that interest under section 29 of the 1940 Act.[894] The court should exercise discretion under section 29, but this should not be done mechanically or arbitrarily. For instance, where an arbitrator declined to award interest, and the court granted interest without considering the decision of the arbitrator, the court was

891. *Lahore Development Authority v. Faisal International Construction Corporation Limited,* 2004 CLC 594; *Ascon Engineers (Pvt.) Ltd. v. Province of Punjab,* 2002 SCMR 1662; *K. F. Development Corporation Ltd. v. Dawood Cotton Mills Ltd.*, 1999 MLD 2953; *Punjab Province v. Chauhan & Company,* PLD 2000 Lahore 314; *Province of Punjab v. Awan Engineering Enterprises,* 2006 YLR 881; *Millat Tractors Ltd v. Millat Tractor House,* 1999 YLR 295.

892. Section 34. Interest:

(1) Where and in so far as a decree is for the payment of money, the Court may, in the decree, order interest at such rate as the Court deems reasonable to be paid on the principal sum adjudged, from the date of the suit to the date of the decree, in addition to any interest adjudged on such principal sum for any period prior to the institution of on the aggregate sum so adjudged, from the date of the decree to the date of payment, or to such earlier date as the Court thinks fit.

(2) Where such a decree is silent with respect to the payment of further interest on such aggregate sum as aforesaid from the date of the decree to the date of payment or other earlier date, the Court shall be deemed to have refused such interest, and separate suit therefore, shall not lie.

893. For more detail, *see Ghulam Abbas v. Trustees of The Port of Karachi,* PLD 1987 SC 393; *Maqbool Associates Ltd. v. Sindh Sugar Corporation Ltd.*, 1990 CLC 55; *Province of Sindh v. Hmi Khan,* 1993 MLD 2349; *Pakistan Steel Mills Corporation Ltd. v. Syed Altaf Hussain,* PLD 1991 Karachi 386; *Sezai Turkes Feyzi Akkaya Construction Company,* 2007 CLC 879; *Muhammad Saleem Butt v. Trading Corporation of Pakistan, Karachi,* 1986 CLC 254; *Hassan Brothers & Company v. Maqbool Cotton Ginning & Pressing Factory and another,* PLD 1986 Karachi 21; *Safia Bai and others v. Karachi Cooperative Housing Societies Union Ltd,* PLD 1967 Karachi 598.

894. *Ghulam Abbas v. Trustees of The Port of Karachi,* PLD 1987 SC 393; *Province of Sindh v. Waseem Construction Co.*, 1991 CLC 66; *University of Engineering and Technology, Lahore v. Moderate Builders,* 2001 MLD 233.

termed to have exercised its discretion mechanically and arbitrarily; therefore, its judgment was set aside by the High Court.[895]

An inconsistent judgment from the Supreme Court surfaced on the landscape of Pakistani jurisprudence.[896] In this judgment, it held that the court had the power to award interest only from the date of the decree on the award and not prior to that. Criticizing this judgment, it may be submitted that the arbitrator cannot award interest subsequent to the date of the award if the conditions empowering him to grant post-award interest are absent. If this judgment were followed, the court would not be able to award interest prior to the decree on the award. This implies that the award creditor will not be able to obtain anything between the rendering of the award and the decree on that award. The gravity of this fact increases if the enforcement proceedings on appeal and after appeal are prolonged considerably.

To conclude, it may very safely be inferred from the permission given to the arbitrator by the parties, law or trade usage to impart interest in his award that courts will not declare a contract containing such permission to be void on public policy grounds.

12.5. CONCLUSION

The term public policy has not been defined by statutory law on arbitration in Pakistan. It has then been defined by the courts very broadly and vaguely. Furthermore, this concept of public policy was crafted exclusively for domestic affairs, which did not take into consideration the international perspective of public policy respecting international arbitral awards. This may be termed as the outcome of absence of some global standard for the construction of public policy whose vague meaning leaves so much room for courts to use their discretion.

It seems to be settled that the public policy of Article V in the New York Convention is that of the enforcing court. Pakistani courts need to redefine the categories of public policy by giving due regard to the pro-enforcement bias of the New York Convention as well as its aim of establishing a uniform concept of public policy to be followed by the Convention signatories. Loose and inharmonious categorization of public policy that is viewed differently by Pakistani courts cannot serve that purpose. It is submitted that these categories should be of very basic and of fundamental nature as, for instance, if notions of morality and justice are to be considered ingredients of public policy, it must be the violation of the most basic notions of justice and morality justifying refusal to enforce. To achieve that purpose, apart from a narrow interpretation of public policy, the courts might distinguish between the public policy relevant to international awards (international public policy) and that for domestic awards (domestic public policy). Bifurcation of public policy into domestic and international seems desirable because the application of the public policy concept formulated exclusively for domestic matters (including award) and coated primarily with the

895. *The Project Director, Peoples Program v. Khawaja Muhammad Sarwar*, 1989 CLC 1030.
896. *Dawood Cotton Mills Ltd. v. K. F. Development Corporation Ltd.*, 2006 SCMR 1555.

state's public interest will not allow the court to interpret it narrowly for the advantage of international awards.

Thus, the current situation demands that Pakistani courts, by divorcing themselves from the territorial approach of public policy, should internationalize their public-policy approach. This suggestion is due to the fact that at this point, to expect from Pakistani court to lay down a uniform and narrow conception of public policy applicable equally for both domestic and foreign arbitration awards may not be a fulfillable dream.

It may also be submitted that instead of putting courts in a difficult position to give a very narrow interpretation to public policy or expect them to apply international (or truly international) public policy for the enforcement of awards, it looks more appropriate for the legislature to incorporate a favourable regime on public policy. It may be said that such an arbitration-friendly attitude from the legislature will make the courts even more arbitration friendly.[897]

897. James D. Fry, *Desordre Public International under the New York Convention: Wither Truly International Public Policy*, 8 Chinese J. Int'l L. 81 (2009).

CHAPTER 13

Pakistani Treatment of Due Process in Arbitration

It is the fundamental right of parties to have their disputes resolved by an unbiased arbitrator. However, to safeguard this cardinal right, the Pakistani legal regime could not engrave on its legal landscape the predictable and consistent principles governing due process in general and independence and impartiality of arbitrator in particular. This chapter goes into the Pakistani jurisprudence on points as to what general principles govern the ascertainment of arbitrator's bias, whether arbitrator bias is a valid ground to thwart the enforcement of foreign arbitral awards in Pakistan and whether the judgments decreed on non-arbitration matters in Pakistan are of any help to conceive the standards for arbitrator bias. It concludes, inter alia, that the approach prevalent in Pakistan as a vantage point to discern arbitrator bias and the test respecting thereto calls for adjustment.

13.1. INTRODUCTION

It is a fundamental right of the parties to an arbitration agreement to have their disputes resolved by an unbiased arbitrator. However, to ensure the protection of this fundamental right, the Pakistani legal regime could not establish well-organized and crystallized standards respecting due process in general and arbitrator bias in particular. On the other side, the predictability and consistency requisites of law demand that a potential party in arbitration resisting or seeking the enforcement of an award in Pakistan, particularly if he is a foreign party, should be able to foresee beforehand the scope of this defence in Pakistani courts.

The need for clarification concerning the independence and impartiality standards include but not limited to the following: the proliferation in challenges against arbitrators on the basis of impartiality and independence; a growing number of participants in arbitral dispute resolution; and the phenomenon of the world getting more and more complex.[898] The fact that arbitral institutions do not publicize challenge decisions seems to have further exacerbated the situation because the courts decide such issues by employing the standards used for judges or on the basis of the perception developed in the court by reading the circumstances. What is left for the parties is nothing more than a question if there is sufficient feeling to make a justified challenge based on given circumstances.

In this chapter, first, the relation between independence and impartiality of arbitrators is discussed to demonstrate that they are not so independent from each other and that the term 'bias' is more apt as it encompasses both of them. Then, the Pakistani perspective on arbitrator bias is explored in detail. The dissection on the topic will be concluded with suggestions as to what standpoint should be used to examine arbitrator bias and also what test should be used. This chapter finally discusses the standard of evidence needed to prove bias.

13.2. RELATION BETWEEN INDEPENDENCE AND IMPARTIALITY

Impartiality and independence have been considered apart from each other, although independence is either a subordinate part of impartiality or dependence of arbitrators is not actionable or prohibited intrinsically until and unless there is a certainty that it would result in the partiality of arbitrators. It is also patent from the House of Lords' verdict in *Porter v. Magill*[899] where it relied on a judgment of the European Court of Justice[900] to elaborate the close interdependence between these two terms (independence and impartiality), and said as follows:

> The court recalls that in order to establish whether a tribunal can be considered as 'independent', regard must be had *inter alia* to the manner of appointment of its members and their term of office, the existence of guarantees against outside pressures and the question of whether the body presents an appearance of independence. As to the question of 'impartiality', there are two aspects to this requirement. First, the tribunal must be subjectively free from personal prejudice or bias. Second, it must also be impartial from an objective viewpoint; that is, it must offer sufficient guarantees to exclude any legitimate doubt in this respect. The concepts of independence and objective impartiality are closely linked; in both cases, the concept requires not only that the tribunal must be truly independent and free from actual bias, proof of which is likely to be very difficult, but also that it must not appear in the objective sense to lack these essential qualities.

The same approach is prevalent in France, where independence was determined by considering the links (economic, intellectual, social, etc.) of arbitrators with parties, and an arbitrator was disqualified from functioning only where such links proved to have (or were presumed to have) crippled him to act objectively and without any favour or bias. Hence, French courts necessitate that in order to demonstrate the

898. Geoff Nicholas and Constantine Partasides, *LCIA Court Decisions on Challenges to Arbitrators: A Proposal to Publish*, 23(1) Arb. Int'l 1(2007).
899. [2001] UKHL 67.
900. *Findlay v. United Kingdom*, (1997) 24 EHRR 221, para. 73.

disqualification of an arbitrator on the basis of circumstances leaned upon by a party to establish the lack of independence, he must also substantiate that such dependence is spawning 'a definite risk of bias in favour of a party to arbitration'. It should be noted that impartiality is, in fact, 'the absence of risk of bias on part of the arbitrator towards one of the parties'.[901] In the words of the court:

> The circumstances relied on to challenge that independence must constitute, through the existence of material or intellectual links, a situation which is liable to affect the judgment of the arbitrator by creating a definite risk of bias in favour of a party to the arbitration.[902]

The same attitude can be found in the Pakistani regime, where the arbitrator will be disqualified if he has some financial or other personal interest in the subject matter. However, where there is some kind of relationship or links of friendship or animosity between the adjudicator and the parties or their counsel, then the onus lies on the party to prove that such link or relationship (is likely to) gives rise to bias on the part of the adjudicator.[903] Therefore, in this chapter, the term 'bias' is used.

13.3. DISCOVERING THE PAKISTANI PERSPECTIVE ON ARBITRATOR'S BIAS

In the Pakistani perspective, the term bias represents both independence and impartiality, which has been dealt with as a subcategory of arbitrator misconduct. Misconduct of the arbitrator is not something different from the prerequisites of due process because if the requirements prescribed by due process are not abided by the arbitrator, this will amount to arbitral misconduct. For instance, one precondition of due process is that arbitrators should not be biased in favour of one party or against the other. If arbitrators violate this due process condition, they will be declared to have committed misconduct or, in other words, infracted a due process requirement. Therefore, in the sections below, first, the term misconduct will be elaborated to establish that the misconduct is the negative side of due process. Then the discussion will be narrowed down to the arbitrator's bias to evince it as a subcategory of misconduct, followed by a discussion on conflicting judgments on the question if the misconduct (including bias) may become a valid ground to resist the enforcement of a foreign arbitral award. The dilation upon this point is succeeded by a discourse on general principles governing the arbitrator's bias. Since the Pakistani regime seems to have taken these principles from English law, the evolution of principles governing bias in the English

---

901. Emmanuel Gaillard and John Savage, *Fouchard, Gaillard, Goldman on international Commercial Arbitration*, (Kluwer Law International, Netherlands, 1999), para. 1033.
902. Judgment of 2 June 1989, 1991 Rev. Arb. 87 (Paris Cour d'appel); Judgment of 28 June 1991, 1992 Rev. Arb. 568 (Paris Cour d'appel); Judgment of 12 January 1991, 1996 Rev. Arb. 428, 2d decision (Paris Cour d'appel). *See also* Emmanuel Gaillard and John Savage, *Fouchard, Gaillard, Goldman on international Commercial Arbitration* (Kluwer Law International, 1999), para. 1029.
903. *Wajid Ali (represented by legal heirs) v. Syed Sajid Ali (represented by legal heirs)*, 1985 SCMR 401.

regime on this subject is very briefly discussed to appreciate the lacunas in Pakistani interpretation. Then, the issue as to whether the judgments decreed on non-arbitration matters pertaining to the bias of judges can be employed to draw some principles to govern arbitrator bias.

13.3.1. Arbitrator Misconduct: Definition and Explanation

Due process is a constitutional protection afforded to the litigants both in civil and criminal proceedings. Article 10A of the Pakistani Constitution, entitled 'right to fair trial' reads that:

> For the determination of his civil rights and obligations or in any criminal charge against him, a person shall be entitled to a fair trial and due process.[904]

The Supreme Court[905] has prescribed the minimum requirements of due process of law as follows:

- Due notice of proceedings affecting the rights of citizens shall be given.
- Reasonable opportunity to defend shall be given.
- Honest and impartial adjudicatory forum shall be constituted.
- The forum is of competent jurisdiction.[906]

These essentials of due process had already been reflected in arbitration cases relating to the misconduct of arbitrators. The 1940 Act employs the term 'misconduct' without rendering any definition to it.[907] While the courts expressed their inability to constitute an exhaustive definition of 'misconduct', in order to ascertain what would amount to arbitrator misconduct, they have affirmed the very wide import of this term.[908] Although the instances taken into account under the head of 'misconduct' encompass general requirements listed above for due process, the matter of arbitrator misconduct had been approached by the courts from two dimensions. First, they

904. Section 5 of the Constitution (Eighteenth Amendment) Act, 2010 (Act of 2010).
905. *Nadeem Arif v. IG Police, Punjab*, 2011 SCMR 408.
906. These requirements of due process were applied in these cases: *Euro Duty Free Shop (Pvt.) Ltd. v. Federation of Pakistan*, 2015 PTD 790; *Sharafat Kaleem v. Additional District Judge, Bahawalnagar*, 2013 CLC 185; *Ammaris Mehtab Chaudhry v. Vice-Chancellor, Sargodha University*, 2013 CLC 1080; *Muhammad Nawaz v. Zarai Tarqiati Bank Limited*, 2013 CLD 1390; *Uzma Shahzad v. Principal School of Nursing, (BVH)*, 2012 CLC 1464; *Decent Textiles, Faisalabad v. Commissioner (Appeals) Inland Revenue (R.T.O.), Faisalabad*, 2013 PTD (Trib.) 954; *Institute for Development Studies and Practices, Quetta v. Government of Balochistan*, 2014 CLC 1211; *National College of Business Administration and Economics, Lahore v. Higher Education Commission of Pakistan*, 2014 YLR 1967.
907. Section 11 of the 1940 Act.
908. *Province of Baluchistan v. Muhammad Hassan*, 1988 CLC 1583; *Abdullah Contractors v. WAPDA*, 2006 YLR 589; *Civil Aviation Authority, Quaid-e-Azam International Airport, Karachi v. AER Rainta International Pakistan (Pvt.) Ltd., Karachi*, 2003 YLR 1523. In *Syed Faqir Shah v. Haji Inayatullah Khan and another*, 2013 MLD 689 misconduct was defined as 'an act on the part of arbitrators which has prejudicially affected the basic rights of the party or is violation of any law or principles of natural justice and which is not interfered with, may result in grave miscarriage of justice'. In this case, the court also gave an enumerative list of instances amounting to misconduct of arbitrators.

categorized it as moral and legal misconduct and second, they declared that the arbitrator should neither misconduct himself nor the arbitration proceedings.

Moral misconduct essentially involves a lack of good faith.[909] An arbitrator is deemed to have committed moral misconduct if he has some pecuniary interest[910] or has embraced some bribe or favour from the party in whose favour the award is later announced. On the other hand, legal misconduct, which 'in its judicial sense, means failure to perform duty judiciously by some breach and neglect to do justice resulting in substantial miscarriage of justice, though erroneously'[911] was deemed to have been committed, for instance, where the arbitrator performed his duties and conducted the arbitration proceedings honestly and to the best of his capabilities, but issued no notice to the parties and recorded the evidence behind their back, etc. It is conspicuous that this sort of misconduct was not moral, but the court would set aside the award on the basis of legal misconduct.

Dealing with the second approach, the terms 'misconducted himself or the arbitration proceedings' as are brought into play with respect to arbitrators are of such a wide scope to embrace all irregularities which may lead to miscarriage of justice.[912] The misconduct of arbitrators has been said to amount to a failure to fulfil essential and basic duties, eventuating in a substantial miscarriage of justice between the parties. On the other hand, the term 'misconducting the proceedings' implies the mishandling of arbitration proceedings by arbitrators that is likely to become the cause of some substantial miscarriage of justice.[913] The significance and connotation of the term 'misconducting the proceedings' are broader than the arbitrator's personal misconduct. There would be misconduct from an arbitrator if he had failed to decide all the issues or objections submitted; or decided issues not included in the scope of the arbitration agreement, or the award was inconsistent, uncertain or vague; or there was some mistake of fact if this mistake is either admitted or is clear beyond any reasonable doubt. But making an erroneous decision would not be misconduct even if the error was one of law or fact or whether or not his decision was supported by the evidence.[914]

The foregoing makes it clear that due process or misconduct has many facets. This chapter discusses two aspects, i.e., arbitrator bias (in detail) and equal treatment of parties (briefly).

13.3.1.1. Equal Treatment of Parties as a Requirement of Due Process

Arbitrators cannot ignore the basic principles of natural justice. They must afford the opportunity of being heard to the parties and cannot act arbitrarily. Since the proceedings before the arbitrator are meant to dispense justice between the parties,

909. *Gerry's International (Pvt.) Ltd. v. Aeroflot Russian International Airlines*, 2018 SCMR 662.
910. *Sarwat Ali & Sons v. General Manager T&T, W.T.R. Quetta and another*, 2007 CLC 1499; *Civil Aviation Authority, Quaid-e-Azam International Airport, Karachi v. AER Rainta International Pakistan (Pvt.) Ltd., Karachi*, 2003 YLR 1523.
911. *Abdullah Contractors v. WAPDA*, 2006 YLR 589.
912. *Government of Pakistan v. Asian Associated Agencies*, PLD 1974 Karachi 155.
913. *Abdullah Contractors v. WAPDA*, 2006 YLR 589.
914. *Gerry's International (Pvt.) Ltd. v. Aeroflot Russian International Airlines*, 2018 SCMR 662.

therefore justice should not only be done but must be seen to have been done. Where an arbitrator has not given a written notice of the date, time and place of arbitration proceedings, or if he examines no witness, he commits misconduct.[915]

As far as the proceedings before the arbitrator are concerned, the 1940 Act does not mandate that the arbitrator should not proceed ex parte if the defaulting party does not appear in the proceedings. Nevertheless, it is the rule of convenience and prudence that obliges the arbitrator not to move ex parte in one sitting but rather give notice to the party requiring his attendance before the arbitrator. If the party is absent from proceedings, the arbitrator should afford another notice to that party expressing his intention therein to move ex parte in case of omission on his part to make an appearance before the arbitrator.[916]

In one case, a party dispatched a telegram to the arbitrator explaining its inability to reach in time, but the arbitrator decided the case in the absence of that party. The award was set aside on the basis that the party was condemned unheard.[917] Similarly, in another case, the arbitrator proceeded without imparting any pre-emptory notice to the party, clarifying that if he failed to produce the requisite evidence by a specific date, he would proceed ex parte. So the arbitrator proceeded, and finally, the award was pronounced. The court held that the basic decision of going ex parte without issuing any notice was illegal, and hence the entire award was also illegal. As a result, the award was set aside.[918] For that reason, the arbitrator must give a reasonable opportunity to the party to make him well versed with the case and present it. Although the arbitrator has considerable latitude in the arbitral procedure to be followed, if he renders the award without affording reasonable opportunity to the parties and condemns any of these without having heard them, this will be on the peril of setting aside the award.[919] The reason is that the award given without hearing a party would be considered against the principles of justice.[920] In another case, the arbitrator adjourned the proceedings by giving a date for the next hearing and then by overwriting gave another date without intimating the defendant about the new date or his intention to proceed ex parte in case of the defendant's non-attendance of the next hearing. The court held that the arbitrator did not act impartially. Proceeding ex parte without giving

915. *Syed Faqir Shah v. Haji Inayatullah Khan and another*, 2013 MLD 689; *Civil Aviation Authority, Quaid-e-Azam International Airport, Karachi v. AER Rainta International Pakistan (Pvt.) Ltd., Karachi*, 2003 YLR 1523; *Kashmir Corporation Ltd. v. Pakistan International Airlines*, PLD 1995 Karachi 301; *Abdul Hamid Butt v. Government of West Pakistan and another*, PLD 1975 Lahore 1427.
916. *Progressive Methods (Pvt.) Limited v. Shaheen Air Port Services and others*, 1998 CLC 1638; *Shahzad Ali Usmani Chohan v. Managing Director, Sindh Small Industries Corporation*, 1989 CLC 450.
917. *Eastern Services (Pvt) Ltd. Company v. Director-General, Federal Government Employees Housing Foundation and another*, 2000 YLR 503.
918. *Jaycee Pipe Agencies v. Jahangir Chemicals and Plastic Industries*, 1998 MLD 115.
919. *Haji Tayab and Others v. Eastern Textile Mills Ltd., Chittagong and others*, PLD 1970 Karachi 357.
920. *Abdul Razaq and another v. Sharif Khan and others*, 1986 CLC 281.

prior notice to the affected party is a clear violation of the principles of natural justice.[921]

Judgments given by Pakistani courts under the 1940 Act also reveal that the phenomenon of due process in terms of equal treatment of parties is not restricted to arbitral proceedings. The issue of due process may arise in court proceedings initiated for the enforcement of awards, at which time the party against whom the enforcement is sought must be given equal opportunity to present its case against such enforcement. In *Humayun Akhtar v. Pakistan Defence Officers Housing Authority*,[922] it was held that on the eve of filing of the award for making it a rule of court, the parties should have been given a notice of such filing so that the award debtor might file its objections against the award; otherwise, such award would not be made a rule of the court. However, where the filing of the award by the arbitrator was already in the knowledge of the defendant, such notice was not necessary.[923]

13.3.1.2. Arbitrator Bias as a Requirement of Due Process

Under the 1940 Act, Pakistani courts have pronounced that bias is a subcategory of arbitrator misconduct or, on the positive side, of due process. By looking at the illustrations counted as misconduct of arbitrators, it will also be clear that those instances are, in fact, a manifestation of arbitrator bias.

In *Muhammad Farooq Shah v. Shakirullah*,[924] the Supreme Court, while deliberating the phenomenon of arbitrator misconduct, stated that 'arbitrators after entering into arbitration must not be guilty of any act, which could possibly be construed as indicative of partiality or unfairness'. Similarly, in *Mian Corporation v. Lever Brothers of Pakistan Ltd*,[925] the Supreme Court held that to challenge an award on the basis of misconduct from arbitrators, such misconduct should be testified to the satisfaction of the court.[926] For example, if the arbitrator was presumptive, it would result in the annulment of the award.[927] In the same way, awards based on the personal knowledge of arbitrators would be bad in law.[928] The fact that the arbitrator was a creditor of one of the parties to the arbitration agreement and then proceedings thereunder due to business dealings between them were considered to be insufficient grounds to disqualify an arbitrator from performing his duties and resolving the inter-party disputes. The non-disclosure by an arbitrator of the indebtedness of a party to the arbitrator would not amount to judicial misconduct to eventuate his disqualification unless there

921. *Memon Medical Society v. Bantva Housing Enterprises*, 1992 CLC 1093. *See also Water and Power Development Authority (Power Wing) v. Combined Enterprises*, 1993 CLC 970.
922. *Maj. (Retd.) Humayun Akhtar v. Pakistan Defence Officers Housing Authority*, PLD 2002 Karachi 427.
923. Section 14 of the 1940 Act.
924. 2006 SCMR 1657.
925. *Mian Corporation v. Lever Brothers*, PLD 2006 SC 169.
926. Court approved the decision in *Pakistan Steel Mills Corporation v. Mustafa Sons (Pvt.) Ltd.*, PLD 2003 SC 301. *See also WAPDA v. Ghulam Rasul and Company (Pvt.) Ltd.*, PLD 2006 Lahore 314.
927. *National Fibers Ltd. v. Government of Pakistan*, PLD 2004 Lahore 722.
928. *Variety Traders, v. Government of Pakistan*, PLD 1980 Karachi 30.

was some evidence to demonstrate the predisposition of the arbitrator against the debtor party. In the absence of such evidence, the allegation of partiality or bias of the arbitrator must fail. But the situation would be different, in the words of the court, if the arbitrator was indebted to the party and such fact had not been divulged at the time of reference of the matter to the arbitrator. The court reasoned that since by lending money to a party, the arbitrator would not become interested in that party or his matter, no analogy could be made in these two cases.[929] Where an umpire participates in arbitration proceedings,[930] or where during the arbitration proceeding in respect of a property, the arbitrator gets personally involved and makes an offer to purchase the property subject matter of arbitration,[931] that would be misconduct.

It is clear that these judgments are rendered to deal with the misconduct of arbitrators and subsume the examples, which are the specific instances of arbitrator impartiality or independence. It is now established that being a subcategory of misconduct and due process, arbitrator bias will be governed by the same principles applied to the misconduct and due process.

13.3.2. Due Process and Misconduct: Is Arbitrator Bias a Ground to Resist the Foreign Arbitral Award?

The judgment of the Sindh High Court in *Nan Fling Textiles Ltd. v. Shamasuddin*[932] may be termed as the onset of conflict on the point if arbitrator bias and may be contested as a valid ground to resist the enforcement of foreign arbitral awards. In this case, the award originated from foreign arbitration conducted under the Liverpool Cotton Association Rules in England and was tainted by allegations of arbitrator misconduct. But the court held that the grounds on which domestic awards might be set aside were different from those enshrined in section 7 of the 1937 Act[933] for the

929. *S. M. Fazail & Co. v. Overseas Cotton Co.*, PLD 1959 Karachi 320.
930. *Haji Abdul Rahim v. Muhammad Sharif (Deceased)*, 2012 CLD 935.
931. *Masood Ahmad Bhatti v. Raja Imran Yaqoob and others*, PLD 2019 Islamabad 577.
932. *Nan Fung Textiles Ltd. v. Pir Muhammad Shamsuddin*, PLD 1979 Karachi 762.
933. Section 7 of the 1937 Act – Conditions for enforcement of foreign awards:

> (1) In order that a foreign award may be enforceable under this Act it must have
> (a) been made in pursuance of an agreement for arbitration which was valid under the law by which it was governed,
> (b) been made by the tribunal provided for in the agreement or constituted in manner agreed upon by the parties,
> (c) been made in conformity with the law governing the arbitration procedure,
> (d) become final in the country in which it was made,
> (e) been in respect of a matter which may lawfully be referred to arbitration under the law of Pakistan, and the enforcement thereof must not be contrary to the public policy or the law, of Pakistan.
>
> (2) A foreign award shall not be enforceable under this Act if the Court dealing with the case is satisfied that-
> (a) the award has been annulled in the country in which it was made, or
> (b) the party against whom it is sought to enforce the award was not given notice of the arbitration proceedings in sufficient time to enable him to present his case, or was under some legal incapacity and was not properly represented, or
> (c) the award does not deal with all the questions referred or contains decisions on matter beyond the scope of the agreement for arbitration;

foreign award. For example, a domestic award could be annulled if the arbitrator or umpire had misconducted the proceedings,[934] but no such ground was articulated in section 7 of the 1937 Act. However, the subsequent judgments pronounced under the 1937 Act on this point are inconsistent. To explore the judgments under the 1937 Act is a momentous task because they reflect the disposition of Pakistani judges to the absence of an express inclusion of such ground (misconduct or, more specifically, arbitrator bias) in the 1937 Act, which disposition then may be applied to foresee the fate of the New York Convention which also does not include this ground explicitly.

In *Nan Fung Textiles Ltd. v. Nichimen & Co. Ltd*,[935] respecting an award emanating from arbitration with its seat in England conducted under the Liverpool Cotton Association Rules, the Sindh High Court held that as far as section 7(3) of the 1937 Act was concerned, it enabled the party to confront the arbitral award on:

> *Any ground other* than the non-existence of the conditions specified in clauses (a), (b) and (c) of sub-section (1), or the existence of the conditions specified in clauses (b) and (c) of sub-section (2). (emphasis added)

The Sindh High Court further stated that the 'any other ground' encompassed the misconduct of arbitrators and hence, under 7(3) of the 1937 Act, such misconduct might be contested as a valid ground to resist the arbitral award successfully.[936] To clarify the scope of misconduct, the Sindh High Court referred to *Brooke Bon Ltd. v. Conciliator*,[937] wherein the 'misconduct' was considered in relation to an arbitrator

---

> Provided that if the award does not deal with all questions referred the Court may, if it thinks fit, either postpone the enforcement of the award or order its enforcement subject to the giving of such security by the person seeking to enforce it as the Court may think fit.

(3) If a party seeking to resist the enforcement of a foreign award proves that there is any ground other than the non-existence of the conditions specified in clauses (a), (b) and (c) of sub-section (1), or the existence of the conditions specified in clauses (b) and (c) of sub-section (2), entitling him to contest the validity of the award, the Court may, if it thinks fit, either refuse to enforce the award or adjourn the hearing until after the expiration of such period as appears to the Court to be reasonably sufficient to enable that party to take the necessary steps to have the award annulled by the competent tribunal.

934. Section 30 of the 1940 Act – Grounds for setting aside award:

> An award shall not be set aside except on one or more of the following grounds, namely:
>
> (a) that an arbitrator or umpire has misconducted himself or the proceeding;
> (b) that an award has been made after the issue of an order by the Court superseding the arbitration or after arbitration proceedings had been invalid under section 35;
> (c) that an award has been improperly procured or is otherwise invalid.

935. *Nan Fung Textiles Ltd. v. Nichimen & Co. Ltd.*, 1999 YLR 2226.
936. The court did follow in its entirety the case of *European Grain & Shipping Ltd. v. Polychem Company Ltd.*, PLD 1990 Karachi 254 where the Sindh High Court held that the grounds given under section 7 should be interpreted narrowly. *See also Ghulam Ali and others v. Ghulam Sarwar Naqvi*, PLD 1990 SC 1.
937. PLD 1977 SC 237.

who was appointed under the Industrial Relations Ordinance, 1969. In that case, the Supreme Court had said that:

> The term 'misconduct' used in connection with arbitration does not necessarily imply anything in the nature of the fraud or moral turpitude. In the judicial sense, the misconduct of the arbitrator means his failure to perform his essential duty, resulting in substantial miscarriage of justice between the parties.

In this regard, it is noteworthy that some cases[938] adjudged under the 1940 Act were referred by the respondents in furtherance of their contention to get two witnesses residing abroad examined, but these cases were discarded by the Sindh High Court, which held that they pertained to the interpretation of sections 16, 30 and 33 of the 1940 Act and hence were inapplicable to a case involving the misconduct of arbitrator in foreign arbitration. However, it is important to observe that while the Sindh High Court cast aside judgments rendered under the 1940 Act, in order to define the expression and scope of misconduct, it relied on a judgment pronounced in respect of domestic arbitration conducted under the Industrial Relations Ordinance, 1969 which is domestic law.

Hence, it may be safely inferred that jurisprudence in respect of arbitrators appointed domestically would also be apposite to determine and apply to the scope of misconduct in international arbitration to decide the enforcement of arbitral awards.[939] However, it is also noteworthy that in the beginning, courts attempted to cede two sets of rules – one under the 1937 Act for international arbitrations and the other under the 1940 Act for domestic arbitrations – in order to govern the phenomenon of arbitrator misconduct to decide the enforcement or annulment of the arbitral award. Later, however, this bifurcation either could not be established or could not be followed by the courts. Nevertheless, a glimpse of the approach or desire developed by judges in cases concerning the 1937 Act can be stumbled upon from the statement that the grounds for refusal against enforcement of foreign awards, including misconduct, should be interpreted strictly and only in the four corners of the 1937 Act.[940] This statement signals that the principles governing arbitrator misconduct or bias as evolved under the 1940 Act should have no application to a case coming under the 1937 Act. This attitude, which could not continue, seems to be very arbitration-friendly and should be employed in cases under the 2011 Act.

However, the case of *Pacific Lloyds Ltd. v. Blessed Enterprises*[941] took a turn opposite to *Nan Fung Textiles Ltd. v. Nichimen & Co. Ltd.*[942] In the former case, the

938. *Muhammad Keramat Ali & Co. Ltd. v. Amin Jute Mills Ltd.*, PLD 1961 Dacca 452; *Haji Tayab v. Eastern Textile Mills Ltd.*, PLD 1970 Karachi 357; *Leiserach v. Schalit*, (1934) 2 KB 353; *S. M. Fazail & Co.v. Overseas Cotton Co.*, PLD 1959 Karachi 320.
939. The jurisprudence developed under the 1940 Act (domestic arbitration) to international arbitration is not specific to the topic of due process or arbitrator bias. Rather, Pakistani courts have been applying the same principle to review domestic as well as foreign awards. Similarly, the same concept of public policy is applied to both domestic and foreign awards.
940. *Nan Fung Textiles Ltd. v. Nichimen & Co. Ltd.*, 1999 YLR 2226.
941. *Pacific Lloyds Ltd. v. Blessed Enterprises*, 2007 CLD 661. *See also Nan Fung Textiles Ltd. v. Pir Muhammad Shamsuddin*, PLD 1979 Karachi 762 wherein the court held that foreign awards cannot be resisted on the basis of arbitrator misconduct.
942. *Nan Fung Textiles Ltd. v. Nichimen & Co. Ltd.*, 1999 YLR 2226.

enforcement of the award originated from a London-seated arbitration, which was resisted by the defendant on the grounds, *inter alia*, that the umpire was biased. The Sindh High Court noticed that the argument of arbitrator bias had arisen because the arbitrator appointed by the claimant stated in one of his letters the word 'leeway'. The court first held that the 1937 Act did not furnish arbitrator bias as a ground for the refusal to enforce an award. Furthermore, if the arbitrator had employed the word 'leeway' to lend some time to the claimant, it was not proven by the respondent what prejudice had been inflicted on him by this. Hence, the award was made a rule of the court.

To analyse this judgment, it may be submitted that it manifests that arbitrator bias is not *actionable per se*, which is questionable. Similarly, the statement that the 1937 Act did not include bias as a ground to dispute the award might also raise the eyebrows of many. Although *Nan Fung Textiles Ltd v. Nichimen & Co. Ltd*[943] was not binding on the court, the principles laid down in that judgment were discarded without even mentioning them. It may be noticed that the court in *Pacific Lloyds*, although expressly rejected bias as a valid ground to resist the enforcement of the award, implicitly conceded the misconduct ground to resist the award, which was obvious from its discussion on the word 'leeway' and then its impact on the award, because the employment of such words was a clear case of his misconduct (if any). After the acceptance, although implied, of the misconduct ground to avoid the enforcement of the award, the declination to give recognition to arbitrator bias is not understandable despite the fact, as is discussed *supra*, that bias is a subcategory of misconduct. If the ground of misconduct and then arbitrator bias does not accede as a defence against enforcement, it may trigger the abuse of the court's process by enforcing unjust awards.

This disposition of the court is very important after the incorporation of the New York Convention into Pakistani domestic law, which also does not contain any specific ground of arbitrator bias or misconduct. Section 7 of the 2011 Act[944] incorporates Article V of the New York Convention by alluding to it, which suggests that the relevant provision for arbitrator bias is Article V(1)(b), providing that the party was 'unable to present his case'.

13.3.3. Principles Governing Arbitrator Bias

Since the Pakistani regime seems to have taken these principles from English law, the evolution of principles governing bias in the English regime on this subject is very briefly discussed to appreciate Pakistani interpretations.

943. 1999 YLR 2226.
944. Section 7 says that 'the recognition and enforcement of a foreign award shall not be refused except in accordance with Article V of the Convention'.

13.3.3.1. English Perspective

In England, in order to arrive at a decision, the first 'reasonable suspicion test' was formulated in *The King v. Sussex Justices.*[945] This test was then replaced by the 'real danger test' in *Regina v. Gough,*[946] which mandated that the existence of 'real danger' of judicial bias was to be decided from the vantage of judges and hence the court was personified as a reasonable man and hence its knowledge was extended to the evidence employed in the case, the access to which was never available to the person sitting in the courtroom (a reasonable man). The House of Lords then extended the application of this test to all adjudicators, including arbitrators.

The 'real danger test' was later modified by a 'reasonable likelihood test' in *Porter v. Magil,l*[947] and the standpoint of a judge to decide the existence of a danger of arbitrator bias was also adjusted to the vantage of a third fair-minded person. This adjustment was made on the basis that the former test gave excessive primacy to the court's view by giving inadequate regard to the public perception of the irregular incident. According to this test, 'the question is whether the fair-minded and informed observer, having considered the facts, would conclude that there was a real possibility that the tribunal was biased'.[948]

Like English courts, Pakistani courts in non-arbitration cases also expressly mentioned that the premise on which the edifice of Pakistani jurisprudence as to the adjudicator's bias is erected is that justice should not only be done but also seen to be done.[949] It is, however, noteworthy that there may be instances where the courts may be compelled to choose between 'justice should not only be done' and 'but also seen to be done'. This is so where the material before the court instructs it that there was no bias on the part of the adjudicator, in which justice dictates a declaration that the judge was unbiased and upholds his decision if any. This falls into the category of 'justice should not only be done'. However, if the judge follows 'it should also be seen to be done' and discards his own objective opinion by looking at the matter from the perspective of a third person, who in the words of Lord Goff in *Gough*, can never have access to the material before the court, this third person's view may dictate that the adjudicator should be declared biased (where opinion is subjective and based on partial and incomplete facts). If the judge also follows the opinion of third persons, it would amount to giving up the substantial justice in favour of cosmetic justice or reality in favour of appearance, which seems to be a miscarriage of justice. In this regard, the preferable approach seems to be the judge's vantage.

945. [1924] 1 K.B. 256.
946. [1993] A.C. 646.
947. [2001] UKHL 67.
948. For the characteristics of fair-minded observer, *see A and others v. B, X* [2011] EWHC 2345 (Comm).
949. *Asif Ali Zardari and another v. The State*, PLD 2001 SC 568.

13.3.3.2. Pakistani Perspective

In *Ali Mohammad v. Bashir Ahmad,*[950] the Punjab High Court said that 'the main attributes of arbitrator are his disinterestedness, his complete independence and his impartiality. If the arbitrator in the proceedings is influenced from extraneous pressures or seeks dictation from extraneous sources, he cannot be termed as impartial'. These abstract principles could not be effectively brought into operation. In *Pakistan Associates Construction Ltd. v. WAPDA and another*, an Engineer, being an employee of WAPDA, signed a contract with the Contractor on behalf of WAPDA and this contract designated the Engineer as an arbitrator in case of a dispute between the parties. A dispute arose, and the Contractor filed suit to the civil court, which was resisted by WAPDA on the basis of such arbitration clause. The contractor contended that the Engineer being a signatory and employee of WAPDA, is a party to the matter and hence cannot be appointed as arbitrator. The court declined to accept this and held that WAPDA was a party to the contract and not the Engineer who was only an employee of WAPDA.[951] But a party to an arbitration agreement cannot become an arbitrator even if the parties have agreed to that effect because such a person would be the judge of his own cause.[952]

In *Director Housing, A.G'S Branch, Rawalpindi v. Makhdum Consultants Engineers and Architects,*[953] the Supreme Court reiterated the significance of arbitrator impartiality by maintaining that he must act honestly and fairly while adjudging the controversy between the parties. However, the Supreme Court did not prescribe any test or standard to be applied in the subsequent cases in order to ascertain if the arbitrator was biased or not. Rather it said that:

> However, the question, whether the named or selected arbitrator is likely to act in a biased or unfair manner is always a question of fact which must be answered with reference to the facts and circumstances of each case. It is neither possible nor desirable to state with precision the circumstances from which it may be inferred that the arbitrator is not likely to act fairly and honestly. Therefore, reliance on the observations made in one case, on the basis of its peculiar facts, is not always safe and correct for the purposes of recording a finding in another case that the arbitrator is not likely to act fairly and honestly. The observations made in each case of this nature are to be seen in the context of the facts of that case. Despite similarities between the facts of a decided case and the case under consideration, the finding regarding bias or otherwise of the arbitrator must be stemmed from the facts of the case under consideration.

It is submitted that while the matter of arbitrator bias may be dealt with in a case-by-case manner, it does not prevent a court from drawing some general standards

---

950. 1989 CLC 2194.
951. *Pakistan Associates Construction Ltd. v. WAPDA and another,* 1989 MLD 203. Arriving at this conclusion, the court referred to *Province of the Punjab v. Messrs Irfan & Company,* PLD 1956 Lahore 442, in which, in a similar contract, the Secretary of Punjab was designated as arbitrator and an objection against such a nomination was overruled and the court did not consider him as a party to the contract.
952. *News Publication (Pvt.) Ltd. and others v. National News Agency and another,* 1999 CLC 1613.
953. 1997 SCMR 988.

regarding the arbitrator's bias to be utilized by courts by taking into consideration the peculiar facts of each case. Nevertheless, the Supreme Court clarified that the bias that might become the basis for the disqualification of an arbitrator must be a personal bias in its nature to cripple the arbitrator from acting impartially and justly. After having narrated this, the facts involved in this case may be outlined briefly. In this case, the disputes under three contracts for the construction of three Army houses were agreed to be submitted to Adjutant Generals (AG) of the General Headquarters (GHQ) of the Pakistan Army. The district court, although granting the stay of its proceedings in favour of arbitration, directed the parties to approach the Pakistan Engineering Council (PEC) instead of the nominated arbitrator for the resolution of their disputes. The direction of the court to knock on the doors of PEC was challenged by the appellants, which was allowed and the order of the civil court that removed the name of the nominated arbitrator was set aside.

When the case reached the Supreme Court, it noticed that the arbitration agreement concurred with the parties' mutual consent, which stipulated plainly that the disputes would be resolved by AG, GHQ Pakistan Army, or his nominee and held that such arbitration agreement could not be avoided lightly by the respondent. The Supreme Court also took up the argument of the respondent on which it relied before the lower courts that the AG could not be expected to act impartially on the matter because he was the part of the organization that awarded the agreement for construction. Hence, to allow him to be a judge in his cause would be against the principles of justice, equity and good conscience. The Supreme Court highlighted the fact that AG was the President of the Housing Directorate – the controlling authority – which accorded the contract and that the contract could never be awarded without his approval. However, the Supreme Court rejected the apprehensions about the impartiality and honesty of the arbitrator. Rather, it held that it was an acknowledged fact that in the majority of agreements concluded between the government and private parties, the nominated arbitrators in the arbitration agreement lying in those contracts were officers serving either in the same or some other department of the Government. If the above reasoning from the respondent as to the partiality of the arbitrator was approbated, in the words of the Supreme Court, that would result in the disqualification of arbitrators in all the cases where there existed a mere inference of arbitrator partiality.

The Supreme Court further elaborated that the AG was having the office of presidentship of Housing Directorate in his official capacity and nothing on the record signified that he was personally interested in the subject matter of the contract. On the contrary, the admitted position was that the AG under whose presidentship the contracts forming the subject matter of dispute were awarded had retired long ago, and after his retirement, two more AGs had served in the same office in the same official capacity. On these grounds, the Supreme Court maintained that the respondent's plea of bias against the AG with whose concurrence the construction contracts were awarded was not valid. As a result, the Supreme Court held that there could not be any likelihood of bias on the part of the arbitrator. It is submitted that although the arbitrator might not have a personal interest in the matter, nonetheless, the interest of the party whom he was serving and from where he was drawing his salary could never be downplayed. This situation could have been cured by not confining the interest to a personal one in order to qualify a successful challenge against the award.[954]

It was not until *Saleem Ali v. Akhtar Ali*[955] when the standards to check the bias of the arbitrator were discoursed. In this case, one party contended that the arbitrator purchased a property from the other party to the dispute, and such a transaction did not uphold the impartiality of arbitrators. The Punjab High Court observed that such a transaction occurred one year after the pronouncement of the award and hence did not have any bearing thereon. Therefore, the arbitrator could not be termed biased or partial on the score of such a transaction. The award was upheld, and allegations were rejected.

In the same case, by laying down general principles, the Punjab High Court proscribed an arbitrator from behaving even after the edict of the award in a way that might create an apprehension in the mind of one of the parties to arbitration that the arbitrator colluded with his adversary. The court mandated that there must 'be purity in the administration of justice, as well as in the administration of quasi-justice as were involved in the adjudicatory process before the arbitrators'. In this regard, the courts were strict enough to lay down a criterion for the arbitrator who, in the words of the Punjab High Court, must not be found 'guilty of any act which can be construed as indicative of partiality, unfairness or bias'. After saying this, the court went on to lay down the criterion to determine bias and stated that 'bias, signifies a real likelihood of an operative prejudice, whether conscious or unconscious'. The Punjab High Court held that the award would be set aside once the bias of the arbitrator was established. After elucidating the test for arbitrator bias and its repercussions, the court gave instances of bias. It said that:

> The fact that the arbitrator has any dealing with one of the parties does afford a real likelihood of an operative prejudice on his part, and the existence of such relationship with one of the parties, unknown to the other, may induce the court to set aside the award ... Doubtless, a party may not be required to prove a cast-iron case in order to bring home the charge of misconduct, but the facts and circumstances should be such as to *convince the conscience of a reasonable person* that the fountain of justice has not remained unsullied and unpolluted ... *The apprehension must be judged from a healthy, reasonable and average point of view, and only the apprehension of an average honest man can be taken note of.* Vague suspicions of whimsical, capricious and unreasonable people cannot be made the standard to regulate the Court's vision.

Despite their clarity, these principles of 'real likelihood' and a third, honest reasonable observer were not brought into use by the courts in subsequent cases. For example, in *Surriya Rehman v. Siemens Pakistan Engineering Company Ltd.*,[956] the plaintiff was involved in the business of rendering services of medical care on an

954. The condition of presence of personal bias for a successful challenge to an award was then followed subsequently. *See Saleem Ali v. Akhtar Ali and others*, PLD 2004 Lahore 404; *Ibrahim Fibres Limited through Managing Director v. Hameed Masood (Pvt.) Limited through Director and others*, 2006 YLR 1523.
955. *Saleem Ali v. Akhtar Ali and others*, PLD 2004 Lahore 404.
956. PLD 2011 Karachi 571.

agreement basis to the employees of various companies. The plaintiff concluded two contracts with Siemens Pakistan Engineering Company Limited (defendant) that was the subsidiary of a well-known international engineering company. These agreements obliged the plaintiff to make a supply of medicines daily to the defendant's employees along with the provision of comprehensive medical consultation and other related paramedical staff services. Both the contracts included an arbitration clause as follows:

> 5.1. In case of dispute or difference between the parties arising during the period of the job contract in connection with any of the terms and conditions of this job contract, the same shall be referred to the MD of Siemens Pakistan whose decision shall be final and binding on both the parties.

Later, disputes arose from the termination of the contracts on which the plaintiff filed suits to the court. The defendant sought the stay of the suits, which was resisted by the plaintiff on the ground, *inter alia*, that the arbitration agreement spoke to refer the dispute to the Managing Director (MD) of the defendant and hence 'the result of any arbitration proceedings was a foregone conclusion'. The Sindh High Court was not satisfied with this objection from the plaintiff. It reiterated the stance of the plaintiff, who was asserting that the arbitrator being an MD of the defendant would be biased against the plaintiff or, at best, would be prejudiced in favour of the defendant. Even so, the court declared that it was well established that the mere fact of an officer or director of a company having been selected to function as arbitrator was 'no ground in and of itself not to refer the parties to arbitration'. Moreover, the Sindh High Court also noted that in the instant case, the arbitrator had been chosen by his office and not by his name, i.e., the holder of the office of MD for the time being would act as an arbitrator to resolve the dispute. Then the court concluded that 'the question of bias, if any, would arise in respect of the acts or omission of an individual and allegations of bias cannot be made against an office as such'. After this, the court granted the stay of its proceedings by finding that nothing on the record transpired to prove the bias of MD against the plaintiff.

In *Pak. U.K. Association (Pvt.) Ltd. v. The Hashemite Kingdom of Jordan*,[957] the court, however, decided the case of arbitrator bias by saying that this is not the apprehension felt by the party justifying to attribute bias to the adjudicator, but rather 'apprehension must be judged from a healthy, reasonable and average point of view and not on mere apprehension of any whimsical person'.[958]

13.3.4. Disclosure of Conflict of Interest

The known interest of arbitrators does not invalidate their appointment as such. If the interest of an arbitrator is concealed or the interest emerges after his appointment, such appointment will be invalidated. Applying these principles, the Sindh High Court held

957. *Pak. U.K. Association (Pvt.) Ltd. v. The Hashemite Kingdom of Jordan*, 2017 CLC 599.
958. *See also The President v. Mr. Justice Shaukat Ali*, PLD 1971 SC 585; *Azhar Ali v. Punjab Public Service Commission*, PLD 2004 SC 4; *Sain Rakhio v. Abdul Ghaffar*, 2011 CLC 1160; *Syed Tahir Hussain Mahmoodi and others v. Tayyab and others*, PLD 2009 Karachi 176.

that in an arbitration agreement with the government empowering the government to appoint an arbitrator will not make the government the judge of his cause because the parties have agreed to that effect with the knowledge that in case of dispute the government will exercise that authority.[959]

Before accepting the mandate of arbitration, if an arbitrator made a disclosure of all the facts, or the parties by themselves knew those facts which might put a question mark on his impartiality, this would not subsequently afford any party a ground to raise objections against an arbitrator's impartiality. This is because the court would not release a party from a bargain he concurred to, however 'improvident it may consider it' so long as the court was persuaded that the party complaining of arbitrator bias knew or with due diligence could have known the fact of his impartiality at the time of his appointment.[960] For instance, when a party appointed his permanent auditor as an arbitrator without making the disclosure of this fact to the other party, such appointment was declared improper.[961]

Similarly, in *Dar Okaz Printing and Publishing Limited v. Printing Corporation of Pakistan Private Limited*,[962] the appointment of an MD of the respondent company as sole arbitrator was found by the Supreme Court to have been consented to by the appellant by its free will. So, the decision of such an arbitrator would be binding on the appellant. The other fact which the Supreme Court highlighted was that the respondent company was controlled by the government. In such a company, the MD was appointed by the Cabinet Division of the Government of Pakistan. Therefore, the MD was expected to be a brilliantly qualified person in both corporate as well as legal affairs, including 'contractual liabilities of the parties, fiscal aspects, administrative and management skills as well as a sense of propriety, equity and justice'. The Supreme Court stated that with these qualifications and skills, the MD could not be conjectured to arbitrate a dispute between the parties with favour or fear. Hence, on the basis of the foregoing, the appointment of the MD as a sole arbitrator was not denominated as against the principles of natural justice.[963] It is submitted that this interpretation might not be warranted due to the reason that the MD was dependent on the company for his salary and job, which also makes it a case of unequal treatment of parties along with that of disclosure. The important thing to note is that in so many cases, due to the frail bargaining power, the party contracting with such company is weaker and has no choice other than to agree on the appointment that the CEO, MD, etc., of such a company, will serve as an arbitrator in future disputes.

959. *Haji Naimatullah v. Federation of Pakistan*, PLD 2013 Sindh 406.
960. *Saleem Ali v. Akhtar Ali and others*, PLD 2004 Lahore 404. *See also Director Housing, A.G'S Branch, Rawalpindi v. Makhdum Consultants Engineers and Architects* 1997 SCMR 988.
961. *Bata Shoe Co. Ltd. v. Government of Pakistan*, PLD 1970 Karachi 784.
962. PLD 2003 SC 808.
963. *See also Lahore Stock Exchange Limited v. Fredrick J. Whyte Group*, PLD 1990 SC 48 and *Director Housing, A.G'S Branch, Rawalpindi v. Makhdum Consultants Engineers and Architects*, 1997 SCMR 988.

The requirement of prior disclosure and its importance were also elaborated by the Punjab High Court in *Saleem Ali v. Akhtar Ali,*[964] wherein it declared that the arbitrator appointed by the parties must unveil every fact:

> Which might in the least affect the minds of those who are proposing to submit their disputes to the arbitration of any particular individual ought to be made, so that each party may have every opportunity of considering whether or not to make a reference to him.

For instance, the court stated that if the arbitrator was under an obligation to repay some amount of money to one of the parties at the time of reference or became indebted to any of them thereafter and did not get that fact across to the other party in either case, such party, upon discovery of this fact might revoke the reference. Similarly, an award rendered by an arbitrator without disclosing such facts would be declared invalid on the basis of judicial misconduct.[965]

13.4. BIAS FROM NON-ARBITRATION JUDGMENTS

In Pakistan, the judgments decreed with regard to judicial bias in civil litigation have been very frequently alluded to and relied on by the courts in arbitration matters, although there are some judgments wherein judge-centric principles were applied by courts in arbitration matters without referring expressly to these parent judgments. So, the relevance and impact of litigation judgments on the evolution of arbitration jurisprudence on the point of arbitrator bias cannot be overlooked. For instance, in *Director Housing, A.G's Branch, Rawalpindi v. Makhdum Consultants Engineers and Architects,*[966] in order to adjudicate the matter of arbitrator bias, the Supreme Court referred to two judgments[967] that were exclusively pronounced in non-arbitration matters. From these two judgments, the Supreme Court derived and applied the principles that the bias should be of personal nature in order to disqualify an arbitrator from his office and; that such bias should be demonstrated as a matter of fact and not merely as an opinion; and, lastly, the mere apprehension in the mind of litigants did not suffice to prove the arbitrator's bias. Hence, all this elucidates that the jurisprudence developed with specific regard to the bias of judges should also be explored and organized to decide the viability, relevance and applicability of these principles to arbitration matters.

In litigation judgments, bias and partiality are synonyms and have been delineated as a condition of mind. Bias has been held 'to refer, not to views entertained regarding a particular subject-matter, but to the mental attitude or disposition toward

964. PLD 2004 Lahore 404.
965. Pakistani court may take into consideration the acceptability of International Bar Association Guidelines on Conflicts of Interest in International Arbitration while deciding cases of bias.
966. 1997 SCMR 988.
967. *Islamic Republic of Pakistan v. Abdul Wali Khan,* PLD 1976 SC 57; *M.H. Khondkar v. The State,* PLD 1966 SC 40.

a particular person and to cover all varieties of, personal hostility or prejudice against him'.[968]

In *Asif Ali Zardari v. The State,*[969] the Supreme Court enumerated how bias might arise. First, if a judge has some kind of pecuniary interest in the matter, however trivial, he will be disqualified from functioning as a judge, even if the likelihood that the decision will be influenced by such pecuniary interest is not proved. Second, when a judge has an interest in the subject matter or has a direct connection with proceedings continuing before him, both of them will result in a legal interest, and he will be considered to be a direct party to the case. Such a kind of bias is named as bias in the subject matter. Third, a judge may have some good relations with one of the parties or, conversely, some hostility towards the other party from some bitter happening before or during the court proceedings. Such disposition will also be tantamount to bias in that judge.[970]

The approach on the test to ascertain the judge's bias is not consistent in Pakistani judgments. Pakistani jurisprudence does not see the presence of bias from the perspective of a judge. Some judgments hold that a reasonable third party should conclude about the subsistence of bias, whereas others postulate that a litigant should have apprehension about the bias. Similarly, some judgments speak about the presence of 'apprehension' while others speak about the 'real possibility' of bias. What proceeds has been organized in this way. There are some judgments where it is not possible to define if the court has prescribed the test of 'real apprehension', 'real likelihood' or 'real danger' and also if such possibility has to be observed from the standpoint of the litigant himself or from the perspective of a third reasonable person. To testify these observations, Pakistani judgments are marshalled below in chronological order by indicating the principles applied in them. The divergence in approach as to the establishment of principles governing the bias sets forth unambiguously that it is difficult to conclude if such judgments may be used for arbitrator bias, as has been done in other jurisdictions, including France and England.

In *Mahbubul Huq v. The Chief Election Commissioner of Pakistan,*[971] the Decca High Court held that where a pecuniary interest of a judge was involved in the matter before him, there would be no need for any kind of evidence to establish the bias. But where the allegations of bias were based on the kinship or relationship between the judge and the party, then the party alleging bias would have to provide evidence that the nature of the relationship in question was such that afforded a reasonable basis for the existence of a real likelihood of bias.

968. *Asif Ali Zardari and another v. The State*, PLD 2001 SC 568.
969. *Ibid.* On this three kinds of categorization, *see also All Pakistan Newspapers Society and others v. Federation of Pakistan and others*, PLD 2012 SC 1; *Federation of Pakistan v. Muhammad Akram Shaikh and Civil Review Petition No. 30-R of 1989 Haji Muhammad Saifullah v. Federation of Pakistan,* PLD 1989 SC 689; Civil Review Petition No. 33-R of 1989.
970. *See also* to *Government of NWFP v. Dr. Hussain Ahmad Haroon and others*, 2003 SCMR 104.
971. PLD 1969 Dacca 741. *See also President-Referring Authority v. Mr. Justice Shaukat Ali*, PLD 1971 SC 585.

In *Chairman, Federal Land Commission v. Sardar Ashiq Muhammad Khan Mazari,*[972] the Supreme Court, while dictating the test, held that 'in such cases the test is not whether in fact a bias has affected the judgment; the test always is and must be whether a litigant could reasonably apprehend that a bias attributable to a member of the tribunal might have operated against him in the final decision of the tribunal'. The judge would be disqualified from acting as a judge if he had some pecuniary interest in the matter before him.

In *Benazir Bhutto v. The President of Pakistan,*[973] the Supreme Court stated in order to disqualify a judge from performing his functions as judge, 'a real likelihood of bias must be established. The court does not see if there was a real likelihood that he would or did, in fact favour one side at the expense of the other. The court looks at the impression which would be given to other people'. In this regard, mere suspicion of bias, even if very reasonable, is not sufficient unless it is established.

When faced with an allegation of personal bias, the Supreme Court held in *Asif Ali Zardari v. The State*[974] that the question to be quenched was whether 'there is in the mind of the litigant a reasonable apprehension that he would not get a fair trial'. To entertain such a question, the test used was 'whether there is a real likelihood of prejudice, but it does not require certainty'. The court approached the definition of 'real likelihood' by asserting that it meant the apprehension begot in the mind of a reasonable person who was fully apprised of the facts and not of the foolish or capricious man.

In another case, the court held that the test of bias was not as to whether there was some suspicion in the mind of the party, but rather the test was if a reasonable person abreast fully with the facts would come to a conclusion that there existed a likelihood of bias or suspicion of bias to a reasonable extent.[975]

In *Government of N. W.F.P v. Dr. Hussain Ahmad Haroon,*[976] the Supreme Court stated that 'the test always is and must be whether a litigant could reasonably apprehend that a bias attributable to a member of the Tribunal might have operated against him in the final decision of the Tribunal. It is in this sense that it is often said that justice must not only be done but must also appear to be done'. It further stated that the adjudicator should not have any kind of 'personal interest in the outcome of the matter under issue before him', nor should the litigant or the public at large feel any kind of apprehension from the conduct of proceedings that bias lies in the mind of the adjudicator against him.

In *Federation of Pakistan v. Mian Muhammad Nawaz Sharif,*[977] the Supreme Court said that 'if a prudent man considers the facts and circumstances of a case demonstrating and to be creative of bias in the mind of a Judge and the real danger of

972. 1985 SCMR 317.
973. 1992 SCMR 140.
974. PLD 2001 SC 568.
975. *Gharibwal Cement Ltd., v. Secretary, Revenue Division, Islamabad,* 2003 PTD 2872.
976. *Government of NWFP v. Dr. Hussain Ahmad Haroon and others,* 2003 SCMR 104.
977. PLD 2009 SC 284.

having no fair trial at the hands of the aforesaid Judge is apparent and existing, then the question would be relevant'.[978]

A person can neither be the judge of his own cause nor of the person related to him. The judge in such a case is not restricted to adjudicate the matter for the reason that the decision will come out in his favour; rather, justice should not only be done but also seen to be done. This object will not be achieved however impartial and honest the judge is because the public in general and the litigant, in particular, will not be satisfied with his finding, and resultantly, such verdict will be set aside on appeal.[979] If a litigant has an apprehension of bias from a judge, he has to level that allegation before the same judge at the earliest opportunity with a statement that he apprehends that he would not get the just and impartial trial of the case from that judge.[980]

13.4.1. Instances of Judicial Bias

The instances of bias extracted from Pakistani judgments on non-arbitration matters are enlisted below:

- In the course of his practising career, a lawyer contested a case against a party (a corporate entity) in court, and later, the same lawyer was elevated as a judge. If that party appears in the court of that judge and contests the partiality and bias of that judge against it on the basis of past appearance against it in court and does not provide anything further to substantiate his plea of personal bias against that party, such plea would not sustain, especially if such party is a corporate person.[981]
- In the course of proceedings before a judge, if the judge makes tentative observations with regard to the relevant questions of law, which cannot be counted as a final opinion of that judge, those observations will not furnish a valid ground for the bias of judge.[982]
- A judge may keep on hearing the case where any one of the parties was having recourse to contest the bias of the judge with an ulterior motive to stop that judge from hearing that case. This may be the case, for instance, when a party engages a counsel who was not allowed to appear before that judge for

978. *Federation of Pakistan and others v. Mian Muhammad Nawaz Sharif and others*, PLD 2009 SC 284.
979. *Asif Ali Zardari and another v. The State*, PLD 2001 SC 568. *See also Federation of Pakistan v. Muhammad Akram Shaikh and Civil Review Petition No. 30-R of 1989 Haji Muhammad Saifullah v. Federation of Pakistan*, PLD 1989 SC 689; Civil Review Petition No. 33-R of 1989.
980. *Al-Khair University and others v. Al-Khair Trust of Pakistan and others*, 2004 YLR 138. In *Chief Justice of Pakistan v. President of Pakistan*, PLD 2010 SC 61, Supreme Court held that 'judge of superior court is a Judge of conscience and he himself has to decide about his competency to hear a case'. Same principle was laid down in following judgment: *Zulfiqar Ali Bhutto v. The State and Another*, 1977 SCMR 514.
981. *State Life Insurance Corporation of Pakistan v. Mrs. Surraya Sajjad*, 2000 CLC 1813.
982. *Ardeshir Cowasjee and others v. K.B.C.A. and others*, 2000 CLC 606.

reasons, *inter alia*, that counsel was a junior associate for a long time with that judge when he was practising as a lawyer.[983]

- Similarly, if one of the parties appearing before the judge has been his client and had a relation of long association, he should not hear that case. But it does not mean that the judge should decline to sit in the bench in every case where one of the parties happened to be his client.[984]
- Opinion stated by a judge in a particular case does not amount to bias because every case has its own peculiar facts giving birth to opinions specific to that very case.[985] Similarly, the judge cannot be said to have a bias on the ground that he has expressed an adverse opinion in some case in the past carrying the facts similar to the instant case.[986]
- Bias will not be established by the fact that a specific judge, while dealing with another case, imparted his decision by way of interlocutory orders against a party now pleading before him.[987]
- If a judge, when he was practising as a lawyer, filed a suit on behalf of his client (a banking company) against a person (now borrower/defendant), the plea of bias from the borrower, now a litigant before that judge, cannot succeed merely on that incident unless such plea is substantiated with some eminent evidence.[988]

13.5. NEED TO PROVE THE ARBITRATOR'S BIAS

Addressing the standard of evidence to prove the arbitral bias, Lahore High Court stated that the party pleading the bias carried the burden to prove it, who had to cede

983. *Ibid.*
984. *Ibid.*
985. *Muzaffar Hussain v. The Superintendent of Police, District Sialkot,* 2002 PLC (C.S.) 442.
986. *Sain Rakhio v. Abdul Ghaffar and others,* 2011 CLC 1160. *See also, Azad Government and others v. Genuine Rights Commission and others,* 1999 MLD 160; *Syed Tahir Hussain Mahmoodi and others v. Tayyab and others,* PLD 2009 Karachi 176. In this judgment, by admitting that an open mind will not mean to be an empty mind for a person can never free himself from the social influences, court quoted the following paragraph from Jerome Frank of US Second Circuit Court of Appeals, in Rt. JP Linahan, Inc. (138 F.20.650), quoted by Sir Louis Blom-Cooper, in his comments on *Bias on Appeal,* published in Public Law (2005), p. 227 observed:

> The human mind, even at infancy, is no blank piece of paper. We are born with predispositions, and the process of education, formal or informal, creates attitudes which precede reasoning in particular instances and which, therefore, by definition, are prejudices. Without acquired slants and preconceptions, life could not go on. Every habit constitutes a prejudgment; were those prejudgments, which we call habits, absent in any person, were he obliged to treat every event as an unprecedented crisis presenting a wholly new problem, he would go mad. Interests, points of view, preferences, are the essence of living. Only death yields complete dispassionateness, for such dispassionateness signifies utter indifference. To live is to have a vocation, and to have a scheme of values is to have a point of view, and to have a point of view is to have a prejudice or bias.

987. *Benazir Bhutto v. The President of Pakistan and another,* 1992 SCMR 140.
988. *Mazhar Butt v. Jawaid Iqbal and another,* 2009 SCMR 1027.

the particulars of bias, and that vague and bald statements on bias could not be elevated to the status of evidence. The court reasoned that the allegations of bias of arbitrator had to be proved beyond doubt because judicial presumption inclined to the favour of upholding the award. It further held that the court would not indulge in the activities of investigating or sifting the record before the arbitrator or arbitration proceedings in order to know the faults in the award. In this regard, the fact which statedly amounted to misconduct or bias must be stated with specification and particularity.[989] In this regard, while challenging arbitrator on the ground of bias, the party must come with grounds stronger than those required to challenge a judge.[990] Although the ground that the award was procured by collusion with the arbitrator was a valid one to set aside the award, such allegation, in order to succeed, must be substantiated with substantial proof and be established with evidence.[991] For instance, the allegation that the applicant made gifts to get the award was not proved.[992] Similarly, the allegation of misconduct was rejected by the Supreme Court on the basis that the petitioner did not give any particulars and other important details regarding the misconduct of the arbitrator. Hence, it rejected such allegation by declaring them vague and nebulous[993] for the award could not be set aside on the basis of mere allegations of collusion without any substantial and compelling evidence.[994] In *Wilayat Bibi v. Hayat Bevi*,[995] an award was rendered in favour of the plaintiff on the day when the arbitration agreement was concluded. The Supreme Court noticed the fact that nothing existed on the record to explain how the notices were issued to the respondent on the day when the arbitration agreement and then award resulted and to clarify as to how the arbitration proceedings took place. From this Supreme Court concluded the fact that arbitration agreement was a tool to get the award in collusion with the arbitrator to grab the property of Mr X, who died without having any male issue. So the award was declared invalid.

13.6. CONCLUSION

As far as the Pakistani regime is concerned, it is not clear what vantage is used to decide the impartiality for the arbitrator. On the basis of the discussion above, it may be

989. *Saleem Ali v. Akhtar Ali and others*, PLD 2004 Lahore 404; *Pak. U.K. Association (Pvt.) Ltd. v. The Hashemite Kingdom of Jordan*, 2017 CLC 599; *The President v. Mr. Justice Shaukat Ali*, PLD 1971 SC 585; *Azhar Ali v. Punjab Public Service Commission*, PLD 2004 SC 4; *Sain Rakhio v. Abdul Ghaffar*, 2011 CLC 1160; *Syed Tahir Hussain Mahmoodi and others v. Tayyab and others*, PLD 2009 Karachi 176.
990. *Syed Munir Syed v. Sardar Muhammad Kamal Khan and others*, 2019 YLR 209.
991. *Al-Abdullah Constructors (Pvt.) Ltd. v. Pakistan Water and Power Development Authority through Chief Engineer*, 2008 CLC 798; *Badruddin H. Mavani v. Government of Pakistan, Ministry of Food and another*, 1981 CLC 339; *Jam's Construction Company (Pvt.) Limited through Managing Director v. Province of Punjab*, 2006 CLC 791. *Fateh Bevi and others v. Additional District Judge, Khushab and others*, 2008 SCMR 1262.
992. *Ibid.*
993. *Province of Punjab v. Sufi Construction Company*, 2005 SCMR 1724.
994. *Al-Abdullah Constructors (Pvt.) Ltd. v. Pakistan Water and Power Development Authority*, 2008 CLC 798.
995. *Wilayat Bibi and others v. Hayat Bevi and others*, 2005 SCMR 1697.

suggested that the standpoint of the judge is more secure than the third reasonable man perspective. Similarly, the arbitrator's bias should be *actionable per se*, i.e., when the bias is proved, then to set aside the award, the party should not be required to prove the miscarriage of justice inflicted upon him by such bias because no loss greater than the adjudication by a biased arbitrator can happen to the party. In that respect, the tradition to extract such standards from litigation judgments may be shunned. The significance of this suggestion is manifest when we see very inconsistent judgments on judge's bias from the Pakistani judiciary. The other reason is that the judgment and jurisprudence under the 1940 Act were evolved under the effect that courts of Pakistan have been utilizing their supervisory role for the arbitration conducted in Pakistan as per sections 14-17 and sections 30 and 33.[996] Jurisprudence compiled under such an effect and with such a purpose may not justifiably be extended to the arbitration proceedings or arbitral award resulted outside the domain of such supervisory jurisdiction of Pakistani courts.

996. *Zakaullah Khan v. Government of Pakistan*, PLD 1998 Lahore 132.

CHAPTER 14

Appealable Orders of Pakistani Court

The appeal is entering the superior court to get its aid and interpretation to remedy errors committed by the court below.[997] *Pakistani law does not give such a right of appeal against the orders of award of the arbitrator. Rather, the right of appeal on orders of the court, as enshrined in section 39, is available only against those emanating from the court. As to orders not appealable, revision is available. It is to note that the procedure followed by the arbitrator to issue an award and by the court, both trial and appellate, proceeding on the orders in their original or appellate jurisdiction is different. There are some restrictions attached to the right of appeal in the form of the limitation period, specification of appealable orders and unavailability of the second appeal on the decision of the first appellate court. Appealable orders are only those given in section 39 of the 1940 Act.*[998] *Right of appeal under section 39 is a complete right in itself and is not affected in any way by any provision of the CPC.*[999]

14.1. INTRODUCTION

Courts issue numerous orders about arbitration, and it is natural for a party to be dissatisfied with the order or judgment of the court. Pakistani courts have acknowledged that the courts of law are not infallible and can commit an error, and resultantly, in civilized systems of administration of justice, there is provision for at least one appeal to a superior court.[1000] This is important to identify those orders, the procedure

997. *Province of Baluchistan v. Sardar Muhammad Usman Khan*, PLD 1987 Quetta 33.
998. *Noble (Pvt.) Ltd., Karachi v. Federal Government Employees Housing Federation, Shaheed-e-Millate Secretariat, Islamabad*, 2002 CLC 1670.
999. *District Council Haripur v. Zaheer Ullah Khan*, PLD 1994 Peshawar 228. For CPC, *see* sections 2(2), 104 and 115 and Order XXXIX, Rules 1, 2, Order XLIII Rule 1.
1000. *Ch. Zahur Ilahi, M. N. A. v. The State*, PLD 1977 SC 273.

being followed by Pakistani courts while issuing those orders and the remedy available to a party feeling aggrieved from such order of the court.

Against the orders of the trial court, remedies of appeal and revision are available. This chapter scrutinizes the concept of appeal and revision and compares both. This chapter also elucidates the procedure followed by Pakistani courts, both trial and appellate, while dealing with the matters in relation to arbitration. In this connection, the procedural compulsions of the arbitrator are also dilated upon. Then right of parties to appeal and ancillary issues related thereto like limitation period, right of second appeal and non-appealable orders are also explicated in light of Pakistani judgments. In the final segment of this chapter, the appealable orders as listed in section 39 of the 1940 Act are discussed in detail with a specific note on the interplay between section 17 and section 39 of the 1940 Act.

14.2. REMEDIES AGAINST THE ORDERS OF TRIAL COURT: APPEAL AND REVISION

Section 39 of the 1940 Act enlists the orders which are appealable, and for orders not included in this list, the revision is available. This section explains the concept of appeal and revision.

14.2.1. Appeal

In an appeal, the superior court examines the soundness of the decision of the subordinate court[1001] by hearing the whole dispute.[1002] In this sense, the appeal is the continuation of the suit,[1003] and the appellate court has the power to issue all the orders

1001. *Juma Khan v. Mst. Gul Ferosha*, PLD 1972 Peshawar 1; *Din Muhammad v. Hidayat Hussain*, PLD 1968 Lahore 207.

1002. *F. A. Khan v. The Government of Pakistan*, PLD 1964 SC 520; *Muhammad Ayyub and another v. Muhammad Yaqoob and another*, PLD 1975 Lahore 445.

1003. *Wajid Ali v. Sajid Ali*, 1985 SCMR 401; *F. A. Khan v. The Government of Pakistan*, PLD 1964 SC 520; *Sherin and others v. Fazal Muhammad and others*, 1995 SCMR 584; *Muzaffar Ali v. Muhammad Shafi*, PLD 1981 SC 94; *Alaf Din v. Mst. Parveen Akhtar*, PLD 1970 SC 75; *The Province of East Pakistan v. Muhammad Hossain Mia*, PLD 1965 SC 1; *Khalid Saigol v. The State*, PLD 1962 SC 495; *Muhammad Salim and others v. Lahore Development Authority and others*, 1993 MLD 2312; *Mst. Anwar Mai v. Ghulam Qadir Shah and others*, 1986 CLC 1457; *Trading Corporation of Pakistan Ltd. v. General Industrial Machines, Handelsgesellschaft Mbh, Frankfurt*, 1986 CLC 1999; *Karachi Metropolitan Corporation v. Associated Constructors Ltd.*, 1984 CLC 1077; *Suleman Haji and another v. The State and others*, PLD 1983 Quetta 84; *Mst. Nazir Begum and other v. Mst. Qamarunnissa and others*, 1982 CLC 2271; *Standard Printing Press v. Sindh Employees' Social Security Institution*, PLD 1978 Karachi 945; *Juma Khan v. Mst. Gul Ferosha*, PLD 1972 Peshawar 1; *Roshan Din v. S. M. Badruddin*, PLD 1969 Karachi 546; *Flour Mills Employees' Union v. Karachi Steam Roller Flour Mills Co. Ltd.*, PLD 1964 Karachi 587; *Shahmir Transport Company Limited v. Member (Colonies and Transport) Board of Revenue, West Pakistan and others*, PLD 1964 Lahore 710.

that a trial court can issue.[1004] The appellate court can set aside or revise the decisions from the lower court.[1005]

The original decree from the lower court merges into the appellate decree on the disposal of the appeal[1006] and remains binding until the appellate court sets it aside;[1007] therefore, the decree of the appellate court holds the ground even if the appellate court merely affirms the decree of the lower court.[1008] However, the original decree will sustain where the appellate court has passed no decree[1009] or has dismissed the appeal in limine, or the appeal is withdrawn.[1010]

The whole of the decree of the lower court should be appealed.[1011] Where lower court gave one judgment in two consolidated suits, one appeal would suffice.[1012] However, the appellant cannot raise new issues or grounds in the appeal, which he has not taken before the lower court,[1013] nor can he depart from his case, which he has contested before the lower court.[1014]

1004. *Sherin and others v. Fazal Muhammad and others,* 1995 SCMR 584; *Mst. Anwar Mai v. Ghulam Qadir Shah and others,* 1986 CLC 1457.
1005. *Tahir Ali and others v. Chief Judge, Karachi Small Causes Court and another,* PLD 1963 SC 147; *Province of Baluchistan v. Sardar Muhammad Usman Khan,* PLD 1987 Quetta 33; *Haji Suleman v. Eastern Rice Syndicate Karachi and others,* PLD 1976 Karachi 263; *Din Muhammad v. Hidayat Hussain,* PLD 1968 Lahore 207.
1006. *Glaxo Laboratories Limited v. Inspecting Assistant Commissioner of Income Tax and others,* PLD 1992 SC 549; *Maulvi Abdul Qayyum v. Syed Ali Asghar Shah and others,* 1992 SCMR 241; *Abdul Ghafoor. v. Ahmad Kunhi,* PLD 1969 SC 424; *F. A. Khan v. The Government of Pakistan,* PLD 1964 SC 520; *Nabi Bux v. Land Acquisition Officer,* 2003 CLC 1914; *Saeed Ahmad v. Messrs. Indo Enamel Works Ltd., Lahore (In Lahore),* PLD 1954 Lahore 490; *Nizam-ud-Din and others v. Ch. Muhammad Saeed and another,* 1993 CLC 2130; *Zahoor Din v. Anjuman Himayat-i-Islam,* 1989 MLD 480; *Jhangimal v. Abdul Aziz Khan,* PLD 1971 Karachi 147; *Walayat Shah v. Ghafar Shah and others,* PLD 1952 Peshawar 6.
1007. *Wajid Ali v. Sajid Ali,* 1985 SCMR 401; *Province of East Pakistan v. Muhammad Hussain Mia,* PLD 1965 SC 1; *F. A. Khan v. The Government of Pakistan,* PLD 1964 SC 520; *Waris Mean v. The State and the State Bank of Pakistan,* PLD 1957 SC 157; *Zahoor Din v. Anjuman Himayat-i-Islam,* 1989 MLD 480; *Haji Ismail Dossa v. Monopoly Control Authority,* PLD 1984 Karachi 315; *Roshan Din v. S. M. Badruddin,* PLD 1969 Karachi 546; *Nawabshah Cooperative Housing Society v. Government Employees Cooperative Housing Society, Nawabshah, and Government of West Pakistan,* PLD 1969 Karachi 1.
1008. *Sherin and others v. Fazal Muhammad and others,* 1995 SCMR 584; *Maulvi Abdul Qayyum v. Syed Ali Asghar Shah and others,* 1992 SCMR 241; *Siddique Khan v. Abdul Shakoor Khan,* PLD 1984 SC 289; *F. A. Khan v. The Government of Pakistan,* PLD 1964 SC 520; *Nabi Bux v. Land Acquisition Officer,* 2003 CLC 1914; *Haji Ismail Dossa v. Monopoly Control Authority,* PLD 1984 Karachi 315; *Sri Lakshmi Narayan and others v. Sri Surath Lal Chakraborti and others,* PLD 1964 Dacca 177.
1009. *Toor v. Abdul Qadir,* 2001 CLC 108.
1010. *Haji Muhammad Boota and Others v. Member (Revenue), Board of Revenue, Punjab and others,* PLD 2003 SC 979.
1011. *Budho and others v. Ghulam Shah,* PLD 1962 Karachi 344.
1012. *Haji Syed Ainullah v. Abdul Rashid,* 1985 SCMR 1991; *Shukar Din and others v. Nazir Ahmed and others,* 1993 CLC 1367; *Sh. Muhammad Riaz Diwana through his legal heirs v. Sh. Muhammad Sharif and others,* 1989 MLD 3663.
1013. *Haji Abdullah Khan and others v. Nisar Muhammad Khan and others,* PLD 1965 SC 690.
1014. *Haji Abdullah Khan and others v. Nisar Muhammad Khan and others,* PLD 1965 SC 690; *Ismail v. Abdullah and another,* PLD 1963 Karachi 161; *Begun v. Mst. Kazbanoo and others,* PLD 1957 Karachi 884.

A statute creates appeal.[1015] Parties cannot create it through mutual consent nor snatch or defect the appellate jurisdiction of an appellate court.[1016] Therefore, appeal being a substantive right must be conferred by law[1017] and should be confined within the confines imposed by the relevant law.[1018]

14.2.2. Revision

Revisional jurisdiction is the creation of statute[1019] Section 115 of the CPC deals with the revisional jurisdiction of the court. The right to move in revision is not a substantive right but is merely a privilege granted to a party and ensuring proceedings before the revisional court is, in substance, proceedings between a higher court and lower court.[1020] Section 115 applies only to cases involving the illegal assumption, non-exercise, or the irregular exercise of jurisdiction.[1021] The higher court will not exercise this jurisdiction if the conclusion as to the fact or law does not in any way affect the jurisdiction of the court,[1022] even if such conclusion is erroneous, wrong or perverse

1015. *Muzaffar Ali v. Muhammad Shafi*, PLD 1981 SC 94; *Ibrahim v. Muhammad Hussain*, PLD 1975 SC 457; *Pir Muhammad Farid Jan v. Colonisation Officer, Sukkur Barrage, Hyderabad and others*, PLD 1965 SC 399; *Muhammad Aslam v. The State*, PLD 1959 SC 119; *Miss. Parveen v. Kh. Muhammad Ashar*, PLD 1975 Lahore 334.
1016. *Malik Ghulam Jilani v. Government of West Pakistan*, PLD 1967 SC 373.
1017. *Mst. Zahida Sattar and others v. Federation of Pakistan and others*, PLD 2002 SC 408; *Anjum Zafar v. Abbas Ali Shah*, 2000 SCMR 59; *Governor, NWFP and another v. Gul Naras Khan*, 1987 SCMR 1709; *S.A. Rizvi v. Pakistan Atomic Energy Commission and another*, 1986 SCMR 965; *Pakistan International Airlines Corporation v. Messrs Pak Saaf Dry Cleaners*, PLD 1981 SC 553; *Muzaffar Ali v. Muhammad Shafi*, PLD 1981 SC 94; *Mian Manzar Bashir and others v. M. A. Asghar & Co.*, PLD 1978 SC 185; *Ibrahim v. Muhammad Hussain*, PLD 1975 SC 457; *Hussain Bakhsh v. Settlement Commissioner, Rawalpindi and others*, PLD 1970 SC 1; *Saeedur Rehman v. Cklef Election Commissioner*, PLD 1965 SC 157; *Muhammad Aslam v. The State*, PLD 1959 SC 119; *Afsar Khan and others v. The State, Ghulam Qadar v. Ahmad Gul and others*, PLD 1964 Peshawar 205; *Ghazi and others v. The State and another*, PLD 1962 Lahore 662; *Ghulam Fatima v. Fazal*, 1986 CLC 2057; *Bahadur v. Muhammad Shoaib and others*, PLD 1981 Karachi 788; *Abdul Ghani v. Settlement Commissioner, Lahore Division, Lahore and others*, PLD 1971 Lahore 59; *Bahadur v. Mirza Abdul Qayyum and another*, PLD 1969 Lahore 636; *The Essential Industries v. Central Board of Revenue*, PLD 1969 Lahore 24; *Hart Mean v. The State*, PLD 1958 Dacca 333.
1018. *Muzaffar Ali v. Muhammad Shafi*, PLD 1981 SC 94; *Ibrahim v. Muhammad Hussain*, PLD 1975 SC 457; *Pir Muhammad Farid Jan v. Colonisation Officer, Sukkur Barrage, Hyderabad and others*, PLD 1965 SC 399; *Muhammad Aslam v. The State*, PLD 1959 SC 119; *Miss. Parveen v. Kh. Muhammad Ashar*, PLD 1975 Lahore 334.
1019. *Muhammad Khan v. Government of West Pakistan and others*, PLD 1971 BJ 53.
1020. *Maulvi Abdul Qayyum v. Syed Ali Asghar Shah and others*, 1992 SCMR 241; *Mst. Shamero v. Sardaraz Khan and others*, PLD 2001 Peshawar 54; *Miss. Parveen v. Kh. Muhammad Ashar*, PLD 1975 Lahore 334.
1021. *Muhammad Boota v. Allah Ditta*, 1998 SCMR 2764; *S. Zafar Ahmad v. Abdul Khaliq*, PLD 1964 Karachi 149; *Abdul Ghaffar v. Jamaluddin*, 1986 CLC 747; *Muhammad Ashfaq v. Sohail Hameed*, 1986 CLC 2218.
1022. *Anwar Zaman v. Bahadur Sher, Abdul Hakeem v. Habibullah*, 2000 SCMR 431; *Abdul Hakeem v. Habibullah*, 1997 SCMR 1139; *Muhammad Zaman v. Zafar Ali Khan*, PLD 1986 SC 88; *Abdul Rehman Wahla v. Sher Dil Batra*, PLD 1986 SC 234; *Muhammad Bux v. Muhammad Ali*, 1984 SCMR 504; *Gul Roz v. Sargand*, 2003 CLC 116; *Khan Akbar v. Mohib Gul*, 2001 CLC 1899; *Riaz v. Malik Dad*, 2001 CLC 1814; *Hussain Naqvi v. Begum Zakira Chattha*, 2000 CLC 1771; *Tabassam Bibi v. Abdur Rashid Khan*, 1999 CLC 1216; *Riasat Ali v. Muhammad Mushtaq*

unless such conclusion involves a matter of jurisdiction.[1023] If consequent to such erroneous conclusion on the fact or law, the court assumes or declines to assume jurisdiction, then such decision would be revisable.[1024] Revision is not a continuation of the suit,[1025] and the court neither investigates the facts nor bases its jurisdiction on the grounds which were never raised before the lower court.[1026]

The revisional jurisdiction is discretionary[1027] and must be exercised in accordance with the law.[1028] Therefore, the revisional court will not intervene to correct every irregularity under section 115[1029] but will intervene only where a miscarriage of injustice or hardship will result on account of the no interference.[1030] Accordingly, the

---

Ahmad Sindhu, 1999 CLC 1195; *Muhammad Bashir v. Jamal Rashid*, PLD 1995 Karachi 261; *Shahzada Muhammad Umar Beg v. Sultan Mahmood Khan*, PLD 1970 SC 139; *Sher Muhammad v. Ghulam Hussain*, 1992 CLC 204; *Ali Muhammad v. Zahida Parveen*, 1992 CLC 2328; *Abdul Ghaffar v. Jamaluddin*, 1986 CLC 747; *Muhammad Dawood Khan v. Muhammad Usman Ghani*, 1985 CLC 2309; *Rahim Bakhsh v. Civil Judge, Lodhran*, 1985 CLC 387; *Mst. Fazal Begum v. Bahadur Khan and another*, PLD 1983 Lahore 365; *Arshad Mahmoo v. Muhammad Rafique*, PLD 1982 Lahore 660; *Aif-ud-Din Malik v. The Government of West Pakistan through Irrigation and Power Department, Lahore*, PLD 1969 Lahore 506; *Khawaja Noor Muhammad v. Namdar*, PLD 1969 Lahore 105; *Maklemuddin v. Kasem Ali Howlader*, PLD 1960 Dacca 884; *Taj-ud-Din v. Nadar and others*, PLD 1959 Lahore 261; *Haji Abdul Ghafur Rishi v. Pakistan*, PLD 1959 Quetta 21; *Allah Bakhsh v. Syed Ghulam Rasool Shah*, PLD 1957 Lahore 968; *Pir Abdullah Shah v. Humayon*, PLD 1957 Lahore 1054.

1023. *Kanwal Nain v. Fateh Khan*, PLD 1983 SC 53; *Muhammad Hussain Munir v. Sikandar*, PLD 1974 SC 139; *S. Zafar Ahmad v. Abdul Khaliq*, PLD 1964 Karachi 149; *Karachi Building Control Authority v. Muhammad Ismail*, 1989 MLD 2987.

1024. *Utility Stores Corpn. of Pakistan Ltd. v. Punjab Labour Appellate Tribunar*, PLD 1987 SC 447; *Muhammad Hussain Munir v. Sikandar*, PLD 1974 SC 139; *Khizar Hayat Khan Tiwana v. Zainab Begum*, PLD 1967 SC 402; *Abdul Aziz Urfi v. S. G. Jeelani*, 1985 CLC 2415; *Khan Nasrullah Khan v. The Member, Election Commission, Government of Pakistan, Lahore*, PLD 1966 Lahore 850; *Ghulam Moin-ud-Din v. Razia Begum*, PLD 1974 Lahore 173; *Malik Fateh Muhammad v. Malkani Brag Bhari*, PLD 1950 Lahore 253.

1025. *Alaf Din v. Mst. Parveen Akhtar*, PLD 1970 SC 75; *Mst. Majidan Khanum v. District Judge, Vehari*, 1984 CLC 3270.

1026. *Noor Muhammad v. Sher Muhammad*, 1982 CLC 2397; *Karachi Development Authority v. Taj Muhammad*, PLD 1977 Karachi 101.

1027. *Muhammad Bashir v. Province of Punjab*, 2003 SCMR 83; *Abid Hussain v. Aziz Fatima*, PLD 1995 SC 399; *Karamat Hussain and others v. Muhammad Zaman and others*, PLD 1987 SC 139; *Razia Begum v. Hijrayat Ali*, PLD 1976 SC 44; *Manager, Jammu& Kashmir, State Property in Pakistan v. Khuda Yar and another*, PLD 1975 SC 678; *Muhammad Afzal v. Riaz Mahmood*, PLD 2004 Lahore 115; *Ch. Gulzar Khan v. Saghir Ahmed*, 2004 MLD 402; *M. Alam Khan v. Jewan Khan*, PLD 1995 Lahore 181; *Abdul Ghafoor Khan v. Tassawar Hussain Shah*, 1990 MLD 213; *Syed Arif Shah v. Abdul Hakim*, PLD 1986 Karachi 189; *Minochar N. Kharas represented by legal heirs v. Ali Hassan Manghi and others*, 1986 CLC 1378.

1028. *Syed Muhammad Khurshid Abbas Gardezi and others v. Province of Punjab and others*, 1988 CLC 362.

1029. *Qazi Shamsur Rehman v. Mst. Chaman Dasta*, 2004 SCMR 1798; *Abdul Ghani v. Manzoor Ahmad Butt*, 1990 SCMR 441; *Tariq Farooq v. Nasruddi*, PLD 1989 Quetta 1; *Abdul Ghafoor Khan v. Tassawar Hussain Shah*, 1990 MLD 213; *M. Alam Khan v. Jewan Khan*, PLD 1995 Lahore 181; *Nazeer Ahmad v. Additional District Judge, Muzaffargarh*, 1983 CLC 113; *Mst. Jahanara Begum v. Abdus Samad*, PLD 1969 Dacca 322.

1030. *Mst. Anwar Khatoon v. Umar Bakhsh*, PLD 1959 Dacca 143; *Muhammad Din v. Atta Muhammad*, PLD 1957 Lahore 971; *Ghulam Farid Muhammad Latif v. The Central Bank of India, Limited, Lahore*, PLD 1954 Lahore 575.

court will not interfere in revision if the order is just and proper[1031] or where the petitioner has not come with clean hands,[1032] or where the suit before the lower court was filed with ulterior motives[1033] or where the matter can be subsequently challenged in proceedings against the ultimate order.[1034]

Where a subordinate court has decided a case in which no appeal lies, revision will be available if the subordinate court:

- has exercised the jurisdiction not vested in it; or
- failed to exercise a jurisdiction vested in it; or
- acted in the exercise of its jurisdiction illegally or with material irregularity.[1035]

14.2.3. Comparison Between Appeal and Revision

An appeal is a matter *inter partes* on the matter on which parties differ, whereas a revision is an affair between a superior and a subordinate court as to the manner of exercising jurisdiction.[1036] Revision is discretionary and is a privilege granted to a party[1037], whereas an appeal is a substantive right. When the appeal is dismissed, the substantive decision is the one done by the appellate court, whereas, in case of

1031. *Muhammad Swaleh and another v. Messrs United Grain & Fodder Agencies*, PLD 1964 SC 97; *Haq Nawaz Chohan v. Tariq Azam*, 1994 CLC 1530; *Abdul Rahim v. Noor Muhammad*, 1993 CLC 1059; *Syed Tariq Farooq v. Nasruddin and another*, PLD 1989 Quetta 1; *Mst. Majidan v. Shabir Ahmed*, 1989 MLD 1959; *Mst. Fazal Begum v. Bahadur Khan and another*, PLD 1983 Lahore 365; *Nazeer Ahmad v. Additional District Judge, Muzaffargarh*, 1983 CLC 113; *Mst. Ghulam Sakina v. Karim Bakhsh*, PLD 1970 Lahore 412; *Bashir Ahmad v. Mst. Kaniz Begum*, PLD 1969 Lahore 560; *Syed Qasim Ahmad v. Manzoor Hussain Khan ad others*, PLD 1966 Peshawar 70.

1032. *Attaullah Alias Billa and others v. Muhammad Ilyas and others*, 2004 SCMR 830; *Abid Hussain and others v. Aziz Fatima and others*, PLD 1995 SC 399; *Syed Tariq Farooq v. Nasruddin and another*, PLD 1989 Quetta 1; *Abdul Wahid v. Ahmad Din*, 1986 SCMR 704; *Gul Baran and others v. Abdul Zahir and another*, 1988 CLC 65; *Mst. Jahanara Begum v. Abdus Samad and others*, PLD 1969 Dacca 322.

1033. 1989 MLD 213.

1034. *Jamat Ali v. Bahadur*, PLD 1993 Lahore 9.

1035. *Abdul Rahim and another v. Mrs. Jannatay Bibi and others*, 2000 SCMR 346; *Malik Hadayat Ullah and others v. Murad Ali Khan*, PLD 1972 SC 69; *Muhammad Swaleh and another v. United Grain & Fodder Agencies*, PLD 1964 SC 97; *Shau Ahmed v. Ashfaq Ahmed*, 1993 CLC 1669; *Karachi Development Authority v. Hadi Bux Memon*, 1992 CLC 1036; *Mst. Hassan Perveen and others v. Muhammad Zafarullah and others*, PLD 1986 Lahore 409; *Gulab and another v. Fazal Ilahi*, PLD 1955 Lahore 26.

1036. *Maulvi Abdul Qayyum v. Syed Ali Asghar Shah and others*, 1992 SCMR 241; *Karamat Hussain and others v. Muhammad Zaman and others*, PLD 1987 SC 139; *Tahir Ali and others v. Chief Judge, Karachi Small Causes Court and another*, PLD 1963 SC 147; *Muhammad Aslam Mirza v. Mst. Khurshid Begum*, PLD 1972 Lahore 603; *Muhammad Anwar v. Hoechst Pharmaceutical Pakistan (Pvt.) Ltd. and others*, 1989 MLD 171; *Mst. Majidan Khanum v. District Judge, Vehari*, 1984 CLC 3270; *Miss. Parveen v. Kh. Muhammad Ashar*, PLD 1975 Lahore 334; *Din Muhammad v. Hidayat Hussain*, PLD 1968 Lahore 207; *Syed Ali Abid Zaidi and others v. Deputy Settlement and Rehabilitation Commissioner, Gujranwala and others*, PLD 1967 Lahore 836; *Qazi Ghulam Ahmad v. J. F. Elahi, Election Tribunal, Chakwal, and others*, PLD 1962 Lahore 786; *Akhtar Aksi v. Aftab Ahmad Khan and another*, PLD 1960 Lahore 57.

1037. *Maulvi Abdul Qayyum v. Syed Ali Asghar Shah and others*, 1992 SCMR 241; *Miss. Parveen v. Kh. Muhammad Ashar*, PLD 1975 Lahore 334.

dismissal of revision, the substantive order is that of the lower court.[1038] Both jurisdictions – appellate and revisional – are the creation of the statute.[1039] While to avail the remedy of appeal, unrestricted grounds have been provided; a revision lies only on the ground enumerated above.[1040]

14.3. PROCEDURE IN ARBITRATION PROCEEDINGS

Different rules of procedure and evidence are applicable to arbitration proceedings before a court and arbitrator. This issue, in fact, primarily pertains to the discussion of the applicability of the CPC and Qanun-e-Shahadat Order 1984.

14.3.1. Procedure Before a Court

Section 23(2) says when the matter is referred to arbitration, the court will deal with such matters only in the manner provided by the 1940 Act. For instance, section 32 prohibits suit for challenging validity, existence or effect of an arbitration agreement or arbitral award. Similarly, sections 17 and 39 are pressed in service for filing appeal. But if some order is not covered by these two sections, then revision under section 115 of the CPC will be applied, and section 41 of the 1940 Act makes the provisions of CPC applicable to the proceedings of arbitration before the court unless the applicability of the provisions of CPC expressly is excluded by the Act or Rules made under section 44 of the 1940 Act or where the 1940 Act itself has been made applicable to any case or procedure.[1041]

Where no provision of the 1940 Act prohibits a court from applying the provisions of the CPC, the court resorts to the relevant provisions of the CPC. For instance, to entertain cases wherein the validity of an order, judgment or decree is challenged on the basis of fraud, misrepresentation or want of jurisdiction of issuing court, the issuing court itself is empowered to apply the provisions of section 12(2) of CPC in arbitration suits to invalidate its orders, judgments or decrees obtained in this way.[1042] Similarly, when the remedy of appeal is available within the framework of the 1940 Act, no revision is maintainable. When an appeal is not available in a certain case, the revision will lie on the ground enumerated in section 115 of the CPC.[1043] Similarly, interim orders issued under Order 39, Rules 1 & 2 of the CPC and the entertainment of application filed under Order 7, Rule 11 of the CPC for rejection of application filed under the provisions of the 1940 Act are the reliefs granted by courts under the

1038. *Mst. Majida Begum v. Sh. Zulfiqar Ali and another,* PLD 1987 Lahore 112; *Syed Ali Abid Zaidi and others v. Deputy Settlement and Rehabilitation Commissioner, Gujranwala and others,* PLD 1967 Lahore 836; *Akhtar Aksi v. Aftab Ahmad Khan and another,* PLD 1960 Lahore 57.
1039. PLD 1975 BJ 53.
1040. *Sardar Muhammad v. Mst. Shakuran Bibi,* 2002 CLC 760; *Qurban Ali v. Hoor Bux and others,* 1991 CLC 248.
1041. *Tribal Friends Co. v. Province of Balochistan,* 2002 SCMR 1903.
1042. *Ch. Fazal Muhammad Through L. Rs v. Pakistan through Secretary Ministry of Defence and others,* 2007 CLC 148; *Sh. Saleem Ali v. Sh. Akhtar Ali and others,* PLD 2004 Lahore 404.
1043. *Tribal Friends Co. v. Province of Balochistan,* 2002 SCMR 1903.

provisions of CPC which are applicable due to section 41(b) read with Second Schedule of the 1940 Act.[1044] The applicability of the provisions of CPC, by virtue of section 41 of the 1940 Act, is extended to all proceedings, suits, and appeals so far as the application of these provisions is not in conflict with those of the 1940 Act.[1045]

14.3.2. Procedure Before an Arbitrator

Provisions of CPC are applicable to the arbitration proceedings before the court but not to the proceedings before the arbitrator.[1046] In the conduct of arbitration proceedings, the arbitrator is not to indulge itself in the technicalities of Qanun-e-Shahadat Order 1984 or the CPC by virtue of section 41 of the 1940 Act.[1047] Arbitration proceedings are in the nature of proceedings before a domestic tribunal which is why arbitrator cannot be insisted upon strict compliance of procedural law or the law of evidence.[1048] The arbitrator has the authority to regulate its own procedure and is not bound to follow any specific procedure.[1049]

The arbitration agreement should lay down the manner and mode of arbitration proceedings.[1050] Parties can either agree on the procedure in their agreement or can incorporate the rules of some institution in their agreement. In *Afiluddin Brothers Ltd. v. Pak. Jute Balers, Narayanganj*, the dispute was referred to Narayanganj Chamber of Commerce and Industries as per the arbitration agreement, and an award was given. The contentions of the appellant that the arbitrator made an award without holding a formal hearing, without issuing notice to the parties or calling for evidence from them or giving the opportunity of being heard were not accepted by the court. The court, referring to Rule XVI of the rules of Narayanganj Chamber of Commerce and Industries,[1051] held that neither party has any grievance on the conduct of proceedings in such a manner. In the present case, parties had submitted to the arbitrator their

1044. *Excel Techno Solutions FZE, UAE and another v. Oil and Gas Development Company Limited and another*, 2019 CLC 416.
1045. *Mst. Afroz Jehan v. Mst. Noor Jehan and others*, 1988 CLC 1318. On this account, an application under section 12(2) of the CPC for setting aside an order making rule of the court and not the award itself would be competent.
1046. *Abdul Sattar Mandokhal v. Port Qasim Authority*, 2001 YLR 758.
1047. *Kashmir Corporation Ltd. v. Pakistan International Airlines*, PLD 1995 Karachi 301; *Kashmir Corporation Ltd. v. Pakistan International Airlines*, PLD 1995 Karachi 301; *Zakaullah Khan v. Government of Pakistan*, PLD 1998 Lahore 132; *National Engineering Services Pakistan (Pvt.) Ltd. v. Steel Mill Corporation*, 2003 YLR 1696.
1048. *Managing Director, Karachi Fish Harbour Authority v. Hussain (Pvt.) Ltd.*, 2014 CLC 1519.
1049. *Ibid.*
1050. *Jamshed Alam Khan v. Haq Nawaz and another*, PLD 1973 Karachi 31. The court held that otherwise the arbitration agreement may be declared uncertain and vague and may be declared void on that account.
1051. The rule XVI read as:

> The dispute will be decided by the Board on the Written Statement of the parties and oral evidence will not be taken nor will the parties be entitled to appear, nor any formal hearing be held provided that the Board shall have power to take such evidence as, in its absolute discretion, it thinks proper and for such purpose the Board may, if it thinks fit, appoint a time and place for hearing such evidence. At such hearing none of the parties to the reference or their representatives shall be entitled to examine or

admitted contracts, written statements and rejoinders along with a series of letter exchanged between them. The arbitrator examined these documents by treating both parties equally. Therefore, arbitrators cannot be said to have conducted proceedings arbitrarily.[1052]

The arbitrator is not bound by the law of procedure or evidence, but he cannot proceed in disregard of all the evidence or without calling upon parties to lead the evidence; otherwise, he would be guilty of misconducting the proceedings. For instance, after submission of claims and counterclaims from parties, the arbitrator should have called parties to submit their evidence in their support which he did not do, rather called parties for arguments by bypassing the evidence stage, which was counted as misconduct[1053] because an arbitrator is not allowed to act arbitrarily.[1054] The fact that arbitrators are chosen by parties does not mean to allow the arbitrator to deviate from the principles of justice by not affording the right of being heard to parties or recording evidence at the back of parties or proceeding without giving requisite notices to the affected parties.[1055]

An arbitrator has considerable latitude in the procedure to be followed in the conduct of arbitral proceedings. In *Gul Hasan Shah v. Sardarali Shah and others*, Peshawar High Court stated that there is nothing in the 1940 Act compelling an arbitrator for recording 'oral evidence, or statements of the witnesses or admissions of the parties. There is no bar in the 1940 Act against relying on oral evidence. Failure of the arbitrator to reduce the evidence into writing is not an omission fatal to the award and does not constitute misconduct on the arbitrator's part'.[1056] Unless mandated by parties, an arbitrator is not bound to record evidence on oath. The arbitrator can decide a case merely on the basis of documents produced before him if parties have not asked him to examine any witness.[1057] The arbitrator is not bound to the frame issue.[1058]

14.4. AVAILABILITY OF APPEAL

Right of appeal is available only in respect of orders mentioned in section 39 of the 1940 Act with the fact that no second appeal is available on the decision of the first appellate court. Then, there are certain orders not included in this section justifying the remedy of revision. This section deals with these issues, including the point of the limitation period with regard to the appeal.

---

cross-examine any witness or the other party or his representatives but the Board only shall have power to examine the witnesses, the parties or their representatives.

1052. *Afiluddin Brothers Ltd. v. Pak. Jute Balers, Narayanganj*, 1970 SCMR I.
1053. *Design Group of Pakistan v. Clifton Cantonment Board*, 1990 MLD 261.
1054. *Afiluddin Brothers Ltd. v. Pak. Jute Balers, Narayanganj*, 1970 SCMR I.
1055. *Syed Faqir Shah v. Haji Inayatullah Khan and another*, 2013 MLD 689. *See also, Abdul Razaq and another v. Sharif Khan and others*, 1986 CLC 281; *Managing Director, Karachi Fish Harbour Authority v. Hussain (Pvt.) Ltd.*, 2014 CLC 1519.
1056. *Gul Hasan Shah v. Sardarali Shah and others*, PLD 1960 (W. P.) Peshawar 14. *See also, Province of Balochistan and another v. Malik Haji Gul Hassan*, PLD 1982 Quetta 52.
1057. *Akhtar Trading Co. v. Food Department and others*, 1991 CLC 258.
1058. *Alpine Construction Co. Ltd. v. University of Karachi*, 1990 MLD 1764.

14.4.1. Second Appeal

39(2) says that 'no second appeal shall lie from an order passed in appeal under this section' which clearly implies that the decision from the first appeal is not open to challenge in the second appeal.[1059] The term 'second appeal' in section 39(2) means an appeal from a lower forum or court to a superior court whereas, Letters Patent appeal is not an appeal in that sense.[1060] Letters Patent appeal, even if it is termed as an appeal, is a special kind of appeal. In an appeal, the superior tribunal determines the correctness of the decision rendered by the lower tribunal, whereas in a Letter Patent appeal, there is no inferior or superior forum. In it, first, a single judge gives his decision which is then reviewed by a Letter Patent bench of the same court. Therefore, decisions from both benches are from the same court. It may be said that the full and final decision comes only after the matter is heard and decided by the Letter Patent bench.[1061]

14.4.2. Non-appealable Orders

Non-appealable orders that are not enlisted in section 39 include court's declination to grant interim measures under section 41 of the 1940 Act,[1062] are the orders of the court to remove an arbitrator,[1063] order of trial court extending time under section 28 of the 1940 Act[1064] and dismissal of appellant's application to make award rule of court for want of evidence.[1065]

The orders not included in the list given in section 39 are not appealable. These non-appealable orders include the court's declination to grant interim measures under section 41 of the 1940 Act,[1066] order of the court to remove an arbitrator,[1067] order of

1059. *Abdul Razzak v. Mst. Qaiser Sultan and others,* 1984 MLD 147; *Muhammad Nawaz v. Mian Khan and others,* 2019 CLC 413. The court stated that since no right of revision has been given under 1940 Act against the appellate judgment pronounced by first appellate court under section 39, there is no forum available to contest first appellate judgment in revision. In this case, at the most, this judgment or orders given under first appeal can be challenged through a constitution petition if these are passed without any jurisdiction.

1060. *Mrs Keays Byrne v. M. Obaidullah Khan,* PLD 1961 (W. P.) Lahore 256. The court relied on *Muzaffar Din v. Allah Wasai,* PLR 1953 Lah. 529; PLD 1953 Lahore 284.

1061. *Sh. Mahboob Alam v. Sh. Mumtaz Ahmad,* PLD 1960 (W. P.) Lahore 601.

1062. *Petrosin Products (Pvt.) Limited v. Government of Pakistan and others,* 2000 MLD 785; *Arbab Abdul Qadir v. Mst. Bibi Fatima and another,* 1984 CLC 546; *Excel Techno Solutions FZE, UAE v. Oil and Gas Development Company Limited,* 2019 CLC 416; *Pakistan Water and Power Development Authority, Hyderabad v. China International Water and Electric Corporation, Karachi and another,* PLD 1999 Karachi 235.

1063. *Province of East Pakistan v. Abdur Rashid,* PLD 1970 Dacca 69.

1064. *Noble (Pvt.) Ltd., Karachi v. Federal Government Employees Housing Federation, Shaheed-e-Millate Secretariat, Islamabad,* 2002 CLC 1670.

1065. *Farid Majid and another v. Mohammad Nawab,* PLD 1976 Karachi 891.

1066. *Petrosin Products (Pvt.) Limited v. Government of Pakistan and others,* 2000 MLD 785; *Arbab Abdul Qadir v. Mst. Bibi Fatima and another,* 1984 CLC 546; *Excel Techno Solutions FZE, UAE v. Oil and Gas Development Company Limited,* 2019 CLC 416; *Pakistan Water and Power Development Authority, Hyderabad v. China International Water and Electric Corporation, Karachi and another,* PLD 1999 Karachi 235.

1067. *Province of East Pakistan v. Abdur Rashid,* PLD 1970 Dacca 69.

trial court extending time under section 28 of the 1940 Act[1068] and dismissal of appellant's application to make award rule of court for want of evidence.[1069]

14.4.3. Availability of Revision in Arbitration Matters

To examine the validity of a decree of court on matter enlisted in section 39, revision is the only remedy available for the judgment debtor,[1070] but the scope of revisional jurisdiction is limited. In *Tribal Friends Co. v. Province of Balochistan*,[1071] the Supreme Court held that when no appeal is available but 'court has exceeded jurisdiction; acted without jurisdiction, committed material irregularity in conduct of proceedings, passed order in violation of principles of natural justice and the same cannot be assailed under the 1940 Act then High Court may exercise its jurisdiction under S.115, C.P.C., on an application of a party or suo motu'. In other words, the revision petition would lie in a case where sections 30, 33 and 39 are not applicable.[1072]

Section 115 of the CPC says that a revision will lie where there is no appeal. In its revisional jurisdiction, High Court can correct the order of the lower court issued under section 8 of the 1940 Act, which is involving jurisdictional error or procedural irregularity.[1073] Revision will also lie where the arbitrator held the inquiry behind the back of the parties and the trial court ignores this material fact,[1074] or where the arbitrator gave an award without giving notice to the petitioner and without affording the opportunity to parties.[1075] However, where the trial court has set aside the award, and the petitioner has not availed his right of appeal, nor has he given any reason for non-availing of remedy of appeal, the revision will also be denied.[1076]

In cases where revision is available but no appeal is there, and appeal has been filed, the court can *suo motu* turn the petition into revision. For instance, section 21 of the 1940 Act says that a court can make reference to arbitration of a matter pending before it only after all the parties to the suit consent to such reference. However, in *WAPDA and another v. Pakistan Associated Construction*, despite the absence of consent from one party to the suit, the court made a reference to the arbitration. Such party wrongly appealed this order of reference, and the appellate court *suo motu* exercised its revisional jurisdiction to set aside this order made without jurisdiction by the trial court.[1077]

1068. *Noble (Pvt.) Ltd., Karachi v. Federal Government Employees Housing Federation, Shaheed-e-Millate Secretariat, Islamabad,* 2002 CLC 1670.
1069. *Farid Majid and another v. Mohammad Nawab,* PLD 1976 Karachi 891.
1070. *Ejaz Ali Siddique and another v. Rana Irshad Ahmed and another,* 1998 CLC 1684.
1071. *Tribal Friends Co. v. Province of Balochistan,* 2002 SCMR 1903.
1072. *See also Abdul Razzak v. Mst. Qaiser Sultan and others,* 1984 MLD 147; *Rahim Jan v. Mrs Z. Ikram Gardezi and others,* PLD 2004 SC 752.
1073. *Combined Enterprises v. Water and Power Development Authority, Lahore,* PLD 1988 SC 39.
1074. *Province of Baluchistan v. Haji Muhammad Hassan and another,* 1988 CLC 1583.
1075. *Meer Muhammad Sharif v. Mirza Muhammad Ashraf and others,* 1980 CLC 1984.
1076. *S.H. Malik v. Additional District Judge, and others,* 1990 MLD 1924.
1077. *Water and Power Development Authority and another v. Pakistan Associated Construction,* 1992 CLC 771.

14.4.4. Appeal and the Limitation Period

The appeal should be filed within the limitation period; otherwise, it will not be entertained. The limitation period for filing an appeal is ninety days to be reckoned from the date when the order was made.[1078] In case of an appeal barred by limitation period, application for condonation of delay may be filed, which will be granted only if strong reasons for delay are given, and delay is explained on a day-to-day basis.[1079] In *Punjab Province v. Muhammad Arif*, after getting a decision from the trial court, the appellant spent time on the wrong forum, due to which the limitation period to file an appeal in the right forum expired. The court held that the appellant has to show that he had prosecuted the appeal before a wrong forum in good faith and stated further that the mistake of the lawyer in filing the appeal before the wrong forum is not an act done in good faith because that act was not done with due diligence and care.[1080] However, in *Taj Muhammad Khan v. N. W. F. P. Forest Development Corporation and another*, the appellate court held that although the contention of filing an appeal with an innocent mistake before a wrong forum as a reason to condone the delay is not supported by section 39, it would be unjust and improper to penalize the appellant for the wrong advice by his counsel.[1081] If the appellant files an appeal on an order mentioned in section 39 under the wrong provision of law, like section 96 of the CPC, the court would treat the appeal as having been filed under section 39 of the 1940 Act.[1082] Where the trial court has rejected the objections as being time-barred, the appellate court will not consider these objections at the appellate stage.[1083]

14.5. APPEALABLE ORDERS: SECTION 39 OF THE 1940 ACT

Section 39(1) says that an appeal can be made against an order:

(i) superseding an arbitration;
(ii) on an award stated in the form of special cases;
(iii) modifying or correcting an award;
(iv) filing or refusing to file an arbitration agreement;
(v) staying or refusing to stay legal proceedings where there is an arbitration agreement;
(vi) setting aside or refusing to set aside an award.

Provided that the provisions of this section shall not apply to any order passed by a Small Cause Court.

This section discusses these orders and appeal thereon.

1078. *National Highway Authority v. China Petroleum Engineering Corporation*, PLD 2017 Islamabad 1.
1079. *Chief Engineer, Building and Road Department, Quetta v. Umar Khan*, 2015 MLD 1332.
1080. *Punjab Province v. Muhammad Arif*, 2003 MLD 1677.
1081. *Taj Muhammad Khan v. NWFP Forest Development Corporation and another*, PLD 1984 Peshawar 64.
1082. *Muhammad Iqbal v. Riaz Sabir*, 1984 CLC 2375.
1083. *Government of Pakistan v. Malik Muhammad Azeem & Bros.*, 2000 YLR 2706.

14.5.1. Superseding an Arbitration

Clause (i) of section 39(1) provides a right of appeal against an order of court superseding an arbitration. This clause was discussed by Punjab High Court in *M. A. Aziz & Sons v. Lt. Col. M. Daud Khan and Pakistan*. In this case, the court held that the order rejecting the authority of arbitrator under section 11 of the 1940 Act is not appealable under section 39(1)(i) because the order superseding the arbitration does not include the order refusing to supersede an arbitration. The court stated that the inclusion of a few orders in section 39 implies the confinement of the right of the appeal to a very limited number of orders. If the legislature had intended to make some orders appealable, it would have specifically mentioned those orders in section 39 and an order refusing to supersede arbitration is not included in that list. Hence, the contention that the word 'arbitration' in this clause includes the revocation and appointment of arbitration was not accepted.

Referring to section 25 of the 1940 Act,[1084] Punjab High Court held that this section draws a clear distinction between removal of arbitrator and supersession of arbitration. It said that:

> The word 'arbitration' has been used to mean the arbitration agreement as distinct from the removal of an arbitrator, which is only a stage in the arbitration proceedings. It is a well-known principle in the interpretation of statutes that when a word has been given a certain meaning in a statute, that word has to be given the same meaning throughout the statute. Accordingly, the word 'arbitration' in subclause (i) of section 39 must have the same meaning as in section 25 of the Arbitration Act and, therefore, the words 'superseding an arbitration' do not mean or include an order revoking the appointment of an arbitrator. Therefore, no appeal lies against the order dismissing an application under section 11 of the Act for removal of an arbitrator.[1085]

In *Amanullah Khan and others v. Kohat Cement Co. and others*, the arbitrator entered upon the reference on 30 July 1983 but did not pronounce the award till 30 November 1984. Hence, the award was beyond the statutory period of four months and extensions given to him by the court. Therefore, such an award was declared by the trial court to be *void ab initio*, and this order of setting aside the award was also upheld in appeals. The question remaining for consideration was if the arbitration agreement has been superseded or (if not) should it be superseded. The appellant court held that this is always discretionary for a court to declare under section 19 of the 1940 Act

1084. Section 25. Provisions applicable to arbitrations under this chapter:

> The provisions of the other Chapters shall, so far as they can be made applicable, apply to arbitrations under this Chapter: Provided that the Court may, in any of the circumstances mentioned in Section 8, 10, 11 and 12, instead of filing up the vacancies or making the appointments, make an order superseding the arbitration and proceed with the suit, and where the Court makes an order superseding the arbitration under section 19, it shall proceed with the suit.

1085. *M. A. Aziz & Sons v. Lt. Col. M. Daud Khan and Pakistan through C. M. E. S.*, PLD 1968 Lahore 847.

whether or not the arbitration agreement will cease to have effect after the setting aside of the award because, in this situation, the arbitration agreement may still continue. So far as the circumstance in which the court may order the suppression of arbitration agreement cannot be identified exhaustively but may include the following:

- Where arbitration agreement itself contemplates that it will come to an end on the emergence of a certain contingency.
- When a particular person chosen by parties on account of his special skill or knowledge to act as arbitrator is unable to perform the duties of an arbitrator.
- Where the procurement of arbitration agreement is tainted with undue influence, misrepresentation, or its terms are unconscionable or otherwise against the law or public policy.
- Where a court comes to a conclusion that intricate questions of law, like the interpretation of legal provisions, involve these and can be decided more authoritatively by the court.

The court concluded that the arbitration agreement should prevail and continue to exist until the court concludes that such a decision would result in a miscarriage of justice. Therefore, the discretion of the court to annul an arbitration agreement is not automatic and must be exercised judiciously and not as mechanically or matter of course. The suppression of the arbitration agreement must be based on sound reasons justifying this annulment, but if the court decided to keep the arbitration agreement intact, it does not need to give reasons. High Court decided that neither the eventualities mentioned above are attracted, nor any miscarriage of justice is apprehended, so the arbitration agreement, in this case, should remain intact since deciding otherwise would leave parties to file a suit in civil court over construction work completed eighteen years ago.[1086]

14.5.2. Modifying or Correcting an Award

Clause (ii) of section 39(1) says that an aggrieved party can file an appeal against an order of court modifying or correcting an award. For instance, in *Ascon Engineers (Pvt.) Ltd. v. Province of Punjab,*[1087] Government of Punjab, Housing and Physical Planning Department (Department) awarded a contract to Acson Engineers (Company) for the up-gradation of Karachi Pumpwali Pond to be completed in one year after the award of contract. Dispute arose, and arbitration ensued, which culminated in an award of PKR 45,83,555 payable by the Department to the Company. The trial court made award rule of the court whereas in appeal, on the point of misconduct of arbitrator, the High Court remanded the award to the trial court, which again made the award rule of the court with an additional order of payment of interest at the rate of 10% per annum from the date of the award. Department appealed this judgment/decree in the High Court, which in appeal reduced the award from PKR 45,83,555 to PKR 31,39,035 and held that the

1086. *Amanullah Khan and others v. Kohat Cement Co. and others,* 1997 MLD 2419.
1087. *Ascon Engineers (Pvt.) Ltd. v. Province of Punjab,* 2002 SCMR 1662.

interest shall be payable on this amount from the date of the decree of the trial court. When the matter was appealed to the Supreme Court, it upheld the decision of the High Court along with the modifications made by it. The Supreme Court held that under section 39(1)(iii), the appellate court has the power to modify or correct an award despite the fact that the objections which are filed are barred by time. Similarly, in *Project Director, Workers Welfare Board and others v. Awami Construction Co.*, the court reduced the interest rate from 14% to 8%.[1088] It is to note that the court can convert the revision petition challenging the modification of award done by the court into appeal and decide it under section 39(1)(iii).[1089]

14.5.3. Filing or Refusing to File an Arbitration Agreement

Under clause (vi) of section 39(1) of the 1940 Act, an appeal is competent against an order 'filing or refusing to file an arbitration agreement'. After the court has decided the validity and existence of the arbitration agreement, the process of arriving at a decision on the filing of an arbitration agreement is concluded, and the decision of the court on this process is appealable. After the court has decided that the arbitration agreement should be filed, on parties' failure to agree on the person to be appointed as arbitrator, the court can make that appointment. This order of the court to appoint an arbitrator is not appealable.[1090] The application to file the arbitration agreement is treated as a suit, and the decision over this application, if not appealed against under section 39(1)(vi), becomes final.[1091] After the reference is made to arbitration, if parties participate before the arbitrator without questioning the validity of such reference nor the jurisdiction arbitrator, they later cannot challenge the award on such basis.[1092]

The appeal is the continuation of the proceeding initiated before the lower court, and the appellate court has all the powers which the lower court enjoys, which have been exercised by it in different manners and cases. The order of the trial court to file the arbitration agreement and appoint a two-member arbitral tribunal can be modified by the appellate court by appointing a sole arbitrator in terms of the arbitration agreement.[1093] In another case, the appellate court directed the parties to appoint the arbitrators by setting aside the order of the trial court.[1094] In *Province of Punjab v. Sufi Abdul Hameed*, the trial court, without first deciding application on the filing of the arbitration agreement, ordered to appoint arbitrators who were appointed accordingly to give the award. This award was made a rule of the court. The appellant court set aside the award on the ground that the lower court should have first decided the

1088. *Project Director, Workers Welfare Board and others v. Awami Construction Co.*, 1991 MLD 686.
1089. *Mirza Muhammad Siddique v. Muhammad Abdullah*, 1989 MLD 54.
1090. *Province of Baluchistan v. Sardar Muhammad Usman Khan*, PLD 1987 Quetta 33.
1091. *Sh. Fazal Hussain v. Board of Governors, Divisional Public High School, Lyallpur*, 2001 MLD 407.
1092. *Muhammad Nadeem v. Additional District Judge, Bhakkar and others*, 2012 CLC 441.
1093. *Pakistan Real Estate Investment and Management Company (Pvt) Ltd v. Sohail A. Khan, Associates*, PLD 2018 Islamabad 115.
1094. *Sports Star International (Pvt.) Ltd. v. Shalimar Recording and Broadcasting Company Ltd.*, 2018 CLC 1892.

application to file the arbitration agreement and remanded the matter to the trial court to decide it afresh.[1095] The court in whose jurisdiction the contract, including the arbitration agreement, was not executed, ordered to file the arbitration agreement. The appellate court set aside the order for want of jurisdiction on the matter.[1096]

14.5.4. Staying or Refusing to Stay Legal Proceedings Where There Is an Arbitration Agreement

Clause (v) of section 39(1) says that where an application for stay of court proceedings is accepted or rejected, such decision of the lower court can be appealed.[1097] An appeal would be maintainable where, for instance, the court refused to stay its proceedings on the ground that the defendant has taken steps in the proceeding,[1098] and the appellate court can set aside the decision of the lower court. In *Haji Muhammad Zaffar v. Muhammad Sikandar and others*, the defendant did not challenge the contentions of the plaintiff as made in the latter's plaint and then filed section 34 application which was allowed by the trial court by staying its proceedings in favour of arbitration. The High Court, in appeal, concluded that for the defendant has not denied the averments of the plaintiff, the arbitration agreement has come to an end and set aside the decision of the trial court.[1099] Similarly, where the court stayed its proceedings in favour of arbitration despite the absence of any dispute between the parties, in appeal, the appellate court directed the trial court to proceed with the matter.[1100] It is to note that non-preference of appeal against such order would imply as 'no ground stands made out for interference with the said order passed by' the trial court.[1101]

14.5.5. Setting Aside or Refusing to Set Aside an Award

Clause (vi) of section 39(1) makes an order of the trial court 'setting aside or refusing to set aside an award' appealable.[1102] Where the court sets aside the award, either on the application of a party or on its own, this order of setting aside is appealable. If no objections to award are filed by the party and the court makes the award rule of the court, this order would not be appealable because this order cannot be termed as an order 'refusing to set aside an award'. However, the petitioner can file a revision petition against his order.[1103] If the court refuses to make the award rule of the court, the arbitrator cannot appeal such a decision.[1104]

1095. *Province of Punjab v. Sufi Abdul Hameed*, 2003 CLC 355.
1096. *Special Communication Organization v. Ibell (Pvt.) Ltd., Lahore*, 2007 CLC 248.
1097. *Infospan (Private) Limited v. M/S Shaheen Foundation and another*, 2019 CLC 750.
1098. *Province of Punjab v. Muhammad Asghar*, 2008 YLR 300.
1099. *Haji Muhammad Zaffar v. Muhammad Sikandar and others*, 2000 YLR 2503.
1100. *Province of Punjab v. Ehsan Fazal & Company, Lahore*, 1986 CLC 2800.
1101. *Province of Punjab v. Muhammad Asghar*, 2008 YLR 300.
1102. *Zafar Hussain Rizvi v. Muhammad Hanif*, 1980 CLC 2177; *Taj Din and another v. Muhammad Sharif and another*, PLD 1970 Lahore 840.
1103. *Major Muhammad Nouman v. Usman Habib and another*, PLD 2019 Islamabad 255.
1104. *Inayatullah Khan v. Obaidullah Khan and others*, 1999 SCMR 2702.

Where party failed to file objections despite sufficient notice and opportunity, or he submitted a statement to the court that they will not file the objections and thereafter, the court made award rule of the court, such decree would not be appealable[1105] because in this case, the question of setting aside of award would not arise. The court will also reject the objections filed beyond the limitation period by refusing to set aside the award. However, an appeal against such an order would be maintainable.[1106] In *Muhammad Ather Hafeez Khan v. Sangyong and Usmani J.V. and others*, the award was objected to having filed beyond the limitation period. The trial court first decided that objections are filed within the limitation period independently of the merits. The appeal was made to challenge such a decision of the court with the fact that its decision on the enforcement of the award was still pending. The appellate court held that independent orders are not appealable. It, however, said that the appellant would be at liberty to contest the issue of limitation if the court rejects his objection by making the award rule of the court, whereafter he chooses to appeal against the final award, then he can contest the issue of limitation.[1107]

The matters considered appealable under this clause cannot be enlisted exhaustively, but some instances may be summarized here. Although the court did not say in so many words that it is setting aside the award, its refusal to make the award rule of court by terming the award illegal will amount to an order setting aside the award to be appealable under section 39. However, if this was not appealable, then such appeal would be treated as a revision under section 115 of CPC.[1108] The order of court remitting award to the arbitrator is appealable under section 39(vi), which includes an order to remit the award because 'same amounts to and takes effect in fact setting aside the award'.[1109] When the award is set aside under section 30(c) on the ground that the main contract, including the arbitration agreement incorporated in it, are non-existent, such order of court setting aside the award is appealable under section 39(iv).[1110]

14.5.5.1. Relation Between Section 17 and Section 39 of the 1940 Act

Sections 17 and 39 are independent of each other without any overriding or overlapping effect and cater to two distinct eventualities. Section 39(1)(vi) gives the right to an aggrieved party to file an appeal against the order of court setting aside or refusing to set an award. If a court has issued a composite order wherein it has refused to set aside an award and in the same judgment/order has made the award rule of the court with the fact that the decree followed this judgment, the part of judgment comprising refusal to set aside the award is a distinct and independent part of the judgment amenable to appeal under section 39, whereas against the other part of the judgment, the appeal will

1105. *Province of Punjab and others v. Mirza Muhammad Latif*, 1996 MLD 1115.
1106. *Tribal Friends Co. v. Province of Balochistan*, 2002 SCMR 1903.
1107. *Muhammad Ather Hafeez Khan v. Sangyong and Usmani J.V. and others*, 2017 CLC Note 135.
1108. *Haji Muhammad Latif v. Farman Ali*, PLD 1994 Lahore 40.
1109. *Government of East Pakistan v. A. Rab & Sons and another*, PLD 1967 Dacca 797.
1110. *Combined Enterprises v. Water and Power Development Authority, Lahore*, PLD 1988 SC 39.

be available only on the ground mentioned in section 17. In this way, section 17 in no way circumscribes the right of appeal of a party given under section 39.[1111]

In *Sayed Hussain Shah v. Haji Ghulam Hassan Khan,* the court eloquently explained the relation between section 17 and section 39. When no ground mentioned in section 30 of the 1940 Act exists, the court proceeds to give a judgment according to award, and upon such judgment pronounced, a decree has to follow. Under section 39, order setting aside or refusing to set aside is appealable. Whereas, under section 17, a decree following a judgment pronounced in accordance with the award is not appealable except on the ground that it is in excess of or not otherwise according to the award. This is the policy of the 1940 Act that the court has to pass distinct order of either setting aside or refusing to set aside the award, as is clear from the combined reading of section 17[1112] and section 39 because it is only after such order is passed, the right to appeal accrues. The right to appeal such an order exists even if the court omits to pass such an order. After the court has passed this order of setting aside or refusing to set aside the award, the court will move to pass another order of pronouncing judgment according to the award. The decree is the final stage of arbitration which arrives only after the above-mentioned orders are made in clear and explicit words. There is no appeal against the decree under section 17. It may be said that when the court rejects the objections of a party against the award and issues a decree in terms of award, the order of refusing to set aside the award is implied in this decree, but it is imperative that the court should not leave anything obscure so that the right of a party to appeal an order which has been given to him is not divested.[1113]

In *Muhammad Ramzan and another v. Nazir Ahmad and others,*[1114] the relationship between sections 17 and 39 was further elaborated. The court stated under section 17 that no appeal can be brought against a decree passed in terms of the arbitral award except on the ground that the decree is 'in excess of, or not otherwise in accordance with, the award'. This means that the decree cannot be challenged on the ground that the award should be set aside. The reason for this bar is obvious, as in the words of the court:

> Before the stage of passing a decree is reached, objections can be raised against an award, and if the objection petition be dismissed, an appeal against such dismissal is provided under section 39 of the Arbitration Act. Therefore, an award cannot be allowed to be challenged twice, once by filing an appeal against the order of

1111. *Rashida v. Ch. Muhammad Anwar and others,* PLD 2003 Lahore 522. *See also Qazi Masud-Ul Haq v. Sh. Fateh Muhammad,* 1980 CLC 553.

1112. Section 17. Judgment in terms of award:

> Where the Court sees no cause to remit the award or any of the matters referred to arbitration for reconsideration or to set aside the award, the Court shall, after the time for making an application to set aside the award has expired, or such application having been made, after refusing it, proceed to pronounce judgment according to the award, and upon the judgment so pronounced a decree shall follow, and no appeal shall lie from such decree except on the ground that it is in excess of, or not otherwise in accordance with, the award.

1113. *Sayed Hussain Shah v. Haji Ghulam Hassan Khan,* PLD 1953 Peshawar 59.

1114. *Muhammad Ramzan and another v. Nazir Ahmad and others,* 1979 CLC 95.

dismissal of the objection petition, and subsequently again after a decree is passed in terms of the award. The Legislature having provided in section 39 of Arbitration Act for an appeal against an order of refusal to set aside the award, at a stage prior to the passing of the decree, had to prohibit the re-agitation of the same matter at a stage after the passing of the decree.

Muhammad Ramzan relied on *Muhammad Yousaf and others v. Nazir Ahmad and others*. In this case, the court held that when a party (plaintiff) files an application under section 14 for a direction to the arbitrator to file the award, the court serves notice to the other party (defendant). In this situation, the defendant can either confess the judgment before the court or file a section 33 application challenging the existence or validity of the award. If the court decides both applications as submitted under sections 14 and 33 in the same judgment by refusing to set aside the award, the defendant has the right to appeal under section 39. This is so because section 17 prohibits challenging a decree passed on an award, and it is an award that is to be set aside. Therefore, such a decree was treated as an order from the trial court refusing to set aside the award.[1115]

14.5.5.2. Challenging a Decree under Section 12(2) of the CPC

The object of an application under section 12(2) of CPC is to save parties from filing a civil suit, which normally takes years to conclude. This provision gives every court jurisdiction to recall or review its orders procured through fraud, misrepresentation or issued without any jurisdiction. In this situation, the aggrieved party can file an application to the court that made such an order. Judgment and then the decree passed in terms of the award is passed by a civil court.[1116]

14.6. CONCLUSION

Pakistani regime, in its statutory and precedential law, clearly elucidates and consistently applies the concept of appeal and revision. Then through, section 41 of the 1940 Act, the provisions of CPC and Qanun-e-Shahadat Order 1984 are made applicable to arbitration proceedings before the court. The application of these laws has meaningfully been excluded from the arbitration proceedings before arbitration. However, by application of these laws, it has been established that where the appeal is not available, another very effective remedy – revision – is available. Absenting an appeal on the awards and providing it for judicial orders has laid down the very effective regime in support of arbitration.

1115. *Muhammad Yousaf and others v. Nazir Ahmad and others,* PLD 1989 Lahore 485. *See also, Trading Corporation of Pakistan Ltd. v. General Industrial Machines, andelsgesellschaft Mbh, 6-Frankfurt,* 1986 CLC 1999.

1116. *Ch. Fazal Muhammad v. Pakistan through Secretary Ministry of Defense and others,* 2007 CLC 148.

Appendices

APPENDIX I

The Arbitration Act, 1940

(X OF 1940)

An Act consolidate and
amend the law relating to Arbitration

Preamble: Whereas it is expedient to consolidate and amend the law relating to arbitration in Pakistan.

It is hereby enacted as follows:-

CHAPTER -- I
Introductory

1. Short title, extent and commencement:

(1) This Act may be called the Arbitration Act, 1940.
(2) It extends to the whole of Pakistan.
(3) It shall come into force on the 1st day of July, 1940.

2. Definitions: In this Act, unless there is anything repugnant in the subject or context,-

(a) "**arbitration** agreement" means a written agreement to submit present or future differences to arbitration, whether an arbitrator is named therein or not;
(b) "**award**" means an arbitration award;
(c) "**Court**" means a Civil Court having jurisdiction to decide the question forming the subject-matter of reference if the same had been the subject-matter of a suit, but does not, except for the purpose of proceedings under Section 21, include a Small Cause Court;

(d) **"legal representative"** means a person who in law represents the estate of a deceased person, and includes any person who intermeddles with the estate of the deceased, and where a party acts in representative character, the person on whom the estate devolves on the death of the party so acting;

(e) **"reference"** means reference to arbitration.

CHAPTER -- II
Arbitration Without Intervention of a Court

3. Provisions implied in arbitration agreement: An arbitration agreement, unless a different intention is expressed therein, shall be deemed to include the provisions set out in the First Schedule in so far as they are applicable to the reference.

4. Agreement that arbitrators be appointed by third party: The Parties to an arbitration agreement may agree that any reference there under shall be to an arbitrator or arbitrators to be appointed by a person designated in the agreement either by name or as the holder for the time being of any office or appointment.

5. Authority of appointed arbitrator or umpire irrevocable except by leave of Court: The authority of an appointed arbitrator or umpire shall not be revocable except with the leave of the Court, unless a contrary intention is expressed in the arbitration agreement.

6. Arbitration agreement not to be discharged by death of party thereto:

(1) an arbitration agreement shall not be discharged by the death of any party thereto, either as respects the deceased or any other party, but shall in such event by enforceable by or against the legal representative of the deceased.

(2) The authority of an arbitrator shall not be revoked by the death of any party by whom he was appointed.

(3) Nothing in this section shall affect the operation of any law by virtue of which any right of action is extinguished by the death of a person.

7. Provisions in case of insolvency:

(1) Where it is provided by a term in a contract to which an insolvent is a party that any difference arising there out or in connection therewith shall be referred to arbitration, the said term shall if the receiver adopts the contract, be enforceable by or against him so far as it relates to any such differences.

(2) Where a person who has been adjudged an insolvent had, before the commencement of the insolvency proceedings, become a party to an arbitration agreement and any matter to which the agreement applies is required to be determined in connection with, or for the purposes of the insolvency proceedings, then, if the case is one to which sub-section (1) does not apply, any other party to the agreement or the receiver may apply to the Court having jurisdiction in the insolvency proceedings for an order directing that

the matter in question shall be referred to arbitration in accordance with the agreement and the Court may, if it is of opinion that, having regard to all the circumstances of the case, the matter ought to be determined by arbitration, make an order accordingly.

(3) In this section the expression "receiver" includes an Official Assignee.

8. Power of Court to appoint arbitrator or umpire:

(1) In any of the following cases-

(a) where an arbitration agreement provides that the reference shall be to one or more arbitrators to be appointed by consent of the parties, and all the parties do not, after difference have arisen,concur, in the appointment or appointments; or

(b) if any appointed arbitrator or umpire neglects or refuses to act, or is incapable of acting, or dies, and the arbitration agreement does not show that it was intended that the vacancy should not be supplied; and the parties or the arbitrators, as the case may be, do not supply the vacancy; or

(c) where the parties or the arbitrators are required to appoint an umpire and do not appoint him; any party may serve the other parties or the arbitrators, as the case may be, with a written notice to concur in the appointment or appointments or in supplying the vacancy.

(2) If the appointment is not made within fifteen clear days after the service of the said notice, the Court may, on the application of the party who gave notice and after giving the other parties an opportunity of being heard, appoint an arbitrator or arbitrators or umpire, as the case may be, who shall have like power to act in the reference and to make an award as if he or they had been appointed by consent of all parties.

9. Power to party to appoint new arbitrator or, in certain cases, a sole arbitrator: Where an arbitration agreement provides that a reference shall be to two arbitrators, one to be appointed by each party, then, unless a different intention is expressed in the agreement:-

(a) if either of the appointed arbitrator, neglects or refuses to act, or is incapable of acting, or dies, the party who appointed him may appoint a new arbitrator in his place;

(b) if one party fails to appoint an arbitrator, either originally or by way of substitution as aforesaid, for fifteen clear days, after the service by the other party of a notice in writing to make the appointment, such other party having appointed his arbitrator before giving the notice, the party who has appointed an arbitrator may appoint that arbitrator to act as sole arbitrator in the reference, and his award shall be binding on both parties as if he had been appointed by consent:

Provided that the Court may set aside any appointment as sole arbitrators made under clause (b) and either, on sufficient cause being shown, allow further time to the defaulting party to appoint an arbitrator or pass such other order as it thinks fit.

Explanation: The fact that an arbitrator or umpire, after request by either party to enter on proceed with the reference, does not within one month comply with the request may constitute a neglect or refusal to act within the meaning of Section 8 and this section.

10. Provisions as to appointment of three or more arbitrators:

(1) Where an arbitration agreement provides that a reference shall be to three arbitrators, one to be appointed by each party and the third by the two appointed arbitrators, the agreement shall have effect as if it provided for the appointment, of an umpire, and not for the appointment of a third arbitrator, by the two arbitrators appointed by the parties.

(2) Where an arbitration agreement provides that a reference shall be to three arbitrators to be appointed otherwise than as mentioned in sub-section (1), the award of the majority shall, unless the arbitration agreement otherwise provides, prevail.

(3) Where an arbitration agreement provides for the appointed of more arbitrators than three, the award of the majority, or if the arbitrators are equally divided in their opinions, the award of the umpire shall, unless the arbitration agreement otherwise provides, prevail.

11. Power of Court to remove arbitrators or umpire in certain circumstances:

(1) The Court may, on the application of any party to reference, remove an arbitrator or umpire who fails to use all reasonable dispatch in entering on and proceeding with the reference and making an award.

(2) The Court may remove an arbitrator or umpire who has misconduct himself or the proceedings.

(3) Where an arbitrator or umpire is removed under this section, he shall not be entitled to receive any remuneration in respect of his services.

(4) For the purposes of this section the expression "proceeding with the reference" includes, in a case where reference to the umpire becomes necessary, giving notice of that fact to the parties and to the umpire.

12. Power of Court where arbitrator is removed or his authority revoked:

(1) Where the Court removes an umpire who has not entered on the reference or one or more arbitrators (not being all the arbitrators), the Court may, on the application of any party to the arbitration agreement, appoint persons to fill the vacancies.

(2) Where the authority of an arbitrator or arbitrators or an umpire is revoked by leave of the Court, or where the Court removes an umpire who has entered on

the reference or a sole arbitrator or all the arbitrators, the Court may, on the application of any party to the arbitration agreement, either-

(a) appoint a person to act as sole arbitrator in the place of the person or persons displaced, or

(b) order that the arbitration agreement shall cease to have effect with respect to the difference referred.

(3) a person appointed under this section as an arbitrator or umpire shall have the like power to act in the reference and to make an award as if he had been appointed in accordance with the arbitration agreement.

13. Powers of arbitrator: The arbitrators or umpire shall, unless a different intention is expressed in the agreement, have power to-

(a) administer oath to the parties and witnesses appearing;

(b) state a special case for the opinion of the Court on any question of law involved, or state the award, wholly or in part, in the form of a special case of such question for the opinion of the Court;

(c) make the award any clerical or in the alternative;

(d) correct in an award any clerical mistake or error arising from any accidental slip or mission;

(e) administer to any party to the arbitration such interrogatories as may, in the opinion of the arbitrators or umpire, be necessary.

14. Award to be signed and filed:

(1) When the arbitrators or umpire have made their award, they shall sign it and shall give notice in writing to the parties of the making and signing thereof and of the amount of fees and charges payable in respect of the arbitration and award.

(2) The arbitrators or umpire shall, at the request of any party to the arbitration agreement or any person claiming under such party or if so directed by the Court and upon payment of the fees and charges due in respect of the arbitration and award and of the costs and charges of filing the award, cause the award or signed copy of it, together with any depositions and documents which may have been taken and proved before them, to be filed in Court, and the Court shall thereupon give notice to the parties of the filing of the award.

15. Power of Court to modify award: The Court may by order modify or correct an award-

(a) Where it appears that a part of the award is upon a matter not referred to arbitration and such part can be separated from the other part and does not affect the decision on the matter referred; or

(b) where the award is imperfect in form, or contains any obvious error which can be amended without effecting such decision; or

(c) where the award contains clerical mistake or an error arising from an accidental slip or omission.

16. Power to remit award:

(1) The Court may from time to time remit the award or any matter referred to arbitration to the arbitrators or umpire for reconsideration upon such terms as it thinks fit-
  (a) where the award has left undetermined any of the matters referred to arbitration, or where it determines any matter not referred to arbitration and such matter cannot be separated without affecting the determination of the matters referred; or
  (b) where the award is so indefinite as to be incapable of execution; or
  (c) where an objection to the legality of the award is apparent upon the face of it.

(2) Where an award is remitted under sub-section (1) the Court shall fix the time within which the arbitrator or umpire shall submit his decision to the Court: **Provided that** any time so fixed may be extended by subsequent order of the Court.

(3) An award is remitted under sub-section (1) shall become void on the failure of the arbitrator or umpire to reconsider it and submit his decision within the time fixed.

17. Judgment in terms of award: Where the Court sees no cause to remit the award or any of the matters referred to arbitration for consideration or to set aside the award has expired, or such application having been made, after refusing it, proceed to pronounce judgment according to the award, and upon the judgment so pronounced a decree shall follow, and no appeal shall lie from such decree exception the ground that it is in excess of, or not otherwise in accordance with, the award.

18. Power of Court to pass interim order:

(1) Notwithstanding anything contained in Section 17, at any time after the filing of the award, whether notice of the filing has been served or not, upon being satisfied by affidavit or otherwise that a party has taken or is about to take steps to defeat, delay or obstruct the execution of any decree that may be passed upon the award, or that speedy execution of the award is just and necessary, the Court may pass such interim orders as it deems necessary.

(2) Any person against whom such interim orders have been passed may show cause against such orders, and the Court, after hearing the parties, may pass such further orders as it deems necessary and just.

19. Power to supersede arbitration where award becomes void or is set aside: Where an award has become void under sub-section (3) of Section 16 or has been set aside, the Court may by order supersede the reference and shall there upon order that the arbitration agreement shall cease to have effect with respect to the difference referred.

CHAPTER -- III
Arbitration with Intervention of a Court where there is no Suit Pending

20. Application to file in Court arbitration agreement:

(1) Where any person have entered into an arbitration agreement before the institution of any suit with respect to the subject-matter of the agreement or any part of it, and where a difference has arisen to which the agreement applies, they or any of them, instead of proceeding under Chapter II, may apply to a Court having jurisdiction in the matter to which the agreement relates, that the agreement be filed in the Court.

(2) The application shall be in writing and shall be numbered and registered as a suit between one or more of the parties interested or claiming to be interested as plaintiff or plaintiffs and the remainder as defendant or defendants, if the application has been presented by all the parties, or, if otherwise, between the applicant as plaintiff and the other parties as defendants.

(3) On such application being made the Court shall direct notice thereof to be given to all parties to the agreement other than the applicants, requiring them to show cause within the time specified in the notice why the agreement should not be filed.

(4) Where no sufficient cause is shown, the Court shall order the agreement to be filed, and shall make an order of reference to the arbitrator appointed by the parties, whether in the agreement or otherwise, or, where the parties cannot agree upon an arbitrator, to an arbitrator appointed by the Court.

(5) Thereafter the arbitration shall proceed in accordance with, and shall be governed by, the other provisions of this Act so far as they can be made applicable.

CHAPTER – IV
Arbitration in Suits

21. Parties to suit may apply for order of reference: Where in any suit all the parties interested agree that any matter in difference between them in the suit shall be referred to arbitration, they may at any time before judgment is pronounced apply in writing to the Court for an order of reference.

22. Appointment of arbitrator: The arbitrator shall be appointed in such manner as may be agreed upon between the parties.

23. Order of reference:

(1) The Court shall, by order, refer to the arbitrator the matter in difference which he is required to determine, and shall in the order specify such time as it thinks reasonable for the making of the award.
(2) Where a matter is referred to arbitration the Court shall not, save in the manner and to the extent provided in this Act, deal with such matter in the suit.

24. Reference to arbitration by some of the parties: Where some only of the parties to a suit apply to have the matters in difference between them referred to arbitration in accordance with, and in the manner provided by Section 21 the Court may, if it thinks fit so, refer such matters to arbitration by Section 21 the Court may, if it thinks fit so, refer such matters to arbitration (provided that the manner provided in that section, but the suits shall continue so far as it relates to the parties who have not joined in the said application and to matters not contained in the said reference as if no such application had been made, and an award made in pursuance of such a reference shall be binding only on the parties who have joined in the application.

25. Provisions applicable to arbitrations under this Chapter: The provisions of the other Chapters shall, so far as they can be made applicable, apply to arbitrations under this Chapter:

Provided that the Court may, in any of he circumstances mentioned in Sections 8, 10, 11 and 12, instead of filling up the vacancies or making the appointment, make an order superseding the arbitration and proceed with the suit, and where the Court makes an order superseding the arbitration under Section 19, it shall proceed with the suit.

CHAPTER – V
General

26. Application of Chapter: Save as otherwise provided in this Act, the provision of this Chapter shall apply to all arbitrations.

26-A. Award to set out reasons:

(1) The arbitrator or umpire shall state in the award the reasons for the award in sufficient detail to enable the Court to consider, any question of law arising out of the award.
(2) Where the award not state the reasons in sufficient detail, the Court shall remit the award to the arbitrators or umpire and fix the time within which the arbitrator or umpire shall submit the award together with the reasons in sufficient detail:
Provided that any time so fixed may be extended by subsequent order of the Court.

(3) An award remitted under sub-section (2) shall become void on the failure of the arbitrator or umpire to submit it in accordance with the direction of the Court.

27. Power of arbitrators to make an interim award:

(1) Unless a different intention appears in the arbitration agreement, the arbitrators or umpire may, if they think fit, make an interim award.
(2) All references in this Act to an award shall include references to an interim award made under sub-section (1).

28. Power to Court only to enlarge time for making award:

(1) The Court may, if it thins fit, whether the time for making the award has expired or not and whether the award has been made or not, enlarge from time to time the time for making the award.
(2) Any provision in an arbitration agreement whereby the arbitrators or umpire may, except with the consent of all the parties to the agreement, enlarge the time for making the award, shall be void and of no effect.

29. Interest on awards: Where and in so far as an award is for the payment of money the Court may in the decree order interest, from the date of the decree at such rate as the Court deems reasonable, to be paid on the principal sum as adjusted by the award and confirmed by the decree.
30. Grounds for setting aside award. An award shall not be set aside except on one or more of the following grounds, namely:-

(a) that an arbitrator or umpire has misconducted himself or the proceeding;
(b) that an award has been made after the issue of an order by the Court superseding the arbitration or after arbitration proceedings had been invalid under section 35;
(c) that an award has been improperly procured or is otherwise invalid.

31. Jurisdiction:

(1) Subject to the provisions of this Act, an award may be filed in any Court having jurisdiction in the matter to which the reference relates.
(2) Notwithstanding anything contained in any other law for the time being in force and save as otherwise provided in this Act, all questions regarding the validity, effect or existence of an award or an arbitration agreement between the parties to the agreement or persons claiming under them shall be decided by the Court in which the award under the agreement has been, or may be, filed, and by no other Court.

(3) All application regarding the conduct of arbitration proceedings or otherwise arising out of such proceedings shall be made to the Court where award has been, or may be, and to no other Court.

(4) Notwithstanding anything contained elsewhere in this Act or in any other law for the time being in force, where in any reference any application under this Act has been made in a Court competent to entertain it, that Court alone shall have jurisdiction over the arbitration proceedings and all subsequent application arising out of that reference and the arbitration proceedings shall be made in that Court and in no other Court.

32. Bar to suit contesting arbitration agreement or award: Notwithstanding any law for the time being in force, no suit shall lie on any ground for a decision upon the existence, effect o validity of an arbitration agreement or award, nor shall any arbitration agreement or award be set aside, amended, modified or in any way affected otherwise than as provided in this Act.

33. Arbitration agreement or award to be contested by application: Any party to an arbitration agreement or any person claiming under him desiring to challenge the existence or validity of an arbitration agreement or an award or to have the effect of either determined shall apply to the Court and the Court shall decide the question on affidavits:

Provided that where the Court deems it just and expedient, it may set down the application for hearing on other evidence also, and it may pass such orders for the discovery and particulars as it may do in a suit.

34. Power to stay legal proceedings where there is an arbitration agreement: Where any party to an arbitration agreement or any person claiming under him commences any legal proceedings against any other party to the agreement or any person claiming under him in respect of any matter agreed to be referred, any party to such legal proceedings may, at any time before filing a written statement or taking any other steps in the proceedings, apply to the judicial authority before which the proceeding: and if satisfied that there in no sufficient reason why the matter should not be referred in accordance with the arbitration agreement and that the applicant was, at the time when the proceedings were commenced, and still remains, ready and willing to do all things necessary, to the proper conduct of the arbitration such authority may make an order staying the proceedings.

35. Effect of legal proceedings on arbitration:

(1) No reference nor award shall be rendered invalid by reason only of the commencement of legal proceedings upon the subject-matter of the reference, but when legal proceedings upon the whole of the subject-matter of the reference have been commenced between all the parties to the reference and a notice thereof has been given to the arbitrators or umpire, all further proceedings in a pending reference shall, unless a stay of proceedings is granted under section 34, be invalid.

(2) In this section the expression "parties to the references" includes any person claiming under any of the parties and litigating under the same title.

36. Power of Court, where arbitration agreement is ordered not to apply to a particular difference, to order that a provision making an award a condition precedent to a action shall not apply to such difference: Where it is provided (Whether in the arbitration agreement or otherwise) that an arbitration agreement shall be a condition precedent to the bringing of an action with respect to any matter to which the agreement applies, the Court, if it orders (whether under this Act or any other law) that the agreement shall cease to have effect as regards any particular difference may further order that the said provision shall also cease to have effect as regards that difference.

37. Limitations:

(1) All the provisions of the Limitation Act, 1908,shall apply to arbitrations as they apply to proceedings in Court.

(2) Notwithstanding any term in an arbitration agreement to the effect that no cause of action shall accrue in respect of any matter required by the agreement to be referred until an award is made under the agreement, a cause of any such matter at the time when it would have accrued but for that term in the agreement.

(3) For the purposes of this section and of the Limitation Act, 1908, an arbitration shall be deemed to be commenced when one party to the arbitration agreement serves on the other parties thereto a notice requiring the appointment of an arbitrator, or where the arbitration agreement provides that the reference shall be to a person named or designated in the agreement, requiring that the difference be submitted to the person so named or designated.

(4) When the terms of an agreement to refer future differences to arbitration provide that any claims to which the agreement applies shall be barred unless notice to appoint arbitrator is given or an arbitrator is appointed or some other step to commence arbitration proceedings is taken within a time fixed by the agreement, and a difference arises to which the agreement applies, the Court, if it is of opinion that in the circumstances of the case undue hardship would otherwise be caused, and notwithstanding that the time so fixed has expired, may on such terms, if any, as the justice of the case may require, extend the time for such period as it thinks proper.

(5) Where the Court orders that an award be set aside or orders, after the commencement of an arbitration, that the orbit have effect with respect to the difference referred, the period between the commencement of the arbitration and the date of the order of the Court shall be excluded in computing the time prescribed by the Limitation Act,1908, for the commencement of the proceeding (including arbitration)with respect to the difference referred.

38. Disputes as to arbitrator's remuneration or costs:

(1) If in any case an arbitrator or umpire refuses to deliver his award except on payment of the fees demanded by him, the Court may, on an application in this behalf, order that the arbitrator or umpire shall deliver the award to the

applicant on payment into Court by the applicant of the fees demanded, and shall, after such inquiry, if any, as it thinks fit, further order that out of the money so paid into Court there shall be paid to the arbitrator or umpire by way of fees sum as the Court may consider reasonable and that the balance of the money, if any, shall be refunded to the applicant.

(2) An application under sub-section (1) may be made by any party to the reference unless the fees demanded have been fixed by written agreement between him and the arbitrator or umpire, and the arbitrator or umpire shall be entitled to appear and be heard on any such application.

(3) The Court may make such orders as it thinks fit respecting the costs of an arbitration where any question arises respecting such costs and the award contains no sufficient provision concerning them.

CHAPTER – VI
Appeals

39. Appealable orders:

(1) An appeal shall lie from the following orders passed under this Act (and from no others) to the Court authorised by law to hear appeals from original decrees of the Court passing the order:
An order-
(i) superseding an arbitration;
(ii) on an award stated in the form of a special case;
(iii) modifying or correcting award;
(iv) filing or refusing to file an arbitration agreement;
(v) Staying or refusing to stay legal proceedings where there is an arbitration agreement;
(vi) setting aside or refusing to set aside an award;
Provided that the provisions of this section shall not apply to any order passed by a Small Cause Court.

(2) No second appeal shall lie from an order passed in appeal under this section, but nothing in this section affect or take away any right to appeal to the Supreme Court.

CHAPTER – VII
MISCELLANEOUS

40. Small Cause Court not to have jurisdiction over arbitrations save arbitration in suits before it: A Small Court shall have no jurisdiction over any arbitration proceedings or over any application arising save on application made under Section 21.

41. Procedure and powers of Court: Subject to the provisions of this Act and of rules made there under-

(a) the provisions of the Code of Civil Procedure, 1908, shall apply to all proceedings, before the Court, to all appeals, under this Act, and
(b) the Court shall have, for the purpose of, and in relation to, arbitration proceedings, the same power of making orders in respect of any of the matters set out in the Second Schedule as it has for the purpose of, and in relation to, any proceedings before the Court:

Provided that nothing in clause (b) shall be taken to prejudice any power which may be vested in an arbitrator or umpire for making orders with respect to any of such matters.

42. Service of notice by party or arbitrator: Any notice required by this Act to be served otherwise than through the Court by a party to an arbitration agreement or by an arbitrator or umpire shall be served in the manner provided in the arbitration agreement, or if there is no such provision, either-

(a) by delivering it to the person on whom it is to be served, or
(b) by sending it by the post in a letter addressed to that person a this usual or last known place of abode or business in Pakistan and registered under Chapter VI of the Post Office Act, 1898.

43. Power of Courts issue processes for appearance before arbitrator:

(1) The Court shall issue the same processes to the parties and witnesses whom the arbitrator or umpire desires to examine as the Court may issue in suits tried before it.
(2) Persons failing to attend in accordance with such process, or making any other default, or refusing to give their evidence, of guilty or any contempt to the arbitration or umpire during the investigation of the reference, shall be subject to the like disadvantages, penalties and punishments by order of the Court on the representation of the arbitrator or umpire as they would incur for the like offences in suits tried before the Court.
(3) In this section the expression "process" includes summonses and commissions for the examination of witnesses and summonses to produce documents.

44. Power to High Court to make rules: The High Court may make rules consistent with this Act as to-

(a) the filing of awards and all proceedings consequent thereon or incidental thereto;
(b) the filing and hearing of special cases and all proceedings consequent thereon or incidental thereto;

(c) the staying of any suit or proceeding in contravention of an arbitration agreement;
(d) the forms to be used for the purposes of this Act;
(e) generally all proceedings in Court under this Act.

45. Government to be bound: The provisions of this Act shall be binding on the Government.

46. Application of Act to statutory arbitrations: The provisions of this Act, except sub-section (1) of section 6 and Sections 7, 12, 36and 37, shall apply to every arbitration under any other enactment for the time being in force, as if the arbitration were pursuant to an arbitration agreement and as if that other enactment were an arbitration agreement, except in so far as this Act is inconsistent with that other enactment or with any rules made there under.

47. Act to apply to all arbitrations: Subject to the provisions of Section 46, and save in so far as is otherwise provided by any law for the time being in force, the provisions of this Act shall apply to all arbitration's and to all proceedings there under.

Provided that an arbitration award otherwise obtained may with the consent of all the parties interested be taken into consideration as a compromise or adjustment of a suit by any Court before which the suit is pending.

48. Saving for pending references: The provisions of this Act shall not apply to any reference pending at the commencement of this Act, to which the law in force immediately before the commencement of this Act shall, notwithstanding any repeal affected by this Act, continue to apply.

49. Repeals and Amendment: [Rep. by the Repealing and Amending Act,1945 (VI of 1945), S. 2 and First Schedule.]

THE
FIRST SCHEDULE
(See Section 3)
IMPLIED CONDITIONS OF ARBITRATION AGREEMENTS

1. Unless otherwise expressly provided, the reference shall be to a sole arbitrator.
2. If the reference is to an even number of arbitrators, the arbitrators shall appoint an umpire not later than one month from the latest date of their respective appointments.
3. The arbitrators shall make their award within four months after entering on the reference or after having been called upon to act by notice in writing from any party to the arbitration agreement or within such extended time as the Court may allow.
4. If the arbitrators have allowed their time to expire without making an award or have delivered to any party to the arbitration agreement or to the umpire a notice in writing stating that they cannot agree, the umpire shall forthwith enter on the reference in lieu of the arbitrators.
5. The umpire shall make his award within two months of entering on the reference or within such extended time as the Court may allow.

6. The parties to the reference and all persons claiming under them shall subject to the provisions of any law for the time being in force, submit to be examined by the arbitration or umpire on oath or affirmation in relation to the matters in difference and shall, subject as aforesaid, produce before the arbitrators or umpire all books, deeds, papers, accounts, writings and documents within their possession or power respectively, which be required or called for, and do all other things which, during the proceedings on the reference, the arbitrators or umpire may require.
7. The award shall be final binding on the parties and persons claiming under them respectively.
8. The cost of the reference and award shall be in the discretion of the arbitrators or umpire who may direct to, and by whom, and in what manner, such costs or any part thereof shall be paid, and may tax or settle the amount of costs to be so paid or any part thereof and may award costs to be paid as between legal practitioner and client.

THE
SECOND SCHEDULE
(See Section 41)
POWERS OF COURT

1. The preservation, interim custody or sale of any goods which are subject-matter of the reference.
2. Securing the amount in difference in the reference.
3. The detention, preservation or inspection of any property or thing which is the subject of the reference or as to which any question may arise therein and authorising for any of the aforesaid purposes any person to enter upon or into any land or building in the possession or any party to the reference, or authorising any samples to be taken or any observation to be made or experiment to be tried, which may be necessary or expedient for the purpose of obtaining full information or evidence.
4. Interim injunctions or the appointment of a receiver.
5. The appointment of a guardian for a minor or person of unsound mind for the purposes of arbitration proceedings.

THE
THIRD SCHEDULE
&
THE
FOURTH SCHEDULE:

[1][Repealed]

Legal Amendments

1. Rep. by the Repealing and Amending Act, 1945 (VI of 1945), S.2 and First Schedule.

APPENDIX II

Recognition and Enforcement (Arbitration Agreements and Foreign Arbitral Awards) Act, 2011 with the New York Convention in Its Schedule

ACT XVII OF 2011

An Act to provide for the recognition and enforcement of arbitration agreements and foreign arbitral awards

[Gazette of Pakistan, Extraordinary, Part-I,
19th July, 2011]

No.F.9(3)/2011-Legis., dated 19-7-2011.--The following Act of Majlis-e-Shoora (Parliament) received the assent of the President on 15th July, 2011, is hereby published for general information:--

Whereas Pakistan is a signatory to the United Nations Convention on the Recognition and Enforcement of Foreign Arbitral Awards, 1958;

Whereas it is expedient to provide for the recognition and enforcement of arbitration agreements and foreign arbitral awards pursuant to the said Convention and for matters connected therewith;

It is hereby enacted as follows:--

1. Short title, extent, application and commencement.---

(1) This Act may be called the Recognition and Enforcement (Arbitration Agreements and Foreign Arbitral Awards) Act, 2011.
(2) It extends to the whole of Pakistan.
(3) It shall apply to arbitration agreements made before, on or after the date of coming into force of this Act.

(4) It shall not apply to foreign arbitral awards made before the 14th day of July, 2005.
(5) It shall come into force at once.

2. Definitions.--- In this Act, unless there is anything repugnant in the subject or context,--

(a) "Article" means an Article of Convention;
(b) "Contracting State" means a State which is a Party to the Convention;
(c) "Convention" means the United Nations Convention on the Recognition and Enforcement of Foreign Arbitral Awards, done at New York on 10th June, 1958, set forth in the Schedule to this Act;
(d) "Court" means a High Court and such other superior court in Pakistan as may be notified by the Federal Government in the official Gazette; and
(e) "Foreign arbitral award" means an arbitral award made in a Contracting State and such other State as may be notified by the Federal Government, in the official Gazette.

3. Jurisdiction of Court.---

(1) Notwithstanding anything contained in any other law for the time being in force, the Court shall exercise exclusive jurisdiction to adjudicate and settle matters related to or arising from this Act.
(2) An application to stay legal proceedings pursuant to the provisions of Article II of the Convention may be filed in the Court, in which the legal proceedings are pending.
(3) In the exercise of its jurisdiction, the Court shall,---
    (a) follow the procedure, as nearly as may be provided in the Code of.Civil Procedure, 1908 (Act V of 1908); and
    (b) have all the powers vested in a civil court under the Code of Civil Procedure, 1908 (Act V of 1908).

4. Enforcement of arbitration agreements.---

(1) A party to an arbitration agreement against whom legal proceedings have been brought in respect of a matter which is covered by the arbitration agreement may, upon notice to the other party to the proceedings, apply to the court in which the proceedings have been brought to stay the proceedings insofar as they concern that matter.
(2) On an application under sub-section (1), the court shall refer the parties to arbitration, unless it finds that the arbitration agreement is null and void, inoperative or incapable of being performed.

5. Furnishing of documents.--- The party applying for recognition and enforcement of foreign arbitral award under this Act shall, at the time of the application, furnish documents to the Court in accordance with Article IV of the Convention.

6. Enforcement of foreign arbitral award.---

(1) Unless the Court pursuant to section 7, refuses the application seeking recognition and enforcement of a foreign arbitral award, the Court shall recognize and enforce the award in the same manner as a judgment or order of a court in Pakistan.

(2) A foreign arbitral award which is enforceable under this Act, shall be treated as binding for all purposes on the persons as between whom it was made, and may accordingly be relied on by any of those persons by way of defence, set off or otherwise in any legal proceedings in Pakistan.

7. Unenforceable foreign arbitral awards.--- The recognition and enforcement of a foreign arbitral award shall not be refused except in accordance with Article V of the Convention.

8. Inconsistency.--- In the event of any inconsistency between this Act, any other law, or any judgment of any Court and the Convention, the Convention shall prevail to the extent of the inconsistency.

9. Power to make Rules.--- The Federal Government may, by Notification in the official Gazette, make rules to carry out the purposes of this Act.

10. Repeal and saving.---

(1) The Arbitration (Protocol and Convention) Act, 1937 (VI of 1937) (hereinafter in this section referred to as "the Act") is hereby repealed.

(2) Notwithstanding the repeal of the Act, it shall continue to have effect in relation to foreign arbitral awards made---

(a) before the date of commencement of this Act; and

(b) within the meaning of section 2 of the Act which are not foreign arbitral awards within the meaning of section 2 of this Act.

SCHEDULE

[See Section 2(b)]

CONVENTION ON THE RECOGNITION AND ENFORCEMENT OF FOREIGN ARBITRAL AWARDS

Done at New York on 10th June, 1958
Entry into force: 7th June, 1959

ARTICLE I

1. This Convention shall, apply to the recognition and enforcement of arbitral awards made in the territory, or a State other than the State where the recognition and

enforcement of such awards are sought, and arising out of differences between persons, whether physicals or legal. It shall also apply to arbitral awards not considered as domestic awards in the State where their recognition and enforcement are sought.
2. The term "arbitral awards" shall include not only awards made by arbitrators appointed for each case but also those made by permanent arbitral bodies to which the parties have submitted.
3. When signing, ratifying or acceding to this Convention, or notifying extension under Article X hereof, any State may on the basis of reciprocity declare that it will apply the Convention to the recognition and enforcement of awards made only in the territory of another Contracting State. It may also declare that it will apply the Convention only to differences arising out of legal relationships, whether contractual or not, which are considered as commercial under the national law of the State making such declaration.

ARTICLE II

1. Each Contracting State shall recognize an agreement in writing under which the parties undertake to submit to arbitration all or any differences which have arisen or which may arise between them in respect of defined legal relationship, whether contractual or not, concerning a subject-matter capable of settlement by arbitration.
2. The term "agreement in writing" shall include an arbitral clause in a contract or an arbitration agreement, signed by the parties or contained in an exchange of letters or telegrams.
3. The court of a Contracting State; when seized of an action in a matter in respect of which the parties have made an agreement within the meaning of this Article shall, at the request of one of the parties, refer the parties to arbitration, unless it finds that the said agreement is null and void, inoperative or incapable of being performed.

ARTICLE III

Each Contracting State shall recognize arbitral awards as binding and enforce them in accordance with the rules of procedure of the territory where the award is relied upon, under the conditions laid down in the following Articles. There shall not be imposed substantially more onerous conditions or higher fees or charges on the recognition or enforcement of arbitral award to which this Convention applies than are imposed on the recognition or enforcement of domestic arbitral awards.

ARTICLE IV

1. To obtain the recognition and enforcement mentioned in the preceding Article, the party applying for recognition and enforcement shall, at the time of the application, supply:

(a) The duly authenticated original award or a duly certified copy thereof;
(b) The original agreement referred to in Article II or a duly certified copy thereof.

2. If the said award or agreement is not made in an official language of the country in which the award is relied upon, the party applying for recognition and enforcement of the award shall produce a translation of these documents into such language. The translation shall be certified by an official or sworn translator or by a diplomatic or consular agent.

ARTICLE V

1. Recognition and enforcement of the award may be refused, at the request of the party against whom it is invoked, only if that party furnishes to the competent authority where the recognition and enforcement is sought, proof that:

(a) The parties to the agreement referred to in Article II were, under the law applicable to them, under some incapacity, or the said agreement is not valid under the law to which the parties have subjected it or, failing any indication thereon, under the law of the country where the award was made; or
(b) The party against whom the award is invoked was not given proper notice of the appointment of the arbitrator or of the arbitration proceedings or was otherwise unable to present his case; or
(c) The award deals with a difference not contemplated by or not falling within the terms of the submission to arbitration, or it contains decisions on matters beyond the scope of the submission to arbitration, provided that, if the decisions on matters submitted to arbitration, can be separated from those not so submitted, that part of the award which contains decisions on matters submitted to arbitration may be recognized and enforced; or
(d) The composition of the arbitral authority or the arbitral procedure was not in accordance with the agreement of the parties, or, failing such agreement, was not in accordance with the law of the country where the arbitration took place; or
(e) The award has not yet become binding on the parties, or has been set aside or suspended by a competent authority of the country in which, or under the law of which, that award was made.

2. Recognition and enforcement of an arbitral award may also be refused if the competent authority in the country where recognition and enforcement is sought finds that:

(a) The subject-matter of the difference is not capable of settlement by arbitration under the law of that country; or
(b) The recognition or enforcement of the award would be contrary to the public policy.of that country.

ARTICLE VI

If an application for the setting aside or suspension of the award has been made to a competent authority referred to in Article V (1) (e), the Authority before which the award is sought to be relied upon may, if it considers it proper, adjourn the decision on the enforcement of the award and may also, on the application of the party claiming enforcement of the award, order the other party to give suitable security.

ARTICLE VII

1. The provisions of the present Convention shall not affect the validity of multilateral or bilateral agreements concerning the recognition and enforcement of arbitral awards entered into by the Contracting States nor deprive any interested party of any right he may have to avail himself of an arbitral award in the manner and to the extent allowed by the law or the treaties of the country where such award is sought to be relied upon.
2. The Geneva Protocol on Arbitration Clauses of 1923 and the Geneva Convention on the Execution of Foreign Arbitral Awards of 1927 shall cease to.have effect between Contracting States on their becoming bound and to the extent that they become bound, by this Convention.

ARTICLE VIII

1. This Convention shall be open until 31st December, 1958 for signature on behalf of any Member of the United Nations and also on behalf of any other State which is or hereafter becomes a member of any specialized agency of the United Nations, or which is' or hereafter becomes a party to the Statute of the International Court of Justice, or any other State to which an invitation has been addressed by the General Assembly of the United Nations.
2. This Convention shall be ratified and the instrument of ratification shall be deposited with the Secretary-General of the United Nations.

ARTICLE IX

1. This Convention shall be open for accession to all States referred to in Article VIII.
2. Accession shall be effected by the deposit of an instrument of accession with the Secretary-General of the United Nations.

ARTICLE X

1. Any State may, at the time of signature, ratification or accession declares that this Convention shall extend to all or any of the territories for the international relations of which it is responsible. Such a declaration shall take effect when the Convention enters into force for the State concerned.
2. At any time thereafter any such extension shall be made by notification addressed to the Secretary-General of the United Nations and shall take effect as from the ninetieth day after the day of receipt by the Secretary-General of the United Nations of this

notification, or as from the date of entry into force of the Convention for the State concerned, whichever is the later.
3. With respect to those territories to which this Convention is not extended at the time of signature, ratification or accession, each State concerned shall consider the possibility of taking the necessary steps in order to extend the application of this Convention to such territories, subject, where necessary for constitutional reasons, to the consent of the Governments of such territories.

ARTICLE XI

In the case of a Federal or non-unitary State, the following provisions shall apply:

(a) With respect to those Articles of this Convention that come within the legislative jurisdiction of the Federal Authority, the obligations of the Federal Government shall to this extent be the same as those of Contracting States which are not Federal States;
(b) With respect to those Articles of this Convention that come within the legislative jurisdiction of constituent States or Provinces which are not, under the constitutional system of the federation, bound to take legislative action, the Federal Government shall bring such Articles with a favourable recommendation to the notice of the appropriate authorities of constituent States or Provinces at the earliest possible moment;
(c) A Federal State Party to this Convention shall, at the request of any other Contracting State transmitted through the Secretary-General of the United Nations, supply a statement of the law and practice of the federation and its constituent units in regard to any particular provision of this Convention, showing the extent to which effect has been given to that provision by legislative or other action.

ARTICLE XII

1. This Convention shall come into force on the ninetieth day following the date of deposit of the third instrument of ratification or accession.
2. For each State ratifying or acceding to this Convention after the deposit of the third instrument of ratification or accession, this Convention shall enter into force o' n the ninetieth day after deposit by such State of its instrument of ratification or accession.

ARTICLE XIII

1. Any Contracting State may denounce this Convention by a written notification to the Secretary-General of the United Nations. Denunciation shall take effect one year after the date of receipt of the notification by the Secretary-General.
2. Any State which has made a declaration or notification under Article X may, at any time thereafter, by notification to the Secretary-General of the United Nations, declare

that this Convention shall cease to extend to the territory concerned one year after the date of the receipt of the notification by the Secretary-General.
3. This Convention shall continue to be applicable to arbitral awards in respect of which recognition or enforcement proceedings have been instituted before the denunciation takes effect.

ARTICLE XIV

A Contracting State shall not be entitled to avail itself of the present Convention against other Contracting States except to the extent that it is itself bound to apply the denunciation take effect.

ARTICLE XV

The Secretary-General of the United Nations shall notify the States contemplated in Article VIII of the following:

(a) signatures and ratifications in accordance with Article VIII;
(b) accessions in accordance with Article IX;
(c) declarations and notifications under Articles I, X and XI;
(d) the date upon which this Convention enters into force in accordance with Article XII; and
(e) denunciations and notifications in accordance with Article XIII.

ARTICLE XVI

1. This Convention, of which the Chinese, English, French, Russian and Spanish texts shall be equally authentic, shall be deposited in the archives of the United Nations.
2. The Secretary-General of the United Nations shall transmit a certified copy of, this Convention to the States contemplated in Article VIII.

Index

B

C

J

P